HOMEWARD TO ZION

HOMEWARD TO ZION

The Mormon Migration from Scandinavia

WILLIAM MULDER

University of Minnesota Press
Minneapolis • London

Published in cooperation with Brigham Young University Press

TO MY FAMILY

Published by the University of Minnesota Press
111 Third Avenue South, Suite 290
Minneapolis, MN 55401-2520
http://www.upress.umn.edu

A Cataloging-in-Publication record for this book is available from the Library of Congress.

ISBN 0-8166-3674-5

Printed in the United States of America on acid-free paper

11 10 09 08 07 06 05 04 03 02 01 00 10 9 8 7 6 5 4 3 2 1

Foreword to the Anniversary Edition of Homeward to Zion

"THINK of it as a book." That was Oscar Handlin's advice when I began writing my Harvard dissertation about the Mormon migration from Scandinavia. That admonition meant keeping an eye on style as well as substance. The progress from proselyte to emigrant to settler seemed a natural narrative sequence, and the chapters began falling into place. They tell a story. The year 2000 marks the 150th anniversary since that story began and nearly half a century since I undertook the telling.

Though long out of print, *Homeward to Zion* has enjoyed a continuing presence in the world of immigration scholarship. Now, like a fly in amber stirring miraculously to life, the book is available again in time for the sesquicentennial observance of the opening of the Mormon mission in Scandinavia. As the ancestral story of numerous Scandinavian Latter-day Saints, *Homeward to Zion* may now find its way into the hands of the descendants of those original missionaries and their converts, whether still in the Mormon fold or not.

I am deeply grateful to the University of Minnesota Press, which considers *Homeward* one of the titles on its permanent list worth reprinting and which has enabled Brigham Young University Press to put its imprint on an anniversary edition enhanced by helpful maps and historic photographs. I owe special thanks to the Joseph Fielding Smith Institute of Latter-day Saint History and to its director of publications and his staff at Brigham Young University for their initiative and collaboration.

It may be a mark of the book's durability that I find myself, at 84, rereading it with pleasure, as though it were someone else's work.

I feel again the old excitement that came with reading the original sources—letters, diaries, reminiscences, church records, and emigration archives—that sprang to life as I thought of the human hopes and fears behind them. I can identify with Canute Peterson, who figures in the Prologue and Epilogue: there was an early promise and now a late fulfillment.

WILLIAM MULDER

Salt Lake City, Utah
December 1999

Foreword

THE fact that the Mormons long presented a political and cultural problem to their fellow citizens for many years obscured the true character of their migration to the United States. An obsessive fear of strangers and nonconformists generated such hostility toward the Mormons that many Americans, in the 1850s and later, regarded this movement as entirely foreign and even threatening. Traces of that prejudice have lingered on to our own times.

Yet just as the migration of the Mormons to Utah was but a part of a larger American westward movement, so the arrival of some of them from across the ocean was but an element, although a unique element, in the total stream of American migration. Between 1850 and 1905, some 30,000 proselytes from Norway, Denmark, and Sweden came to Utah. Their experience was enlightening, for it reveals both the forces at work in the transplantation of Scandinavian culture to the New World, and also those that shaped Mormon institutions in the second half of the nineteenth century.

The men and women who left their homes in Europe to share the life of the Mormons were moved by much the same impulses as other immigrants. Discontent with conditions in the homeland and hopes for a better future in America led them across the ocean. But this movement was also distinctive in the religious motivations involved in it, and in the extent to which it was organized and directed by conscious policy. It thus bore striking similarities to the Utopian colonies set up in the middle of the century in the open spaces of the New World. Once in the United States the immigrants faced serious problems of adjustment, both in their transmitted culture and in their expectations as to future livelihood. The story of their reactions, vividly told by Dr. Mulder, is a fascinating chapter in the history of migration and of the settlement of the American West.

OSCAR HANDLIN

Cambridge, Mass.
December 1, 1956

Preface

AMERICA in 1830 could have taken Joseph Smith's *Book of Mormon* as portent and symbol. Itself the narrative of an ancient religious migration, the book begot a greater wandering, an epic ingathering of believers from Europe and the States seeking New Jerusalem on the American frontier. Every Mormon proselyte knew by heart and in his own tongue the words of Father Lehi, refugee from Babylon, American immigrant circa 600 B.C.: "We have obtained a land of promise, a land which is choice above all other lands. . . . Yea, the Lord hath covenanted this land unto me, and to my children forever, and also all those who should be led out of other countries by the hand of the Lord." That was the book's portent, big with history and promise. America, it said, had always been a land of promise.

A nation seized with a conviction of manifest destiny should have rejoiced in the book as symbol. It was so very national. It was, in fact, aboriginal. It gave the young country the immemorial past its poets yearned for. With its central theme of the continent as a favored land providentially preserved for the gathering of a righteous people, it improved the American dream with scripture and endowed it with sacred legend. More faithfully than the Prophet's neighbors in New England and western New York ever realized, his revelation reflected their most cherished myth. Descendants of Puritans and Patriots should have recognized the doctrine.

Having given America its primeval migration story, Mormonism proceeded to make migration history—in two directions, both stemming from the same impulse to establish Zion: pioneering in the West and proselyting in Europe. In secular terms, call it building America.

The Mormons called it building the Kingdom. Pioneering and proselyting, the frontier and immigration, forces which have so largely determined the national character, gave Mormonism the shape of the American tradition, with a difference. How traditional and how different may appear by looking at what seems hardly more than a ripple in the mainstream of American immigration.

During the second half of the nineteenth century thirty thousand Mormon converts left Scandinavia to follow the gleam to Zion, a movement as large as the Puritan migration of the 1630s, though over a longer period. England, earliest of Mormonism's foreign fields, had already been yielding a rich harvest of convert-emigrants for thirteen years when in 1850 operations were extended to Scandinavia. It is a peculiar circumstance that at a time their countrymen were homesteading the richer and more expansive acres of the Old Northwest and the prairies, Scandinavian Mormons chose to join latter-day Israel in the rainless valleys of far-off Utah. Unlike the general movement from Scandinavia, in which the Norwegians and Swedes were early and most numerous, in the Mormon migration the Danes were first and predominant. The Danes, proverbially reluctant to sail out farther than they could row back and traditionally considered poor pioneers, nevertheless, as Mormons, left their homeland in years of actual prosperity to become hardy grass-roots settlers well beyond the frontier of Scandinavian occupation in the United States.

Mormon migration from Scandinavia was a planned migration, every detail already rehearsed by Mormonism's experience in Britain and on the frontier; it had a special motivation and momentum — a dramatic rise and a marked decline, a rhythm independent of the general immigration to the United States; it saw an unusual mingling of Danes, Swedes, and Norwegians with one another and with Yankee and English converts in the act of colonization; it received a disproportionate amount of popular and official attention during the 1870s and 1880s, part of the country's obsession with the "Mormon Question"; and it has been the object of persistent misconceptions concerning the Mormon policy and program, even among reputable historians.

Mormonism's career in Scandinavia was only part of its larger European enterprise. As an American influence abroad, as part of the current of ideas and attractions which have washed back upon the Old World from the New in the intellectual free trade that has always marked the exchange of isms between Europe and America, Mormonism was a particularly dynamic version of America's romantic hope, its optimistic early nineteenth-century gospel. Yet, the European experience, not less dramatic than the story of Mormonism's successive dislocations on the frontier until its final desperate remove to the mountains, is not nearly so well known. The Yankee exodus, the historic trek of 1847, and the pattern which Yankee leadership gave to Mormon colonization have overshadowed the transatlantic events. Perhaps because the immigrant was also pioneer his original identity has been lost in the dust of covered wagons. And because the history of Mormonism and of Utah, as of so much of America in fact, has been written from the English-speaking sources, it has not been seen through immigrant eyes.

Judged by national standards, by the history of other immigrant groups, the story seems placid: no Irish turbulence, no Lutheran factional wrangles, no Teutonic push for power, no desperate Ghetto struggle for survival; hard work, yes, but a living assured, and a place in the sun; a transplanting but no tragic uprooting. The story is rich in significant trifles, as Willa Cather might say. And it has a borrowed drama, reflecting much of Utah's colorful history—the continuing warfare of the Saints against their enemies, the drama of any attempt to found a commonwealth in the wilderness. It has an inherent drama, too, as the story of many unknown lives which, taken together, assume a grander sweep.

The story comes down to 1905, an arbitrary date but meaningful, because by then Scandinavian Mormon unity both abroad and at home had radically altered. By this time, too, organized emigration was a thing of the past; the honored names, the first convert-heroes, the patriarchs, were almost gone; and a marked change in church policy and program fixed the end of an era.

The Mormon immigrant, like every immigrant, crossed more than an ocean and a continent—his traveling was, in John Ciardi's phrase,

> . . . across the sprung longitudes of the mind
> And the blood's latitudes.

From earliest voyager to latest refugee the personal record of that experience holds an unfailing fascination, whether set down in William Bradford's "plaine stile; with singuler regard unto the simple trueth in all things," or in the broken tongue of the lowly Scandinavian Mormon. The constant renewing of this experience has in fact determined the course of United States history and given it a characteristic literature. If the present study has any value at all, it springs from the immigrant himself, who wherever possible is permitted to tell his own story.

In the course of this study, presented originally as a doctoral dissertation in the History of American Civilization at Harvard University, I have incurred many obligations. I give sincere thanks to Professor A. M. Schlesinger, Sr., who saw me through a critical period in my graduate career and spoke well of a seminar paper which proved to be forerunner of the present work; to Professor Oscar Handlin, who was patient and encouraging in the early stages of research and writing; to Professor John M. Gaus, who so willingly took over the chore of reading and proved an inspiring counselor; to Professors Perry Miller and Kenneth B. Murdock, who gave me an ideal of scholarship; to Dean Theodore C. Blegen of the University of Minnesota for his warm interest as the work came to his attention; to the staffs of many institutions, but especially to the Historian's Office, Church of Jesus Christ of Latter-day Saints, to the Utah State Historical Society, the University of Utah Library, and the Royal Library at Copenhagen for generous use of their resources; to many Scandinavian immigrants themselves and their descendants who have given me of their time and frequently of their treasure; to Virginia Sorensen, a fine American novelist, who shares my interest in these matters; and, not least, to my wife, Gweneth Gates Mulder, who worked hard and waited long.

I give special thanks to the University of Minnesota Press itself for making publication possible and for a humane and expert handling of the manuscript. Finally, for permission to use certain parts of the work which have appeared in revised form as articles, I am grateful to the following professional journals: *Church History*, *Mississippi Valley Historical Review*, *Norwegian-American Studies and Records*, *Pacific Historical Review*, *Swedish Pioneer Historical Review*, *Utah Historical Quarterly*, and *Western Political Quarterly*.

WILLIAM MULDER

Salt Lake City, Utah
September 1956

Contents

PROLOGUE

Promise

CANUTE PETERSON, just turned twenty, wanted a blessing, and Uncle John Smith, Mormon patriarch, had one for him. The old man laid strong hands on the young Norwegian's head and spoke slowly for the recorder: "City of Joseph," he datelined it, "October 21, 1844 . . ."

> . . . Thou art one of the horns of Ephraim and appointed to push the people together from the ends of the earth, and thou shalt go with mighty power. . . . Thou shalt have power to gather very much for the building up of Zion; thou shalt have power to feed many in the wilderness in the time of famine, cause streams to flow out of the dry and thirsty land; thou shalt have an inheritance in Zion with thy brethren, have a companion for thy comfort and assistance, and raise up a posterity to keep thy name in remembrance.[1]

To a youth still single, accustomed only to breaking prairie sod and threshing grain, that seemed a heady promise. *An inheritance in Zion.* With the Prophet dead, cut down that very summer, and with Nauvoo a doomed city? Canute had already left one inheritance—the ancestral farm in Eidfjord, Hardanger, Norway, where his forefathers for six centuries had farmed and fished and hunted. He thought of the snug house built of skillfully hewn logs, the solid barn, and summers spent as herd boy in the mountain meadows. He remembered, at eight, a trade, a change in family fortunes, a smaller farm, and then, in 1837, the family's departure for America to join the renowned Fox River settlement in Illinois. He thought of his father, dead after eight months of discouraging railsplitting. He thought of his mother, an invalid, tended now by goodhearted neighbor Johanna Dahl. He thought of his own hire among different farmers and how, laboriously, month by month, he had at last paid the family's emigration debt to kindly Tove Kettleson. Yes, he would like an inheritance.

With mighty power. By what poor gifts? Perhaps the blessings of the restored gospel? Canute recalled the coming of Mormon elders to Fox River in 1842, and the Lutheran minister's displeasure when some of the very founders of the colony embraced the new faith with its urgency about the Second Coming, its living Prophet, and its visible Zion. The congregation now numbered nearly a hundred Saints, rich in spiritual gifts. Canute reflected that he himself had on one occasion given the interpretation of tongues, and in a Norwegian so perfect and unlike his common, untutored speech that his mother, daughter of a schoolteacher, was astonished and took it as a sign her son had found favor with the Lord. And now, attending a Mormon conference in Nauvoo, Canute had been ordained a Seventy, which meant a missionary assignment, probably to Koshkonong in Wisconsin or Sugar Creek in Iowa to proselyte among his countrymen.

The promises were great, and he would take them on faith. Perhaps even now they were being fulfilled, for Brigham Young and some of the Twelve had left Nauvoo for Fox River, where tomorrow, it was rumored, they would lay out a settlement for the gathering of the Norwegian Saints. Perhaps the old patriarch meant what he said about an inheritance. Had not the Prophet himself once predicted that the Scandinavians would become a power in the Kingdom? "God hath made of one blood all nations." Zion was for the Scandinavians too.

And so it would prove. But before Canute Peterson – missionary, emigrant guide, colonizer, Indian peacemaker, temple builder, legislator, and himself finally a patriarch – died full of years in a Rocky Mountain settlement and in the bosom of a large posterity begotten of not one companion but three, he would think often of his early blessing, of Joseph Smith's vision of Scandinavians strong in the church, and of Brigham Young's blueprint for a Nordic colony, and ponder how these reached fulfillment in unexpected ways.

I. PROSELYTE

CHAPTER 1

Forerunners

"HERE ON THE GRANARY DOOR WAS PAINTED IN LARGE SIZE THE PICTURE OF MY GRANDFATHER AND HIS BROTHER ERIK RIDING HORSES. . . . THEY WERE NOBLE LOOKING MEN."[1]

THE earliest Scandinavian converts to Mormonism were won not in Europe but in the United States among the Norwegian immigrants in the historic settlements at Fox River in Illinois, Sugar Creek in Iowa, and Koshkonong in Wisconsin Territory, all within missionary striking distance of Nauvoo, the rising Mormon capital of the 1840s. Traveling elder George P. Dykes first found them in his tireless preaching up and down the country. In March 1842, he visited the Fox River settlement in LaSalle County and within a month secured a following of some distinction: a number of respected Haugean lay leaders like Ole Heier, "a winning personality and gifted speaker" who in Telemarken had been regarded a pious Reader; the schoolteacher Jörgen Pederson; Endre Dahl, one of the famous sloop folk of 1825 and a first settler at Fox River; and another slooper, Gudmund Haugaas from Stavanger, whom Dykes ordained an elder and described in a letter to Joseph Smith as "a man of strong mind, and well skilled in the scriptures; he can preach in Norway, Sweden and Denmark, having an understanding of their languages" – indication that among them the Prophet hoped to recruit missionaries for Scandinavia who would lead their countrymen to settle in and around Nauvoo to strengthen Zion as converts from the British Isles were already doing.[2] Eighteen-year-old Knud Peterson of Hardanger, immigrant of 1837, better known to history as Canute, was baptized soon after, with his widowed mother and "two best friends and comrades, Swen and John Jacobs." Canute remembered Dykes as a very able man: "Many of our most intelligent men, including the minister, came to his meetings and opposed him, but none were successful in argument against him, or the doctrine he was advocating." [3] History would take note of another convert – Aagaata Sondra Ystensdatter, also eighteen and an immigrant of 1837, from Telemarken, who as Ellen Sanders Kimball, wife of Brigham Young's counselor Heber C. Kimball, would be one of the three women in the first company of Mormon pioneers to enter Salt Lake Valley in 1847.[4]

In May 1843, Dykes wrote the Prophet reviewing the year's work: the LaSalle Branch, as he named the Fox River congregation, numbered fifty-eight, "in good standing," with Ole Heier presiding. In January 1843, Gudmund Haugaas and J. R. Anderson had spent three weeks among the Norwegians in Lee County, Iowa, and baptized ten, notably Erik G. M. Hogan and his family, who had come from Telemarken on the same ship with the Petersons and Ellen Sanders. After his return to Fox River, Haugaas had set out again, this time accompanied by Ole Heier, to visit "a large body from Norway" in Wisconsin Territory, where, thought Dykes, "they have laid the foundation of a great work to all appearance. There are now fifty-seven members of the church from Norway and the time is not far distant when the saying of Micah 4:2 will be fulfilled." [5]

The Prophet shared his optimism. When the Norwegian Saints at Fox River sent Endre Dahl to Nauvoo with one hundred head of sheep and cattle and "a little money" as a contribution toward building the temple, Father Dahl met Brother Joseph on the street; the Prophet invited Dahl to come home with him, but Dahl protested that he was only *en ganske likefrem Nordmann*, a very simple Norwegian, unworthy to enter a prophet's dwelling. The Prophet, who finally prevailed on Dahl to go with him, was much impressed. He told Apostle George A. Smith soon after that the Scandinavians would in time come to play a significant role in the church.[6]

Dahl must have returned to Fox River flushed with news of this meeting. Like so many converts, the Norwegians found the Prophet personally attractive; they often visited Nauvoo simply to lay eyes on him or hear him preach in a favorite grove. Young Goudy Hogan, one of the converts from Sugar Creek, just across the Mississippi from Nauvoo, came frequently with his father Erik. He sat one day on the boards of a temporary outdoor platform from which the Prophet was speaking close enough to touch him and remembered the light linen coat the Prophet wore with the small holes in the elbows. Goudy heard him declare that both North and South America would become Mount Zion and that the Constitution would hang "on a single untwisted thread" and that the Latter-day Saints would save it. Goudy remembered once that some young men were sparking girls at the back of the congregation and disturbing the meeting with their loud talk; the Prophet, a very human man for all his godliness, rebuked them: they should wait and go home and talk to their "young ladies" by consent of their parents. Goudy wished that all those friends and relatives who had made such a funeral of his family's departure from Norway a few years back could only see the Prophet and his beautiful city.[7]

Goudy and his countrymen visiting Nauvoo in 1844 might well have encountered its two resident Scandinavians – the Dane Hans Christian Hansen and the Swede John Erik Forsgren, their nations' lone representatives in the latter-day Zion. Forsgren and Hansen, both sailors, had embraced Mormonism in Boston in the early 1840s. Hans Christian had written the news of his conversion to his younger brother Peter Ole in Copenhagen, who, finding no Mormons in Denmark, had set out for America at once; Hans Christian went to Boston to meet him and invite him to come on to Nauvoo to see a real prophet. Peter Ole arrived late in 1844, after the Prophet's martyrdom, but Brigham Young set him to work on a Danish translation of the *Book of Mormon*, while Hans Christian's popular fiddle frequently entertained the Saints.[8]

With the British Mission, opened in 1837, already a firm foothold for Mormonism in Europe, Joseph Smith saw in these young Nordics the chance for spreading the faith to Scandinavia. His gospel, the seed, had to be carried to the nations, and here were the sowers. But his death by violence in June 1844 cut short such plans. Peter O. Hansen and John E. Forsgren would indeed introduce Mormonism into their homelands, but only after the Prophet's dream had run west to the mountains and they had followed it. The expulsion of the Saints from Nauvoo would see Forsgren march to California with the Mormon Battalion in 1846 and Hans Christian Hansen enter Salt Lake Valley with the vanguard detachment of pioneers in 1847, with Peter O. following soon after. Only a handful of the Norwegian converts from the Illinois and Iowa settlements would go west, a dearly bought remnant of Mormonism's first adventure among the Scandinavians, but they were men like Erik Hogan and Canute Peterson and Endre Dahl, seed corn for the great growth to come. In their future labors, their recollection of Nauvoo and the Prophet's personal ministry would provide a lasting and powerful motivation; their proselytes would take pride in a laying on of hands by such intimate disciples.

Lutheran leaders, meanwhile, were by no means happy at Mormonism's inroads among settlers whose ties with the mother church were already lamentably loose. Pastor J. W. C. Dietrichson, bitter that sects and schisms were destroying Lutheran unity, wrote agitated letters home deploring Mormon activity. He was distressed that by 1845 nearly a hundred and fifty Norwegians in the western settlements – some eighty in the Fox River colony alone – had followed the Mormon delusion. When Gudmund Haugaas and Canute Peterson came to Koshkonong late in 1844, Dietrichson entertained them at his home but also took occasion publicly to oppose their millennial doctrine. At Fox River the next spring he was not afraid to call a meeting of his own attacking Mormon elders who had preached to his Norwegians from an ox-drawn wagon.[9] Johan R. Reiersen, prime mover of the early emigration from Norway, considered the Sugar Creek converts "our credulous and simple countrymen."[10] Ole Andrewson of the American Home Missionary Society, feeling himself between the two extremes of the state church and American revivalism, wrote that Mormonism and fanaticism left the Fox River region like a prairie swept by fire.[11] And at Pine Lake, Wisconsin, Bishop Gustaf Unonius was equally critical. He regretted Fredrika Bremer's "sympathy for . . . Shakers, women's-rights associations, yes even Mormonism" which "judicious Americans regard as more or less noxious weeds sown by the enemy into good ground."[12] It was a judgment the Mormons were used to.

Mormon activity among the Norwegians established a pattern that would prevail again years later in Scandinavia itself: American elders initiated what became a movement with its own momentum, though always centrally directed. The proselytes themselves became the most effective missionaries and able leaders of local congregations, while the brethren on circuit from Nauvoo called on them frequently: Wilford Woodruff, one day to lead the whole church and issue the famous manifesto discontinuing polygamy; George A. Smith, future church historian, who in May 1844 described the Prophet as "general Smith the smartest man in the U. S. and best calculated to fill the presidential chair, which was applauded by the assembly"; G. E. Deuel, returning from a preaching tour of New York, Canada, and Michigan – all spoke in the "Norwegian settlement," as they described Fox River.[13]

But "general Smith" was in trouble. In June 1844 the Fox River Saints heard that he planned to escape to the West. He had crossed the Mississippi on the 22nd and Porter Rockwell, "Old Port," was seeking horses. Canute responded and rode swiftly toward Nauvoo only to learn on the way that the Prophet had returned and given himself into the hands of his enemies. On the 27th he and his brother, Hyrum the Patriarch, were shot down by a mob. Goudy Hogan, fourteen, out picking wild strawberries, wept at the news; with his father he hurried across the river to the city to see the bodies returned from Carthage.[14]

In the ensuing contest within the church for the Prophet's mantle, the strong man Brigham Young, president of the Council of Twelve, visited the outlying congregations of the Saints in quick succession, for a time magnetizing the pieces of Joseph's kingdom and holding it together. Late in October of the martyr year, he went north 144 miles to Fox River. Parley P. Pratt, "Archer of Paradise," author of the persuasive *Voice of Warning* which gave so many converts their picture of the ideal Zion, had a farm within a day's ride of the settlement and went with him, as did Heber C. Kimball and Lorenzo D. Young – a good representation of the Twelve, betokening important business. After conference at nearby Ottawa, they visited the Norwegian Branch on the 23rd, "taught the principles of the Gospel," appointed George P. Dykes, their old familiar, to preside over the branch and Saints in the vicinity, and ordained Reuben Miller bishop. Then, from Gudmund Haugaas and Jacob Anderson they bought a hundred acres of land about nine miles northeast of Ottawa, "laid out a city," called it Norway, and "dedicated it to the Lord." They set aside ten acres for a temple "upon a high and very beautiful spot," selected sites for a "tithing house" and other public buildings, even driving the southeast corner stake for a meetinghouse or "tabernacle."[15] Canute Peterson bought a lot near the temple site for $40, which went to pay the county surveyor. Canute heard Brigham Young say that the new settlement would be "a gathering place for the Scandinavian people, and that they would build the temple on the site selected . . . that in this temple they would have the privilege of giving and receiving the Endowments in their own language."[16] Despite the martyrdom, Zion's tent, it seemed, was lengthening her cords and strengthening her stakes.

High Priest Gudmund Haugaas might soon be sent abroad to proselyte for Mormonism's promising Scandinavian stronghold.

But the Mormons were torn by dissension within and the mounting threat of violence without. By spring of 1845 Brigham Young was assembling the Saints from the surrounding country at Nauvoo to prepare for no one knew exactly what. Canute Peterson at Fox River remembered "exciting rumors" that the Saints would leave the city and go to the Rocky Mountains. Anxious to receive his temple endowments before such an evacuation took place, Canute and a small company from Fox River made a wagon journey down to Nauvoo in mid-January 1846, where he saw "preparations for the great exodus going on both night and day." He offered his help for the trek, but the brethren advised him to remain with his invalid mother.[17]

In the Iowa settlement across the river Erik Hogan's family had seen the troubles coming. Goudy remembered how in his neighborhood anything amiss was always laid to the Mormons. After robberies, the warrants were always made out to search Mormon houses, and at school, where he was the only Mormon boy, he was often called "Joe Smith." "There was considerable talk in Nauvoo and all around privately that the Saints would have to move and go into the wilderness in order to have peace."[18] In February Goudy saw the first of the evacuees cross the frozen Mississippi and camp along Sugar Creek in the snow not two miles from his father's farm; he would remember how the family gave what they could and how his father, enraged at the inhumane treatment the Mormons suffered, threw in his lot with the "Camp of Israel." He traded his grubbed land with its fine Norwegian granary for a yoke of cattle and an old wagon, the best bargain he could get because so many in and around Nauvoo were selling out. In April, in a heavy rain that mired everyone down, the Hogans joined the exodus. Goudy wanted to enlist in the Mormon Battalion being mustered at Mt. Pisgah, but his father found his sixteen years too young.

The family stayed the winter of 1846–47 at Plum Hollow, eight miles east of the Missouri River, on whose banks Brigham Young had established Winter Quarters. They cut wild hay, built a log house and corral, and Goudy hunted deer and collected wild honey. Father Erik went down to Missouri with a team to haul back food obtained in trade for his broadcloth suit, and in the spring he let Heber Kimball and his Norwegian wife Ellen take the family's work horse for the pioneer trek west, while he remained behind to clear and fence fifteen acres and raise corn which he could not sell even at ten cents a bushel. Goudy meanwhile went down to Fort Kearney to hire out as teamster for four months at $20 a month, the only Mormon, he remembered, among twenty-three hands. He earned enough to outfit the family for the journey west. In the spring of 1848 Erik traded his Plum Hollow holding with George P. Dykes, back from Mormon Battalion duty, who said he had a house in "the fort" in the infant settlement at Salt Lake. But when the Hogans arrived in September they found no house belonging to "said Dikes." They went north a few miles, instead, to Sessions' Settlement, which their labors soon christened Bountiful. There, because their log house was the largest, they and their Yankee neighbors held meetings and thanked the Lord for their deliverance.

In the fall of 1849 Erik and Goudy beefed one of the family's work oxen and made moccasins of the hide; and Goudy could sell his "fine boots" for a bushel and a half of wheat seed to their old Nauvoo acquaintance John Forsgren, about to leave on a mission to Scandinavia. The grasshoppers cleaned out the hoped-for crop, and when Goudy and his sister Caroline had gleaned what was left, using the family butcher knife for a scythe, Goudy joined a company of "Mormon boys" headed for the gold fields with Brigham Young's blessing. In a year he was back, in time to see his father off on a mission to Norway with Canute Peterson. And in a few years, when the Knut Nelsons arrived from Denmark and Goudy took the three daughters to wife, he began to see that like the branches of Jacob's vine his father's family were running over the wall and becoming fruitful in their new home—a vision his twenty-five children and his hardy pioneering in three Deseret communities would confirm. It was a foretaste of experiences awaiting all the Scandinavians who would follow the forerunners to Zion.

Meanwhile, the Norwegian congregation at Fox River, to which Canute returned after his Nauvoo visit in January 1846, was thrown into confusion by the whirlwind visitations and strident claims of the quick-tongued James J. Strang. The Twelve, he said, were subject to the First Presidency, and Strang was the president and true successor. He vigorously opposed the plan of Brigham Young and the Twelve to move the Saints west. Operating out of Voree, Wisconsin, Strang proselyted the Fox River region in December and January, 1845–46. He found Bishop Miller very much "bound up with the rule and authority of the Twelve" and ready to organize a company of one hundred families to rendezvous at Ottawa "and emigrate to unknown regions in the west under the direction of the Twelve to found there in connection with twenty-four other companies a New Empire to be governed by priestly authority."[19] Miller had called "an extensive meeting" of the "breathren" at the Norwegian settlement on the first day of January to set the company in order. Strang found they were "generally making great efforts" to start as soon as possible and were "very near unanimous in favour of going." On the 20th Strang countered by meeting with "about one hundred brethren and sisters, mostly Norwegians" who "seemed to receive his testimony." He was heard with attention, opposed with warmth, but managed to unsettle most of them. Miller vacillated. Ole Heier and Gudmund Haugaas were won over. "Hougus himself and the brethren generally were so well persuaded of the strength of our positions that three loads of them went to Nauvoo to call on the Twelve to justify their position and show them the first Presidency." Strang believed his winter's forays had brought "some three hundred breathren [*sic*] and sisters back to the true order of the Church . . . saving them from that most hopeless undertaking the Emigration to the western wilds."[20]

The roll call of the "Saints assembled in Conference at Norway, LaSalle Co. Ill." the following April revealed the extent of Strang's influence among the Norwegians: stalwarts like Gudmund Haugaas, Endre Dahl, Ole Heier, and Shure Olson and a score of "high priests and elders" pledged themselves to support Strang and "labor faithfully in the upbuilding of the Church and Kingdom of God as he hath revealed it." Haugaas was ordained an apostle "to open the gospel to the nation of Norway," together with five others.[21] Had they gone, as Strangites, they would have anticipated Brigham Young's emissaries to Scandinavia by four years.

There was no mission; loyalties to the impossible Strang were short-lived, and there was a falling away instead. In July Louisa Sanger of nearby Ottawa, troubled over the disaffection of Reuben Miller, wrote Strang, "These are indeed trying times and I fear that but few will be able to endure. . . . The Norwegian brethren are down very low. . . . Goodman is entirely off. . . . Ole has maintained his integrity until he saw Buzzard [Philip Busard] but now I hear he is clean down and if *he falls* what can we hope for the rest?"[22] Haugaas at one time almost decided to go west but finally joined the reorganization under Joseph Smith III, son of the Prophet, who in the 1850s united many splinter groups and individuals adrift around Nauvoo following the Brighamite exodus. Smith remembered "Goodman Hougas, Christian Hayer [Heier], Hans Hayer, and Oliver Hayer, with their families" as a "band of thrifty, industrious farmers . . . occupying in one of the richest localities in the state of Illinois" whose union with his church added considerable strength.[23]

The Norway branch remained captive to the reorganization; a son succeeded Gudmund Haugaas as its minister and, some fifty years after its planting by Brigham Young, could be found preaching there to a congregation of about 140.[24] Ole Heier, who for a few months served the Strangites as "presiding High Priest over the district of North, Eastern [*sic*] Illinois," finally joined the Close Communion Baptists. He had visited Nauvoo, a son recalled, during preparations for the evacuation, but "was one of the first to get his eyes open to the terrible work of the church he had espoused."[25] Shure Olson and Endre Dahl, the slooper, perhaps remembering his visit with the Prophet, recovered themselves and went west: Shure, skilled cabinetmaker, to help build the organ in the great tabernacle; Endre, entered in Utah Territory's first census in 1850 as "Andrew Dolle, 60, Farmer," to engender a grandson who would sit in the state's constitutional convention.[26]

Canute Peterson, like the Hogans at Sugar Creek, had made up his mind to go west when the chance came, and remained unmoved by the contrary winds of doctrine at Fox River. While others blew hot and cold, he hired out in the spring and summer of 1846 breaking prairie and threshing grain. In 1847, with a good team which he later traded for forty acres of land, he freighted between Ottawa and Chicago. In 1848 he hauled lumber for an Ottawa sawmill. When his mother died, he recalled, "my desire to gather with the Saints in Utah became stronger and stronger and I gradually made the necessary preparations."[27]

Brigham Young meanwhile had not forgotten the Fox River Saints. In December 1847 he sent George W. Bratten from Council Bluffs to visit the Norwegian settlement. "I arrived at Norway Jan. 10, 1848 and on the 12th had a large and very attentive congregation in a school house. . . ." The "great Erick Janson Prophet of Sweden" happened to be there at the same time and in a morning service in the schoolhouse declared "the Mormons were most particularly damned." Bratten disposed of him by calling on Gudmund Haugaas, still in the fold, to answer him in his own language and challenge him to public debate. "The house was crowded we had a most excellent meeting but no Prophet of Sweden." Bratten reorganized the branch, received "eight dollars and some cents" and a pledge from twenty members – Canute Peterson and Gudmund Haugaas among them – that they "would support the Twelve and go to the west." [28]

A year later, on April 18, 1849, twenty-two Norwegians left Fox River in six wagons, mostly those who had pledged Bratten their support, with the notable exception of Gudmund Haugaas. A notable addition, from Canute's point of view, was "Sister Sarah Ann Nelson," daughter of the slooper Cornelius Nelson Hersdal. She had been teaching English in the settlement school to scholars from twenty to forty years old. Canute married her on July 2 in camp a few miles east of Kanesville.[29]

After passing through Burlington, Iowa – which they found deserted except for the ferrymen and a few guards, with the streets and porches strewn with new lime in the wake of a cholera epidemic – the company joined Apostle Ezra Taft Benson's camp at Kanesville on the east bank of the Missouri River and became known in Mormon history as the Norwegian Company. In Apostle George A. Smith's camp, also on the grounds, was a group of Welsh Saints under Captain Dan Jones. From Kanesville the companies traveled together, a mingling of tongues typical of Mormon migration. "We are composed of Yankees, English, Welsh, Norwegian, etc.," wrote Smith, "yet we are one, although of different dialects and nations." [30]

At Elkhorn River young Canute and his friend Ira Sabe won everyone's admiration when they volunteered to swim a rope to the ferry on the other side of the river, dangerously swollen by heavy rain. "After this," said Canute, "when there was any swimming to be done, I was generally asked to do it, and became quite popular." And modestly he admitted that he was also "a lucky hunter." At Independence Rock they were met by brethren from the Valley with cattle and wagons for their assistance. Brother Thomas E. Ricks was assigned to help the Norwegians. He won their love and confidence, which, Canute could reminisce fifty years later, "he has to this day." It forecast a characteristic relationship among the Mormons between Yankee settlers and Scandinavian immigrants.

On October 25, after battling waist-deep snows in the mountains, the company reached the Valley. Canute, Shure Olson, Christian Heier, and the Jacobs brothers were so eager to see "the great Mormon city" they "went up about the Temple Block and other places. We found the city to be more than we had expected and so were agreeably surprised."[31] Three or four of the young men in the company, hailed by goldseekers on their way to California, joined them, only to return in two years with a fortune "rather small" compared with their expectations. Canute found the land around Salt Lake City already taken up. "The water was very scarce and to get five acres of water right was an impossibility." Apostle Benson, who treated Canute as "a favorite," told him about some land "rich as a cream pot" on the other side of the Jordan River, but, unable to bring water to it, Canute soon gave it up. In July he was glad to be called thirty miles south to settle what became known by the *Book of Mormon* name of Lehi. "Now my occupation was plowing, sowing, making water ditches, and fences. . . ." But not for long, for in 1852 Brigham Young would call Canute and his Sugar Creek friend, Erik Hogan, now of Bountiful, on a mission to old Norway, where Mormon activity had already begun.

The Norwegian Company had encountered Apostle Erastus Snow and their recent Nauvoo neighbors, John Forsgren and Peter O. Hansen, in the mountains eastward bound for Scandinavia. The October conference of the church just past had renewed Mormonism's old determination to carry the gospel to the continent of Europe. It was part of the latter-day "gathering" which by 1849 already had a history, a philosophy, and a program. Its keys and covenants had moved the forerunners and would sustain them and all who followed after. The doctrine of the gathering was the mainspring of Mormonism and its coming work in Scandinavia.

CHAPTER 2

Keys and Covenants

"THE BEARDS ON NEW YORK FARMERS' JAWS
GREW TOO HEAVY FOR SMALL LAWS.

A MOSES OR AN ABRAHAM
FELT THAT NATIONS IN HIM SWAM."[1]

THE gathering," not polygamy, was Mormonism's oldest and most influential doctrine.[2] It was the signature of the "new and everlasting covenant" which the Lord had made with his elect in this last of all gospel dispensations.[3] The doctrine reflected a tradition of golden dreams and fierce desires reaching back to the promises made to Israel and forward to the Second Coming. The gathering was as new as the latest proselyte, as old as prophecy. It was a still small voice and a mounting whirlwind, at once the product of a thousand personal decisions and of the Divine Will unfolding itself in history. A little girl in Sweden plays a game, rocking back and forth in the family rocker: she calls it "Going to America." A Danish shoemaker toasts his friends on New Year's Eve: "May next year find us together in Zion." A Norwegian, released from his labors as a missionary, rejoices in his return to Zion: "My absence has been to me an exile."[4] It was all one and the same manifestation: it was the spirit of gathering. The phrase abounds in the literature, personal and official, the theme of countless songs and sermons and endless exposition.[5] It describes a universal yearning among the proselytes, an experience private yet common to which they loved to bear witness after their arrival in Zion, spellbinding the young with tales of the Lord's wonder-working providences on their behalf. After baptism by immersion, they said, and the laying on of hands at confirmation, came the baptism of desire, a strange and irresistible longing which ravished them and filled them with a nostalgia for Zion, their common home.

Oh Zion when I think of thee
I long for pinions like the dove
And mourn to think that I should be
So distant from the land I love.[6]

In some it leaped up like a flame and led them to leave kin and country in one fine careless rapture; in others it produced a steady glow, warming friends and family by its light and accomplishing through patient labor the final long journey to the sanctuary. "Gathering" came to be regarded the sign of one's faithfulness, and the convert who did not feel the pull was considered a queer fish in the gospel net.

The gathering was Mormonism's way of channeling what the nineteenth century called the religious affections; it disciplined into action the fervor that in revival faiths was dissipated in an aimless love affair with Christ. Though Mormonism, like other adventist faiths, was a millennial proclamation, a warning that the days were at hand when "kingdoms, governments and thrones are falling . . . plague, pestilence, and famine are walking abroad; and whirlwind, fire, and earthquake proclaiming the truth of prophecy . . ."[7] it was also a program designed to deal with these eventualities: "Let the Saints be faithful and diligent in every duty and especially in striving to stand in chosen places, that they may watch the coming of the Holy One of Israel."[8]

The invitation and the promise were as magnetic as the warning and involved more than a trip to the sinner's bench. "To stand in chosen places" meant getting out of Babylon and uniting with God's people to build up the Kingdom and await greater spiritual endowments. The gathering was to be a roll call of Saints without halos, in whom divinity had yet to breed wings—of a people not already saved and sanctified but, one in faith and fellowship, eager to create conditions under which sainthood might be achieved. Building the Kingdom meant providing an environment that would regenerate the adult and rear the young so that they would never know themselves otherwise than as Saints. Salvation was an on-going process: "As man is, God once was; as God is, man may be."[9] To become like God required an eternity, an endless unfolding of regenerated powers by study, faith, experience, and the intelligence which was the glory of God. George Q. Cannon, visiting Scandinavia in 1862, expressed this developmental aspect of the doctrine when he promised that

Transplanting the Saints to Zion will benefit them in every way if they will do right. With all the rest, their physical beauty will be increased. They are already strong and robust, but handsome forms and faces will . . . become common. The heavenly influence of the Spirit of the Lord, with more favorable circumstances and a more generous diet, will effect this.[10]

Inspiration for the gathering sprang from a literal interpretation of Scripture, from a providential reading of history, and from the circumstances of free-land society in early nineteenth-century America. Joseph Smith, a "restorer among restorationists,"[11] saw the idea of the Kingdom of God as the unifying theme of Scripture, and he made the assembling of the Saints which would have to precede that Kingdom – to him no mere parable – the great unifying theme of Mormonism. Fired by a biblical imagination which fused history and myth, Old Testament and New, into one consuming vision, he reflected the high-wrought excitement of the millenarians all around him expecting an imminent divine event in America, a state comparable to the confident expectation of the Reformers in Milton's England before the disappointment of the Commonwealth.[12]

The Prophet would re-enact an old drama, rehearsed in every gospel dispensation when the righteous sought to separate themselves from the wicked in special gatherings: Enoch's holy city, Noah's seaworthy ark, Abraham's intrepid family, the great migration of the tribes under Moses, the flights of *Book of Mormon* peoples under Lehi, Mulek, and the brother of Jared, the establishment of the Primitive Church – momentous gatherings followed all too often by heartbreaking captivities and dispersions or dissolutions. But now, in the fullness of times, after the long night of Christian apostasy, Israel by blood and by adoption was being called home.[13] Rachel would weep no more for her children, Ezekiel's dry bones were being quickened, the clay of Jeremiah's potter reworked, Isaiah's remnant ransomed. It was Daniel's stone ready to roll forth, and St. John's heavenly city about to come to earth. The proof texts were abundant and the signs of the times unmistakable.[14] This was to be the summing up. This was the last dispensation, and the Prophet had received the keys. The date is exactly recorded.

On April 3, 1836, in Kirtland, Ohio, at the dedication of the Saints' first temple – no bigger than a New England meetinghouse but already hallowed by their labor and sacrifice – Joseph Smith and his schoolteacher companion Oliver Cowdery declared that they saw the heavens opened and Moses appear, committing to them "the keys of the gathering of Israel from the four parts of the earth, and the leading of the ten tribes from the land of the north"; and Elijah, who came, he said, "to turn the hearts of the fathers to the children, and the children to the fathers, lest the whole earth be smitten with a curse." The young New Englanders were charged with a great responsibility: "The keys of this dispensation are committed into your hands; and by this ye may know that the great and dreadful day of the Lord is near, even at the doors."[15] It was a double commission: to inaugurate the resettlement of Israel and to build temples to perform gospel ordinances on behalf of the unredeemed dead. Throughout Mormon experience this visitation related and motivated proselyting, emigration, and colonizing—which meant communities of temple-building Saints, for they held the Old Testament conviction that all that Jehovah could do and all that he could be for his people depended upon the existence of his temple. Only there could the Saints be washed clean from the blood and sins of their generation. In the minds of the converts, emigration and temple-building would be inseparable: the injunctions of Moses and Elijah would be reflected in mission ledgers where savings funds for the journey to Zion and for the temple there would be entered side by side.

If Moses and Elijah lifted the curtain on what was to be the last act in the centuries-old drama of Israel's dispersion and promised restoration, America was to be the stage. While other millenarians set a time, the Mormons appointed a place. Joseph Smith split the Hebrew metaphor of Zion and Jerusalem: he saw Judah returning to Jerusalem, Israel to Zion. And America was the land of Zion. To accommodate this stupendous homecoming would, in fact, require both continents, North and South.[16] For this, all history had been mere prologue. The discovery of America by Columbus, the Reformation, the coming of the Pilgrim Fathers, the founding of the Republic, and the raising of "that glorious standard," the Constitution, were all preliminary to this design, while "the happiness of America," as Washington himself believed, was in turn to be but "the first link in a series of universal victories."[17] The Mormons made this common Protestant view of providence controlling America's destiny peculiarly their own.

Joseph Smith's vision of Zion, a holy commonwealth, was nothing new in his America, freckled with communitarian societies, secular and religious, protesting a wicked and competitive world. What was different was the Prophet's continental imagination, the magnitude of his dream, and its nativism. The *Book of Mormon* and the *Doctrine and Covenants*[18] naturalized biblical prophecies and events to the American scene. America was the promised land, and Missouri, heart of the continent, was to be the site of the New Jerusalem. It had been, in fact, the site of old Eden; not Mesopotamia, but the great valley of the Mississippi had been the cradle of mankind, and the Prophet pointed to the very spot where Adam, Ancient of Days, had once built an altar and where he would come again to preside over his righteous progeny.[19] America as the promised land was the grand refrain of the *Book of Mormon*, which chronicles several migrations. Centuries before the Pilgrim Fathers, America had sheltered refugee bands from the Old World: the Jaredites from the Tower of Babel, the Mulekites and the followers of Lehi from Jerusalem in the days of Zedekiah. Their survivors were the Lamanites, Columbus' Indians, who were to be won back to a knowledge of their forefathers and become a "white and delightsome people." How many other migrations had peopled the Americas the ruins of ancient cities and forgotten mounds could only begin to tell. The *Book of Mormon* was just one record, but its message was unmistakable: only by serving the God of the land – Jesus Christ, who himself had trod American soil just before his ascension – had any civilization flourished. America on these terms, taught the Prophet, had been held in special remembrance for the righteous in ages past, was even now fulfilling its characteristic role as a sanctuary, and for the redeemed would provide an inheritance in eternity.

The doctrine of inheritances went hand in glove with the doctrine of the gathering, domesticating and eternizing for the American freeholder the promises made to Abraham. Joseph Smith's foursquare plat of the City of Zion, an idealized New England village with adjacent farm lands – pattern for the communities with which he hoped to fill up the earth – could have been conceived only in a free-land society. A simon-pure agrarian concept, the doctrine of inheritances taught that the meek would inherit the earth. Orson Pratt, early Mormonism's brilliant materialist, demonstrated by simple arithmetic how many acres the arable globe could afford the righteous who had lived since creation: 150 acres, or, if the New Earth contained only the same proportion of land as the old, about forty acres for every redeemed soul.[20]

When the earth, purified by fire in a baptism of the spirit as it had been baptized by water in the days of Noah, received its celestial glory and became the abode of the blessed, they could claim their inheritance. It was their stake in the Kingdom, and, since life here and hereafter was a continuum, the living Saints could make a head start: the communities they founded through their gathering were the prelude to the Kingdom, in which they were first settlers.

What for other millenarian faiths marked the end, for the Saints was just the beginning. Their expectation of the Second Coming was momentary, but they planned for mansions on earth rather than in the sky. The Advent itself would bring no more than a change in administration, so to speak – the benevolent monarchy of the King of Kings. The Kingdom, already established, would go right on, and its yeomanry would keep their inheritances, tilling their fields and tending their shops as they had done the day before. The materialism of this vision filled the Saints with security and made them eager to plant their vines and fig trees.[21]

The earliest revelations and removals were the image and shadow of the gathering as it was to develop, giving Mormonism a history and largely determining its institutions. The Kirtland visitations actually culminated a series of pronouncements and looked to a worldwide expansion of what had been a stateside movement. At Fayette, New York, in September 1830, the Prophet first specified a gathering of the elect "unto one place upon the face of this land," and, though "no man knoweth where the city of Zion shall be built," it was to be "on the borders of the Lamanites," or Indian country.[22] The church was already looking west. Kirtland, where Mormonism's strongest congregation flourished – the result of successful proselyting among Sidney Rigdon's Campbellites – became an early center and the jumping-off place for "the regions westward," into which a revelation in February 1831 directed elders to proceed, to raise up churches "until the time shall come when it shall be revealed unto you from on high, when the city of the New Jerusalem shall be prepared, that ye may be gathered in one, that ye may be my people, and I will be your God."[23] The Saints were being called a "covenant people" and told to look to the day when the temple would be built. In March they were instructed to "gather out from the eastern lands . . . go ye forth into the western countries. . . . And with one heart and with one mind, gather up your riches that ye may purchase an inheritance which shall hereafter be appointed unto you." This was to be the New Jerusalem, "a land of peace, a city of refuge, a place of safety. . . ."[24]

In June the Prophet and over twenty leading elders left Kirtland, traveling west two by two by different routes to build up branches, agreeing to meet in conference in western Missouri, where the land of inheritance would be made known.[25] At length, in July, at the frontier village of Independence, Jackson County, a thousand miles west of Kirtland, the Prophet proclaimed Missouri the land consecrated for the gathering. He selected a temple site and, in the published revelation, urged the Saints to buy "every tract bordering by the prairies" and "every tract lying westward, even unto the line running directly between Jew and Gentile . . . inasmuch as my disciples are enabled to buy lands. Behold, this is wisdom, that they may obtain it for an everlasting inheritance."[26] He appointed a land agent to make purchases for the Saints and a bishop to allot inheritances as they arrived.

Some converts from New York were already on the ground. Mormonism's oldest congregation, the Colesville Branch, keeping time with Joseph Smith's westering revelations, had made its way in the spring and summer of 1831 the 1250 miles from Broome County, New York, to Independence: to Buffalo, by lake sloop to Fairport, Ohio, settling briefly at the neighboring town of Thompson, then taking passage to St. Louis, arriving on June 25 by the river boat *Chieftain* at Independence, actually ahead of the Prophet. "I found it required all the wisdom I possessed," recorded Newell Knight, "to lead the company through so long a journey in the midst of their enemies." But the blessings were great: quite overcome at finding themselves at last "upon the western frontiers" and enraptured by the "pleasant aspect" of the country – its rich forest, beautiful streams, and widespread prairies, deep and rolling, "inviting the hand of industry to establish for itself homes upon its broad bosom" – they spoke the spirit of the gathering: "Our hearts went forth unto the Lord desiring fulfillment, that we might know where to bestow our labors profitably."[27]

In August the Prophet assisted the New Yorkers to lay the first log for a house as the foundation of Zion in Kaw Township, west of Big Blue a few miles from Independence. At the same time, Sidney Rigdon dedicated the land of Zion for the gathering. The next day the temple site was dedicated, a short distance west of Independence; and on the day following, the Saints held their first conference in Jackson County.[28] With a mercantile house, a printing office, and a periodical – *The Evening and the Morning Star* – soon to follow, it was a hopeful beginning for the central stake[29] of Zion's tent, which would "lengthen her cords and strengthen her stakes" as the arriving Saints filled up the countryside, establishing title to the Kingdom in good legal tender at the federal government's going rate of $1.25 an acre. The Saints had to purchase their inheritances; they were no handout. In 1833 the *Star* had to admonish mistaken zealots in realistic terms that would characterize all future immigration and settlement and be echoed in the instructions in coming mission periodicals, reflecting a sober and practical economics that once more distinguished the Saints from the adventists of the time: the "disciples of Christ" should not come without means to purchase their inheritances and the necessities of life; the Lord would not open the windows of heaven and rain down "angel's food" when their whole journey lay through "fertile country, stored with the blessings of life from his own hand for them to subsist upon." It was vain for them to build air castles. ". . . notwithstanding the fulness of the earth is for the saints, they can never expect it unless they use the means put into their hands to obtain the same in the manner provided by our Lord."[30]

But in 1833 the drivings began. Less imaginative frontier neighbors, mistaking thrift and industry for high-and-mightiness, had little sympathy with the pretensions of New Jerusalem, and the Saints, temporarily abandoning the lands of their inheritance in successive withdrawals across Missouri counties – Jackson, Clay, Caldwell, and Daviess – at length in 1839 redeemed a swamp at a bend of the Mississippi River in Illinois and renamed the squalid hamlet of Commerce, Nauvoo the Beautiful. In a few years it was teeming with thousands from New England, the East, and the Ohio country, and from the British Isles. For in 1837, spurred by the Kirtland revelations of 1836, Mormon evangelists – persuasive and powerful figures like Wilford Woodruff, John Taylor, and Heber C. Kimball, and shortly Brigham Young – went to Great Britain, the first step in making the gathering as wide as Europe itself. By 1840 converts were arriving in Nauvoo from England – over three thousand before the fateful city's evacuation in 1846.[31] With the migration from the States, Nauvoo became the regional capital of communities of Saints who were colonizing all around it in Illinois and across the river in Iowa. The Kingdom seemed here to stay, and the Prophet, pleased beyond his expectations in the flow from abroad, told his apostles in 1843 that he planned to go with them to England and from there throughout the world conducting a great revival. "I will yet take these brethren through the United States and through the world, and will make just as big a wake as God Almighty will let me; we must send kings and governors to Nauvoo, and we will do it." [32]

But despite such optimism, Nauvoo also had to be abandoned, torn by hostilities as much from within as from without, and it became a silent and deserted city providing not even the hospitality of a way station on the road west. In January 1847 from the Camp of Israel's Winter Quarters among the Omahas on the west bank of the Missouri River, Brigham Young rallied the Saints and hinted the new gathering place: in the Rocky Mountains, beyond the malice of the States, they would seek refuge. "Zion shall be redeemed in my own due time. . . . I am he who led the children of Israel out of the land of Egypt; and my arm is stretched out in the last days to save my people Israel." [33]

Let the Saints only covenant to keep all the commandments, and the promises would yet be fulfilled. Let them be organized into companies of hundreds, fifties, and tens with their captains, and let each company choose a number of "able-bodied and expert men, to take teams, seeds, and farming utensils" to go as pioneers for putting in spring crops. Let each company look to the poor, the widows, the fatherless, and the families of those who had gone into the army headed for Mexico; and let the companies prepare houses and fields for those remaining behind that season. Let all use their "influence and property to remove this people." Let them keep their mutual pledges, ceasing to contend with one another, ceasing drunkenness. Let them return what was borrowed, restore what they found that another had lost. Let them be wise stewards. And if they felt merry, let them "praise the Lord with singing, with music, with dancing, and with a prayer of praise and thanksgiving." If sorrowful, let them "call on the Lord . . . with supplication, that [their] souls may be joyful." Let the ignorant learn wisdom by humbling themselves. The nation had rejected the testimony of the Saints; now would come the day of its calamity unless it speedily repent. The blood of the Prophet cried out against it. As he sealed his testimony with his death, so let the Saints seal theirs with their diligence. The "Word and Will of the Lord" to Brigham Young was the Deuteronomy of the Saints' last journey into the wilderness. A renewal of their covenants and a strengthening of their hopes in the face of defeat, it was their Mayflower Compact, the civil and religious order of a people uprooted but saved by the ideology of the gathering from disintegration.[34]

"We have created in the wilderness of the western world a commonwealth for Christ, a spiritual New Jerusalem," wrote the divines of New England. "We have established the political Promised Land, and have set up the Lamp of Liberty for a beacon light to all nations," wrote the fathers of the American Revolution.[35] In the eyes of an astonished country, the New Canaan in the Valley of the Great Salt Lake seemed no less the work of zealots and rebels: Deseret would prosper, coming so clearly within the American tradition.

Though some wept at its desolation, to Brigham Young this was the destined place, and the Saints, turning readily to Scripture that spoke of deserts blossoming like the rose and of the mountain of the Lord's house being established in the tops of the mountains, found ample proof that the choice was prophetic.[36] It was a land of promise and possibility, a region requiring only to be wrested from the dual menace of drouth and the squalid aboriginals who clung precariously to its hills. Communities could be founded by faith and nourished by irrigation, and the Indians could be fed, fought if necessary, and converted. If one believed, the land lay, almost, in the lap of God, who sent the sea gulls to save the grain from marauding crickets and covered the hills with sego lilies whose roots sustained the hungry settlers through the second hard winter.

The beginnings had been severe. "It has been hard times for bread," wrote Parley P. Pratt on July 9, 1849, to his brother Orson in England; but he could report that harvest had commenced and he had cut some fine wheat. Rye, oats, barley, corn, and vegetables were all doing well, and, in his opinion, "the best foundation for a living in this country would be a herd of young heifers, driven from the States, or a drove of sheep." To the scores, the hundreds, of travelers arriving in the valley daily on their way to the gold fields of California,

> this spot suddenly bursts upon their astonished vision like a paradise in the midst of the desert. So great is the effect, that many of them burst forth in an ecstasy of admiration on emerging from the kanyon,

and gaining a first view of our town and its fields and gardens. Some shed tears, some shout, some dance and skip for joy; and all doubtless feel the spirit of the place resting upon them, with its joyous and heavenly influence bearing witness that here live the industrious, the free, the intelligent, and the good.[37]

By the fall of 1849 the First Presidency of the church, in a general epistle addressed to "the Saints scattered throughout the earth," could review an encouraging year. A provisional government for the new state of Deseret had been formed, with a constitution and elected officers, and Congress was being petitioned for admission into the Union. A good carriage road ran a hundred miles from the Weber River on the north to Provo River on the south, with "fine cultivated fields and civilized dwellings more or less from one extreme to the other." Good frame bridges crossed many of the streams, and ferries had been established on the Upper Platte during high water and at each crossing of Green River – important for next spring's immigration.

Some fifteen to twenty thousand immigrants from the States bound for the coast had passed through the city, "filling the valley with goods" as in their haste they exchanged three heavy wagons for one light one and disposed of clothing, goods, and equipment at one quarter their New York or St. Louis wholesale value. The immigration of the Saints involved some five to six hundred wagons during the season, "besides many who come in search of gold, hear the gospel for the first time and will go no farther, having believed and been baptized . . . many of whom are among the most respectable and wealthy." New valleys were being explored and sites selected for settlement. Timber was abundant; three grist mills were operating.

In Salt Lake City itself a spacious bowery for public worship had been built on the temple block; a council house was nearly completed; a foundation had been laid for an extensive storehouse and granary. A fund for helping poor Saints to immigrate had been created, since it had been covenanted that "we would never cease our exertions, by all the means and influence within our reach, till all the Saints who were obliged to leave Nauvoo should be located at some gathering place." The need now in all Zion was for laborers and multiplied means of farming and building: "We want men. Brethren, come from the States, from the nations, come! and help us to build and grow, until we can say, enough, the valleys of Ephraim are full."[38]

With the prospect so fair for the future of Zion, it was time to turn once more to the wider obligations which the gospel of the gathering imposed: the warning, the invitation, and the promise must go to the oppressed continent of Europe:

> Ye Saints who dwell on Europe's shore,
> Prepare yourselves with many more
> To leave behind your native land,
> For sure God's judgments are at hand.[39]

At a general conference of the church in October 1849, the appointments indicated that Mormonism was going to "the nations" in earnest: Apostle John Taylor to France and Germany, Apostle Lorenzo Snow to Italy and Switzerland, Apostle Erastus Snow and Elder Peter Hansen to Denmark, Elder John Forsgren to Sweden.[40]

They were a small company for so great an undertaking. But they went as the Lord's husbandmen, confident the harvest was waiting for them to thrust in the sickle before the great field of the world should be burned as stubble. That confidence was to die with them and their convert generation. They themselves could never imagine that the millennial hope would burn out, the program of the gathering come to a halt, and the doctrine itself, though its language remained the same, suffer a change. Only the fact that Utah's turbulence gave each new generation of Saints its own provocations with the enemy, making it as militant as the first with its own memories to pass on to the children, kept the ideology incandescent so long. The intoxicant biblical images, the apocalyptic rhetoric disappeared as the expectations subsided and as, with the renunciation of polygamy in 1890, the whiplash of persecution ceased to sting. Legislation aimed at drying up Mormon immigration hastened what changing social and economic conditions were already accomplishing.[41]

Zion meant "the pure in heart," a people and a condition, and it meant the place where the pure in heart dwell. For the first generation it was Zion as a place that was preached with so much passion and commitment and that found expression in the practical program of immigration and settlement. But as outside influences broke in upon the harmony of one faith, one Lord, and one people, Zion became less provincial; the idea and the ideal expanded to mean any place where the pure in heart dwell. It meant permanent churches and at last even temples in Europe, once condemned as Babylon.[42] The great events which had seemed so imminent retreated into a future comfortably remote, and Mormonism settled down to an indefinite postponement of prophecy.

It was an accommodation to changing times. Abroad as at home, the newer generation, less literal in their reading of Scripture – if they knew the Bible at all – were apathetic to issues that spelled the end of the world, and the beginning of another, to the earlier age. Europe, moreover, was finding itself by the end of the century less oppressed, and domestic programs which provided economic opportunities for more people and an outlet for social pressures weakened the old longing for distant utopias. Besides, the sky was no longer the limit in Zion. Once the encyclicals had urged, "Let all who can procure a bit of bread, and one garment on their back, be assured there is water plenty and pure by the way, and doubt no longer, but come next year to the place of gathering, even in flocks, as doves fly to their windows before a storm."[43] But in 1891, forty years later, they played a different tune: "Respecting the gathering, the elders should explain the principle when occasion requires; but acting upon it should be left entirely to the individual."[44] To talk of emigration only "when occasion requires" reveals a startling transition from the days when the clarion call was to redeem the faithful and bring them singing to Zion. It was a day of pruning – the Saints were welcome, but at their own risk.

In 1849, however, when the handful of redoubtable elders stood ready to carry their gospel abroad, Salt Lake City, the City of the Saints, as the British traveler Sir Richard Burton called it,[45] seemed the city set on a hill. It was Zion visible and growing. Its citizen missionaries would soon be found all over northern Europe spreading its fame, especially in Scandinavia, the "land of the north," where the blood of dispersed Israel was supposed to run thick. In the coming siege of Babylon, the elders' untroubled image of Zion as a refuge would prove their brightest weapon.

CHAPTER 3

The Siege of Babylon

"THE KINGDOM IS BELEAGUERED BY THIS MISSIONARY ARMY FROM UTAH."[1]

THE conference call of 1849 marked the beginning of a significant expansion of Mormonism's transatlantic career with important consequences for the peopling of Deseret.[2] Soon strange tongues would be heard in the meetinghouses of Zion, and Yankee frontiersmen would teach inexperienced villagers from the Old World the mysteries of irrigation. Of all the countries—France, Switzerland, Italy, Germany, and Scandinavia—"opened" by Mormon elders the following year, Scandinavia would prove most fruitful, in time the annual number of conversions even surpassing that of Great Britain, where for thirteen years the movement had been reaping a remarkable harvest. At the moment, there were actually more Mormons in England than in America.[3] The British Mission, which had already given Mormonism a lifesaving stability and continuity during the troublous days following the martyrdom, now became the base of operations for the thrust to the European mainland. It was Zion's stoutest stronghold in Babylon, a source of wealth and manpower, securely anchoring provincial Deseret's spectacularly lengthened line of communication. Headquarters at Liverpool served as Mormonism's busy European clearinghouse for arriving missionaries and departing converts. The mission, launched in 1837 in a desperate moment following the failure of Mormon affairs at Kirtland, had been a bold enterprise. Characterized by aggressive leadership and strenuous self-help, it established the pattern for the Scandinavian adventure, to which it gave as the first of many fostering acts some timely assistance: the Saints in England and Scotland took up a collection for Apostle Snow and his companions as they preached their way to Copenhagen.

Erastus Snow, a stocky Vermonter, deliberate in speech and action, was only thirty-two but already a veteran missionary and colonizer, who had once been imprisoned with Joseph Smith and had quoted Blackstone in his own defense. He had carried the chain for surveying the first town lots of Nauvoo and, after enduring the rigors of Winter Quarters, where he lost a child, had scouted the Salt Lake Valley ahead of Brigham Young's pioneers. He had traveled some eighty thousand miles in the ministry in the eastern states and had crossed "the backbone of the continent," as he put it, four times – on one occasion, in 1848, to solicit aid in New York and Boston for the destitute Saints scattered between Illinois and the Rocky Mountains. After nearly two years in Scandinavia he would stop in England on his way home to organize the Deseret Iron Company and, back in Utah Territory, strengthen the Iron County settlement; in 1854 he would be in St. Louis directing Mormon migration from the frontier; and in 1861, after two other tours of duty in the states, he would establish the Cotton Mission in Utah's Dixie, where he would remain the rest of his life, serving as a kind of regional administrator, Mormonism's nearest approach to an archbishopric. A polygamist who eventually married five wives, he was typical of the strong men to whom Brigham Young entrusted the affairs of the Kingdom.[4]

Snow's missionary journey to Scandinavia – he was underway eight months – illustrates the resourcefulness of the early Mormon elders.[5] He had to leave his family in primitive circumstances: his two households were sheltered in rude one-room huts, one of adobe, the other of logs, connected by a shed, with wagon boxes drawn alongside for sleeping. It was nine months before he heard from them again, only to learn of his eldest son's death. On October 19, 1849, driving a light wagon drawn by a span of skinny horses (the goldseekers had bought the best animals in the valley), he joined Peter Ole Hansen and John Erik Forsgren in a twelve-wagon caravan of thirty-five missionaries and merchants at the mouth of Emigration Canyon, where Brigham Young gave them a parting blessing and where in a few years he would welcome their return at the head of the first companies of immigrant converts.

Braving mountain snows which more than once nearly foundered their underfed animals, they made their way together as far as the Mormon settlement of Kanesville, Iowa, across the frozen Missouri, where late in December the Saints hailed them with songs and gun salute, overjoyed at seeing friends from "the Valley." The company had encountered Apostle Ezra T. Benson's westbound train, including Canute Peterson and his Norwegians, on the Weber River, somewhat the worse for storms endured at South Pass and had given them fresh oxen for the final pull. From Kanesville the missionaries made their separate ways to the sea, the Saints in St. Louis and Boston and New Orleans helping them along. They planned to meet in England.

Snow himself went to St. Louis, where, in February, he sold his outfit and sent some foodstuffs back to his needy family. He stopped at Canton, Ohio, where he baptized his brother Zerubbabel and his family. When the next year Zerubbabel received an appointment as judge of the supreme court of the new Utah Territory, Erastus felt it was "from the Lord, though it came through the President."[6] Calling on lukewarm Saints wherever he stopped, Snow made his way by steamboat to Pittsburgh and by rail to Washington, where Mormons Almon Babbitt and J. M. Bernhisel were lobbying for admission of Deseret to the Union. For a week in March he called on senators and congressmen in the same cause, but felt it hopeless. Listening to Calhoun, Clay, Webster, Cass, Benton, and Douglas debate the California and slavery questions, he realized how incidental in the great compromise his own crusade seemed. Of greater immediate consequence were the letters to the ministries in Europe which he had the foresight to obtain from the secretary of state and various members of Congress.

In Philadelphia, where he preached in a hall familiar to him in the days of the Prophet and where he found most of the Saints poor and getting ready to emigrate west in the spring but still able to contribute fifteen dollars toward his journey, he called on Colonel Thomas L. Kane, renowned friend of the Mormons, and met the Danish minister to the United States, though he does not say what happened.

En route to old haunts in New England, Snow spent a few days in New York, inquiring about passage to England, visiting Saints, and enjoying the hospitality of Colonel John Reese, one of the gentile merchants with whom he had left Salt Lake in October, beginning a friendship that brought the colonel to the edge of conversion. In Boston and Cambridgeport, in Marblehead and Salem, as in every other place, the Saints gave their mite toward his mission, though one old neighbor locked the door against him and some backtrailers whom he had known in happier days in Nauvoo had lost the faith. With Apostle Wilford

Woodruff, who was getting ready to lead several New England congregations west in April, he sent some money home, with a $50 donation besides toward the church's Perpetual Emigrating Fund for the removal of the poor Saints from the Iowa frontier. Finally, on April 4, after a briefing on European affairs from Apostle Orson Pratt, fresh from England and on his way to Salt Lake, Snow left Boston on the steamer *Niagara*, arriving in Liverpool on the 16th. Hansen had arrived a week before; Forsgren came in three days later.

Hansen went to Scotland, where the Saints gave him clothes and a little money. Then, without waiting for Snow, he set out for Denmark, only to be rejected by his father's family. While waiting for Snow and Forsgren, he wrote a little tract, *En Advarsel til Folket*, "A Warning to the People," the first piece of Mormon literature in Scandinavia.[7] Snow tarried two months to make a twelve-hundred-mile preaching tour of the British Mission. In Bradford he found George P. Dykes, who had been the first Mormon elder to the Norwegian settlements in Illinois, and invited him to come along to Copenhagen. Dykes had seen service with the Mormon Battalion, where he had won a reputation for "military" sermons and testiness, a trait which would prove more hindrance than help to Snow, but for the moment he seemed a strong addition. After a rendezvous in London with Apostle Lorenzo Snow, who was headed for Italy, and Apostle John Taylor, who was headed for France, Snow, Dykes, and Forsgren embarked at Hull on June 11 and crossed the North Sea to Zealand, largest of the Danish isles.[8]

They arrived in Copenhagen on Friday, June 14. Hansen met them and led them to a room in a cheap hotel where they knelt in thanksgiving for their safe deliverance and dedicated themselves to God's service. But the gaming at the billiard tables and the clatter of carriages on the street distressed Snow, and after a sleepless night he wandered the city calling on different families "to try their spirit and examine rooms." At Lauritz B. Malling's house on Bredgade "the ark came to rest." In a pleasant upper room overlooking the garden, the elders were soon receiving visitors curious to see "the Americans," and Snow, as yet unable to speak Danish, communicated by pointing to passages in their own Bible which they seemed to discover for the first time. The landlord and his family liked to hear them sing and pray and were soon numbered among their earliest converts.

The elders wasted no time. On their first Sunday they attended the

Baptist meeting of the reformer Peter C. Mönster, who, often imprisoned for his agitation against the Establishment, welcomed them as allies in dissent. It was a fellowship he would sadly withdraw with the discovery the Mormons had a program of their own which lost him followers. On Tuesday, with a letter of introduction from Senator Cooper, the elders called on the Honorable Walter Forward, United States minister to Denmark. A Pennsylvanian and former member of President Harrison's cabinet, he proved "an openhearted and honorable gentleman of the old school" who regretted the persecution of the Mormons at home and promised the elders due assistance as American citizens. On Wednesday Forsgren left for his native Gefle, six hundred miles away on Sweden's Baltic coast, where he hoped for a kindly reception from the father he had not seen in twenty years. Dykes meanwhile proselyted Mönster's congregation, Hansen worked over his manuscript translation of the *Book of Mormon*, and Snow, pondering how best to proceed in his momentous calling on alien soil, studied the language and the laws, observed the life of the city, and strove to become familiar with the customs of the country.

"From my first appointment," he wrote Brigham Young in August, "my mind rested upon Copenhagen as the best place in all Scandinavia to commence my work, and every thing has since strengthened my convictions." [9] He found the capital "a beautiful city, the seat of learning for northern Europe," though given, he felt compelled to add, to "priestcraft, infidelity, and politics." It was still lighted with "the old oil lamps" and served by fire companies that hauled their hose and water "on sleds with tubs and barrels." But the fortifications, the public buildings, the walks and gardens were impressive, though in July the hospitals of the city looked like "slaughter-houses and the surgeons, butchers" as they tended the three thousand wounded brought in from the Schleswig-Holstein battlefield, one of the bloody wrangles, as it seemed to him, that was ripening Europe for final destruction.

Snow often saw the clergy on the street in their black gowns and white ruffles and observed they could be seen as often at the popular amusements. Sunday, indeed, was lightly esteemed: balls flourished in the evening and the theaters were thronged. Churchgoing seemed to be out of fashion, with audiences of eight or ten not uncommon in even the popular churches. In the country, where the villagers lived in "miserable houses, with thatched roofs and clay floors, and are generally filthy and uncouth in their habits," he did not fail to notice that the church nevertheless stood ready to receive their tithes. The man with the hoe was priest-ridden, and Snow longed to free him from bondage.

In Copenhagen's splendid Frue Kirke he sat through a consecration service with mounting indignation. A marble statue of Jesus overlooked the altar and statues of the apostles ranged the walls. If these were living figures, Snow mused, what would they say to the archbishop surrounded by his clergy in their sacerdotal robes? By the influence of this clergy and at the instigation of this bishop, P. C. Mönster had repeatedly been imprisoned for exhorting the people to follow the example of Jesus in going down into the water. This was the bishop who believed it the duty of the government to protect Denmark from the Mormons as a dangerous sect. These were the men who padlocked the Bible and pocketed the key. "Surely," Snow raged inwardly, "the great mother of abominations with her numerous progeny of the protestant family, after their fathers martyred Jesus and his apostles, transgressed his laws, changed his ordinances, broke his everlasting covenant and drove the last vestige of his kingdom from the earth, have now placed their statues in her temples to grace her triumph." [10] What a work, not for reformation merely, but for the new broom of the restored gospel. The obstacles, he knew, would be great:

> The novelty of a new religion in the country, the excitability of the people, the control of the priests over churches and schoolhouses; the fear of violence and damage that deters men from leasing us houses; the restrictions of law upon street preaching and promiscuous assemblages; the spleen and jealousy of a well organized national police. . . .[11]

Snow determined to work quietly. The time would come when he and his companions and their new followers could emerge from retirement and seek, as he put it, notoriety. For the moment they met privately in small family gatherings. "Our preaching is mostly fireside preaching." In the lowly homes of a potter, a shoemaker, a bargeman, a clerk, an ex-soldier, they read aloud from the pages of Hansen's manuscript translation of the *Book of Mormon* and the *Doctrine and Covenants*, kept Orson Hyde's "German work" moving among "the Dutch," and English tracts among those who could read them. Early in August, within two months after their arrival in Copenhagen, the Americans baptized their first converts – twenty-six Germans, Swedes, and Danes, most of them Mönster's followers "and the best he had." Snow felt reassured. "We thank God that the seed has sprung up and has deep root . . . if we are banished from the country, the work will spread."[12]

By September he had sufficient confidence to form "Jesu Kristi Kirke af Sidste Dages Hellige" in Denmark with a Copenhagen congregation of fifty members and sought recognition from the national Ministry of Culture and from Copenhagen's Board of Magistrates, who granted permission for a place of worship though without the promise of protection. The new Saints found a hall on Lille Kongensgade, near the heart of the city, and, as poor laboring folk, did what they could to furnish it, Snow advancing fifty rigsdaler for three months' rent. There, on September 18, Elder Forsgren, banished from Sweden and just arrived in Copenhagen, gave their first assembly an exciting account of his three months, a foretaste of difficulties to come.

At Gefle he had found his brother Peter Adolph and sister Christina Erika at the old homestead; they had seen him coming in a dream. His old father was absent on a sea voyage to America, actually seeking his son. Forsgren raised Peter from a consumptive sickbed and baptized him. (The event would be remembered fifty years later at a great Scandinavian reunion in a Utah town when Peter Forsgren, weaver and patriarch, with a head like Walt Whitman's, received a gold-headed cane as the Scandinavian Mission's first convert.) Encouraged by his family's warm reception, Elder Forsgren translated one of Orson Pratt's pamphlets on the rise and doctrine of the church, but the printers refused to touch it. Neighbors on whom he called warned him Sweden imposed grave penalties for religious activity outside the Establishment. The *Landskansliet*, or county authorities, moreover, retained his passport to immobilize him. Forsgren determined to go to Stockholm, but he missed his steamer and while waiting for another he heard of a shipload of farmers about to sail. He looked them up in their warehouse lodgings to learn they sought religious freedom and their fortune in America. With interest they heard Forsgren, whose enthusiasm led to a public meeting in a grove outside town. He baptized seventeen of the farmers and organized them into a church community, ordaining and instructing them as the short time allowed, and saw them off, to be lost to history, though Forsgren later claimed some reached Zion.

Flushed with his success, Forsgren risked a second public meeting. "Some wept, others rejoiced, and nearly all seemed to feel that surely a prophet had come among them." But the marshal took him into custody and marched him into town, amid the crowd's shouts of "the dipper" and "the prophet," to be arraigned successively before county, clerical, and municipal officers. He seemed another instance of the *Praedeke Sygdom*, the preaching sickness, and doctors were ordered to examine him. But Forsgren's American passport and prosperous appearance prompted them to send him to Stockholm, where he was kept a prisoner at large for a month until he could be shipped off to America. The endorsement on his passport warned that the "North American consul . . . rejects him, and leaves him without protection," and described his infractions: ". . . disturbed the general peace by illegal preaching in warehouses and in the open air before several hundred persons, and has even performed the act of baptizing several grown persons on the seashore." In Stockholm Forsgren gained considerable notoriety in the press and through his court appearances, until the city put him, with passage paid, aboard an American vessel with strict instructions not to put him ashore anywhere in Scandinavia. But at Elsinore, where the vessel stopped to pay Danish toll, he was permitted to leave by a sympathetic captain, only to be picked up on grounds of vagrancy by the police, who had been alerted by the Swedish consul. As luck would have it, Ambassador Walter Forward was in Elsinore; he assumed responsibility for Forsgren and accompanied him to Copenhagen, where to the young Saints hearing his recital the zealous missionary seemed the hero of the hour.[13]

As *persona non grata* in his native Sweden, Forsgren busied himself instead among the Swedes in Copenhagen, and with one or another of the new converts took missions to various Danish isles, while Snow went to England to raise funds for printing a Danish edition of the *Book of Mormon* and Dykes, at first disgruntled to be sent from Copenhagen, went up to Aalborg, Jutland, where once more the Baptists proved the readiest converts and provided the core of a soon thriving congregation. Snow felt "quite willing that the Lord should use the Methodists and Baptists to prepare the way for the fulness of the gospel; for their systems are less exceptionable to the wicked, and they have more sympathy to sustain them."[14] But the Baptist leaders were not so willing, and in Aalborg, where the town was constantly confusing Mormons and Baptists and once even stoned a Baptist meeting by mistake, the Baptists followed in the wake of Mormon tracting in an attempt to win back old members.

At the close of a first year in Scandinavia, Snow could look back on gratifying accomplishments: a membership of three hundred, half of it in Copenhagen; the beginnings of a local ministry; a clear indication that the government was disposed to allow the Mormons their course unobstructed; a Danish edition of the *Book of Mormon*, a psalm book, selections from the *Doctrine and Covenants*, an effective tract *En Sandheds Röst*, "A Voice of Truth," all published, with a monthly periodical about to be undertaken. There had been, to be sure, a few mobbings in Denmark and banishment from Sweden, and no work had yet been attempted in Norway. But Snow could exult in his report to Brigham Young that "the shell is broken in old Scandinavia, and the work of the Lord will advance."[15] Before another year had passed and Snow was recalled, membership stood at one thousand, with one hundred fifty in the local ministry.[16] From the beginning, visitors from European headquarters at Liverpool had high hopes for the Scandinavian Mission. In 1855 when Daniel Spencer asserted that "the good order in the meetings, the due respect paid to each individual officer in his place, the manner of keeping records and books, and the peace and union which pervade the hearts of the Saints are not surpassed in the oldest Conference in England," he was sounding highest praise; he was confident the time was "not far distant when this will be the most important mission in Europe."[17]

Snow felt that he and his companions had come at the right moment, that an earlier mission probably would have proved a failure. The leaven of religious dissent and social unrest at work in all three Scandinavian countries had prepared the way. In Denmark the nationalistic followers of N. F. S. Grundtvig, dissatisfied with the rationalism and dead formalism of the Establishment, were trying through poetry, myth, and saga to return Lutheranism to "old-fashioned, living Christianity," rendering it pure and patriotic, and were getting ready to establish their folk high schools. By 1854 a very different movement of otherworldly pietists founded the Indre Mission, or Inner Mission Society, whose laymen went from house to house exhorting and selling religious tracts, their doctrine of depravity a far cry from the robust paganism of the Grundtvigians.[18]

The unrest in Denmark had produced a liberal constitution just the year before the Mormons arrived. Snow's first act was to have Hansen translate the document into English for close study. Snow concluded that the country now enjoyed as much political freedom as England and the chances for religious liberty were reassuring. Had they come earlier, under the old law they would not have been permitted to proselyte on pain of expulsion as foreigners. Noting the banishment of some Methodists and Baptists from Sweden, and "quite a war going on in the Swedish papers about it," Snow prayed that it might grow until Norway and Sweden followed Denmark's example. "French philosophy, infidelity, and republican principles" in that once absolute monarchy had so increased that "at the death of the old king [Frederick VII], the nation had kept the heir to the throne at bay" until they were granted the liberal *Grundlov* of June 5, 1849, securing to them an elected legislature and generous provisions on behalf of dissenters.[19] In session when the elders arrived in Copenhagen, this first people's Rigsdag, it was hoped, would annul old laws obnoxious to the new spirit.

An important reform was the abolition of the "odious" passport system. Formerly even natives had been subject to arrest and imprisonment if caught overnight beyond the limits of their own town or parish without a passport. The continual renewing of passes, their signing and countersigning by the police at every stopping place, and the attendant expense and inconvenience would have paralyzed Mormon proselyting in Denmark; as it was, recurrent "vagrancy" charges vexed the elders for years.

Snow found the press sufficiently "free and untrammeled" for his purposes, and though it supported the Establishment it did defend the right of citizens to organize dissenting societies, whose privileges, however, still had to be defined by law. But Snow found the popular mind lagging behind the enlightenment: "We have to preach the Constitution to prepare the way for the Bible, and the Bible to prepare the way for the Book of Mormon."[20] An ingenious provision had long ago given a clergy-controlled charitable institution, Veisenhuuset, the exclusive right to distribute the Bible in Danish. Snow found "a few honorable exceptions" among the clergy who favored reformation and showed zeal for the diffusion of Scriptures, but "We sometimes may hunt whole neighborhoods over and not find a copy of the Scriptures, except, perhaps, in church, or with the priest."[21]

It took time for Denmark's official liberalism to soak in. Snow lamented that the provisions for dissenters were permissive merely, without the guarantee of protection in free worship which he had been used to in England and the United States. "The Danish Constitution allows religious freedom, but it is not supported by other existing laws, nor the moral strength of the land, and with the exception of Copenhagen and the larger commercial centers, it is hardly known such freedom exists." [22] The Mormons knew their rights better than many local prosecutors, who, while often sincere enough, did not always know what the new religious freedoms were or to whom they might be extended. Many were not at all aware that normal civil and social privileges like marriage could now be extended to those not "sprinkled, educated, and confirmed" by the Establishment. Local officials had to write to the Ministry of Culture for clarification: in 1851 the mayor of Aalborg had to know whether he could permit public meetings; the police had closed up the Mormon hall because, as if the Baptists weren't enough, the Mormons were throwing his town into an uproar. The Kultus-minister informed him the government interposed no obstacles to their right to worship.[23] In 1852 eight hundred fifty names appeared on a petition to the Rigsdag itself asking that "our persons, goods, and property may be protected in our worship according to the freedom which the Constitution grants," but nothing ever came of it. Unluckily, the memorial came just when the slanders of the federal judges who had deserted their posts in Utah were appearing in the Copenhagen press.[24]

The following year the Rigsdag heard a full-dress review of the Mormon question when Counselor Hjorth of the Ministry of Justice asked the Kultus-minister what his intentions were toward the energetic and growing movement—not that he wished to see the civil power invoked against a religious sect, for that was contrary to the spirit of the new constitution; but the common people, many of whom seemed sincere enough in joining the Mormons—though some seemed to hope for temporal gain—put great store by what the administration would say. Wouldn't the government publicly condemn the Mormons as corrupt? The Kultus-minister refused the bait; he firmly insisted that the government could take a stand only against what openly threatened the morals and good order of the kingdom, in which event the Ministry of Justice would have to act. Member Haas felt the Mormons had as much right to live in Denmark as polygamous

Mohammedans. Member Lindberg defended the ideal of perfect religious liberty. Member Hansen urged that the Mormons be allowed to worship in their own way but not be permitted to go about the country advertising their faith – a proposal which met strong disapproval from all sides of the house. The discussion concluded on the self-satisfied note that Mormonism was an upstart religion hardly to be compared with Christianity's 1800-year-old revelation. The Establishment, it was hoped, would be more vigorous in opposing its spread.[25]

Individual diet members took friendly notice of the Mormons from time to time. The smith Anders Winberg, while proselyting in the Randers area in 1851, impressed Sören Kjaer, who as a prominent Rigsdag member later proved a steadfast defender of the Mormons. When the sister of a Rigsdag representative from the island of Bornholm joined the Mormons he asked them only not to influence her to leave home for Zion.[26]

In 1856, in the Lolland and Falster diocese, chamberlain Esquire Wickfeldt persuaded several hundred peasants to petition His Majesty to take steps to stop "that awful delusion, Mormonism." The king told the deputation who presented the signatures that he would take the matter into consideration, for "it had been upon his mind a long time." But the liberals got wind of it and ridiculed the petitioners for taking a step against their own interests: the intervention they sought was unconstitutional and threatened the whole cause of religious liberty. Better leave it to the learned and well-paid clergy – on whom the irony was not lost – to carry on the war against the Mormons. And if the Establishment could not stand without the help of the police, let it totter.[27]

Twenty years later the liberals, as the *Venstre*, or party of the Left, championed the cause again. The municipal authorities in various places sought to forbid Mormon meetings. The case went to the Rigsdag, where a lively debate ensued, with the *Venstre* insisting Mormons should have the same privileges as other sects. One member declared the Mormon elders had done ten times more to enlighten the people on religion than all the Lutheran priests together had done; and besides, he felt it unfitting for the honorable members of the Rigsdag to trouble themselves with religious questions. Once again the argument was that the Establishment should fend for itself.[28]

On a few other occasions the government took official notice of the Mormons. In 1879 it received a solicitation from United States Secretary of State William Evarts to cut off the stream of Mormon migration at its source, on grounds that as theoretical polygamists they were potential criminals – a request the Danish government politely pointed out was manifestly absurd.[29] In 1885 United States consuls abroad were instructed not to extend protection to American citizens engaged as Mormon missionaries. And in the 1880s and 1890s Denmark's so-called Foreigners' Law, designed to keep out anarchists, was mistakenly invoked to banish half a dozen missionaries whom a new generation of officials viewed as radicals.[30] Except for these lapses, Denmark was from the beginning officially hospitable. It was left-handed recognition, but it gave Mormonism needed legal status, for which it had to wait considerably longer in Norway and Sweden.

Those countries fought dissent with the powerful voices of pulpit and press and with conventicle acts from the preceding century forbidding public preaching, religious gatherings in the home, the "enticing" of anyone from the mother faith in any manner, or administering any of the ordinances and sacraments which were the proper business of official Lutheranism.[31] The Establishment, chief vested interest of governments virtually theocratic, resisted whatever threatened to disturb the rigid mold of society and its four estates. "To educate the peasants beyond the requirements of religion was to encourage social disorder,"[32] and "the requirements of religion" were the strict province of the state church. Sweden, alarmed at the spreading "preaching sickness" and the increasing participation of laymen in religious services, was particularly severe with nonconformists during Mormonism's first decade in Scandinavia. The Conventicle Placate of 1726, long a dead letter, was revived to cope with the rising tide of dissent. Even after 1858, when it was revoked, everyone was born a legal member of the state church, paid it an automatic tithe, and could separate from it only by formal application.[33] But much was left up to local jurisdiction, and what went unnoticed in one province was harshly dealt with in another. Though popular thought was fast liberalizing, sticklers held out for their pound of flesh. In the 1840s the radical acts of the Jansonists, who burned all religious books except the Bible, may have put the authorities on guard against the Methodists, Baptists, and Mormons.

Not until the spring of 1852, when Anders Winberg went to Skane, did Mormonism get a foothold in Sweden. Nils Capson's big barn in Lund, festooned with evergreen boughs, housed the first meetings, miraculously undisturbed, and the first baptisms were performed in a tanner's vat. Though old Father Capson himself later sought refuge in Copenhagen, indignant at his country's narrow policy, times improved rapidly and the 1880s found official attitudes of Denmark and Sweden reversed; the elders who were banished from Denmark as undesirable foreigners finished out their missions in Sweden, where they encountered "great good will among the people and houses full of attentive listeners." [34] In 1886, in fact, not the Mormons but those who disturbed their meetings were for once arrested and fined – a startling turnabout from the days when Mickael Johnson, one of the first missionaries, was shaved and chained and carted from town to town as a shameful exhibit of what the Mormons were supposed to look like.[35] The clergy were not particularly happy with the new tolerance. One pastor in 1900 looked enviously to Germany's arbitrary exclusion of the missionaries; the least Sweden could do, he felt, was to appoint a pair of priests to tour the country in the Mormons' wake and, further, strengthen the work of the Augustana Synod in Utah, where it had maintained a counter-mission for some five or six years.[36] In 1902 it was only because the Mormons encouraged emigration that they were denied a petition seeking recognition of their proselytes as separated from the state church, one in a long series of such memorials.[37]

Norway had passed measures as early as 1845 which tolerated dissenters belonging to duly recognized societies, but only after formal, personal application at nineteen years of age or older to the parish priest – a difficult condition which none of the Mormon converts seemed to observe.[38] The theological faculty at Christiania and the bishops of the Establishment periodically debated whether Mormons were true Christians and as such an admissible sect, but fear of the supposed Mormon ideal of setting up a state within a state forbade their recognition. "Have the Mormons actually come to this city?" asked the incredulous provost of Osterrisor in September 1851, when tailor H. F. Petersen, fresh from Aalborg, asked permission to hold a meeting in the schoolhouse.[39] The plague could not have startled him more.

The Mormons repeatedly memorialized the Storting for recognition under existing dissenter provisions. In 1852, 1854, 1856, and 1862 petitions signed by as many as eight hundred names got nowhere. In 1865

Mormon Iver Isaksen, influential owner of a large mechanics works in Oslo, approached parliament representatives in vain.[40] Finally, in 1882, a petition bearing 638 signatures produced a change in a section of the law which, without specifically naming the Mormons, legalized their services.[41] Meanwhile, except for frequent imprisonments and fines in the first few years, the Mormons operated unmolested, local authorities, much less severe than in Sweden, often winking at the letter of the law or applying it regretfully and making confinement as endurable as possible. Carl Widerborg—former schoolteacher who had joined the Mormons after a compassionate visit to two of them in prison, and who was himself arrested three times thereafter in Oslo—was on affable, hat-tipping terms with local officials when they met on the street:

"Have you preached lately, Mr. Widerborg?"
"Yes."
"Have you baptized anyone?"
"Yes."
"But you know that is against the law of the land?"
"Yes, I know that, but it is according to God's law."
"Yes, but we must judge you according to the law of the land."
"Very well! You do your duty, and I will do mine."[42]

The law was one thing, popular feeling another; and the popular mind, like the official, was divided. The law could nominally permit or restrict or be ignored as a dead letter, but owners could refuse halls, police withhold protection, the clergy rouse resentment, the press misinform, and neighbors monger scandal. Mormonism reaped a double harvest: converts from among the social and religious discontents, and abuse already generated against these. "The many uneducated colporteurs and itinerant preachers," reported the governor of Westmanslandlän, Sweden, in 1860, "prepare the way for proselyters of the Baptist and Mormon faiths."[43] Of American origin, Mormonism may have seemed doubly fearful to those who regarded any influence from abroad as dangerous, adding fuel to ideas already unsettling the social order. "To the clergy and official classes in Sweden, America was anathema. . . . a Godless country, ravaged by sects. . . . emigrants [were] 'traitors' and 'unfaithful sons.'"[44]

Erastus Snow and a successor, probate judge Hector C. Haight, feared most the unbridled enthusiasms of their own converts, whose "harsh preaching" and whose appetite for "reproving and reproaching both priest and people for their religion" often reaped the whirlwind.[45] Snow urged caution. But his companion Dykes was himself a fire-eater. In Aalborg, where Dykes had published an unauthorized chronological table attempting to prove that the last days were at hand, two of his converts, ironmaster Hans Peter Jensen and tailor Christian Larsen, enraged a crowd of a thousand gathered at the seashore to witness a Mormon baptism. Told their church and clergy were of the devil, the crowd became a mob; they stoned the men, razed the meeting place, and broke every Mormon's windows. The town was in a tumult for nine days, "the police quarreling among themselves, the citizens with each other, and the lower classes fighting among themselves."[46] Snow, in England at the time, was dismayed at this imprudence. "Where a cold indifference prevails," he admonished, "a little *healthy excitement* to arouse the public mind to investigation may be profitable, provided it can be controlled and the *truth kept before the people*." But the voice of truth could not be heard above outraged feelings. A little fire upon the hearth on a cold day was very convenient, if it didn't burn down the house.[47]

A more uncontrollable provocation of mob violence was the scandalous stories editors, ministers, and the man in the street told about the Mormons. On August 20, 1850, Snow noted that "a very scurrilous letter about the Mormons, from America, has just appeared in a Copenhagen paper translated from a French paper. It is the first of the kind that has appeared."[48] The papers were soon teeming with misrepresentations, "the usual catalogue of transatlantic lies," ill winds of rumor that sorely buffeted the Saints. Copenhagen, in and around which was concentrated a fourth of Denmark's population, witnessed some turbulent scenes. The humbler sections of the city yielded willing listeners but, along with them, the rabble. Services were so regularly disturbed by students from the university out for a lark, by mobilized artisans and apprentices, by roughnecks, that they were suspended for several months during the first year. Unruly elements would interrupt services, abuse the speakers, threaten the Saints as they came and departed, and in their vandalism pile up the benches, rip the casements, stave in the doors. Poor landlord Nehm could no longer afford to rent his hall to the luckless Mormons, who tried in vain to secure a government building as sanctuary. One early convert, a burgher of the city, at times used the privileges of his class to obtain militia who were posted with fixed bayonets at the door or in the aisles during the service.[49]

Sometimes the violence was personal. Homes of new converts were attacked. It became the common saying that to join the Mormons was to have one's windows broken. What was mere diversion in Copenhagen turned to special vengeance in the villages, thanks to the intensity of distrust in a neighbor tainted with a foreign delusion. A mob burned down the cottage of tailor Jacob Bohn, crying, "Let's baptize the Mormon priest in his own blood." Bohn, searching the ruins after the debacle, praised God his journal containing fifty hymns for the new faith had not been destroyed. Hans Peter Jensen, during the Aalborg troubles, had to flee from a crowd that stormed his dwelling, tore the tiles from the roof for brickbats, and made a shambles of the place. Peasant girls held stones in their skirts while others pelted. "Call on your God now and see if he will help you." In Osterrisor skipper Svend Larsen was determined not to take the abuse lying down. "If your sheep enter my house," he told the provost, "they'll come upon a sharp ox."[50]

After the first fearful decade, as the novelty of the movement wore off and apprehensions about it proved unfounded, the general violence subsided, flaring only sporadically. In the summer of 1856, visiting apostle Ezra T. Benson addressed a Mormon conference of one thousand in Copenhagen's Coliseum without disturbance.[51] Name-calling, of course, and the subtler persecution of job boycotts and social ostracism persisted.

The banishments from Sweden, the imprisonments on bread and water in Norway, the mobbings in Denmark – altogether a tremendous stirring in the early years – paid tribute to Mormonism's vitality in Scandinavia, a vitality that was as native as the violence. The mere foursome from America – Snow, Forsgren, Dykes, and Hansen – could never have produced such an agitation by themselves. Their new followers proved as valiant in sowing the American seed as their antagonists were bold to uproot it. Mormonism's Scandinavian oak, once planted, struck deep into home soil. It was Snow's express policy to nurture local congregations into hardy growth and to recruit his ministry from among the proselytes themselves, many of whom had been ardent and articulate dissenters. With the first baptisms he hoped before long to have converts "scattered over the country preaching the word."[52] In 1859, for a large tabernacle audience in Salt Lake City, Snow recalled his circumstances:

> I was there comparatively alone, and the harvest great, and the laborers few, and the Spirit bore testimony that the Lord had much people there. I saw if they were all to be sought out and gathered home by the labors of men sent from America, and after traveling so long a journey to learn their language, that it was a great work. . . . And I cried unto the Lord, saying, "O Lord, raise up laborers and send them into this harvest, men of their own tongue, who have been raised among them and are familiar with the spirits of the people." He has done it. Before I left there was quite a little army of Elders and Priests, Teachers and Deacons, laboring in the vineyard, and thousands have rejoiced in the testimony of the gospel borne to them by their fellow countrymen.[53]

By the end of the first year, twenty-five of the three hundred members were "ordained in branches and traveling," and a conference in Copenhagen voted that the contributions received in the meetings every second Sunday of the month should be given to "the poor sisters whose husbands are doing missionary labor." By the end of 1852, the number in the local ministry had increased to one hundred fifty in a membership of one thousand.[54] These native elders, mostly former Baptists, were young journeymen or masters in a variety of occupations. "I laid my hands upon the men that were raised up around about me and sent them to preach the gospel, and they were just such men as the Lord sent me, no matter if they were shoemakers, carpenters, chimney sweepers, or any other kind of trade."[55]

They were hardly "past masters at tilling the soil of religious, social, and political discontent."[56] They were homespun evangelists preaching the old Bible in the new light of the American gospel which seemed like a key to the prophecies of Scripture. Baptized one day and sent on missions almost the next, they had no indoctrination but their sense that these promises were being fulfilled. Given a laying on of hands by the young Americans who had been commissioned by a living prophet, they felt a powerful spur. Hans Christensen of Rakkeby, who herded sheep and courted his employer's daughter, lost both his job and his girl when at twenty-one he joined the Mormons, but he sold his ewe lamb and his clothes chest – he had been ordered to leave home in disgrace – and forthwith became a missionary, confident the Lord would provide.[57]

The charge given the "traveling elders" was twofold: by word confound the unbeliever out of his own Book, and by deed confound his slanders. Mormonism, so unsavory in repute, could afford no scandal. The elders must keep themselves unspotted. With unblushing Yankee baldness Willard Snow, who followed his brother Erastus as mission leader, told them early in 1853 to "keep their heads out from under the petticoats, as they would be shorn of their influence and powers in the Priesthood, like Sampson [*sic*] was shorn of his strength by the treachery of Delilah." He had a revelation on the subject of matrimony, he said, which had never been published in Scandinavia, and which "unfolded the everlasting covenant of marriage, and extended into the Worlds to come; and if the Elders would seek to build up the Kingdom and attend to their duties faithfully in the ministry with clean hands, they should never want for mothers, sisters, wives, or children." [58] The doctrine of polygamy, not yet announced but already widely rumored, by no means meant promiscuity. The stakes were high and elders who fell from grace were forthwith excommunicated.

Frequent correspondence with headquarters in Copenhagen, the organization of the mission into districts or conferences each with a resident elder to supervise the itinerants, and regular visitations in the field from the mission leadership all went far toward educating Mormonism's untried native ministry. Peder Nielsen's five years as a traveling and presiding elder were typical.[59] A shoemaker, he was converted in Copenhagen in June 1854, at the age of thirty. Aside from entertaining Saints who came to Copenhagen to attend the conference or to join the next company of emigrants, his first service was to visit members as a deacon, collecting for three established funds: the Temple Fund, the Perpetual Emigrating Fund, the General Fund of the Copenhagen congregation. In January 1855, President John Van Cott asked him if he were willing to leave his wife and infant son "in the hands of the Lord" and go out to preach the gospel. Though the "powers of darkness" nearly overcame him, he made immediate preparations and left within a few days with "very solemn feelings," authorized, according to his certificate of calling, to labor in the Lolland Conference under the supervision of another native elder, Johan Svendsen. After a few months he was "set apart" as president of the Valse Branch on Falster and as traveling elder for the whole island. The ordination prayer urged him to "be humble before the Lord . . . and go forth in holiness and righteousness," and he was promised that he should be "blessed exceedingly both temporally and spiritually together with your family. You shall never lack food or clothing. You shall be called home with the children of God, and stand saved in Zion the day the Savior will come and receive His kingdom. . . ." This, his own greatest desire, was the hope he sought to bring his hearers.

Nielsen knew little rest; his mission became his whole life and his constant preoccupation. He entered any cottage that would invite him in – a weaver's, a farmer's, a shepherd's, frequently the servants' quarters on some estate. He found many who believed but dared not confess their faith, though frequently he could record with joy that he had baptized someone in spite of the Devil, who seemed at times working hard in a particular neighborhood, especially through the Lutheran ministers. He sold tracts and books and regularly received a bundle of the mission periodical, *Skandinaviens Stjerne*, from Copenhagen, for which he sought subscriptions from among members and strangers, noting frequently that *Stjerne* was "light and truth" to him. Now and then he read "a good letter from Zion," which built up his faith tremendously and stimulated his study of English. He heard the complaints of backsliders and sat in judgment on transgressors. He assisted intending emigrants to get their passports and arranged their transportation to Copenhagen. Sometimes he helped a needy brother get in the harvest, or – very rarely – indulged a whole day in mending boots, recording almost ruefully, "I worked temporally." He kept the district accounts for the mission's several funds – tithing, temple, emigration, books – and sent amounts and reports faithfully to Copenhagen. On occasion he took up a special collection for an overcoat or a pair of boots or for the traveling expenses of some faithful about to leave for Zion or for visiting brethren from England. He met in council with the presiding officers of the local congregation and once or twice a year journeyed to Copenhagen for missionwide conferences, when he could see his family, report to the warden of his guild, renew his passport, and perhaps drop in at the waxworks or at Tivoli, the great amusement park, to ponder both the good and the evil in the world, or visit the Anatomic Museum to see "the development of man from the sperm cell and many other interesting and instructive things." Better still, on such occasions he might find a new mission leader from America, "full of a father's love and a blessed man," or see a visiting apostle like Ezra

T. Benson, and his heart would swell with gratitude for the privilege. Once he encountered the Honorable S. Jorgensen, Rigsdag member, who was staying at the same hotel, and they had "an enlightening talk."

Back in the field, in Fredericia, Jutland, where he was assigned after nearly two years on Lolland, he occasionally "enjoyed the good things of the earth" with the Saints themselves and "danced a few dances, sang a song, and united in prayer," finding greater fellowship with them than with his "self-righteous and indifferent" parents and relatives in Bodelsker parish, whom he visited for the first time in twelve years. He fasted more often than he feasted, however, and in hours not taken up with walking miles and miles in his pastoral duties he studied church books diligently and tried to learn English. He was glad and ready to be released from his arduous voluntary ministry when in 1860 he received permission to go to Zion. In token of his devotion the Saints in Vejle gave him a watch and chain and his wife a gold pin as a parting gift.

The first elders after serving brief apprenticeships under Hansen, Dykes, and Forsgren were, like Nielsen, soon on their own, traveling two by two through most of the provinces of Denmark and venturing into Sweden and Norway to carry on their work as fortune favored them and the letter of the law allowed. If standing up was construed as preaching, they preached sitting down; if religious services were forbidden in homes, they held "conversations"; if after imprisonment or court examination in one place they agreed not to proselyte, they went on to another and sent fresh laymen in their stead who had made no such promise. Where they were shut out as missionaries, they found work at their trades and passed the contagion of their message to fellow workmen. A shoemaker stuffed Mormon tracts into his customers' shoes; a tailor sermonized as he sewed. They baptized by night along river banks and on the seashore. Every proselyte bore witness to his neighbor. The new gospel was a germ which spread by contact.

The Mormon elders were so well known they were celebrated in the street ballads of the time.[60] In 1856 the itinerant artist Christen Dalsgaard encountered them in a carpenter's cottage and recorded the scene in "Mormon-praedikanter," a colorful genre painting notable for its sympathetic realism.[61] In a workshop interior whose hewn beams and whitewashed walls reflect the elemental sturdiness of its inhabitants, he shows a young missionary in boots and jacket addressing the household, with raised arm and stretched finger expounding from a Bible held open on one of the carpenter's rests as a makeshift pulpit. A summer sun pours in through a cobwebbed casement window, flooding a workbench still littered with the dishes of the *mellemmad*, or noon meal, as they stand congenially side by side with the carpenter's tools. The light reveals each member of the speaker's intimate audience as an intense and individual creation; it winks on the silver buttons of a gnarled and quizzical old farmer seated next to the workbench, looking well-to-do in his town clothes, and rests finally on the upturned face of a blind girl beside him. A leaflet sticks out from the farmer's upturned hat on the floor near him, its title clearly legible, *En Sandhed's Röst*, Erastus Snow's "A Voice of Truth," Mormonism's most widely read tract in Scandinavia. The old man's heavy hand knuckles stoutly around his cane; a figure resolute in the experience of his years, he will not easily be persuaded.

The blind girl, her whole body taut and listening, drinks in the vision of the zealous elder's words as she sits in the sunlight. Behind the workbench stands the carpenter himself, stolid and confident, a barely perceptible smile playing upon his lips as he glances through a tract while an older companion of the young missionary stands at his shoulder. Not to be overlooked, an awed little girl, balancing on one foot, hides under the bench. Another curious but bashful member of the household peers in at the window, a face half wonder, half fear—for there have been stories about these Mormons. By a door leading into a back room leans a bolder girl, hands behind her back, perhaps the barefooted servant in the house, comely and skeptical. In the other room a woman tends a cradle. The painting captures Mormonism's most characteristic early setting in Scandinavia. To Dalsgaard it seemed natural to depict the Mormon elders as Denmark's *Indremissionaerer*, or evangelicals, who, along with the Haugeans in Norway and the *Läsare*, or Readers, in Sweden, were tuning the religious fiddles of the times.

Familiar figures in Dalsgaard's countryside, the Mormon itinerants were especially well known in civil courts and church councils, where priests and judges found them impious and stubborn, to be handled like nettles. Erastus Snow counseled a realistic compliance with the civil power, however arbitrary, rather than languishing in prison, but his brother Willard felt otherwise. He published an account of Joseph

Smith's Liberty Jail experience and infused a martyr spirit into the brethren, urging them never to accept freedom if it meant capitulation. He would stay in prison until they "picked him out piecemeal through the keyhole" rather than promise to cease preaching and baptizing.[62] It was an honor to suffer imprisonment for the sake of conscience. And in Norway, where the whole missionary force of eight was in prison at one time for five months, most of the brethren held out grimly, to be feted by the Saints on their release.[63] In years to come, some of them would defy the government of their adopted country in the same spirit on the polygamy issue.

Local officials, not a little perplexed by the changing status of dissenters, often reverted to old laws and prejudices and gladly handed the Mormons on from jurisdiction to jurisdiction – from magistrate to mayor to crown, from pastorate to bishopric, the police disclaiming responsibility, judges vacillating, and parliaments debating. Shoemaker Christoffer S. Winge, released from a winter's confinement in Molde in 1859 and on his way to Christiania, found letters preceding him at every town warning the authorities not to allow him to stay over twelve hours in one place. Threatened by the accompaniment of a guard from constable to constable unless he went straight to his destination, he made a cold march of two hundred miles, broken only by a single friendly sleighride. On another occasion, emerging from the courthouse at Stavanger, mothers of daughters he had baptized spat on him and pointed accusing fingers. But someone dared to defend him, claiming that the Mormons, far from being seducers, had reformed the town's drunkards.[64] Anders Olsen, arrested in Oslo for baptizing and fined ten daler, on his release found his wife and children on the floor at home eating out of a kettle with two knives between them – the police had auctioned off the furniture to pay the fine.[65] It irritated the officers to find that the elders' passes were usually in order, but the police could withhold them annoyingly long times. After 1860, when the converts returned to Scandinavia as missionaries after a sojourn in Zion, they came as untouchable American citizens, and it was a special satisfaction to taunt their erstwhile jailors with the fact. A luckless two or three of the early brethren, tripped on a technicality as vagrants, were drafted into the army for five- and six-year stretches. It was not uncommon for local hostelries to be told not to lodge "that class of people," the Mormon missionaries. On several occasions the authorities burned literature or confiscated a treasured diary, more than one missionary in after years lamenting that loss and apologizing in his memoirs that his history of those great days had to be written from memory.

But the arrests often proved only petty annoyances which served to advertise the work of the elders, one way in which they saw the Lord using their enemies toward good ends. Svend Larsen, whose pilot boat *Zions Löve*, the *Lion of Zion*, plied constantly between Norwegian and Danish ports on mission errands, persuaded the authorities of Osterrisor, who had come to respect his sterling qualities, to send a crier through the town warning the inhabitants not to molest the Mormons; and the policeman stationed at the meeting to maintain order was himself converted, as was his relief. One jailor was even willing to send his child to America with his missionary prisoner.[66] And, despite their bread and water diet, which only induced visions and fierce joy, they kept a sense of humor. As late as 1896, Peter Ernstrom, given lodgings by an ironworker from the factory in Borgvik, Sweden, where he had been distributing tracts and holding conversations during the lunch hour, found himself threatened with forced removal. It would be a pleasure, Ernstrom told the constable, to ride back; it had been a long way on foot. More than one magistrate, baffled and exhausted by his inability to wear down these zealots, heartily wished them far away in their Zion. "O tempora, O mores!" lamented the *Fredrikstad Avis* at the pretensions of "shoemakers, smiths, and tailors."[67]

The trouble they caused the civil authorities was mild compared with the way they vexed the clergy. Pastor often worked with constable in attempts to limit their activities and curb their zeal. To the Mormons it was an unholy alliance. The clergy were Satan's hirelings, the Prince of Darkness raging the more as the work of the Lord advanced, and the Mormons were busy casting out devils. The clergy in turn saw the elders, these farm hands and artisans who were their own parishioners, as upstarts, ignorant fanatics, perverting Scripture and unsettling the minds of their fellow villagers. The priests could see dwindling tithes, emptier pews, a breakup of a snug and time-honored village order in which their estate had been secure. It was an economic threat, and, for those genuinely interested in the cure of souls, a still more serious spiritual one. Alarmed to think their cottagers should be misled, they took measures. They solicited signed pledges from their flock not to house or feed the Mormon itinerants; they cut off assistance to wards of the parish so foolish as to be baptized; they attended Mormon meetings and disputed doctrine; they put counternotices in the papers and reprinted anti-Mormon accounts; and later, after they received letters from disillusioned emigrant-converts, they industriously circulated these as tracts; they prayed for the souls lost to the Mormons, naming them from the pulpit – to the Mormons a fiendish device for identifying converts and setting neighbor against neighbor, a call to ostracize, to boycott, and to persecute; they redoubled their pastoral visits, often to be spurned by converts who said that since the priest had neglected them in the past they could do without him now; in Copenhagen the clergy held Sunday evening services for the first time in years to compete with the lure of the Saints; they stooped to spying in attempts to blacken the character of the Mormon leaders; they persuaded farmers to dismiss Mormon hands; they offered the native missionaries special schooling if they would return to Lutheranism.

The elders were unabashed. Invariably they knocked boldly on the pastor's door when they entered a village and announced themselves; they would give him the first chance to hear the truth. Exasperated, all he could do sometimes was sick the dog on them or notify the constable in hopes they could be shut up as vagrants or harried beyond the outskirts of town.

Through the labors of these tenacious laymen, ardently preaching a Zion they had never seen, Mormonism gained its own momentum in Scandinavia. They were its mustard seed. They formed a redoubtable brotherhood and established a tradition that warmed them years afterward when, transplanted to Utah's settlements, they recalled their native service as the Lord's handymen when life had been at high tide. The first ten years of the mission were largely their story. They did not merely dominate the scene down to 1859; they were the scene, some of them serving six and seven years before emigrating. During that first decade, Utah itself sent only thirteen missionaries to Scandinavia, and six of these were Scandinavians who had joined the church in America.[68] The period saw no more than four elders – usually but two or three – from abroad in the mission at any one time except when on occasion a few Americans serving in England toured the mission briefly. The "elders from Zion" arrived in greater numbers with each passing year, the average annual force increasing from fourteen in the 1860s and twenty-three in the 1870s to sixty-six in the 1880s and 109 in the 1890s. Altogether 1361 missionaries were sent out from Utah during the half century 1850–1900, after the first decade gradually supplanting the missionaries recruited in the field. "The Kingdom is beleaguered by this missionary army from Utah," reported a Swedish official.[69] Denmark to the later comers, when missionary work, less spectacular than in the early days, had settled down to house-to-house tracting, appeared to have been "very thoroughly warned by our elders," for Mormon tracts were to be found in nearly every house they visited.[70] Observers unaware of the lay character of the Mormon priesthood, in which nearly every male member holds an office, pictured the movement as a Jesuitical cabal, alternately fearing and envying its "great strength," its "energy and confidence."[71]

The strength was more than numerical. To a surprising degree the manpower from America was Scandinavian – converts and the sons of converts who had emigrated and had answered a call to devote two or three years in the homeland as elders from Zion. Of the 1361 missionaries sent from Utah by 1900, only 24, or less than 2 per cent, were non-Scandinavian; 516, or 41 per cent, were first-generation Danes, 417, or 30 per cent, first-generation Swedes (the Swedes nearly equaling the Danes after 1886), and 130, or about 10 per cent, first-generation Norwegians. Ten were Icelanders. The American-born missionaries of Scandinavian parents, the first of whom arrived in 1882, numbered 247, or about 19 per cent. The proportion of these second-generation missionaries rose sharply after 1896, for the five years 1895–1900 surpassing the first generation. By June 4, 1905, when the Scandinavian Mission was divided into separate Swedish and Danish-Norwegian administrations, another 388 missionaries had spent the usual two and a half years in the field, totaling 1749 for the life of the undivided mission since Erastus Snow and his three companions had founded it in 1850. Some sixty-seven of these returned to Scandinavia on second and even third missions, among them many of the old-timers who had formed the earliest native ministry. Anthon Skanchy, Norwegian ropemaker who became a building contractor in America, served five terms.[72] It became a matter of pride in many families that a son, or the father himself, should return to the Old Country "on a mission." "We have no desire to return to Sweden," wrote the brothers L. F. and K. A. Kvalberg in 1878, "unless it is to preach the gospel." [73]

It was a return of the native on a grand scale, and it began in 1859 with Ola Nilsson Liljenquist, master tailor, one-time burgher of Copenhagen and emigrant of eighteen months before.

> I was the first elder that had received the gospel in Scandinavia to return and testify of Zion. It was a wonder and a marvel to many who thought that no one could ever return after he got to the Rocky Mountains. . . . I went to the magistrate's office [in Copenhagen] to report my arrival. All the officers and clerks left their chairs and desks and completely surrounded me, and bid me heartily welcome. I spent a very agreeable time with them, testifying about Zion and my experience while I had been gone.[74]

Two years before, Iver N. Iversen, converted in America, had visited among his relatives on Als island. "The Saints and many who were not in the church had long desired to see some of their countrymen who had lived in Utah return to preach among them. His labors have been particularly beneficial." [75] One Jutland convert recalled the profound impression Christian Christiansen, whom Snow had ordained as the first elder in the local ministry, made when he returned in 1865: "Brother Christiansen, just arrived from Zion, gave us an account of the Saints' mountain home, his parting with wife, children, and friends, and his journey across the prairies. All this was naturally something new to us and so moved us that there was not a dry eye in the assembly." [76]

With such witness the siege of Babylon entered a new phase and the early sixties brought Mormonism its greatest victories in Scandinavia. Within a year after Liljenquist's arrival there were 2000 baptisms; when he left in 1862 he was in charge of a company of emigrants numbering 484, one of four groups totaling 1556 to leave that year.[77] The Montreal *Gazette* in 1869 urged Canada to take a leaf from the Mormons' book:

> . . . men are chosen from among the Transatlantic Saints of Utah who are natives of the country to which they are sent; missionaries speaking the same tongue and particularly known to the people they are sent among. . . . How much may be done in the way of selecting good emigrants if only the proper means are employed. . . . Send some of their own number, choosing always the most intelligent and worthy of the working or agricultural class from among our adopted citizens.

... to return periodically laden with a wealth of heart and hand that would soon populate Canada with the true gems of humanity, even honest hard working men and women.[78]

Though the missionaries were more numerous toward the close of the century—as many as 165 in 1900—they were no longer so effective. They were in the main second-generation Scandinavians without the intimate acquaintance with the language and customs that had made their fathers so successful. Conditions, too, had changed: the openhanded hospitality of the countryside had disappeared; they could no longer travel without purse or scrip, and they missed the intimate household contact that had made proselytes in the early days. They missed, moreover, the bracing air of persecution which had once invigorated the movement; they encountered instead a discouraging indifference to religion. The elders felt themselves gleaners rather than harvesters of stout sheaves.

The native strength of Mormonism in its prime in Scandinavia also marked the leadership of the mission.[79] Although Americans naturally dominated the founding period, of the twenty-six presidents through 1904, only seven were old-stock Americans; seven were Danish, nine Swedish, two Norwegian, and one born of Danish parents in America. The non-Scandinavians, representing 27 per cent of the total number, served altogether fourteen years, or 26 per cent of the total time. The mixed nationality of the leadership for a mission serving all three countries reflected its unity; the missionaries, too, served in the different countries without regard to nationality—an ignoring of traditional lines which was to characterize the colonizing of their proselytes as well.

Of these mission leaders, two were in their twenties, eleven in their thirties, eight in their forties, four in their fifties, and one (on his fifth mission) was sixty-two. Ten of the Scandinavians had emigrated in their twenties, two in their thirties, one in his forties, one in his teens, one as a child of seven. They returned as American citizens after residences ranging from eleven to thirty-five years, although nearly all had returned on an earlier mission. And nearly all, before emigrating, had been schooled as local elders in the trying days of the mission's founding. At least thirteen of the mission leaders were polygamists; seven of them had known Joseph Smith and most of them knew Brigham Young, who had personally given them their assignment.

Among them were a mason, teacher, merchant, judge, journalist, woolgrower, foundryman, tailor, co-op store manager. Several were farmers, colonizers really, skilled in the arts of organization and human relations learned in building communities from the stump up. Whatever the particular skill, the whole vocation of most of them had been "settlers," a calling giving them a world of civic and church experience as bishop or mayor, watermaster or postmaster, councilor or justice of the peace. Their service to their proselytes extended far beyond their mission years as they assisted the newcomers to establish homes in Zion. Their own origins had been humble, but America, Zion, had given them a chance to rise. Strong-faced, intelligent, energetic men who had proved they could take care of themselves, they were the men Brigham Young could trust with the greater stewardship of the Scandinavian vineyard.

The missionaries from Zion were called directly from the plow and the shop twice a year at general conference time, after spring planting and the fall harvest. Their names were announced without forewarning from the Tabernacle pulpit in Salt Lake City, followed by a written summons from the First Presidency of the church. Friends returning from conference to the settlements were sometimes the first to announce the news to the startled elder. Some communities seemed bled of their ablest manpower in response to these summons: Ephraim, the Little Denmark of the settlements, had supplied forty-four missionaries by 1886 to Salt Lake's seventy-five, and the hamlet of Hyrum sent eighteen in the same period.[80] Congregation minutes proudly recorded the names of the missionaries, their date of call, departure, and return – a single line summing up the drama of the man and his family's struggles while he was away. Meanwhile, Zion's communities were filling other calls: sending men and equipment to the frontier to convey immigrants to Utah, donating labor tithing to the construction of temples, or responding to assignments to settle new areas.

The call often worked a hardship. The missionary usually had little time to put his house in order and report to headquarters to be "set apart" at the hands of one of the Twelve and to receive a certificate of ordination. Peter Hansen of Hyrum, who in 1865 began a *Dag Bog*, or diary, the day he received his appointment, transcribed his certificate in still uncertain spelling:

To All Persons To Whom This Letter Shall Come. This certifies that the bearer Elder Peter Hanson [*sic*] is in full faith and fellowship with the Church of Jesus Christ of Latter Day Saints, and by the General Autorities af said Church has been duly appointed a Mission to Skandinavia, to Preach the Gospel, and administer in all the ordinances thereof partaining to his offis.

And we invite all men to give heed to his teachings, and counsels as a man af God, sent to open to them the Door of life and salvation—and assist him in his travels ind whatsoever things hi may need.

And wi pray God the Eternal Father to blass Elder P. Hansen and all who receive him and minister to his comfort, with the blessings of heaven and earth, for time and for all eternity in the name of Jesus Christ Amen.

Signet at Great Salt Lake City, Territory of Utha. May 22, 1865. in behalf af said Church.—Brigham Young, Heber C. Kimball, First Presidency[81]

Brigham Young's admonitions to a group of missionaries gathered in his office on the eve of their departure in 1860 epitomized the church's unvarying counsel: Be guided by the Spirit; avoid debate and argument; learn all you can of all kinds of things but only to be put to mankind's service. An elder skilled in logic is not so inclined to lean on the spirit of the Lord. Don't give the world cause to speak ill of you. Depend on the Lord in your journeys; means will come in unexpected ways if you live as you should. A few elders have lost their lives in the service, but live for the fulfillment of the patriarchal blessing you have received. When enemies belittle you or you feel you cannot preach as fluently as you want to, rebuke Satan and live so that the spirit of the Lord will guide your understanding. Don't be a burden to the Saints; rather work yourselves or beg from strangers. Don't preach the gospel with a view to becoming rich. Some elders come back in two or three years with downcast eyes, despondent. Come back with head high. Keep yourselves pure from the crown of your head to the soles of your feet. Remember that Satan is most active against the truest and the strongest. Some of you will have a chance to visit relatives and the old home, but don't expect to stay there. There was no more evil spoken of the Redeemer's disciples than is now spoken of Utah's residents; you will be told your religion is one big delusion; tell your enemies you'll give them two delusions for every truth they can give you. Don't preach things you don't understand; if someone poses a question you can't answer or confronts you with a difficult passage of Scripture, say the Lord hasn't revealed it to you or opened your understanding. . . .[82] It was good advice for a lay ministry which felt that one word from a living prophet was worth a whole cartload of scripture.

It was up to the missionary to make his own way to Scandinavia, usually in company with a band of brethren bound for Europe. The home congregation collected what they could at a farewell social or in pre-railroad days perhaps gave him a horse which he could sell in the East to continue his journey. And in neighborly fashion they looked after the "missionary widow," so familiar in Utah, and her family. When Willard Snow died suddenly in Denmark, the Scandinavian Saints, learning that he had sold a badly needed team when he came on his mission, sent the widow a large donation.[83] Niels Wilhelmsen one winter traded his suit of Danish broadcloth for enough flour to see his family through till spring and made his way on snowshoes from Bear Lake to Salt Lake City, quartered along the way by well-wishing friends from the Old Country.[84] Christian Hansen, whose wife had to make him a shirt from one of her petticoats before he could go, solved his farm help problem providentially. Within a few days of his departure with $1.50 in his pocket he married a plural wife, a "big, strong, Danish woman" who as "Aunt Mary" proved a godsend to the otherwise shorthanded family, for she worked alongside the oldest son in plowing, planting, harvesting, and hauling wood.[85] The Scandinavians in Salt Lake City for years maintained a missionary fund for which their choir and dramatic society staged frequent benefit performances. In the early days Brigham Young urged hardship as a salutary discipline for the missionaries:

> I am ashamed of our Elders that go out on missions. It is a disgrace . . . that they do not start from here with handcarts, or with knapsacks on their backs, and go to the States, and from there preach their way to their respective fields of labor. . . . Some ride so much they do not know how to preach, whereas if they would walk, they would be in far better condition to labor in the Gospel.[86]

Once in the field, the elder from Zion traveled "without purse or scrip," living on the open hospitality of Saints and strangers. The early Scandinavian converts were urged to support the missionaries to the utmost as a test of faith: they should give their last pair of shoes, their last piece of clothing, and go hungry themselves, such sacrifices all to be compensated by some day "going up to Zion"; but some in their zeal went into debt and they had to be cautioned.[87] The Copenhagen congregation, particularly, bore the brunt of the burden as the mission's clearinghouse, and had to appeal to other branches to send their offerings. In 1859 the Saints were warned that released elders were not to become a burden to them. They were supposed to support themselves.[88] Tithes, which had been a missionary mainstay, after 1860 were ordered sent to Salt Lake subject to the church presidency's disposition as a general fund for temple building and "for the gathering of the poor from all nations." [89] Elders unwilling to go without purse and scrip in earnest or periodically to turn to manual labor for self-support were released. Tithe-paying was spurred by the thought that the faithful would have their names "sent home to Zion," entered in the books of the church against the day of judgment when they would be rewarded for their good works.[90] At the same time Zion itself was charged with a heavier responsibility. At a bishops' meeting in Salt Lake City in 1860, Brigham Young, thinking perhaps primarily of England, sharply condemned the impositions of the elders upon the Saints, binding them "with chains of oppression." It had to be stopped. "The Saints in Zion must take this burden off from the poor abroad. This subject has pained me for years, but I have never had the power until now to handle it." [91]

In spite of hardships, the joys for the elder from Zion were many. It was satisfying to be a laborer in the Lord's vineyard, to return to the Old Country an object of wonder in the eyes of former neighbors as a villager who had gone to America and made good. His return satisfied any longings for the old home he might have entertained, and provided for the rest of the immigrants in Zion a vicarious outlet for nostalgic yearnings – by pooling their funds to send him back and by exchanging frequent letters with him full of queries about friends and family in *det gamle land*, they made him their proxy. Going and returning he was their living link with the past. And the arrival of Old World newspapers which he sent them, redeeming the isolation of Utah's settlements, informed them of European affairs, if only to make them glad they were in Zion. When their missionary came home, the community turned out to greet him with choir or brass band, and heard a report of his labors at his "homecoming" in the meetinghouse.

It was sweet to be back again with a chestful of comforts for the family, to laugh when the dresses brought back were too large or the long-awaited pair of store shoes, alas, too small; to grieve that the precious china had been broken in transit; to look forward eagerly to the planting of the slips and bulbs and seeds of familiar Old World plants he had brought back with him. Sometimes a missing face from the family circle saddened the reunion; or the addition of a plural wife, Father's recent convert, rendered it uneasy. But Father was home, with stories to tell, a man of stature and respect in the community because he had been "on a mission."

Having recruited for Zion, he now had to turn again to building it. C. F. Olsen, schoolteacher who led a company of emigrants home following his mission in 1886, felt lost when he saw the last of them leave Salt Lake City for the settlements.[92] "I have been busy with the harvest since my return," wrote P. F. Madsen from Brigham City in 1873. "This week I hope to begin building my house. . . . My orchard is heavy with fruit and I have to shore up the branches of my apple trees for fear they will break. I have never seen here a richer harvest of both grain and fruit. . . ."[93] Pictures like this gladdened the hearts of his friends and fellow Saints still in the Old World and made him an effective missionary in his letters.

Rumors floating down the years in Scandinavia formed a far different image of the elders from Zion. They were railroad agents, they were speculators, they were white slavers, they were polygamists sent abroad to avoid prosecution, they were Utah's delinquents farmed out for reform. Heber C. Kimball's salty advice to outgoing missionaries in the 1850s was underscored even in late anti-Mormon works: "You are sent out as shepherds to gather the sheep together; and remember that they are not your sheep; they belong to Him that sends you [a Norwegian pastor commented that "Him" meant Brigham Young]. Then don't make a choice of any of those sheep; don't make selections before they are brought home and put into the fold."[94]

Julie Ingerøe, a Norwegian spinster, and N. Bourkersson, a Swedish small tradesman, who had been to Utah in the middle sixties and been disillusioned, considered the missionaries pious hypocrites. On a mission to Drammen, Norway, in 1891, Andrew M. Israelsen found advance notice of his coming in *Tidende*, local newspaper. A countryman in his home town in Utah, whom Israelsen as justice of the peace had once fined for striking a boy, had written a letter warning people against him and his kind: "The railroads in America take such ignorant fellows almost gratis because they know they will get it back on their deluded converts who emigrate to Utah."[95] That was hard to take for a man who had paid $73 in cold cash for his ticket and who had left a pregnant wife, a boy with a broken arm, and a struggling dairy business in response to "the call."

Whatever the interpretation put upon the activity of the missionaries, there was no mistaking their connection with America. They were usually remembered as having passports "from Washington." And their preaching, their conversation, their literature, their hymns were all about America, the land of Zion.

CHAPTER 4

"Zion, When I Think of Thee"

"OUR PLACE AND OUR PEOPLE ARE BECOMING WELL KNOWN ABROAD."[1]

WITH his finger the Mormon missionary might trace the word "Zion" in a huge scrawl across the smoky ceiling of some lowly cottage. For the wonderstruck household, the moment materialized two myths, uniting them—the Mormons and the American West—and what had been rumor filled the dwelling with its reality, immediate and immense. The advent of the Mormons turned the fabulous into a fact and a disturbing force.

Folk imagination in Scandinavia by 1850 had already been quickened by the growing number of "America letters" and "America books," like Ole Rynning's influential *True Account of America* (*Sandfaerdig Beretning om Amerika*, Christiania, 1838). In the 1840s a few emigrant guides, forerunners of handbooks to come by the score, described the American prospect in engrossing detail. But New Scandinavia, to use Fredrika Bremer's optimistic term, meant Minnesota or Wisconsin or Illinois, the rich lands east of the Mississippi. "The West" in L. J. Fribert's *Haandbog for Emigranter til Amerikas Vest* (Christiania, 1848), a work cited again and again in Danish papers,[2] meant the Old Northwest. The German editions of Josiah Gregg's *Commerce of the Prairies* (1845) and T. J. Farnham's *Travels in the Great Western Prairies* (translated as *Wanderungen über die felsenbirge in das Oregongebiet*, Leipzig, 1846) may have found their way to bookstalls in Scandinavian capitals, but the average villager did not know them. In the schoolbooks and on the maps of the period the Far West was written off as the Great American Desert.

If knowledge of America was fanciful, of the Mormons it was almost pure fable. Europe knew Joseph Smith during his lifetime as "the Western Mohamet," with sword in one hand and his Koran, the

Book of Mormon, in the other. Yet the British press had been alive with notices about the Mormons since their coming to England in 1837, and papers on the Continent occasionally copied stories. Peter O. Hansen in 1843 first read in a Copenhagen paper about "a book found in America called the Book of Mormon," kindling a curiosity that sent him to the United States to learn more.[3] The *Latter-day Saints' Millennial Star*, published in Liverpool, by 1850 had reached a biweekly circulation of 22,000, model of mission periodicals soon to appear in Geneva, Paris, Copenhagen, Stockholm, Hamburg, and Rotterdam. Sometimes official Mormon literature found a place as news from America. In 1850 John Taylor, Erastus Snow's fellow apostle who opened a mission in France, sent Brigham Young's "Fifth General Epistle," a detailed account of the year's developments in Utah Territory, to the *Journal des Debats* in Paris, where "the chief editor made some excellent remarks upon it, and signed his name to them." It was copied from the *Journal* into papers in "Switzerland, Italy, Denmark, and Germany, and thus, in their various languages, it was spread before the nations of Europe. Our place and our people," Taylor told a Salt Lake City audience in 1852, "are becoming well known abroad." He reported the London *Times* as saying, "We have let this people alone for some time, and said nothing about them; we have been led to believe that they were a society of fanatics and fools, etc.; but let this be as it may, their position in the world, in a national capacity, demands at our hands, as public journalists, to report their progress, improvements, and position."[4] In seeking permission to preach in Paris, he said, all he had to do generally was to send his card, "John Taylor, du Deseret."

> The things that are going on here [in Deseret] require talent, force, energy, a knowledge of human nature and of the laws of God. . . . The nations . . . gaze with astonishment at the stand that this people take at the present time in their territorial capacity; to that all the nations and courts of Europe are looking. Talk about preaching; this is a matter of another importance entirely. I do not care how eloquent men are . . . but it is the organization in this place; the wise policy of the Governor who presides here, in the extension of this infant state, by building up new colonies, etc.; making such extensive improvements that preach louder among the courts of Europe, at the present time.[5]

It was a questionable notoriety. In 1858, after a missionary tour of

Europe, Apostle Ezra Taft Benson, who had preached to an assembly of two thousand in Copenhagen, asserted that "Wherever you find a man in England, in Germany, or in Denmark who takes the periodicals of the day, he can sit down and tell you all about the Latter Day Saints; he can tell you what we believe and, providing you could converse with him without his knowing you were a 'Mormon' or a servant of God . . . he would sit down and tell you all about 'Mormonism.'"[6] Benson was being ironic. It was all misinformation, he said, born of "the father of lies," who was determined to destroy the Saints. Benson felt it his duty not only to "vindicate the truths of the gospel" but also to "take up the laws of the Territory of Utah and the laws and Constitution of the United States."

Early ignorance in Europe about the American West in general and the Mormons in particular was matched only in the United States itself. No less a personage than the godlike Daniel Webster once opposed a mail route between Independence and the mouth of the Columbia River, declaring he would not vote "one cent from the public treasury to place the Pacific Coast one inch nearer Boston":

> What do we want with this vast, worthless area? This region of savages and wild beasts, of deserts, of shifting sands and whirlwinds of dust, of cactus and prairie dogs? To what use could we ever hope to put these great deserts, or those endless mountain ranges, impenetrable, and covered to their very base with eternal snow? What can we ever hope to do with the western coast, a coast of 3,000 miles, rock-bound, cheerless, uninviting, and not a harbor on it?[7]

Webster's contemporary and fellow New Englander, Joseph Smith, took a more creative view of the reports coming from California and the Oregon country. In 1842, standing on the Iowa side of the Mississippi with uneasy Nauvoo at his back, he prophesied that the Saints, after afflictions and apostasies, would yet become "a mighty people in the midst of the Rocky Mountains." He was ready to march at the head of one hundred thousand volunteers, if the government would arm them, and secure the "Western Territories" for the United States.[8]

With the discovery of gold in California, both Europe and America took a hurried lesson in geography and sent their thousands to El Dorado. Abridged translations, with maps, of Edwin Bryant's *What I Saw in California* appeared as early as March 1849 in Paris and the next year in Stockholm. J. Hoppe and A. Erman's *Californien* came out in

Copenhagen in 1850. Because the overland route to the gold fields led through Mormon country, Great Salt Lake City unexpectedly found itself athwart a national highway and it became the renowned "Half-Way House in the Wilderness," succoring the travel-weary and doing a brisk trade in flour and fresh animals in exchange for costly eastern goods which the impatient goldseekers were only too glad to unload. The Mormon community was something to write home about, a miracle of life in the desert as great as the wonder of gold in California. Letters gave readers of provincial newspapers in Europe a growing awareness of that life, like Christian Høier's, sent to *Bratsbergs Amtstidende* from Nevada City, describing his encounter with several Thelebønder among the Mormons.[9] Travel books multiplied. Not a few titles reflected the popular image of the Far West as a land of "golddiggers, Mormons, and Indians," or America as a whole, for that matter, as a country of "Yankees, Indians, Mormons." Some early accounts ostensibly about the goldseekers gave the Mormons equal attention.[10]

The gold fever passed, but the Mormons remained a standard curiosity abroad. Down the years few travel books about America failed to advertise that the author had spent some time among them. No subtitle seemed fashionable without them; W. G. Marshall's *Genom Amerika* (Stockholm, 1882), for example, took care to mention "New York, Niagara, the Mormons, and San Francisco." Translations of whole books, English and American, devoted to observations about the Mormons in their western retreat found their way to the Continent as early as the middle 1850s: the surveyor Lieutenant John W. Gunnison's authentic but opinionated *The Mormons, or Latter-day Saints, in the Valley of the Great Salt Lake* appeared in a German edition in 1855. Mrs. Maria Ward's fabrication, *Female Life among the Mormons*, advertised as observations of social, administrative, and religious customs among the Mormons by the refugee wife of a Mormon elder, attained full-length editions in Copenhagen (1855), Leipzig (1856), and Stockholm (1857). More notably, in 1858, Copenhagen was reading *Ved Saltsøen, Et Besog hos Mormonerne i Utah*, the Englishman William Chandless's temperate *A Visit to Salt Lake City*. In 1866 Hepworth Dixon, well-known British journalist, curious about "the changes now being wrought in the actual life of man and woman on the American soil," studied the Shakers and the Mormons and wrote

New America, which by 1868 found its way into French, German, and Swedish editions, in Swedish known as *Vår tids Amerika* (Stockholm, 1868).

Travelers from the Continent, too, published observations in their own tongue, like Jules Remy's *Voyage au Pays des Mormons* (Paris, 1860), which, turnabout, enjoyed an English edition. Apostate Scandinavian Mormons would declaim their disillusionments at book length, but countrymen without an axe to grind and in the spirit of the earlier British travelers came to America most particularly to see the Mormons and make their own observations: Jonas Stadling, Erling Bjørnson, Curt Wallis, among others. The Mormons themselves frequently quoted travelers' accounts; the official mission periodical, *Skandinaviens Stjerne*, taking its cue from the *Deseret News* and the *Millennial Star*, translated columns from a variety of metropolitan papers: Horace Greeley's famous conversation with Brigham Young from the New York *Tribune*; George F. Parsons' "Among the Mormons" from the San Francisco *Times*; "By Foot from the Atlantic to the Pacific" from the Utica *Herald*; "A Visit to the Mormons" from the Glasgow *Sentinel*; "A Traveler's Opinion of Utah," from the Boston *Traveller*, to name a very few.

Travelers continued to find Mormon country fascinating and, now with sympathy, now without, perpetuated Europe's image of it as a religious state with outlandish customs and beliefs. Carpetbaggers and crusaders—and time—at length reformed what had been most outrageous and therefore most attractive, and well before the turn of the century businessmen were celebrating "Utah, her cities, towns, and resources," and dwelling on "her financial, commercial, manufacturing, mining and agricultural enterprises." [11] But that was after the floodtide of Mormon immigration. At the outset Mormon propaganda faced the difficulty of making a forbidding region and a peculiar people sound attractive, of getting a population to the land to undertake the labors that Utah's governors would one day praise in their annual messages. For this the Mormons had enthusiasm and a special vision.

In 1850, at the moment the mission to Scandinavia was launched, Utah admittedly had little to attract either homesteader or speculator. Isolated, rainless, without a railroad and the lure of land grants, without a government survey to ensure title, with a precarious amount of arable land, and with its discovery as the "treasurehouse of the nation" still in the future, the territory seemed an affront to the rest of the country, which officially rejected the land and repudiated its inhabitants; during the debate on the Great Compromise, Senator Seddon of Virginia, glad to see Utah hemmed in between two great mountain walls in a desert basin, was perfectly willing to abandon it to the Mormons for its worthlessness.[12]

But Utah's natural adversities seemed to Brigham Young an advantage. They exactly suited his design – salvation for his people lay in a region where a good living would require hard labor and where the land consequently would be coveted by no one else. No longer could the Mormons advertise Zion as in their lush Nauvoo days when they spoke of "miles in extent of fine rich land, just ready for the plow," and described the "City of Joseph" as a paradise.[13] Zion as a refuge, a place where the pure in heart dwell, a land "where honest labor and industry meet with a suitable reward, where the higher walks of life are open to the humblest and poorest,"[14] became the basic theme of Mormon propaganda. The prospects were brightly pictured, but only on these terms – prospects and terms which gave Brigham Young confidence that, granted ten unmolested years, he would ask no odds of the United States. His messages as governor of the territory and his epistles as president of the church sounded the same enterprising optimism, an enthusiasm for the potentialities of his people and his country that was often mistaken as deliberate deception; he was so eager to fill up his valleys and pre-empt a domain of empire proportions, said his enemies, that he did not stop short of gross misrepresentation.[15] The railroad financiering of the nineteenth century, with capitalization based on earning power rather than actual assets, could have given these critics an understandable analogy: the claims for Zion did not seem disproportionate to a people who felt they were all rich, which is to say, who believed there was no real poverty "where all men have access to the soil, the pasture, the timber, the water-power, and all the elements of wealth without money or price."[16]

It was a different kind of wealth, certainly, from that which lured men to California. As governor, Brigham Young in 1852 noted rather scornfully that, whereas Utah Territory was self-supporting, California, despite her annual $100,000,000 in gold, had to receive heavy federal appropriations for every public improvement and her Indian Department. She had to import her flour, beef, and other supplies. Her

200,000 population, moreover, was transient. Utah, on the other hand, producing no precious metals, receiving comparatively little from the "General Government," had "her mills and manufactories, her roads and her bridges, raising her own bread and beef, besides exporting considerable quantities; preserves peaceful relations with the Indians at her own expense; and still is free from debt. . . ."[17] It was wealth not very different from that which labor created on the land in every other frontier community, except that in Utah the land was grudging and the labor more sweaty, but it was labor, as the London *Times* had the insight to observe, "lightened so that it is never sordid and never penurious, and some kind of image is reproduced of patriarchal sufficiency and contentment."[18]

As governor, Brigham Young put the welcome mat out for all, proselyte or gentile, who understood these terms – to the

> overpopulated districts of the older states and countries, where every avenue seems closed against the poor, who linger out a miserable existence in hunger and want, bequeathing their children the same fate – a hopeless and thankless legacy. . . . These pursuits and their results [cultivating the soil, improving stock, erecting dwellings, encouraging domestic manufacture] . . . are laying for us and our children a foundation broad, deep, strong and durable, upon which, through the blessings of our God, to rear a super-structure for the temporal well being of ourselves and the thousands upon thousands who will seek us for sustenance and the enjoyment of the inalienable rights of civil and religious liberty.[19]

Later, gentile governors, striving to wrest Utah from Mormon domination, would glorify its resources, particularly its mineral wealth, its climate, its industrious population, its capacities for "commercial empire, power and greatness," but the appeal was wholly secular and as such could scarcely compete, abroad at least, with the literature of boards of immigration and railroad land agents common to other states.

Utah had no board of immigration. It needed none with Mormon missionaries in Europe. To be sure, after Mormon proselyting was successful enough to draw thousands to Utah, others got on the band wagon to advertise the state: one or two of the immigrants themselves wrote handbooks, something not needed by the shepherded companies of Mormon converts; business houses with immigrant names advertised in the state's foreign-language papers which were sent abroad – but even these were church-sponsored; and, in 1895, a Lucerne Land

and Water Company issued an "Invitation to Danish Farmers and Dairymen," Utah's closest approach to the immigration literature of other states.[20] Utah's early invitation to prospective settlers clearly required a special motivation and indoctrination, a mingling of spiritual and practical inducements. For anyone to be content in Zion, conversion—at least conditioning—had to precede immigration. Mormon missionaries were "heralds of salvation" first and only incidentally immigration agents.

In Scandinavia, Zion was proclaimed in a vigorous literature ranging from the sober and moralizing to the extravagant and apocalyptic that sometimes failed to distinguish between Zion as metaphor, the city of the prophets, and Zion as the city by the Great Salt Lake. Hymns reflected the tendency, identifying Deseret with Zion of the Psalms. Converts who mistook allegory for reality were in for trouble: "They read and sing about Zion as she was seen in visions of the Prophets . . . and do not appear to have any conception that this is not all to be enjoyed now. . . . let every Saint remember that Zion is composed of such as he." [21] The description was not literal, any more than the songs of praise of other evangelicals, but as a reflection of the mood of yearning they were real enough. At other times the description of an American and western Zion was unmistakable. "O Du Zion i Vest" [22] was the Danish version of "O Ye Mountains High," where the sky was blue, the streams clear, the air breathing liberty. The color was often local and particular; Zion was by a salt sea; the way to it led through the haunts of red men and buffalo; and life was bucolic:

We plow, we sow and irrigate,
  To raise the golden grain;
And diligently labor
  To independence gain;
Some haul the wood from canyons wild,
  Some tend the flocks and herds,
And all our moments are beguiled
  By industry's rewards.
My Valley Home, my Mountain Home,
  The dear and peaceful Valley.[23]

The songs were doctrinal as well as descriptive; they spoke of restoration, gathering, millennium, resurrection, the everlasting covenant, the Second Coming, Babylon's darkness. The imagery was appealing. Joseph Smith was a "fattig Bondedreng, total ulaerd," a poor peasant boy, wholly unlearned, like so many Scandinavians themselves. Zion was frequently "Zion's ship," an appropriate image for expectant voyagers. The songs promised poetic justice – the defeat of the clerics, the redemption of the poor. They were sometimes jaunty and militant, always joyful and spirited, songs of invitation and gratitude, anticipation and encouragement, of hail and farewell. The farewell hymns, like "I Vestens Bjaergeland," all spoke the same sentiments: we're not sorry to go; we'll not forget you; we hope to see you in Zion soon; our home is in the West, that is our Fatherland; there are to be found the living water of the Word and prophets and a people obeying God's laws; here, in Babylon, are want and war and misery; when the Prince of Darkness is bound, the millennium will come; soon God will bare his mighty arm; Zion will be glorified and Babylon will fall.[24]

A little collection of twenty-eight hymns "adapted to the tunes used in Zion" and devoted to the themes of the gathering of Israel, the restoration of the gospel, and the kingdom of God appeared in March 1851, one of the Scandinavian Mission's first publications. Destined to go through many augmented editions, it was fully as effective as scripture. Forty-five years after her conversion a woman, though disaffected, recalled "the glory of those first impressions," the thrill of the hymn "O Babylon, O Babylon, we bid thee farewell!"[25] The converts themselves wrote many hymns, setting their new emotions to old tunes. A surprising number of private journals yield hymns from unlikely pens, the mood of Zion touching clerks, tailors, schoolmasters, and shoemakers. The fourteenth edition of *Salmer til Brug for Jesu Kristi Kirke af Sidste Dages Hellige*, which by 1900 had run to over 40,000 copies, contained 275 hymns, 40 of them translated from English Latter-day Saint songs, a few selected from other denominations, and all the rest originals by Scandinavian converts, ample fulfillment of Erastus Snow's wish, when he issued the first collection in 1851, that "these few will be kindly accepted until the Lord shall raise up gifted poets and give a greater abundance of the songs of Zion."[26]

Ahead of these expressive and influential hymns, however, came tracts, a veritable chorus of "voices" with but a single melody: *A Voice of Truth*, *A Voice of Warning*, *A Voice from the Land of Zion.* Peter Hansen's *Advarsel til Folket*, "A Warning to the People," which he wrote before Snow's arrival, was ephemeral and can hardly be counted, except as indicating the adventist mood in which most of the early literature was written. Snow's *En Sandheds Røst til de Oprigtige af Hjertet*, "A Voice of Truth to the Honest in Heart," was the first official tract and remained the most popular.

From a first edition of 2000 copies in September 1850, it reached 140,000 by 1882 and was still being read during Mormonism's centennial in Scandinavia.[27] It made only casual mention of Zion and the gathering as an article of the new faith. Its masthead, "Repent ye, for the kingdom of heaven is at hand," was its most insistent message. A clear, succinct account of the new gospel's first principles, its arguments were biblical, its tone tempered but urgent, appealing to minds trusting in Scripture but dissatisfied with the formalistic creed of the state religion and its indifferent clergy. Through homely example it taught the doctrine of works as well as grace – the farmer must plow and sow though God sends the rain and provides the earth, an illustration that for many effectively refuted Lutheran dogma. Every man must think and act for himself in religious matters. Knowledge follows faith as fruit follows seed, and Snow employed another homely, and unmistakably American, example when he described the Indian's faith in the white man's ability to make bread from certain seed.

Skillfully, without using the words "Mormon" or "Mormonism" or "Latter-day Saints" or "Church" in the first thirteen of its sixteen pages, the tract clarified basic doctrines: the fall and redemption, faith, repentance, baptism, infant sprinkling, priesthood authority, the Second Coming. It concluded with sixteen articles of faith and a declaration avowing Mormon belief in monogamy and admonishing obedience to the marriage laws of the land, a declaration which remained in later editions despite Mormonism's public admission of polygamy in 1852. Snow's sixteenth article of faith remained too, professing a belief "that this generation now living on the earth will not all disappear before the second coming of the Savior, when he will begin his thousand-year reign." A 1902 edition had not yet revised this hope, but to readers in 1850 it seemed more urgent.

Snow had difficulty finding a printer who would handle these heresies, but a young journeyman recommended by Peter Hansen's wife needed a start in business and took the risk. F. E. Bording of Copenhagen continued thereafter to do all Mormon printing until his death in 1884, and his son after him. Though every word of the mission's propaganda passed through his hands he never became converted, but the long business relationship spoke well for the Mormons' credit rating. Between September 1850 and June 1881, they paid 100,000 kroner ($25,000) to him for a total of 1,840,750 pieces of literature—tracts, periodicals, and books—in Danish and 275,600 in Swedish.[28]

A tract comparable to *En Sandheds Røst* in effectiveness and popularity was Snow's *En Røst fran Landet Zion*, "A Voice from the Land of Zion," which he issued in February 1852 for Swedish circulation, and which ran to 7000 copies by 1882. Primarily a translation of Lorenzo Snow's *The Voice of Joseph*, which had just appeared in Liverpool after its first European publication in Turin in 1851 as *La Voix de Joseph*, it reviewed the "rise, progress, and persecutions" of the church, its "present position and prospects in Utah Territory," favorable observations of Mormon life from American newspapers, and included the "American Exiles' Memorial to Congress." Though in *En Sandheds Røst* Erastus Snow had mentioned the gathering only in passing, in this, with his following no longer a bird in the bush, he could be specific: he concluded with two paragraphs on the best routes for emigration, the New Orleans and Panama routes, from which emigrants could find colonies of Saints at Kanesville and San Pedro to help them on their way.

A Danish translation of the *Book of Mormon* itself, full of doctrinal disquisitions but at the same time an intriguing story of migration to the promised land, immediately followed Snow's successful first tract. In August 1850, he wrote Brigham Young that he had "the promise of backers in England" and hoped to have the work appear "in its own native simplicity and truth." During his stay in America, Peter Hansen had become "very dull in his native tongue" and the translation begun in Nauvoo was imperfect. Snow needed help but did not wish to confide the book to "learned professors who were not imbued with the spirit of the work."[29] He did engage a language teacher, Mme. Mathiesen, to assist, greatly to Hansen's discomfiture, because she sought to convert the style "to modern taste," which would have ruined the book's "peculiar, ancient style" which Hansen had been charged to preserve.[30] Snow exhausted himself in keeping vigil over the translation as it proceeded, distributing two hundred press sheets weekly from January to May 1851, when the completed *Mormons Bog* of 568 pages in an edition of 3000 came from the printer. Even at the last moment Snow's vigilance was rewarded: when he glanced at the first copies of the title page he found to his horror that they said the book was "to come forth by the gift and power of God unto the destruction (*Ødelaeggelse*)" instead of the "interpretation (*Udlaeggelse*)" of the ancient record. "I looked upon it as another daring attempt on the part of the Adversary, and I hurried down to the printing office to have the error corrected before anymore title pages were printed."[31]

Two hundred pounds sterling from the British Mission and a loan of one hundred rigsdaler from a recent convert, Hans Jensen Simpsen, had made publication possible. Snow would have issued a smaller edition first "if I could have found a stereotype foundry in the kingdom, but Denmark is a little behind the age in this as in most other improvements. They are now being thrown into circulation by the brethren, and by a bookdealer of Copenhagen." "As the Saints began to peruse its sacred pages," he wrote Brigham Young, "the Holy Ghost descended upon them, and bore record of it in a marvelous manner, speaking to some in dreams, visions, and divers manifestations, which caused our hearts to magnify the Lord."[32] By 1882 Scandinavia had absorbed 8000 Danish and 3000 Swedish copies of "America's strangest book."

Laerdommens og Pagtens Bog, a translation of Joseph Smith's revelations and epistles found in the *Doctrine and Covenants* – another distinctively American scripture – appeared in February 1852; the printing of a thousand copies was once more subsidized by English benefactors with an outright gift of two hundred pounds from a Mr. Tennant. *Pagtens Bog*, a 318-page volume in its first edition, was less a proselyting instrument than indoctrination for members, setting forth the order of the church, introducing them to the responsibilities of a lay leadership whose forms and procedures had been born on the American frontier, and in the process incidentally acquainting them with a good deal of American geography. Successive Danish editions by 1882 totaled 6800 copies. Snow explained to Brigham Young that because the "literature of the great university of Copenhagen has long taken the lead in this north country . . . works read in Danish may be read and understood by a large portion of the Swedes. . . . and as for Norway, although they have their rustic dialects, yet the Danish is the public language of the state"[33] – which explains why the preponderance of Mormon publication was in Danish.

The early years saw a profusion of books and pamphlets, most of them theological, pre-eminently translations from the prolific Pratt brothers: Parley Pratt's *Voice of Warning* and *Marriage and Morals in Utah*; Orson Pratt's *Remarkable Visions*, *Divine Authority*, *Celestial Marriage*, *The New Jerusalem*, *The Divine Authenticity of the Book of Mormon*, and *True Principles of the Gospel*. These went through several editions during the half century, running into thousands of copies. Other works widely distributed, their titles suggesting their emphasis, were Orson Spencer's *Patriarchal Order or Plural Marriage*, John Taylor's *Is Mormonism False?*, Joseph W. Young's *The Gathering of Israel and the Redemption of Zion*, John Van Cott's *Invitation to God's Kingdom*, Lorenzo Snow's *The Only Way to Salvation*, John Jacques' *Catechism for Children*, Orson Pratt's *God's Kingdom in the Last Days*. Pratt's *Celestial Marriage* was recalled because its arguments went beyond sound scripture. A curiosity never reprinted was George P. Dykes' *Chronologisk Tabel*, of which he published 800 copies in Aalborg in 1851 to show that the current year was 6080 since Creation and the Second Coming was at hand.[34] Editions of *Bibelske Henvisninger*, or "Bible References," with multiple categories, were a staple, evidence of the proof-text method of Mormon preaching.

These titles were a far cry from tales whispered to Welsh miners of "unworked lodes in the Wahsatch Mountains," and "pleasant legends told to land-hungering Norsemen of free 'gaarder' in the West, such as no 'Herremand' in the North possesses," and assurances of "food and an endless elysium of beer" given to rude millworkers of Lancashire "clemmed" for want of bread – which were supposed, by some journalists at least, to be Mormonism's characteristic appeal.[35]

Publication was a striking aspect of Mormon activity in Scandinavia. Clearly the proselyte had to be able to read. By 1873 eighteen titles of *Bøger og Skrifter* – books and pamphlets – were actively in print, advertised for sale at mission headquarters in Copenhagen or at any of the Latter-day Saint meetings.[36] The editions, measured by the standards of modern mass propaganda, were not large, but their distribution was personal and effective. Congregations were instructed to use a portion of the tithing fund monthly or quarterly to buy a supply of books and tracts. As their property, these could be sold or given away, and members were urged to spread the literature as widely as possible to correct misunderstandings about the Mormons. But it was much better, the missionaries and the local ministry who served as book agents were told, to sell. "God's word is free, but paper, printing, binding, and our sustenance all the same cost money."[37] It was poor policy to sell literature to the poor without collecting for it; it created feeling. "Let the poor band together, three or four, to buy a Book of Mormon together and other scriptures, to their enlightenment and salvation." If it was still necessary to give or lend books and tracts to "the honest poor," let congregations or able individuals pay for such use, thus sharing the burden.[38]

Persons "who can keep good accounts" were appointed book agents in each conference and congregation and reported quarterly. Peder Nielsen, serving Vejle district, reflected the concern and incidentally the difficulties of amateur colportage: "I balanced the book accounts and received the whole material from R. Mikkelsen; the whole thing was in poor shape and a lot of debt for which there were no books or pamphlets. . . . All books and pamphlets were delivered to me and checked; the brethren were given 50% discount, otherwise the debt would have been much greater."[39] In 1863, despite such devotion, accounts receivable from the conferences stood at 6618 rigsdaler ($3309), an indication, at least, of the size of the book business. Copenhagen called for united effort on the part of the whole mission to pay it off, which was done within the year.[40]

Many of the titles which appeared eventually as tracts and books first appeared serially in the mission periodical, *Skandinaviens Stjerne*, founded in October 1851, and hailed by its sister publication in England as "another star in the moral firmament of celestial lights." Quaintly the first number recommended that readers preserve each issue, for it would be of great value to them and their children after them when the kingdoms of the earth had passed away and God's kingdom became general on the earth. *Stjerne*'s editors were the incumbent mission presidents assisted by talented young converts as writers and translators, a number of whom after this apprenticeship and their emigration founded church-subsidized news weeklies in their own tongue in Zion. These weeklies were sent to the Old Country by the hundreds to be used in proselyting, affording a picture of thriving communities and a lively round of Scandinavian-language activities, the advertisements themselves showing how well the converts were faring in the new land.

Stjerne began as a monthly but became a biweekly by general vote of the mission the next year. It sold for twenty-four skilling the quarter, single copies for the equivalent of three pennies; subscriptions could be placed with any royal post office or with bookdealers in Copenhagen. Those too poor to subscribe in advance were urged to be faithful in buying each issue from the elders in the field, who were sent bundles for the membership and for door-to-door soliciting. By 1861 it reached its highest circulation of 2700, leveling off to an annual average of about 1500. *Stjerne*'s nonmember circulation in 1861 was 500, suggesting the extent to which it was a proselyting instrument. In 1877 it was augmented by a parallel publication in Swedish, *Nordstjärnan*, and from 1880 to 1887 by *Ungdommens Raadgiver*, or "Young People's Counselor," to give them an indoctrination in the field that Zion would have afforded them during their growing up, reflecting a period when emigration was not so general and members were being urged metaphorically to become "saviors on Mt. Zion" by doing genealogical work in the mission field.

Stjerne's convert readers learned to look forward to it, often continuing their subscriptions after removal to America, to which, in 1870 at least, Copenhagen would send it for "to [two] Dollars Greenbacks." Scandinavian Mormons temporarily settled in St. Louis, Weston, and Mormon Grove in 1855 expressed joy in *Stjerne* and asked for other literature too, for various nonmember Danes and Swedes were visiting the meetings.[41] H. J. Christiansen, subscribing in America to the *Nordstjärnan* in 1892, recalled its great work as missionary: "A poor fisherwoman brought it to my mother and blessed will she be for it."[42] Ropemaker Anthon Skanchy found it being read and reread by some Norwegian Saints in 1879 who had no other contact with the church.[43] On Falster Island, where, so recalled a disaffected member, one third of the congregations were married women whose husbands hated the church, a missionary used to leave copies of *Stjerne* in a moss-covered box buried near a certain grain house, where he always found two marks, milk, and food left there by the women in return.[44] *Stjerne*'s colorful history even included a government ban: the Finnish post office once considered it subversive and sent only its empty wrappers on to the subscribers.[45]

The influence of *Stjerne*, at once so pious and practical, was wider than its modest circulation. "Several periodicals," wrote Willard Snow, "have copied some important pieces from it; and, I am happy to say, to their credit." [46] Issues passed from hand to hand, and it attained considerable notoriety as the local press engaged it in forensic warfare, an aspect of the great debate being waged generally on the virtues and vices of America. Like the *Millennial Star* in England, it was an organ in Europe devoted to American interests, providing an indoctrination far broader than its Mormon bias.

Provincial as the minutes of local conferences and cosmopolitan as the farthest traveler's account, *Stjerne* was scripture, mission historical record, newssheet, emigrant guide, and above all a serialized "America Book." As carrier of Zion's sermons and epistles, letters from emigrants, excerpts from American newspapers, and reprints from the *Millennial Star* and Salt Lake City's *Deseret News*, it was a storehouse of information about a new world. Here Zion was pictured in engrossing detail: Indian raids, grasshopper plagues, the hardness of a winter or the dryness of a summer, the size of the harvests, the founding of new settlements, the coming of the telegraph and the completion of the railroad, the appointment of federal officials, the convening of the territorial legislature, congressional debates about Utah, Fourth of July celebrations – in short, the praying, the working, and the dancing in Zion. Scandinavian readers learned more of what was happening in Utah Territory than in their own community and, fascinated, followed the fortunes of the Mormons in their conquest of the desert and their continuous conflict with the world, a drama in which apostate and gentile were the stock villains.

In its physical descriptions and minute reports of developments in the territory, *Stjerne* served Utah as the railroad and land commission circulars served other states. One early issue advertised real estate in Salt Lake Valley which had been donated to the Perpetual Emigrating Fund – lots, farms, and houses evaluated for Scandinavian readers in rigsdaler, suggesting a membership affluent enough to be interested, and certainly creating a vivid image of the homesteads all hoped to have some day in Zion: "A brick house and a timber house, together with 32 acres well enclosed in two fields by stone and adobe walls, Davis County, 3½ Danish miles north of Salt Lake City, 3,000 rigsdaler. . . . Goddard's property, a shop on East Temple Street, bakery and residence in one building, Salt Lake City, 21,000 rigsdaler . . . 10

acres near Little Cottonwood stream, south of Salt Lake, 150 rigsdaler . . . Half a town lot, Salt Lake City, 200 rigsdaler. . . . "[47]

The "Fifth General Epistle of the Presidency of the Church . . . from Great Salt Lake Valley, State of Deseret, to the Saints scattered throughout the Earth," which was issued April 7, 1851, and published in the *Millennial Star* in July and in *Skandinaviens Stjerne*'s first issue in October, was typical of the literature, concrete and colorful, that provided a firsthand view of pioneering, a closeup of a working model of American state building. Zion was perhaps more theocratic than democratic, but it was Zion in American terms, familiarizing Scandinavians with words like "Congress" and "settlement" and acquainting them with leading personalities in the national arena.

In the "Epistle" the Saints at home were pictured as making preparations to receive the Saints from abroad, who were urged to bring with them all choice seeds, hedges for fencing, lath and shingle nails, glass, wire "#9," raw cotton, yarn, machinery, and "domestics." An expedition had set out to found a colony near San Diego, the first of a chain of settlements planned between there and Salt Lake City to facilitate emigration by way of Panama. Grain and lumber mills had been erected; furniture was being made, a pottery nearly completed, a cutlery established; the state had given $2000 toward a woolen manufactory; two or three threshing machines had operated during the past fall and winter, which last fact warranted the observation that labor-saving machinery could be employed to greater advantage in Deseret than anywhere else because it could release more elders for missions. The Council House was nearly completed; the Warm Springs Bath House and the Tithing Storehouse were finished; a Seventies Hall of Science was to be built on shares. A State House was planned on Union Square for the new territorial capitol, though so far it was only a rumor that Utah Territory had been organized – when official notice came Deseret contemplated a peaceful transition to the new order and would be grateful to "our mother land," the United States, for its relief. The university lands had been enclosed by a stone wall; most wards had schoolhouses with winter sessions and looked forward to continuous sessions; a Parent School to train teachers was aborning; and Congress had appropriated $5000 for a state library.

Deseret had seen its first jury trial – some transients had been convicted of stealing. The through-emigrants were a trouble; the animals of so many travelers could hardly be pastured in the fields left after enclosure and they were being advised to go by way of Fort Hall. Three hundred of the emigrants quartered in the valley during the winter had left for California in the spring; others had decided to stay; a few had turned out to be hypocrites, "winter Saints" who found it comfortable to join the church and marry Mormon girls until spring when they could desert to the gold fields. Mail came monthly from the Missouri. Salt Lake had rather more sickness than elsewhere because the infirm stopped there, the hardy going on to the settlements. Tithing was needed for a wall around the Temple Block and to start the Temple. The epistle concluded on a note echoed in the tracts:

Amid all the revolutions that are taking place among the nations, the elders will ever pursue an undeviating course in being subject to the government wherever they may be, and sustain the same by all their precepts to the Saints, having nothing to do with political questions which engender strife, remembering that the weapons of their warfare are not carnal but spiritual. . . .

So ran the vital bulletin from Zion, an absorbing miscellany to prospective inhabitants. It was easy to understand why Deseret meant honeybee and had chosen the beehive as its official symbol. The reports breathed confidence. Calamities outside Zion were the Lord's judgments, the signs of the times; inside Zion they were purgative trials of faith. Zion always came off well by comparison; events in Europe and the States – wars, strikes, fires, municipal corruption, and financial panic – showed the gentiles ripening for destruction, often destroying themselves and each other. "We'll prosper both here and in all lands until the honey bee has sucked all the good and strength from the nations till they are ready for damnation."[48] The epistles, and *Stjerne*'s accompanying editorials, met the challenge of adversity from year to year – Johnston's Army, the accusations of unworthy federal officials, the crusade against polygamy, hard times like the panics of 1873 and 1893. Zion never ate humble pie. When Johnston's Army came to Utah in 1857 only to prove Buchanan's move a blunder, and when the States themselves became embroiled in civil war, the note in Zion became triumphant, even overbearing. The Saints saw the Civil War particularly as forerunner of the calamities that would vindicate Zion and were persuaded that the world's worthy, even though not members of the church, would flee the plagues and come dwell with them. These friends were welcome; by exemplary lives they could also assist in building up the Kingdom and at the same time enjoy its blessings.[49]

In the defense of Zion, *Stjerne* was the Lord's quiver, always full. But more absorbing even than the official communiqués, more intimate, having the authority of personal witness from known friends, were the letters from Zion that found their way into *Stjerne* after the departure of the first emigrants. Emigration itself, once begun and growing yearly, was good advertising for Zion: "I am happy," wrote Brigham Young to F. D. Richards, the Mormon agent in Liverpool, "to learn of your forwarding so many Saints to America. . . . I believe it helps the cause, not only by coming to assist in the works of Zion, but has a beneficial influence in the world, and aids those who go to proclaim the Gospel, in obtaining hearers and believers."[50] Next to the return of the emigrants as missionaries, whose influence has already been suggested,[51] emigrant letters proved Mormonism's most persuasive witness, informing, motivating, compelling. Peder Nielsen recorded that a daughter's letter from Zion helped reconvert her disaffected father. By the same token, letters from apostates, which often found their way into provincial papers or were industriously circulated by the parish priest in "skillings-brev" or chapbook form, hurt the cause.

Stjerne published the faithful and the enthusiastic, like tailor Christian Larsen, who, arriving at the mouth of the Mississippi River on February 15, 1854, in charge of three hundred Scandinavian Mormons, felt that "I have already seen enough of America that even if I were not a Mormon I would not want to remain in Denmark"; and a generation later Johan Sandberg, who, though the times were "nothing to shout about," found them still better in Utah "than in the eastern states." Many like Christoffer J. Kempe wrote "It's impossible for me to write each one of those who requested me; I send you these lines hoping they may find a little place in *Stjerne*."[52]

During the half century *Stjerne* became a rich repository of America letters, hundreds of them, one or two every issue, their postmarks a romantic roll call of Zion's habitations, names of far places yet familiar, endeared by the knowledge of friends and kinfolk writing from their own firesides. From Sanpete Valley, itself an Indian name and the "Little Denmark" of the settlements, came numerous letters bearing lovely names: Springtown, Mt. Pleasant, Fountain Green, and Fairview; a biblical name like Ephraim—at first Fort Ephraim and then Ephraim

City, the change speaking a whole history; a *Book of Mormon* name like Moroni; a historical name like Gunnison. Letters from emigrants en route were an education in United States geography: "Fort Laramie," so explained *Stjerne*'s editor in introducing Niels Wilhelmsen's letter from that outpost in 1861, "lies about midway on the prairies and about 500 English miles from Florence."[53] And of course a great many letters came from "Store Saltsøstad," Great Salt Lake City itself.

In the news from Zion the facts were always more marvelous than fiction, big with reports of health and ownership in the new home, alive with memorable detail, as often heavy with moral observations. Through the letters ran glad refrains like "Children are no burden in Zion," "We have the deeds to this ground," "There is freedom here," "The land cries out to be used." A letter from America must have run like rumor through a village, making the recipient an object of respect, creating a legend even before the letter itself could pass from hand to hand:

> The Nielsens have house and land—two town lots, twenty acres of plowland. They own the deeds! Christian says he built a mill for the town, Danish style. Three hundred Danish families live in their town, and everybody is independent. Daughter Sophie is married to young Jacob Knudsen. They live at the Mormon capital, the city by the Great Salt Lake. Son Fritz is conducting an English school for Danes. They say the children are already talking English and they can speak Indian as well. The Indians are friendly, but dirty, and they sell their children for slaves. One Indian wanted to trade his wife to Christian for an ox. Christian says they miss good Danish rye bread; but they eat all kinds of new things—have you ever heard of squash? It isn't true that the Mormons censor their letters; there is no wall around Utah. . . .[54]

Marie Louise Lautrup, emigrant of 1856, wished that "one of our Danish poets" could see Zion's valleys and mountains; he would have stuff enough for poetry and write a long description of what she could tell only poorly and briefly. She recalled that while living in Copenhagen "in Brother Petersen's house," the Mormons had come talking about the thousand-year kingdom and the promised land. She had thought Mormonism a delusion and had wished she might be rich enough to journey to Utah to see conditions for herself and then return and warn Denmark. "Maybe," she remembered Brother Petersen had said, "you will go and not want to come back." And now, writing of Salt Lake City with its wide streets and water from the canyons running down each side, its young trees just planted and cattle browsing in the high grass on the mountain slope above the city, and of temple endowments and visits to Old Country neighbors in nearby settlements who were doing well on their own land with their own herds and good crops, she was glad to stay: "I enclose two flower petals for you from Zion. . . ." [55]

J. C. Nielsen, writing from St. Louis, wanted to spike the hearsay that Mormon elders did what they would with emigrants once they were in America; he wished all Denmark could see the freedom, both spiritual and temporal, that prevailed:

> If I don't like working for one man, I can go at once to another. Are not servant folk bonded the whole year in Denmark? And if I don't want to be a Latter-day Saint, I can go where I want to. No one can bind me. And I could return to Denmark if I wanted to, for I have already earned enough. The biggest trial for the Saints here is that the earnings are large compared with Denmark.[56]

C. A. Madsen found Abrahamic values in Zion; during the evacuation of Salt Lake City and the northern settlements at the approach of Johnston's Army in the spring of 1858 he was convinced "no other folk in the world has, in proportion to its size, so great a blessing of horses, cattle, mules, oxen, sheep, etc." The caravan of wagons would have stretched, he said, "from Copenhagen to Korsør." He found Zion "glorious to work for by day, to dream of by night, and refreshed, arise to begin the Lord's work in the fruitful morning hours when the snow-clad mountain tops send a refreshing coolness down into the valleys and fill the streams with water. . . ." [57]

P. C. S. Kragskov, sounding like a John Smith on the inestimable virtues of Virginia, found "the healthiest air, the clearest water" in Zion, "the best place for the Saints I have ever seen. . . . But the greatest joy for me is that I can see and hear prophets and apostles Sunday after Sunday who teach us Christ's pure gospel." [58]

M. Pedersen did not want to preach in his letter, but had to relate how a large family of immigrants were cared for by one of the brethren in his town until they got themselves a house, and how the brother refused payment saying, "I desire nothing, but when the Lord blesses you, do the same toward others in similar circumstances." "And such examples in Zion," said Pedersen, "are not rare." [59]

"We built ourselves a stone house last summer," wrote Jens C. A.

Weibye in 1870, "which includes a living room, two bedrooms, kitchen, cellar and loft. We also planted a number of fruit trees, and sowed about fifty kinds of flower seed. I am a sort of farmer, gardener, tithing clerk, and postmaster." [60]

"There is good work with Bro. Rich for two men," wrote a correspondent from Provo in 1869, "namely a tanner and one who can manage property." [61]

A. Christensen in 1863 wished he could send pictures of the new Salt Lake Theater "throughout the world so that they may see that the Latter-day Saints have ability, intelligence, and taste to raise grand buildings, especially in view of the conditions we've had to live under." [62] In 1867 letters were describing the great new Tabernacle and its mighty organ, destined to attract so many generations of tourists.

In 1868 Christian Edlefsen considered the approaching railroad a blessing – it would aid the gathering, and, furthermore, it would bring travelers, "the powerful and the rich," to Utah to see Brigham Young and his people and be amazed at how advanced the Saints were over other peoples.[63] And in 1869, when the railroad came, "We have daily visits from strangers of all classes, and without exception they are amazed over Salt Lake City and over us whom they had judged as a low, ignorant, and leader-oppressed and tyrannized folk, for they see and experience now that the contrary is true." [64]

Ironically, the railroad that the faithful were sure would testify of Zion's virtues itself worked a transformation of Zion from a confident, if struggling, independence to a troubled, and still struggling, dependence. Zion, seen with the eye of faith, continued to be brightly pictured, but sober realizations and rationalizations crept into the literature. Zion had known drouth, grasshopper plagues, and Indian raids; its existence had always been marginal; but by choice as well as by necessity it had been self-supporting. Land, and home industries based on what the land produced, had been the basis of Zion's agrarian beatitude. The railroad, however, made Utah Territory more intimately a part of the national economy, responsive like the rest of the country to the business cycle. Now "hard times" meant a scarcity of money and jobs, particularly in Salt Lake City, Zion's chief glory: "It is very pleasant to settle in a place like Salt Lake City," said a *Deseret News* editorial reprinted in *Stjerne* in 1878, "with its varied attractions and the opportunities it affords of instructions from the general authorities of the

Church. But most of those who settle here may make up their minds to live 'from hand to mouth' for some time to come." Newcomers were urged to push out into the country. "Though much of the land is occupied and labor is not in such demand as in former times, there are still abundant opportunities for men and women of energy, faith and determination." Those who remained in the city in comparative poverty, crying about the scarcity of work and the hardness of times and murmuring against their more prosperous friends, brought upon themselves "the darkness and unbelief that rise out of discontent." [65]

Admittedly there had been "a change in our affairs in this Territory." It was a very different picture from Parley P. Pratt's idyllic description of the Valley as he had found it in 1849: "The joyous and heavenly influence bore witness that here live the industrious, the free, the intelligent and the good," [66] a picture of domestic peace and prosperity which may have been true for a day and excusable in the fancy of a tired people who had just found haven. Unfortunately the picture was perpetuated in a tract that went into a new edition the very year the *News* editorial faced the dilemma: "Israel must be gathered. But a serious question arises after the people arrive here; that is, what shall be done with them?" Pratt's picture was too extravagant for the later time. Brigham Young himself, replying in 1873 to the New York *Herald*'s request for a description of conditions in Utah, was content to point out that Utah had fewer mortgages than any other state, that Zion's Cooperative Mercantile Institution was flourishing, that the mines and local railroads were in good condition, and that he had planted 200 settlements numbering 100,000 inhabitants. To the rumor that he had millions of pounds sterling in English banks he replied that if he had he would use it in gathering the poor from the Old Country and building up the New. But, significantly, he sounded Zion's new and fundamental concern: "We have all kinds of merchants here, but we lack capital." [67] Labor and capital were the divine union that would fulfill Zion. The need had been for labor, being abundantly supplied by the gathering of the converts. Now there was danger that without capital, enough work could not be created to accommodate the immigration. "We lack capital" echoed in all the communiqués, private and official, from Zion after the coming of the railroad, reflecting a change, subtle at first, then marked, straining the rationalizations of the most faithful.

Peter O. Thomassen noted in 1875 that "A deal of unemployment has existed in Utah during the winter, which has brought many to complain and wish themselves 'home again.' Yet the need in Utah bears no comparison with the need in the States."[68] A decade later A. W. Carlson wrote how liberally the poor in Utah were looked after at Christmas time from the provisions in the tithing storehouses, receiving quantities of coal, mutton, flour, and potatoes. "When I read of the conditions of our poor Saints in Scandinavia, I wish they could have shared all this." And C. C. A. Christensen could not resist noting in 1892 that Utah, so lately a wilderness, sent 50,000 pounds of wheat flour to a needy China.[69]

The very protestations betrayed Zion's retrenchment. It was shocking to learn that there were indeed poor in Zion. Two years later C. A. Carlquist had to admit that times were hard, yet Zion once more was not as badly off as other places in the United States. The harvest was good and the leading men of the church were doing all in their power to make work. They were just then holding a meeting in Huntsville to suggest damming the Ogden River to make Ogden into a manufacturing city. "The Lord's spirit works on our leaders in this matter, and their wishes are that as quickly as possible we can become independent, because the times are near when the only place in the world where peace and freedom may be found will be among God's people." The messianic hope was still alive. But newcomers must not expect to find Zion now as it should one day be; it was going through a purification period, cause for deep reflection, and converts must come ready to adjust.[70]

In the 1890s there were official warnings about packing off to Zion without due forethought of the difficulties of earning a living. Missionaries were cautioned not to let the fact of Zion as home, with its personal endearments and associations, lead them to think only of its beauties and to forget to tell its disadvantages to newcomers. "When they are inquired of, let them state the whole situation, especially the untoward circumstances which emigrants and strangers are likely to meet." The principle of the gathering was to be explained only when occasion required, and acting upon it was to be left entirely to the individual.[71] By the turn of the century the discouragement was downright:

Though emigration is not preached by the Elders and those who desire to leave to join themselves with our people in Zion are in many cases emphatically advised against it, still many are so filled with the spirit of gathering. . . . that they stop their work and their business and haste away to the valleys of the mountains as quickly as possible. . . . They do not consider the difficulties which they will meet in a new land, and despite the present information shows they absolutely cannot find work. . . . 75% of European Mission immigration goes direct to Salt Lake. Only few have capital or skill to depend on. On arrival they find nothing to do. . . . They become discouraged when their hopes fail, and they cast the blame on the gospel although the fault lies in their own thoughtlessness.[72]

The Saints were exhorted instead to live as examples in the world, to build up congregations in the mission, which had need of their services, their tithing, and their influence.

Not that Zion had ever been pictured as all clover. From the beginning the literature smelled often enough of western sagebrush and greasewood, the official epistles unsparing in their sober delineation of struggle in a wilderness. But they had never, like these later bulletins, doubted Zion's destiny, its economic opportunity. The cautions had all along been spiritual, an effort to prepare the new converts against disappointment in their fellows. Jedediah M. Grant, two-fisted counselor to Brigham Young, wanted converts and immigrants on the "wholesale principle," but he took missionaries to task who preached "long and pious sermons" representing Zion as "one of the most delightsome places in the world, as if the people in Salt Lake City were so pure and holy that the flame of sanctity would almost singe the hair off a common man's head." The imagination of some of the Saints had been "so exalted that they suppose all our pigs come ready cooked with knives and forks in them, and are running around squealing to be eaten." On the contrary, when the Saints arrived from abroad they would find the people almost too busy to speak to them. "When they find us all active, some rushing to the canyons, and gathering in the crops, and others rearing houses – when they find the people all alive with business, they think that the Mormons are all telegraphs. . . ." The first things newcomers might expect to have to do in Zion, he said, were "to leap into the mire and help to fill up a mudhole, to make adobes with their sleeves rolled up, and be spattered with clay from head to foot." Some would be "set to ditching in Zion."[73]

Heber C. Kimball, another plain-spoken counselor to Brigham Young, expected "many of you who have come in from Denmark, Sweden, Norway, England and the United States will turn away" because they would see faults in their brethren. They would find their firewood stolen, their cow milked, their flour or their pig taken. "Then you will find fault with the authorities because of these things. . . . you will have enough of this milking business. . . . and very likely there are some of you who have come here for the loaves and fishes and to steal from others." [74]

Eliza R. Snow's verses on the gathering echoed the warning; an early translation in the Scandinavian hymnal became a favorite with the Saints:

> Think not, when you gather to Zion,
> That all will be holy and pure,
> That fraud and deception are banished
> And confidence wholly secure. . . .
>
> Think not, when you gather to Zion,
> The Saints here have nothing to do
> But to look to your personal welfare,
> And always be comforting you.[75]

The net had been cast into the sea, they were told, drawing to the shore all kinds of fish, and they must not be alarmed if they found in Zion some curiosities.

If Mormon literature itself was not sober enough, there was always the advice in the general immigrant handbooks: "In Utah Territory . . . the population consists chiefly of a polygamous sect called Mormons, against whose advances the immigrant is earnestly warned." [76]

While Mormon propaganda was one stream of knowledge about Zion, the movement as it grew provoked another, a turbid flood of mingled fact and fiction which took its rise from clerical attack, folk rumor, travelers' accounts, and the testimony of disillusioned immigrants. "The way the Danish priests and editors avail themselves of the old lies of Bennett, Caswell [Caswall], Turner and others might well put to shame even Bowes himself," wrote Erastus Snow in 1851, "and besides these transatlantic wares, there seems to be an abundance of domestic manufacture." [77] It ranged all the way from learned refutations by the archbishop of Zealand to ribald portraiture of "Brigham Young and His Sixteen Wives" in anonymous street ballads.

Most of the anti-Mormon pamphlets which have survived originated in newspapers and periodicals, which devoted an incalculable amount of space to the Mormons, their notoriety securing them an attention quite out of proportion to their numbers. The attack came from all quarters: from the cities—Copenhagen, Christiania (Oslo), Stockholm, Odense, Randers, Aalborg—and from the provinces, wherever a cleric could get hold of a printer. The 1850s were most prolific, as with Mormon propaganda itself. The bishops and the theological faculty at the universities wrote impressive treatises, arming their parish priests with scriptural and historical defenses against Mormon heresies, ranging in specific density from the sixteen-page *Brief Account of the Real Mormonism* (*Kort Begreb om den egentlige Mormonisme*, Christiania, 1855) of C. H. Jensenius to C. B. Garde's ninety-two pages on *The Errors of Mormonism* (*Om de mormonske Vildfarelser Til mine Menigheder*, Copenhagen, 1854), with Alfred Beyer in between devoting thirty pages to refuting Mormonism's opposition to infant baptism (*Et Forsvar for den i Danmark bestaaende Kirkes Daab*, Copenhagen, 1858).[78] Even the illustrious Gustaf Unonius produced an anti-Mormon work, *Mormonismen. Dess upprinnelse, utveckling och bekännelse* (Stockholm, 1883).

Like Carl Fog's article "Mormonerne. En Historisk Skildring" in *Nyt Theologisk Tidsskrift* (Copenhagen, 1851), these intellections could hardly be expected to reach the commoner. The priests themselves knew how to approach him more directly and wrote histories, explications, exposés, and even handbooks like *Everyman's Aid in the Fight against Mormonism* (*Haandsraekning for Menigmand i Kampen mod Mormonisme*, Copenhagen, 1857) and *A Little Antidote to Mormonism's False Teachings* (*En liden Modgift mod Mormonernes falske Laerdomme*, Randers, 1857), works which often abandoned doctrine for diatribe and attempted to frighten parishioners with accounts of Mormon infamies. Anti-Mormon works were a staple in series like Professor Dr. Fredrik Nielsen's *Smaaskrifter til Oplysning for Kristne*.

Church societies in America as well as in Scandinavia were zealous distributors: the Norsk Bogmissions Forlag, the Norske Sedelighetsforeninger, Middelfart's Kirkelig Forening, the Kirkelig Forening for den Indre Mission i Danmark, the Dansk Luthersk Mission in Utah, the Lutheran Publishing House in Blair, Nebraska. Their opposition was long and unrelenting; as late as 1907 the Lutheran Mission in Utah was distributing *Lock Your Door against the Mormons* (*Luk Døren for Mormonerne! Advarsel!*), a title reminiscent of an early anti-Mormon tract in Scandinavia, *Look Out for the Mormons!* (*Vogt Dig for Mormonerne*, Copenhagen, 1862).

Some tracts told the story of experiences with the Mormons in a particular locality, like F. Baumann's *Mormonernes Faerd i Tanderup Sogn* (Odense, 1854). Some lumped Mormons and Baptists together, though the Baptists themselves were "making themselves conspicuous," said Snow, in the "dirty work" of "translating and revamping old English and American lies" with which the newspapers were teeming.[79]

The arguments were tediously alike, the accusations over and over that Mormonism was unchristian, an *imperium in imperio*, its followers ignorant, its leaders scheming, the whole movement a foul hypocrisy, with polygamy its crowning abomination. It was polygamy, of course, that gave Mormonism such wide notoriety, making it fair game at church and carnival. A vaudeville dialogue-and-song sequence in Copenhagen depicted a rake in a dilemma because he had been courting two women who unexpectedly meet and discover his deception; but he has a solution: they'll buy tickets to "Zions Land" where both can be his wives, to which the women agree if he promises to take no more; en route, however, one woman runs off with a Tyrolese, leaving the lover and his lass to return to Denmark and a peaceful, lawful existence.

The Mormon Girl's Lament (*Mormonpigens Klage*, 1873) "together with a true and accurate account of a rich farmer's daughter from Fyen who a short time ago was lured by the Mormons to Utah after giving great sums of money to their priests" bewailed her fate as one of seven wives forced to work in the fields while the husband drank and slept, and recounted her escape and the indescribable trials on her return home, where she soon died, poverty-stricken but repentant. Balladeers hawked "the latest new verse about the Copenhagen apprentice masons" who sold their wives to the Mormons for 2000 kroner and riotously drowned their sorrows in the taverns. And in 1874 Copenhagen was treated to a "song and monologue between the verses" about Ole Peersen and his wife Dorthe who decided to go to the land of the Mormons, where a prophet with four guns stuck in his belt confronted them and where they lived in a broken-down shack until Ole tried to add two more wives to the household; that was enough for Dorthe, who threw them out and with Ole fled the devil amid a number of tall-tale adventures to find that "Denmark is best."

Perhaps most widely known of all the street ballads was one portraying a harassed Brigham Young who had sixteen wives, thirty-two girl friends, and sixty-four "acquaintances" and had real difficulties when he took his family to the theater or ordered refreshments or tried to evade in-laws asking for loans. In the songs, gay and crude and often illustrated with satirical drawings, it was easy to see where Mormonism touched the popular imagination.[80]

Not simply polygamy itself but its delayed acknowledgment discomfited the Mormons abroad. They had called their detractors liars and scoundrels when they were accused of practicing such an outrage and had pointed to the *Book of Mormon*, which hallowed monogamy, and to the declaration on marriage in *Doctrine and Covenants* and *The Voice of Truth* which clearly professed the belief "that a man shall have one wife and a woman only one husband" and called any other arrangement an immorality. Convert F. J. Hahn, translator for *Stjerne*, in his aroused tract *A Few Words* (*Et Par Ord*, Copenhagen, 1852) called the claim of *Dannevirke* and *Theologisk Tidskrift* that Joseph Smith lived in polygamy "a shameless untruth." That was one "general lie" of the many circulating in Scandinavia, he said, that he was eager to quash. Jacob's blessings did not mean that, like David and Solomon, one could have many wives. But public announcement of polygamy at a general conference in Salt Lake City on August 29, 1852, meant exactly that and a *Deseret News* "extra" confirmed the doctrine. Hahn had to eat his words.

The 1852 announcement was signal for attacks at home and abroad unparalleled in fierceness, unabated for forty years, the smoke and smell not cleared away after a century. It provided the Republicans at home with a slogan making polygamy and slavery "the twin relics of barbarism" and auguring for Utah as for the South the insufferable attentions of the professional reformers for two generations. Polygamy practiced by Anglo-Saxons in the enlightened U.S.A. seemed an experiment bold enough to startle many into admiration and win frank spokesmen for it on the grounds of religious liberty, but the multitude could see in it only gross immorality and hypocrisy.

Once the fat was in the fire, *Stjerne* boldly published the revelation, though not until October 15, 1853 (the *Millennial Star* had published it in January),[81] and along with it classic defenses of polygamy by Milton and Luther and most of Orson Pratt's *The Seer*, which had been founded in Washington, D.C., to explain polygamy to the nation. With the announcement, *Stjerne* took care to publish an exhortation to the priesthood to beware of lust and every other unholy desire and to preach nothing but repentance and obedience to the laws of men.

Mormon polygamy abroad was doctrine only, never practice. The covenant of "celestial marriage" had to be approved by the president of the church and solemnized in a temple ceremony, usage Mormonism's defamers never understood. Erastus Snow's *Voice of Truth* oddly enough went through numerous editions without revising its statement on marriage, and the opposition accused the Mormons of deception, of keeping their proselytes in ignorance of the doctrine. Snow's declaration emphasized observance of local civil law, about which the mission was scrupulous; and he might have argued that the Mormons did indeed believe in monogamy – as well as in polygamy. The tract was not a denial. And other publications were plain-spoken enough. *Stjerne* in issue after issue defended the doctrine on scriptural and social grounds, described its practice in Zion, and closely followed the efforts of the United States to outlaw it.

Several titles were exclusively devoted to its exposition. Orson Pratt's *Celestial Marriage* was translated as *Det Celestiale Aegteskab* in 1855, but was recalled when the author's vagaries, such as his contention that Christ was a polygamist, were not considered scriptural. The damage was done, however, and later tracts were obliged to refute the book. Parley Pratt's defense of polygamy, *Marriage and Morals in Utah*, appeared the next year as *Aegteskab og Saeder i Utah*, calling for the death penalty for fornication and adultery, bidding the "monogamic law with all its attendant train of whoredoms, intrigues, seductions, wretched and lonely single life, hatred, envy, jealousy, infanticide, illegitimacy, disease and death. . . . sink with Great Babylon," and inviting the Saints to "fill these mountains, the States, North and South America; the earth; and an endless succession of worlds with a holy, virtuous, and highly intellectual seed. . . ." The tract was still in active circulation through the 1880s, as was Chancellor Orson Spencer's *The Patriarchal Order or Plural Marriage* (*Den patriarkalske Orden eller Fleerkoneri*, 1854), with its concluding sentence, "What reward have the men who have faith enough to forsake their contrary and unbelieving wives to fulfill God's commands? A hundredfold of wives in this world, and eternal life in the world to come."

However theoretical in Scandinavia, such doctrine was dynamite in the hands of Mormonism's opponents, who saw in it the dissolution of their families and put on Mormon proselyting but one interpretation: it was a brazen bid for concubines for Zion. William Budge's *The Latter-day Saints' Views of Marriage* (*De Sidste-Dages Helliges Anskuelser om Aegteskab*), an address given in Coswell Hall, London, in 1879, and circulated in Scandinavia in the 1880s, presented a more rational defense of polygamy. The issue was not dead even after the turn of the century, when Christian Fonnesbeck published an answer to an attack by parish priest A. Bulow and noted that 41,960 illegitimate children were born in Denmark between 1895 and 1900: Denmark had better look to her own morals.[82]

In the late 1880s the mission issued a pamphlet *Mormonerne Skildret af Ikke-Mormoner*, "Mormons as Seen by Non-Mormons," quoting favorable comments from sources as disparate as the *Christian Century*, the New York *Herald*, the Boston *Index*, the *Christian Register*, and the *Congregational Record*. In it Sir Richard Burton, Bishop Daniel S. Tuttle, Bayard Taylor, Col. Thomas L. Kane, Phil Robinson, Helen Hunt Jackson, J. C. Kimball – travelers, adventurers, writers, clergymen, congressmen, philanthropists, and even apostates who were still friendly – all toasted Utah. It sought national and international good opinion at the very moment the United States itself was laying the axe to Mormon institutions in the form of the Edmunds-Tucker Act.[83] But in genteel eyes, no number of quotations could whitewash polygamy and the associations of nearly forty years. The picture of Zion as drawn for so long by less friendly critics had left too deep an impression.

These sources pictured Zion at worst as an Augean stable, its inhabitants wretched in this life and without hope in the life to come; at best as crude and worldly without the spirituality of Lutheranism, its people leading industrious if subjugated lives, and the immigrant settlers longing for the homeland but, having no way to return, resigned to their lot. Pastor Andreas Mortensen, who had been to Utah in the 1880s, made sport of the idea that it was a land flowing with milk and honey where every man sat under his own vine and fig tree; he suggested that his countrymen imagine a peasant or laborer in Scandinavia trying to support six wives and all their children on his small holdings. It was *hundeliv* in Utah, he said, a "dog's life."[84] Credulous seamen at Jørsby,

Jutland, in 1873 solemnly believed that fellow mariners sailing up the west coast of America had seen women in Utah pulling plows.[85] A common saying among the peasantry was that no one ever got away from there alive. It was hardly strange that "evil reports" should circulate about the land of the Mormons when people were asking about the United States itself, "Is it true that those who are brought to America are sold as slaves?" [86]

The disappointed and embittered immigrant was not peculiar to Utah, but Mormon apostates seemed to be particularly virulent. Some, like Andreas Mortensen and Julie Ingerøe, returned to the Old Country (how they managed to escape the Destroying Angels they never made clear), and became anti-Mormon crusaders delivering sensational lectures and writing booklets that could be sold for a few pennies among the poor whom the missionaries were supposed to be deluding.[87] Derogatory letters from the settlements frequently reached the columns of local newspapers in Scandinavia or were used by the clergy in their counterpropaganda as tracts. Though but a fraction of all those that must have been written, the surviving letters reveal the long and intense struggle for the soul of the proselyte, who was no doubt sorely tried by the conflicting portrayals of Zion. It was not curious to find a letter from a Mormon girl and a letter from a goldseeker in Melbourne published together in Copenhagen in 1855, part of Denmark's general anti-emigration campaign.[88] The specific anti-Mormon warnings were numerous. C. H. Jensenius, industrious foe, compiled *Breve fra Amerika om Mormonernas Religion, Saeder, og Vandel* (Christiania, 1856), which contained a letter of disillusionment written from Salt Lake City on December 31, 1854, one of the very earliest, for the first company of converts had arrived there only the year before. In 1861 in Hjorring appeared a *Brev fra Snedkersvend*, "Letter from a Joiner's Apprentice," who wrote from Chicago in 1856 to his father in Jetzmarck parish attempting to dissuade his sister from joining the next Mormon emigrant company. No witness was too humble to be summoned in the attempt to find Zion guilty of every offense.

The bad reports began even before the immigrants reached Zion. Christian Binder wrote from St. Louis in 1854 that the widow Jørgensen from Slesvig lost all her money to the Mormon agent, that seventy to eighty Danes were dead of cholera and smallpox, and that a number did not go far beyond St. Louis, refusing to go on with "such an ungodly pack." [89] Christian Michelsen in 1866 was shocked by the rawness of the Mormon teamsters from the Valley who came to assist the immigrants on the Wyoming frontier: dressed in wide-brimmed hats, short jackets, and leather breeches, with a revolver or bowie knife in the bootleg, a long bull whip around their necks, a quid of tobacco in their mouths, and emitting a stream of curses, these were "Zion's chosen men"! [90]

Jens Laursen Lund of Sjelstrup, who in 1863 "escaped" through "Mormon lines" to join United States soldiers returning east, went to Omaha, from where he wrote horrible reports of the castration of the disobedient in Zion. It had been preached, he wrote, that in two years in Sanpete Valley (where most of the Scandinavians had settled) there would be more geldings than could stand on an acre. Lund's letter, published as an eight-page missive in Aalborg in 1863, sold for two skillings, with special rates for lots of fifty and a hundred, suggesting a determined countermissionary effort to spread these Mormon antidotes far and wide. Most telling of all in the eyes of the cleric who edited the letter was Lund's confession that his Utah experience had cost him all religious faith whatsoever; a doomed soul, he found it impossible to return to the mother church.[91]

Peder Meilhede, emigrant of 1858, also writing from Omaha, in 1862 described the shocking ease of divorce among "twenty-six Danish women" in Fort Ephraim, each of whom had "changed husbands several times." [92] Soren Jepsen Schou of Vandrup, who escaped from "Spanning Fork" (Spanish Fork) to Nebraska, wrote in 1863 that at sea the emigrants were compelled to cast their Bibles overboard and were not permitted to keep any books not pertaining to the new faith.[93] The complaints were as grievous as they were numerous.

Despite free expression on the part of "wicked apostates," as the faithful regarded them, the belief persisted that the hierarchy in Utah censored immigrant letters and that authors of unfavorable accounts were punished. Friends at home consequently received glowing reports with suspicion. What made matters worse was that sometimes they heard nothing at all. As late as 1897 George Christensen, a missionary, lamented that emigrating Saints neglected to write home describing conditions in Utah, a neglect causing "wonder, dissatisfaction, and unpleasant surmisings." Missionaries also broke their promises to write friends made in Scandinavia, an ingratitude not lightly taken.[94]

N. Bourkersson, a gentile who followed his Mormon wife to Utah in 1864, where he lost her to another and thus had cause to be bitter, nevertheless exploded the legend of censorship. He found the federal mails too well regulated, and even intersettlement correspondence untampered with, as he proceeded to demonstrate by quoting several letters freely criticizing "dishonest apostles and bishops." He added the assurance that neither did the United States government censor letters from America, another prevalent notion. Ingeniously, however, he explained why the newcomer to Zion did not generally write unpleasant things: missionaries among his friends in the Old Country might get hold of such letters and send them to his local congregation in Utah, where they would be read aloud and incur social censure; or he did not want to admit that he had made a mistake in coming to Utah against his friends' advice, and pride painted an untruthful picture; or he was ashamed to acknowledge he was illiterate; or, having nothing good to write, he did not write at all; finally, perhaps he wanted to see the rest of the converts come to Utah and be disappointed.[95]

Besides apostate letters there were book-length memoirs like the Swede Johan Ahmanson's *Vor Tids Muhammed* (Omaha, 1876), the Norwegian Julie Ingerøe's *Et Aar i Utah* (Copenhagen, 1868), and the Dane Christian Michelsen's *Livet ved Saltsøen* (Odense, 1872), books devoting one third of their pages to an emotional recounting of personal experiences, one third to a recapitulation of hearsay about blood atonement and Danites, and one third to whitewashing the authors' own careers among the Mormons, explaining how intelligent and respectable people like themselves were for a time carried away by the delusion.[96] When the nostalgic and the disappointed refrained from retailing hearsay and gave an honest report of their grievances, it was clear they were often simply not prepared for the hardships and the crudities of frontier life, faults common to pioneer America but in Zion, of course, laid at the door of the church. It was the rare reporter who stood on neutral ground.

It was not until about 1895 that any purely secular literature advertised Mormon country in Scandinavia. A. Jessen, a civil engineer and former Swedish-Norwegian and Danish vice-consul in Utah, addressed *An Invitation to Danish Farmers and Dairymen from the Lucerne Land and Water Company in Utah*[97] designed for the emigrant who had no particular destination and could perhaps be persuaded that the mountain states offered the most favorable conditions for the industrious. After pointing out the disadvantages of other regions (the South, for example, was unhealthful for Scandinavians, the prairie states too dependent on wheat, a poor risk with a lowered world market and the danger of drouth, hot summers, severe winters, and whirlwinds), he described Utah's fine grasslands and small, sheltered valleys that irrigation could make productive. Land costs, canal construction expenses, yields of various crops per acre and their market value – all these he presented in exact figures, an attractive frame for his own picture of the Lucerne Land and Water Company's development in Uintah County: there it had built ten "Danish miles" of canals intended to irrigate eventually 16,000 acres in Lucerne Valley on the west bank of the Green River, where the earth was "twelve feet deep without stones," lumber abundant for building, coal available, and a market for produce at hand in the nearby mining districts. While land sold generally for $84.25 an acre, the Lucerne Company offered it at $20, with water, to be paid over five years. As a special offer, if a number of Danish farmers would establish a commercial dairy, they would be given the land for a nominal rental. There were few dairies in Utah or its neighboring states and dairy products were high. The circular had every confidence that "the business ability and industry for which the Danes have a reputation" would guarantee large earnings.

It sounded like a fulfillment of Zion's most material hopes, but between Erastus Snow's *A Voice of Truth* and the Lucerne Company's *Invitation to Danish Farmers* lay a difference greater than the half century that separated them. It was a difference in spirit and in conception – a conception by the one of Utah as Zion, a state of mind, and by the other of Utah simply as real estate. Infusing all of Mormonism's propaganda was the notion that what was being done in Deseret was but the beginning of a worldwide reformation. Zion was model for America as America was model for the world, and the calling of the missionary and his literature was to advertise this fact by word as the inhabitants of Zion advertised it by their works.

Parley Pratt's Fourth of July oration in Salt Lake City in 1853 revealed the grand design, the extent to which Mormonism felt itself to be an American influence abroad:

The more I contemplate our country, the providences which have attended it, the principles upon which it is governed . . . and the practical working of it . . . the more I look at the spirit of our institutions, and the more I contemplate the circumstances of mankind in general, the more I realize . . . the greatness of the destiny of those principles. . . . There is a day coming when all mankind upon this earth will be free. When they will no longer be shackled, either by ignorance, by religious or political bondage, by tyranny, by oppression, by priestcraft, kingcraft . . . but when all will positively have the knowledge of the truth, and freely enjoy it with their neighbors. . . .[98]

Observing that "It is hardly possible for one dwelling at home to realize the influence that American and English institutions, which are the best, exert over the nation, and among them," he enumerated the ways in which Europe looked to America first, next to England, "for instruction and example": the railroads, the telegraph, free and universal schools, liberty of the press and of conscience. "These things have a bearing upon their minds; they are ready to converse upon them, and when they have heard the description, they say, 'It is good, far better than our own institutions.'" In the spread of these influences, leading the world to seek deliverance from oppression, "not in the style of revolution, but by voluntary emerging into freedom," Zion and the gathering played a central role. Providence opened the way whereby "the first and best spirits from all countries" might liberate themselves. Though they could not "master their tyrants at home," they could leave "the old constitutions to crumble in their own rottenness" and "one by one, family by family" they could come to America "where they have a right to the elements to sustain them." And in time their influence would "overturn those institutions which they could not conquer in their own country."

In Pratt's peroration the American eagle spread Mormon wings:

Hence we contemplate that small beginning made by the American pioneers, by Columbus as the first pioneer, and by our fathers the pioneers of religion and liberty; we contemplate how that influence has spread and increased in the earth, influencing the feelings of individuals as well as national institutions. . . . We will acknowledge the hand of God in the movements of men, and in the development of minds, the result of which will be the fulfillment of what the Prophet has spoken—the renovation of our race, and the establishment of a universal Kingdom of God, in which His will will be done on earth as it is done in heaven.

Forty years later a gentile governor of Utah recognized this characteristic outlook, its aspiration essentially unchanged despite radically altered circumstances: "The Mormons are . . . informed they are the chosen people of God, and that they must consecrate themselves to his service; and that in the fullness of time all nations and peoples will accept their doctrines and look to them as the great light shining upon the darkness of all nations of the earth. . . ."[99]

This exaltation, whether stated in religious or secular terms, from first to last marked Mormon proselyting and won a host of believers in Eden's nursery, as the mission was called, eager to be transplanted to Zion, the Garden itself.

CHAPTER 5

Ugly Ducklings

"THE GOSPEL . . . IS FOR THE MOST PART RECEIVED BY THE POOR, YET THE SAINTS ARE FAR FROM AMONG THE UNGIFTED."[1]

THE conflicting claims of half a century in the lively tug of war between Zion's advocates and its foes yielded Mormonism a harvest of wheat and tares in Scandinavia: 46,497 converts by 1905 for the life of the undivided mission, nearly a third of whom abandoned the movement almost as soon as they embraced it. But over two thirds of the remaining faithful emigrated, more than 30,000 when their children are included, enough to give Zion a markedly Nordic cast.[2] With the long-sustained immigration from Great Britain, Utah's population was from the beginning, and remained, decidedly Anglo-Scandinavian.

The harvest was most abundant in the compact villages of densely populated Denmark and southernmost Sweden, smallest in far-stretching Norway and northern Sweden, regions where, besides the restrictions placed on Mormon proselyting, the needle of emigration to America was already oriented, and Utah seemed a meager offering alongside the riches of "New Scandinavia." Denmark, through improved methods of tillage and a profitable outlet for its produce, was enjoying agricultural prosperity and did not experience a general exodus of the distressed.[3] But the religious unrest was considerable, product of the discouraging strife over Schleswig-Holstein in which many read God's disfavor with Denmark, of dissatisfaction with the Establishment, and of the effective work of the Inner Mission and the Grundtvig movement. And the Mormons still found many poor.

On the sandy peninsula of Jutland, less fertile than the Danish isles, particularly in the barren province of Vendsyssel at its tip and in the countryside around Aalborg, Aarhus, and Fredericia, they won their largest following outside Copenhagen and its environs. In proportion to its population Vendsyssel, it was said, yielded more converts than any other part of Scandinavia – a hardy, independent stock, descendants of Jutes who had resisted Catholic Christianity centuries before and made Lim Fjord, which separated them from the rest of Jutland, renowned as "the northernmost frontier of righteousness." [4] Missionary Christian Madsen in 1861 described Vendsyssel converts as coming from "the poorer class, mostly peasants from the country districts," but faithful and glad to travel "from ten to fifteen miles on Sunday, in rain or shine to attend meetings." Wherever he preached – "in private houses, barns and outbuildings" – the people willingly heard him. He was "astonished" to see the Saints, despite their poverty, "so glad and happy and full of good works," paying their tithes and responding with "ungrudging willingness to every requirement." [5] Anders Christensen, Madsen's fellow laborer, noted at the same time that a number of converts possessed means and were "very liberal in assisting the Elders to send off the poorer class to the Valley." The "liberality, kindness and freedom of spirit" of Vendsyssel, he was convinced, were the result of its never having been "under the mother church." [6]

Visiting apostle Amasa M. Lyman, who toured Jutland by carriage and found "a good Danish shake of the hand . . . no sickly, indifferent affair," compared the flat country beyond Lim Fjord with "the prairies of the great West," treeless except for occasional isolated islands of growth, the green foliage contrasting with the white walls of the better farmhouses. In contrast to Utah's valleys, he found the soil poor, the "hardy husbandman" only partially repaid for his toil. Five hundred of these north Jyllanders gathered in Johan Petersen's big barn to hear him. On his way back to Aalborg he spent two nights at farmsteads, where he found the "habitations of these sons of toil" very primitive:

> Yet in these hovels (the low ceilings of which keep one in constant remembrance that it is not good to hold the head too high) with all their indications of squalor and poverty, the spirit of genial friendship shed its cheering light; and, although there were no bedsteads, a liberal supply of fresh clean straw, placed on the earthy floor of the best apartment, afforded the traveler an opportunity to think of the rude and humble entertainment extended to the Sinner's Friend, and in sleep to forget the rude couch on which he finds repose.[7]

The island of Fyen, on the other hand, where the Saints numbered but 170 compared with Vendsyssel's 600, reminded him of the richest country districts of England and Scotland, the whole "a sea-girt picture of rural loveliness and beauty." Everywhere in Scandinavia – in Malmo, Oslo, Copenhagen, Odense – he received "most expressive proofs of the hospitality and brotherly love" of the Saints, though it was clear the gospel "at present finds its votaries" among the hardy poor, "sound material for the development of that worldwide nationality, in the broad shadow of which the saved of the world shall repose in the full enjoyment of that liberty which the gospel promises to the honest disciple of truth." [8]

Even a satirical missionary like Joseph W. Young, in whose eyes Jutland had "a very hungry appearance" and who thought the stables connected to the dwellings bred "the finest fleas in the world," was of the same opinion: the country people might be plain and simple with their black bread and strong coffee, their age-old wooden shoes and homespun, and their "hornspoon and finger" manners might be as primitive as their dress, but they were industrious "and certainly the most strictly honest that I have ever met with." [9]

More than half, or 53 per cent, of the Danish converts were won in Jutland – 27 per cent of the total Scandinavian membership.[10] The Copenhagen Conference (representing the whole of Zealand as well as the capital) produced 37 per cent of the Danish membership, or 21 per cent of the Scandinavian total. By 1905 Denmark yielded 23,509 proselytes, slightly more than half of all the following in Scandinavia. Of these, 12,696, or 54 per cent, emigrated; when the disaffected – who amounted to 31 per cent of the original Danish membership – are discounted the emigration looks more impressive: 78 per cent of the faithful. By 1878 it could be asserted of Denmark that perhaps no other country had been "so fully and faithfully warned. People can be found in nearly every section who have friends or relatives in the Church either there or in Zion." [11]

Denmark's general emigration statistics showed graphically how much "wind and sail," as one journalist put it, the Mormons had. The country's early emigrants were principally Mormon: of 3749 departing during the 1850s, over three fourths (2898, or 77 per cent) were Mormon; and of 13,011 during the 1860s, nearly two fifths (4942, or 38 per cent).[12] These converts gave Utah by 1860 nearly 19 per cent of the Danish population in the United States (1824 out of 9962), more than any other state. By 1870 only Wisconsin's Danish-born exceeded Utah's. Of six counties in the United States that year numbering 500 or more

Danes, Utah had four; Wisconsin had one, as did Nebraska – Douglas County, to which numbers of disaffected Danish Mormons had back-trailed. In 1890 still only Iowa (15,519), Nebraska (14,345), and Minnesota (14,133) exceeded Utah (9023) in number of Danish-born.[13]

It was a remarkable showing for a handicapped territory. Mormonism's accomplishment during the early decades was all the more notable in view of the Danes' stay-at-home tradition: in 1860, for example, the ratio of emigrants living in the United States to the total of those remaining in their native lands was highest in Denmark, 1 to 248, a striking contrast to the 1 to 33 ratio for Germany, 1 to 34 for Norway, 1 to 42 for England, and 1 to 187 for Sweden.[14]

Significant for Mormon success in Denmark was the early concentration there of the missionary force. Most of the literature, furthermore, was in Danish, which served Norway well enough, but until 1880 Norway never saw more than half a dozen missionaries at any one time, and Sweden only twice that number.

Most early proselytes in Sweden were made in the readily accessible province of Scania (or Skane) just across the Sound from Zealand and historically and culturally as well as topographically an extension of Denmark. After the periodical *Nordstjärnan* (1877) and the *Book of Mormon* (1878) were published in Swedish, and with the arrival of more elders – themselves Swedish convert-emigrants now returned as missionaries – activity flourished in Sweden. In 1879 baptisms exceeded those in Denmark; the year before, Stockholm had outstripped Copenhagen in membership and never relinquished the lead thereafter. The shift was abetted by a curious reversal of attitudes already noted: Sweden progressively abolished restraints on proselyting though never according the Mormons legal recognition as a sect, while Denmark in the 1880s imposed troublesome prohibitions.[15] Franklin D. Richards, visiting Stockholm in 1867, had noted "an insatiable thirst on the part of the people, that is growing with the ruler and sovereign also, for an extension of human rights, and freedom of thought, of speech, of the press, and of conscientious worship of almighty God. . . ."[16] That spirit predicted the welcome changes of the ensuing years, a far cry from the days when in some places in Sweden meetings had to be held privately and at night, as Carl Widerborg remembered: "We assembled at midnight, enjoyed much comfort of the spirit, transacted our business, and dispersed quietly at 5 o'clock in the morning."[17]

Sweden furnished altogether 16,695 converts, or 36 per cent of the Scandinavian total by 1905, when it became a separate mission. A little over a third of them, 36 per cent, came from Stockholm and its environs; another third, 34 per cent, from Skane. The Stockholm and Skane areas thus each furnished about 11 per cent of the whole Scandinavian membership. The Skane successes were early – in the 1850s and 1860s; Stockholm's prosperity came after 1870, particularly in the 1880s, the shift from rural to urban membership reflected in the predominant number of farmers among the early emigrants and of laborers among the later. Proportionately, emigration among the Swedish converts was less than among the Danish: 32 per cent of the Scandinavian total, or 44 per cent of all Swedish proselytes – 62 per cent if disaffected followers (who amounted to 29 per cent of the original Swedish membership) are not counted. Though conversions in Sweden actually surpassed those in Denmark during the 1880s and emigration of Swedish proselytes nearly caught up with the Danish, it was too late to overcome the handicap of the earlier decades. Yet just prior to 1880 more Swedish-born lived in Utah than in any other mountain state or territory. In 1910 Utah, coming within a fraction of Dakota and Nebraska, emerged as the fifth highest state in percentage of total population formed of Swedish stock. Proportionately the Swedes by this time were more strongly represented in the mountain West than in the United States as a whole.[18] Their actual numbers in Utah were relatively small, but locally important.

Norway, though it had given Mormonism forerunners like the Illinois settlers already described, turned a cold shoulder to Zion's invitation. Missionary A. L. Skanchy complained in 1887 that of Bergen's 41,000 inhabitants only four families were converted, and in the years Mormonism had been preached there only five or six families had emigrated.[19] From 1850 to 1905 Norway contributed but 14 per cent of all converts and 11 per cent of all the emigrants; they were, however, a highly articulate minority as it would prove, largely from Christiania (later called Oslo), producing an intelligentsia easily distinguished among the Scandinavian converts, who were in the main the "respectable farmers and mechanics, with their families," as Daniel Spencer observed in 1855, "who have embraced this work . . . and were constantly inquiring and being baptized wherever we went."[20]

Viewed by decades, the statistics on conversion, excommunication, and emigration for Scandinavia as a whole throw into relief the course of Mormon activity from 1850 to 1905, reflecting in part the declining energies of the movement itself, in part the changing times.[21] A handful of missionaries accomplished far more in the early years than superior numbers later. But if baptisms were numerous, so were excommunications – actually higher than emigration the first ten years. While conversions, after the peak of the 1860s, steadily declined, as did excommunications, the rate of emigration among converts rose. The high percentage – 67 per cent – of emigration in the 1880s in relation to the number of converts was the result of an all-out effort to bring to Zion many of the old converts who had not yet found means to emigrate. The 1850s saw only 26 per cent of the converts emigrate, and the 1860s 48 per cent, but they were a vanguard which, once established in Zion, sent help to the Old Country and made possible the greater emigration, proportionately, of the 1870s and 1880s.[22] The year 1880, incidentally, saw a greater number of Mormons resident in Scandinavia than at any time before or since. The great decline in numbers and the leveling of emigration in the 1890s and early 1900s to an even 50 per cent of conversions, with disaffection as low as 14 per cent, reflect a more stable if far smaller membership and a program aimed at accommodating it abroad instead of transplanting it to Zion.

Altogether, of the 46,497 converts which Scandinavia yielded between 1850 and 1905, 50 per cent were Danish, slightly less than 36 per cent were Swedish, and not quite 14 per cent were Norwegian. Of the 22,653 of these "members of record" who emigrated, 56 per cent were Danish, a little over 32 per cent were Swedish, 11 per cent were Norwegian, and a fraction Icelandic.[23]

All prevalent notions to the contrary, these converts by and large embraced Mormonism in families. Lurid stories of abduction to supply women for Utah's supposed harems had their germ in occasional runaways and desertions, but the statistics and the accounts of the converts themselves provide a convincing, not to say startling, corrective of folklore. Unusual enough to be amusing even in Mormon eyes was the congregation at Svedala, Sweden, in 1859, called the "Sister Branch" because all but six of its forty members were women.[24] Far more typical was the composition of the Vendsyssel Conference for 1861, which tailor Jens C. A. Weibye noted in his journal in detail: the 662 members of record included 115 married couples, 9 widowers, 36 widows,

18 betrothed men, 62 betrothed women, 2 divorced men, 8 divorced women, 58 youths over 15 years of age, 131 girls over 15 years of age, 46 boys between 8 and 15, and 62 girls between 8 and 15.[25]

Of 10,565 converts making up 31 selected companies which left Scandinavia between 1853 and 1882, 7785, or 74 per cent, were in family groups ranging from married pairs to flocks of eleven, with couples most common – 560 of them – followed by 470 families of three, 345 families of four, and so on, in descending order as the families grow larger.[26] Families made up as high as 85 per cent of the passengers on the *James Nesmith* in 1855, and 80 per cent of four companies in the 1860s. When in 1869 the migration shifted from sailing vessel to steam, the family character altered sharply for a time, only 45, 59, and 66 per cent of the next three companies, respectively, comprising family groups. It was no doubt an indication that, what with increased travel costs, fathers or sons found it expedient to go on ahead and send later for their families now easily able to manage alone a journey less hazardous on sea and plain than it had been in earlier years. If this assumption is correct, it explains the rather higher proportion of women in the companies that followed, though part of this increase may reflect more modern trends in Scandinavia itself which permitted young women to strike out for themselves without censure. The parallel movement of Mormons from Great Britain was also markedly a family migration: of 18,791 emigrants counted between 1841 and 1868, 15,112, or 80 per cent, were in family groups, with 32 per cent of these in groups of over five.[27]

Three-generation groups were not uncommon among the Scandinavians, the oldsters content to "die in the Lord" even though they should never reach the promised land. And there seemed to be a surplus of widows, no fewer than 61 among the 1213 emigrants of 1866. The majority of the emigrants, as the family structure would predict, were in their vigorous thirties and forties. Eligible girls and women (at the "spinster" age of 14 years and over) numbered 1515, or 15 per cent, of the 10,565 in the 31 companies being considered, and the eligible boys and men (at the apprentice age of 14 years and over) numbered 1184, or 12 per cent, a difference so slight it renders ridiculous the public headshaking in both Scandinavia and America, where it was assumed that "the females were in the great majority" in every boatload. Critics, besides, did not realize that a great many of the marriageable young women in the emigrant companies married the young men, their own countrymen, before journey's end.

Women did, in fact, predominate – by a slim margin. Of 12,477 emigrants – a somewhat larger sampling of Mormon companies leaving during the half century – 5796 were men, 6681 women, a difference of 885, or 7 per cent. The difference is significant enough because the general emigration from Europe to America was predominantly male: 59.6 per cent from 1820 to 1867, 64.9 per cent from 1869 to 1910. From Denmark it was 60 per cent male from 1869 to 1900; from Norway 57 per cent for the same period; and from Sweden 54 per cent between 1851 and 1900.[28] Among Scandinavian Mormons the ratio was essentially reversed: 46.5 per cent male, 53.5 per cent female. Among 19,017 British converts emigrating between 1841 and 1868, men showed a slight edge to 1860, women thereafter, though final percentages stood at 47 per cent for men and 47.5 per cent for women, with 1038 infants uncertain. English general emigration from 1840 to 1855 was 57.73 per cent male, 42.27 per cent female.[29]

Despite a growing gentile population that was largely male, Utah was the one pioneer territory with a nearly equal male-female ratio, the direct result of Mormonism's family structure. In 1870 men in Utah numbered 44,122, women 42,665; foreign-born men 15,127, women 15,575. In 1890 the ratio was 92 men to every 100 women among the Swedes, 87.2 among the Norwegians (no figure for the Danish),[30] all of which supports the inference that Mormonism's doctrine of polygamy made some impact in Europe, though much less than its critics contended. The Swedish government, noting that from 1881 to 1893 Swedish Mormons leaving for America numbered 895 men, 1303 women, and 1211 children under 12, speculated charitably that perhaps women were more given to religion than men.[31] The doctrine without question made the invitation to Zion practicable for women who could otherwise not have come, and the very family character of the migration made their travel as wards possible.

"The people wherewith you plant," Francis Bacon had advised America's first English colonizers, "ought to be gardeners, ploughmen, labourers, smiths, carpenters, joiners, fishermen, fowlers, with some few apothecaries, surgeons, cooks and bakers." [32] Except for the "apothecaries and surgeons" the Mormon proselytes would have strengthened the "plantations" of the New World as they did in fact strengthen the settlements in Zion. Although the collector of customs at New Orleans in 1853 indiscriminately labeled the first shipload of converts "Labourers and Shoemakers" – and had them coming from "Ireland"[33] – they were in reality Danish farmers and artisans representing the same variety of skills which would mark the whole emigration. The original Mormon roll of the *Forest Monarch* company has not survived, but a partial reconstruction in the Latter-day Saint Church archives from extant journals kept by members of the company mentions several weavers and blacksmiths, a tailor, wagonmaker, seaman, miller, wheelwright, carpenter, cabinetmaker, cooper, government clerk, former Baptist lay preacher, village choirmaster, school trustee, and a good many farmers.[34] The proportions cannot be known, but the occupations of the *Forest Monarch* emigrants must have foreshadowed the pattern of the companies which followed them, made up as they were of converts alike in every respect.

Farmers and their families (including an occasional shepherd and a few called gardeners or agriculturalists) made up fully half the emigration in the 1850s – 57 per cent in one company. In the 1860s they made up about a third, their numbers steadily diminishing with each decade as the proportion of laborers rose – the *Nevada* company in 1882, for example, counted 12 per cent farmers, 37 per cent laborers, and 16 per cent servant girls, reflecting the shift from rural to urban membership already noted. The "farmers" of the shipping lists were small farmers, Europe's familiar peasants – freeholders, tenants, or simply journeyman hands. Their peasant ancestry would figure years later in directives from the Genealogical Society of Utah outlining "how we must go to work if we want to construct a genealogical table of a farmer-family," a matter "of particular interest in Utah because most of the Latter-day Saints of Danish origin have come from the country districts."[35]

They included a few like the well-to-do Peter Thomsen of Bregninge on Falster Island, so prominent his conversion rocked the village, and the landed Anders Eliason of Ennerkulen, Sweden, who provided a hundred of his fellow converts with passage to America. At the other extreme were young hands like Christian Lund, who remembered herding cattle one winter for his board and a pair of wooden shoes, and Hans Christensen, whose sole possession was the sheep his father gave him as his share of the family property. In between were freeholders like Jens Nielsen, who at thirty years of age could buy five acres of land costing 600 rigsdaler, build a house costing 400 rigsdaler, and find himself "looked upon as a respectable neighbor and many times invited to the higher class of society." A small farmer like Hans Jensen Hals took over his father's place, worked it profitably enough to pay it off, and sold it for $1025.[36]

The great majority in the 1850s and 1860s – decades of Mormonism's largest rural membership in Scandinavia – were independent enough to pay their passage to Zion, at least as far as the frontier where wagons from Utah Territory awaited them, and to assist those without enough salable goods to scrape their passage together, an operation costing 65,000 English pounds for the twenty-eight companies who emigrated before 1869.[37] The many accounts of sales and inheritance settlements before departure for America and the considerable amounts recorded in the exchange column of the emigration ledgers speak a surprising means, further evidenced in the 21,069 pounds tithing and temple offering the mission paid during 1856 and the 2352 pounds paid during 1857, a period which saw 2610 members baptized and 990 emigrate.[38] The well-to-do farmers were few enough to be especially noticed; of course, wealth was relative: James Jensen remembered that owning a cow gave his parents "some recognition socially" in the village of Haugerup.[39] But certainly the farmers of those early years were far from the indigent serfs they were commonly imagined to be. Many were still too young when Mormonism found them to have gotten a competence or to have received a family inheritance; they were usually cut off anyway upon joining the church. All told, they were the seed corn for Zion, supplying it with a skill most sorely needed. Better fitted for an agrarian experience than the urban British migration, they were destined to make the valleys where they settled known as the granaries and creampots of Utah.

Like the farmers, the artisans, who outnumbered the unskilled laborers, included the prosperous and the poor – masters, journeymen, and apprentices – at one extreme, established proprietors like Hans Jensen, whose blacksmith works in Aalborg was valued at 8000 rigsdaler, and tailor Jens Weibye of Vendsyssel, who kept fourteen employees busy in his shop and sold a leaflet describing his new way to cut cloth; at the other extreme, a journeyman carriagemaker like Jens Christopher Kempe, who had nothing but the tools of his trade. Others like weaver

Hans Zobell owned their cottage worksteads, which they could sell when they emigrated. Ola Nilsson Liljenquist, Copenhagen tailor, whose wife could afford silks and a servant, was one of the few early converts enjoying the privileges of burghership.[40]

Among the artisans, carpenters and related craftsmen like cabinetmakers, coopers, wheelwrights, joiners, turners, and carriagemakers made up a considerable group, 11 per cent of reported occupations in the selected companies; in the *John Boyd* company in 1855 they formed 17 per cent. The next largest group of artisans were the tailors, seamstresses, dyers, and weavers (7 per cent). Smiths – blacksmiths, ironfounders, coppersmiths, tinsmiths, and an occasional machinist – followed these (6 per cent), with shoemakers, tanners, saddlemakers, and harnessmakers almost as large a group (5.6 per cent), not far outnumbering stonecutters, masons, and bricklayers (4.5 per cent). Speaking of early converts among the workmen in Oslo's factory district along the Aker, Carl Fjeld recalled that "From the foundrymen the gospel went round among the smiths, good and solid material, and from there to the stone masons," a sequence readily illustrated: himself an ironfounder, Fjeld passed his psalmbook and tracts around until they became as black as the workers themselves. They convinced Jonas Otterström, a smith who could no more keep silence, the newspapers noted, than he could from using a sledgehammer. And among those who heard him was stonemason Gustave Anderson, whose wife sold milk on the square, a capital opportunity to proclaim Mormonism at the same time.[41]

There were about the same number of butchers, brewers, bakers, and millers (only 17) as there were fishermen and seamen (only 16). The sailors were few. Landlocked in Zion, they might on some glorious Fourth of July climb the community flagpole like a mast or, like bargeman Hans "Pram Stikker" Larsen, work the block and tackle to hoist the stone for meetinghouses and temples.[42] Four ropemakers, two house painters, a miner, a matmaker, a hairdresser, a hunter, a bookbinder, a printer, a thatcher, a sailmaker, a shipbuilder, five watchmakers or instrument-makers, four clerks, four potters, and a furrier were among the infrequent occupations. Three musicians – all members of the *Monarch of the Sea* company in 1861 – alone saved the day for the professions, though the *B. S. Kimball* emigrants included a homeopath and, to complete the curiosities, a professed golddigger. For a budding artist like young Carl Christian Anton Christensen, whose expert silhouettes won him a scholarship to Copenhagen's Royal Academy until he joined the Mormons, Zion had at first no call. He had to content himself with farming when he emigrated in 1857, though he kept his interest alive as an amateur, painting scenery for the Salt Lake Theater and creating a traveling panorama of church history which won him at last a kind of fame.[43]

The basic skills were all there; others would be developed in the settlements, where as bishops and mayors some of them would help run church and state and where newspapers in their own tongue would one day advertise goods sold and services performed by countrymen adequate enough to serve them from the cradle to the grave. "I would never have believed," wrote C. C. A. Christensen in 1872 after visiting the Utah Territorial Fair, "so much talent could be found among us as a people who are nearly all gathered from among the poor and most downtrodden classes of mankind." Someone from his home town, the Danish settlement of Ephraim, had won the silver medal for a landscape painting showing several children gleaning corn in the field just outside "our town"; a Swedish sister had received the premium for *haararbeide* – hair artistry; "our friend W." (without doubt the Norwegian painter Dan Weggeland) had received the silver medal for his portraits; a young Norwegian brother had taken the prize for wood carving; a Swede for an artistic watch; "and many others won premiums. . . . It's only a small part of what can be accomplished."[44] Twenty years later Christensen observed that he met Scandinavians "nearly everywhere" in his travels and found his countrymen in many places holding "the most responsible positions both in church and civic affairs," which he found "a greatly satisfying witness to our national character by the world's most practical nation – the Americans."

I come to the conclusion that although the Gospel is preached as in Jesus' time, and is for the most part received by the poor, yet are the Saints far from among the ungifted; because by leaving their old homeland where social class conditions pose almost insurmountable obstacles to the economic improvement of the unfortunate they have occasion to use their gifts without narrow restrictions. Thus have many Scandinavians in free America on the whole, and not least in Utah, achieved satisfactory living conditions for themselves and their posterity.[45]

Both Europe and America, however, took a dim view of the Mormon convert-emigrants. They were an embarrassment to Scandinavia, a trouble to the United States, where Secretary of State William Evarts, for example, in 1879 felt uneasy about Utah's "accessions from Europe . . . drawn mainly from the ignorant classes, who are easily influenced by the double appeal to their passions and their poverty." [46] Samuel Bowles, editor of the Springfield *Republican* and no more enlightened, described them in 1865 as "simple, ignorant people beyond any class known in American society, and so easy victims to the shrewd and sharp and fanatical Yankee leaders in the Mormon church." [47] Utah, already outlandish enough as the Mormon refuge, seemed all the more un-American with its alien population recruited, it was feared, to strengthen Mormon subversion of federal authority and Christian morality.

Vilification of the convert in this respect was most vicious in Utah itself, among the gentiles, who made Mormon immigration a major issue in their campaign to bring the church to its knees and the territory to unsullied statehood. The *Deseret News* resented the contemptuous remarks of "the local journalistic maligner" that never lost an opportunity "to defame and belittle everything 'Mormon'" and talked "with frequent scorn about the Scandinavian element, as though the . . . presence of such people was sufficient to show the degraded character of Utah's population." The slurs, plainly enough, stemmed from the notion that "everything American must be superior to anything foreign . . . and the very name of Scandinavian [means] something inferior and to be ridiculed." [48]

In the bitterly anti-Mormon *Handbook on Mormonism* gentiles were Americans, Mormons were foreigners, "low, base-born foreigners, hereditary bondsmen . . . serf blood. . . ." [49] The Reverend J. Wesley Hill's patriotism erupted in odious images of the converts as foreigners: they were "gathered from the slums of Europe . . . brought from the fetid fields of the Old World . . . ignorant peasants entrapped through misrepresentation and fraud . . . refugees from the despotisms of the Old World" who endeavored "in the name of Religion to undermine our liberties and destroy our government. . . ." [50] Governor Caleb West's animosity in 1889 drove him into an extreme allusion: "It is just as if a lot of Chinamen or other foreign people should come here and take possession of that Territory, with ideas entirely distinct and diametrically opposed to ours." [51]

The governor retracted the implication as accidental, but such hyperbole was all too common. In vain did an impartial observer like the Reverend John C. Kimball ask: "Who has implicit confidence in a Californian's denunciation of the Chinese, or in a western squatter's diatribe against the Indians or in a Protestant theologian's strictures on Roman Catholicism? So with the criticisms of Utah gentiles on their Mormon neighbors."[52] And in vain did Apostle George Q. Cannon contend that "a large part of our people are native-born," and that "our proselytes are more largely Americans than any other nationality."[53] It was an ingrained national habit to speak ill of the Mormons: even in their Missouri days, long before they went abroad, Mormons were by definition "the very dregs and sediment of society."[54]

Praise, if any, was always left-handed—amazement at the good results from disreputable beginnings. "It may be true," said the London *Examiner*, "the religious fanatics of Scandinavia are sometimes charmed with this Mohammed's Paradise," but "These bigamous folk . . . their peculiarly unpleasant institution aside, have . . . preserved order and public morality in a manner strange to other Western towns."[55] Rarely did anyone like Hugh McCullough, former secretary of the treasury, applaud the Mormon immigration: "The people of the United States," he said in the New York *Tribune* in 1877, "are under obligation to the Mormons. . . . They have brought to the country many thousands of industrious, peaceable and skilful people, and added largely to its wealth. . . ." The most the gentiles were willing to grant was that "under proper training" the foreign-born "would in time become liberty-loving, patriotic citizens, as they are now industrious and economical."[56]

In a day of phrenological judgments, observers of Mormon audiences thought they noticed "the want of intellectuality in the countenances of the majority," who were "evidently for the most part composed of persons of little education, drawn from humble walks of life in the Old Country."[57] *Harper's*, noting in 1884 "how largely foreigners they are, the predominant nationalities being British and Scandinavian," found "their peasantry stamped upon their faces, though they have exchanged their foreign characteristics for a rusticity of the American type."[58] At ports of entry newsmen usually found the immigrants looking "far from intellectual, and apparently of the class that had been used to hard work"; or the reporters were at best condescending: "The grade of intelligence was apparently low . . . but by no means indicative either of ignorance or stupidity." [59]

There was seldom the open admiration of the New York *Daily Graphic*: "A cleaner, neater, and more comfortable looking set of immigrants than those Mormons were seldom enters our port." [60] The irrationalism of the antipolygamy prosecution in the late 1880s betrayed even the commissioner of immigration into an irresponsible description of one company: "In many instances there were women with children born out of wedlock, wives who had deserted their husbands and brought their children with them, husbands who had left behind their wives, children who had run away from home, and parents who had abandoned their children." [61] It was a perfectly stereotyped picture of Mormon immigrants, as common in Europe as in the United States.

While the United States blamed Europe for supplying proselytes "ignorant enough and sufficiently docile to carry out the schemes of the apostles," [62] and on occasion even sought the help of foreign governments to check them, Europe blamed America for exporting an undesirable ism: the London *Times* considered Mormonism another "invention of the United States" along with spiritualism: "They are both . . . transatlantic in their origin; but it must be confessed that both have been sustained by converts within our own borders." Such isms would continue as long as there were persons in Europe "so imperfectly educated, intellectually and morally, as to accept with facility and even with eagerness creeds that put back the dial of time at least two thousand years," [63] as long as there were people, in the words of a Leicestershire curate, "accustomed on market-days to listen open-mouthed to the lies of 'Cheap John' and to believe whatever he is pleased to tell them about his great-grandfather's marvellous hatchet, or his mother's astonishing mousetrap." [64] It was deplorable, but England, thought an observer like Hepworth Dixon, ought to face the facts: Mormon converts were "a symptom of a disease which may be lying at the seat of life. Has Convocation ever given up a day to the Book of Mormon? Has a bishop ever visited the Saints in Commercial Road?" [65]

Scandinavia found Mormon success equally deplorable. National pride dismissed the converts as not representative – it was consoling to think they were the sick, the poor, the outcast, and that the well-to-do and intelligent among them were the exception, though Denmark expressed surprise, if not concern, that its peasants, traditionally so stable and sober, should be persuaded in such numbers.[66] Worst of all, the Mormon proselytes alienated themselves from both church and country: the Danish Establishment already had its hands full with dissenting Grundtvigians and the pietists of the Inner Mission, but these were at least native movements and patriotic.

Sweden, also on national grounds, was frankly envious: while its missionaries were evangelizing the heathen in Africa, China, and India at a cost of about 1425 kronor for each proselyte, the Mormons were making proselytes in Sweden itself and at a third the cost, with the added difference that the Mormon proselytes, at an economic loss to the country of 5000 kronor capital worth, emigrated to strengthen the community in Utah, where they paid tithing, supported missions, and maintained churches, whereas the Swedish missions had only a handful of black and yellow natives to show for their trouble.[67]

Consular officer John L. Stevens, speaking of Norway and Sweden, wrote angrily in 1879 that "The government and the public sentiment of these countries are averse to having their population victimized and depleted by immoral and criminal means."[68] An elaborate official survey, the result of Sweden's concern over her alarming emigrant loss generally, found Mormonism a "well-ordered emigration recruiting system under the cloak of religion," appealing chiefly to "cottiers, laborers, artisans, and servant classes," but the survey concluded that while it was regrettable any of these should be deluded into joining the Mormons, it was better that they continue to emigrate than harass the mother land as they had certainly harassed the United States: "The sect has freedom in the United States but with unhappy consequences. The government there has been sorely tried."[69]

The bad opinion of the Mormons in Scandinavia was universal: "I knew nothing of the Mormons except very bad reports." "I had always understood them to be a wicked, mean people that ought to be shunned." "Father did not care so much about the Baptists, if my brother would only keep away from the Mormons." Anna Karine Widtsoe, widow of a Trondhjem schoolmaster, felt contaminated when her shoemaker stuffed some Mormon tracts into shoes she had left for repair. It was always a surprise to find any good apples in the barrel. Tailor Olof Hanson remembered his pastor's astonishment: "He asked me how I, who could read so well, could have become a Mormon."[70]

Overnight, established reputations could be blighted. Convert Hannah Sorensen, though twenty-five years a respected midwife in Snedsted, lost her practice and was threatened with the workhouse; Oslo impresarios, eager to engage Agnes Olsen's golden voice to sing Solveig's song from *Peer Gynt*, told her no audience would tolerate her as a Mormon. It was not often that teachers or employers took the part of the proselyte as did Annie Christensen's teacher, who told the children not to make fun of her. On the contrary, Christina Oleson's Swedish pastor, encountering her on the village street one day, struck her with his cane for joining the despised Mormons. She felt she was getting off easy.[71]

An immorality of the clergy's own making gave many early proselytes an unsavory reputation. They came from a class already in bad repute because, cut off from benefits of clergy through fees they couldn't meet or having an antipathy to the authority and ritual of the Establishment, they had entered into common-law marriages. Franklin D. Richards observed in Stockholm in 1867 that one of the brethren went to a Lutheran priest to be married but was refused the ceremony because he was a heretic. Obtaining a writ to that effect, he applied to the Mormon mission president, who performed the rite and gave him a certificate, "since which his neighbors consider him an honorably married man." The clergy, said Richards, had "bastardized" 42 per cent of the population.[72] Erastus Snow must have had this condition in mind when in his *Voice of Truth* he admonished members to observe the civil marriage requirements. With the Mormon position so precarious in the world, it was imperative to avoid even the appearance of evil. Indiscretions were stones in the slings of the enemy. As late as 1899 missionaries were warned, "Don't walk with young ladies across the country holding your arm. Walk with their father or brother. . . . Don't kiss anybody. . . ."[73]

Stories about the Mormons emphasized their credulity and low caste. Folk memory recalled a Mormon who "clung to a cooper, a wagonmaker, and thresher, and would not be shaken"; the wife of Fisherman Stranden, who left her husband at night to be baptized; an uncle who joined the Mormons and looked for the millennium; villagers in Ronbjerg who were baptized in a pond where dogs and cats were drowned; a weaver and his family who sold their house and went "to the prophet in America"; a farmer's daughter about to leave until a furloughed soldier sweetheart changed her mind; a nurse who warned that a great grasshopper plague would come over Denmark and the people had better leave for Utah.[74] Not a few of these tales had to do with runaways, desertions, child-stealing, and broken homes. Once the Mormon elders entered a household, said Pastor Åslev, it was demoralized, divided.[75]

In their zeal, some converts committed follies that rumor easily magnified. They took Christ at his word and left family and friends to form new ties stronger than the old. What private dissatisfactions lay at the root of this is hard to say. Women in the early years were often baptized without their husbands' knowledge—a practice eventually discontinued. There were no abductions as enemies charged, but enough voluntary runaways, abetted by sympathizers, to confirm the bad reputation of the Mormons and get them into trouble with the civil authorities.

More than one frantic parent tried to win back a son or daughter lost to the Mormons—run away, he might say, but very likely turned out of doors. Despite her mother's "heart-rending pleadings" Olina Törasen would not return home from Christiania, where she had gone in 1864 to learn dressmaking and had met the Mormons. Her father, "crazed with grief," came for her, sitting up all night at her boarding-house because he did not dare to leave her alone; but she outwitted him in an unguarded moment and, with the help of a missionary and disguised as a boy, made her way to Copenhagen until the spring emigration of the Saints. She worked meanwhile at a cape factory and wrote home, her mother finally relenting to the extent of sending Olina her "grandmother's feather bed and a few clothes." [76]

What were testimonies of God's providences to the faithful seemed cloak-and-dagger treachery to the bereft. In 1858 the Danish minister to the United States asked the State Department to stop a Dane named Madsen who had two young women with him headed for the Mormon settlements. The State Department authorized the Army to stop the trio if it could and ask the women whether they were proceeding of their own free choice; the Army could try to persuade them to return to their families in Denmark but could not force them to return, for they were of age.[77]

Hardly a company of Mormon emigrants ever left Copenhagen without a warrant being served on someone for child stealing: fearful relatives or suspicious neighbors often tried to interfere when a Mormon family sent some of their young ahead. Efforts of women to take their children with them when the husbands objected were the source of most child-smuggling tales. Midwife Hannah Sorensen's estranged husband was in Chicago, but when he heard that his wife was getting ready to take their three youngest to Zion, he had the authorities take them from her. Distracted, she put her case in the hands of the Lord and the elders, who advised her to go without them, assuring her they would follow in due time. But it was years before she saw them again in a strained reunion in Chicago.[78]

Anna Lucia Krause, wife of a prospering wheelwright and nail maker who was in no mood to give up his thriving shop to go to America, kept her Mormon membership a secret for two years, until her unhappiness persuaded him to go as far as St. Louis. When they sailed, Anna left eight-year-old Maria behind with a Mrs. Frandsen who would soon emigrate with a Mormon company. It was part of Anna's design to get her unbelieving husband to Utah, where he would have to journey to fetch the girl and in the process perhaps be converted and remain. But a brother of Mrs. Frandsen, opposed to her joining the Mormons, had her arrested for stealing a child. Years later Maria remembered being taken to police headquarters and asked whether she wanted to go with Mrs. Frandsen to her mother. She said yes. They claimed she said no.

Maria was eventually left in care of the Lars Madsen family. When the emigrant company passed through St. Louis her father came for her, but zealous Mrs. Madsen was determined not to leave the child among gentiles. Krause, already grief-stricken at the loss of his wife and three children, all victims within a week of the cholera, made a heartbreaking search for his Maria. Going from wagon to wagon, even throwing covers off sick people in his desperate quest, he spied her playthings, but he never found her; and Mrs. Madsen, confident she was doing a good deed, took the child off to Utah, leaving the father, already at odds with the Mormons, more embittered than ever and a source of more damaging evidence against them.[79] Sad histories like this soon became known in Scandinavia and blackened Mormonism's visage the more.

The popular image of the Mormon proselytes – their poverty, their ignorance, their fanaticism – made them Europe's ugly ducklings, objects of scorn and ridicule, though the novelist Ole Rölvaag called emigrants from the same class "giants in the earth." It was precisely the poor and humble the Mormons were after. Poverty and ignorance were ills for which America itself was the remedy, an assurance that was one of Mormonism's enthusiasms. "The people have much to learn," observed Apostle George Q. Cannon. "Transplanting them to Zion will benefit them in every way, if they will do right. . . . The gospel will not only bestow spiritual benefit . . . it will benefit them temporally."[80] Their "habits of industry and the various ways in which they are taught to apply it," felt Apostle George A. Smith, "render them well qualified to develop the resources of new and untried countries, and their former experience greatly enhances their appreciation of the emancipation the gospel brings to them and contentment follows."[81]

The poverty of the Old World was really a blessing; nothing so endangered salvation as a prosperity which killed the urge to gather. Besides, already inured to want, they were better prepared for hardships.[82] The Mormons had no illusions about their converts, but they saw beyond their limitations: the poor were after all the Lord's poor; the ignorant had simply been denied schooling; and the credulous had faith, frequently displaying the "fortitude of patience and heroic martyrdom unsung" which Milton found the essence of Christian humility.

The hidden resources of the humble could be magnificent. "I want to say here that at one time I nearly broke down," Ansine Peterson confessed as she looked back over a long life as convert and emigrant, "and that was at the death of my third child." To lose a husband and three children of diphtheria in a single summer tried her to the limit: "I begged the brethren to pray for me that I harden not my heart." But the woman who as a girl had found herself singing at her work after baptism, who had stood fast when her parents denied the new faith, who had felt herself a stranger at home and lonely whenever a party of emigrants left for Zion, and who had been comforted in dreams and by "the spirit of promise," once more felt "how weak is Humanity, how little we are, and also how good and mercyful God is for truly He places no burden on our Shoulders but He also gives strength to bear."[83]

There was no way to measure the intangibles which were Zion's greatest assets. How could the pastor who caned Christina Oleson for joining the Mormons ever imagine her a pillar of the community, a progenitor of leading citizens? Yet who else in Deseret's wastes would get a precious daily pound of butter into town to sell before the sun could melt it, or be forever knitting as she plowed or read or herded?[84] How could fellow Lollanders ever see in Elsie Rasmussen and Jens Nielsen more than simple, hard-working hands hiring out from one farm to another, now and then walking arm and arm into town to dance away the night and return in time to do the chores? How could anyone predict their heroic history? Underway to Zion Jens' courage would fail him crossing Wyoming's snowbound plateau, and Elsie would load him, his feet frozen, into her handcart and pull him till his courage returned, saving him, though permanently crippled, to pioneer five settlements and build as many homes to make good his dedication to the Lord for the deliverance. As colonizer, Indian peacemaker, merchant, stockman, bishop, and patriarch he would make his broken-tongued maxim *Sticket to trude* – "Stick to the truth" – a badge of honor, while in sandswept Bluff Elsie would plant mulberry trees to raise silkworms, tend beehives to provide the settlement its only sweets, spend long hours at the loom, giving her days to manual labor, her evenings to the Bible and other good books, and devote herself as foster mother to the children of her husband's plural wives.[85]

It was just such recruits Zion needed. Conversion called thousands like Jens and Elsie Nielsen out of obscurity, confirming Mormonism's conviction that "The Lord is gathering out the best and the most pure material for his own use. . . . With them will he build himself a people and name in the earth."[86] No ugly ducklings ever had a greater sense of destiny. Scandinavia might disown them and America not want them, but they felt a singular identity as the Lord's own. In fact, they felt sorry for the unsaved, for the king himself. Apostle Franklin D. Richards, attending the Royal Theater in Stockholm in 1867 and finding himself "in the midst of nobility and gentry, the beauty, elite, and authority of Sweden," thought how much he would like "to impart to His Majesty the testimonies of the gospel restored, and the work of God as it is now progressing on the earth, and inform him how he could assure the stability of his throne. . . ."[87]

But only royalty's humble subjects, their eyes on another kingdom, came to know the high drama of conversion. For them the encounter with Mormonism was the great turning point in their lives, a new beginning to which all previous events, as they now looked back, had unerringly led. They signalized their rebirth by keeping journals in

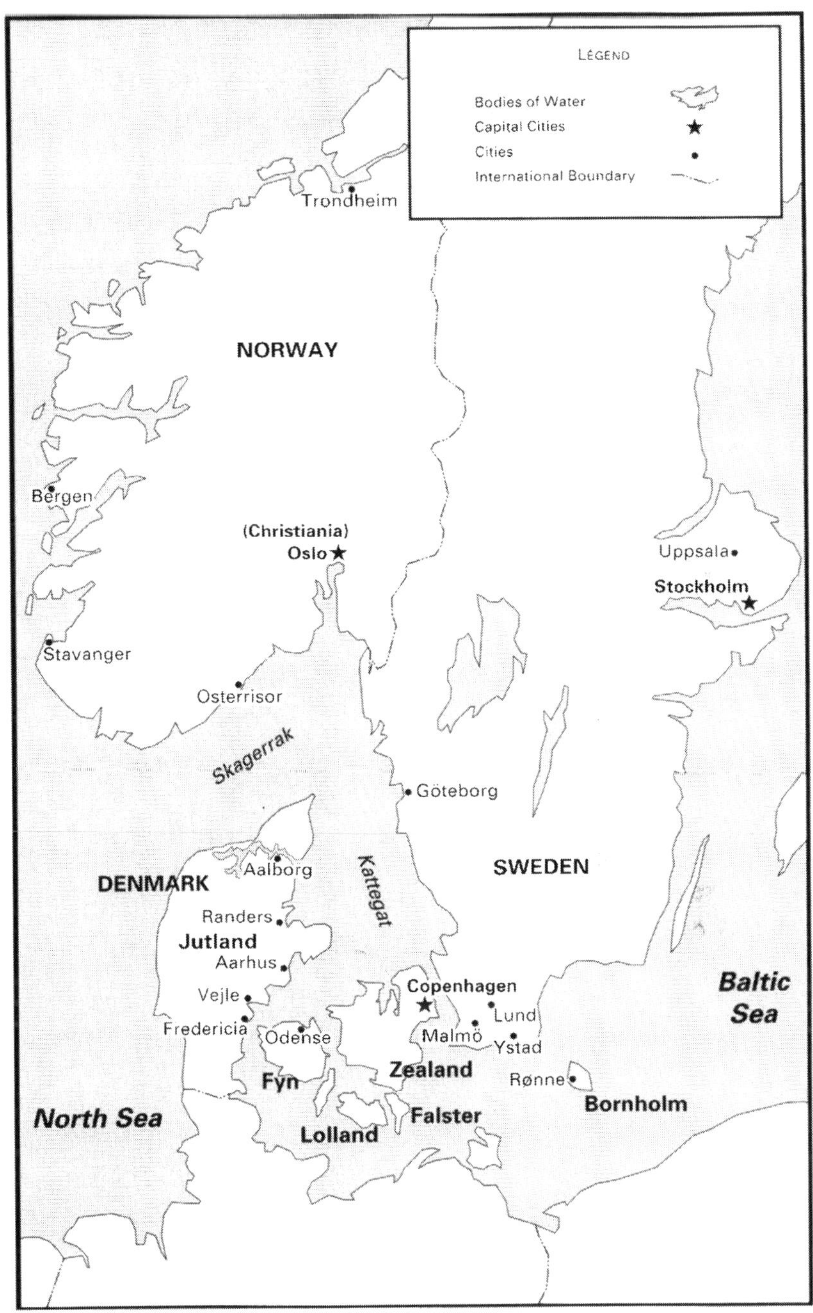

Map 1. Major centers of LDS missionary proselyting in Scandinavia, 1850–1905.

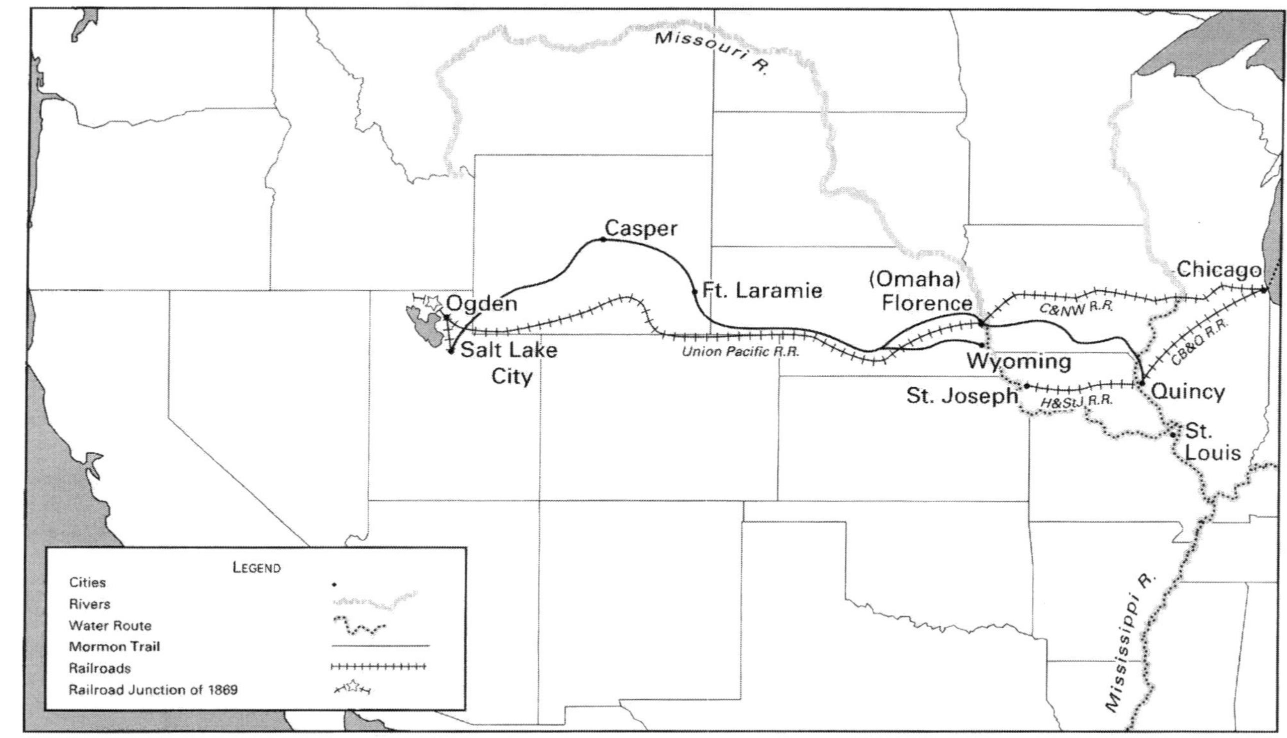

Map 2. Western routes frequently traveled by LDS Scandinavian immigrants, 1853–1905.

Figure 1. *Canute Peterson family, tintype, hand tinted, ca. 1871.* Family sources believe this picture was taken in the spring or summer of 1871, shortly before Canute filled a mission to Scandinavia. Canute, seated in the middle, is surrounded by his three wives (left to right: Sarah Ann, Maria, and Charlotte) and multiple children at the family's home in Ephraim, Utah. Courtesy LDS Church Archives.

Figure 2. *Erastus Snow, ca. 1850.* Born in Vermont in 1818, Snow became a member of the LDS Church's Quorum of the Twelve Apostles in 1849 and was called to initiate missionary work in Scandinavia. Between 1850 and 1852, along with his companion John Forsgren and earlier converts who had become local missionaries, he baptized over six hundred people in Scandinavia. Courtesy LDS Church Archives.

Figure 3. *Anthon H. Lund as a missionary in Denmark, 1871.* Born in Aalborg, Jutland, Denmark, Lund and his family joined the LDS Church and emigrated to Zion. In the early 1880s, Lund served as president of the Scandinavian Mission. He later became a member of the church's Quorum of the Twelve Apostles and a counselor in the First Presidency. Courtesy LDS Church Archives.

Figure 4. *Portrait of LDS missionaries in the Copenhagen Conference, 1874.* Standing: Carl M. Nelson, Thorwall Orlob, Niels Nielsen, Ole Petersen, Niels P. Nielsen, Jörgen Jensen. Sitting: James Hansen, Peter O. Hansen, Peter C. Carstensen, Knud Petersen, Adolph Jörgensen. Courtesy LDS Church Archives.

Figure 5. *Montage of individual portraits of missionaries in the Scandinavian Mission, 1887.* Mission presidents Nils C. Flygare and Christian D. Fjeldsted are pictured in the center. The missionaries are grouped by conference (geographical divisions within the mission): Christiania, Skåne, Aalborg, Aarhus, Stockholm, and Gøteborg. Of particular interest is P. A. Forsgren in the Stockholm Conference, son of John Erik Forsgren who, with Erastus Snow, was the first LDS missionary to Scandinavia, and A. S. Skanchy in the Christiania Conference, son of convert-emigrant Anthon Skanchy. As the family names show, most missionaries were of Scandinavian descent, and it became a matter of pride in many families that a son, or the father himself, should serve a mission to the Old Country. Courtesy LDS Church Archives.

Figure 6. *Group portrait of choir members in the Stockholm Branch, ca. late 1800s.* The group of men on the left include C. J. Selin, L. Ramström, A. Bång, A. J. Olsen, J. J. Pettersen Sangloren, and L. D. Nyberg. Women in center include Tekla Frederikson, Maria Åkerlund, Albertine Rudergren, Charlotte Östergren, Anna Jacobson, Pauline Olsen, Hannah Söderberg, Amalia Olson, Agnes Faben, Josephine Engström, Clara Erickson, Christine Nielsen, and Emma Olsen. Men on right include F. R. Sandberg, Johan Aug. Pattersen, Olof Olsen, and Soward Lindström. Courtesy LDS Church Archives.

Figure 7. S. S. Waesland, *ca. 1890–1902.* View of the ocean liner *S. S. Waesland* before its sinking in 1902. Carl Alfred Carlson (1874–1950), a missionary in Scandinavia, photographed this typical Scandinavian ship. Such vessels transported convert-emigrants from Scandinavian ports to assembly points in England. Courtesy LDS Church Archives.

which, with the introspection of the Puritan diarists, they noted God's providences, an engrossing record of trials and blessings and triumphant spiritual manifestations—the sick made whole, enemies routed, prophetic dreams and visions enjoyed, tongues spoken and interpreted, the signs which follow believers multiplied—a pentecostal outpouring of gifts so widely experienced and reported that it seemed a special dispensation for Scandinavia.

The ancient gifts were a comfort, but extravagant expectations spelled trouble both in the mission and later in Zion, where the frenetic fringe were the first to be disappointed; enthusiasts, immoderate seekers of signs, were a thorn in the side of the quiet ones whose faith ran deeper. During Copenhagen's cholera epidemic in 1852, Sister Matheasen was healed and her husband ran up and down the stairs crying, "A miracle, a miracle!" until Elder Liljenquist took him firmly by the arm saying, "If you do not repent of this spirit and quietly give God the honor, you will apostatize." The Saints began to "boast before the world" that they could not die of the dreadful plague; but the leader of the congregation was himself struck down, bringing the Mormons "a very trying day in many ways."[88] More important to Mormonism's health in Scandinavia was the record of very human works, the Saints performing their own daily miracles of survival even as they stood in the presence of the miraculous.

Conversion itself was primarily such a work and far from simple-minded. Sarah Josephine Jensen did not easily accept the doctrine of polygamy: "I must say that I was thunderstruck. It was so contrary to my feeling and tradition that I stopped; some doubts came to me and after a severe struggle with weeping and praying I saw some light and the Lord spake Peace to my soul and I had a testimony of the divinity of this great revelation. . . ."[89] Often attended by such doubt and indecision, conversion answered a variety of rational and emotional needs felt by the dispossessed looking for a place to belong, the worldly ready for moral reformation, the dissenter unsatisfied by the established creed or piqued with the clergy, the scriptural literalist looking for fulfillment of prophecy.

Many were ripe for a spiritual experience, like so many Bunyans earnestly seeking their abounding grace: "I felt that I had allowed myself to be careless, and to trifle with the most important of all subjects, my soul's salvation." "In school I was the greatest mischief and the worst fighter but always ahead in my studies. When school was done with, my religion was laid on the shelf. . . . I found a piece written by Ap. [Apostle] E. Snow entitled The Importance of a Virtuous Life. I read this to all my associates stating that if ever I could find a people like this I would be willing to go to the ends of the earth to join them." "I had heard other religious people speak of the satisfaction their religion afforded them, but I had never experienced this comfort. . . . I became so deeply afflicted in my mind that I began to think I was alone in the world. . . ." "I got acquainted with much wickedness as the people in this city [Ronne] are very deeply engaged in sin and darkness. . . . For a time I participated in the pleasures of the world, but from 1849 . . . my feelings became very serious and deep." "A stranger introduced himself as an elder from America. . . . In an hour we saw and understood more of our Bible than ever before. . . . Our hearts rejoiced and a new life had opened before us."[90]

They went to their first Mormon meeting on a dare or out of curiosity and universally with the worst expectations. "I went to the meeting that night with the pronounced conviction that they were not even Christians . . . with the thought of spending the evening in mischief."[91] But time and again they were confounded: "As soon as I saw those men's faces I knew the testimony they bore was of God." "It seemed as though every word the Elder spoke went right through me. . . . The sermon had an entirely different effect upon my brother and the other young man. They were greatly amused. I sat there like a statue and could not join them in the merriment." "I heard them speak and the first time I heard them I felt that Mormonism was true, and that it would comfort and satisfy me." "I received a testimony that God had begun this work, therefore all the evil in the world was against it. . . . I felt more happiness than I had ever had before."[92]

Their fears routed at the first encounter, they were ready for more: "We bought some few of their tracts and studied them for a few weeks and were perfectly satisfied the work was of God." "I borrowed the Bible and searched for myself . . . and prayed. . . . It was before me by day and by night that the time had now come for the fulfillment of these promises [of gathering and restoration]. . . . They that went to Zion would save their souls for that time in the last days when the great trials that the prophets had written about would take place."[93]

And then invariably they felt the stigma that their affiliation with the new movement gave them in the eyes of friends and neighbors still prejudiced. "From that time on all my former friends turned against me and spoke all kinds of evil against me, and that falsely." "Half the lies they told about us were not true"! [94] What had seemed so glorious became a nightmare, an agonizing struggle to remain steadfast that crushed some but strengthened others: "All the slurs and insinuations of the hands I was laboring with had no effect upon me." "When my Onkel found I would not leave the Gospel he tore to pieces a will he made in my favour the amount of my loss being about Sixty thousand Dollars I lost no sleep over it however." "All my possessions had no power over me then, my only desire was to sell out and come to Zion." "In this state of affairs there was a fight going on in my own mind, my prospects in life was reasonably bright for a poor boy, should I become convinced of the truth of Mormonism, which was very unpopular, my prospects would be gone. . . . my Parents and friends used their influence with me and sought to draw my attention away from Mormonism, using both religious means and also encouraged me to engage in the pleasures of the world. . . ." "My step-father told me that if I became a Mormon I would become an outcast and would not be permitted to enter their home. This threat filled my heart with bitter anguish, for I loved my home dearly." "I had no idea before I was baptized that I should have to go through so much if I joined the Mormons; if I had known it, I don't think I could have done so." [95]

Conversion cost dearly. No allegory of Christian warfare, the soul against the world, was ever more terribly real. Nearly a third of the proselytes could not pay the price but disavowed the faith in Scandinavia, with others following suit after emigration, some en route to Zion, others after residence in Zion itself. Such wholesale disaffection refutes the easy explanation that Mormonism was such an effective Pied Piper because its tune was America. It was America, but on very special terms, forbidding to any but the most ardent believers. Belated discovery of unacceptable doctrine, inability to endure ostracism and persecution, capitulation to doubt and disbelief created by adverse propaganda, disappointment in the expectation that transportation to America was a handout – all undoubtedly weighed in the scale of apostasy.

Moreover, some of the converts themselves, in church eyes, were weighed and found wanting. The *Stjerne* bluntly published names of those cast out for "whoredoms and abominations," while congregations were quick to censure backsliders for intemperance or for returning to an occasional service in the state church or for failing to pay tithes and offerings. Sometimes personal pique and backbiting, jealousies over positions in the lay priesthood, or misunderstanding about the order of the church led to breaches impossible to mend. In later decades prospective members usually served a long period as "investigators"; conversions were fewer but less ephemeral. The insistence on standards and the severe excommunication policy were evidence Mormonism was not interested in converts and emigrants at any price. It was a winnowing both natural and deliberate, intended to separate the wheat from the chaff so that early and late it could be noted that "many of our brethren have so improved their manner of living, the civil authorities have been obliged to acknowledge the fruits of a good doctrine." [96]

The winnowing was part of a general reformation in which conversion, itself such a profound education, was only the beginning. Mormonism might have blamed Scandinavia for having done so little for its lowest estate, but Mormonism took its converts where it found them and prepared them for the American experience in an indoctrination unique among European emigrants. To this end the mission considered itself "Eden's nursery," where the gospel was sown and the seedlings readied for transplanting to Zion, the Garden itself.[97] The husbandry was both spiritual and mundane, another demonstration of the way Mormonism's practicality gave its vision substance, at once bent on a purification of motives and on a program for improved living intended to win greater respect for Mormonism in Scandinavia and to make its converts better inhabitants of Zion.

Though emigration was the great common impulse among the converts, they were told not to make gathering the sole aim, confusing means and ends. It was an urgent duty to gather, but those not feeling it should not be induced until moved by their own zeal. Simply getting to Utah did not ensure salvation. Motives were all-important. Converts should come to build up Zion, willing to be identified with it in adversity as well as in prosperity, the object not wealth but only serving God. Whatever temporal benefits attended removal from Babylon came through the gospel and through their "own energies under wise direction and the opportunities which the country affords," blessings which were the natural fruits of righteousness.[98]

The Saints were urged to make the most of opportunities while still in the homeland, to add "to the treasury of the Church all useful knowledge and all the benefits of their experience" gained there.[99] The church itself supplied valuable training: converts enjoyed a voice and by the uplifted hand a vote they had never known in the professionalized service of the Establishment; the men served as missionaries, teachers, book agents, congregational leaders, filling a variety of positions in the lay priesthood – all excellent apprenticeship for responsibilities in Zion, where they would serve side by side with the Americans and converts from other lands. In the choirs (in Oslo as early as 1856), the Sunday schools, and the young people's and women's societies (dating from the 1870s) congregations as a whole found important outlets for recreation, an exhilarating experience, and the dances, outings, and visiting among the members satisfying and joyous. The banquet which three hundred of the brand-new Saints tendered Erastus Snow, founder of the mission, at the Hotel du Nord in Copenhagen in 1852 was the most festive occasion most of them had ever known, and the banner which decked the hall, "Zion's Löve," celebrating the apostle as the Lion of the Lord, expressed their buoyant pride.[100]

As notable as any activity, and most directly related to preparation for America, was the sustained effort, the insistent campaign, to learn English, in which classes for children and for adults abetted the private sessions of painful learning. Held often on Sunday morning, a prelude to church service, they were in a real sense religious exercises; a phrase in Peter Nielsen's journal unconsciously reflects the familiar and natural affinity of the worldly and spiritual in their lives: H. T. W. Eriksen, he says, who held an evening school in Nyby for the children, "taught them English, religion, and writing." And he was pleased to note "They made good progress according to the circumstances." [101] The private journals themselves moved from Scandinavian to English, the language mixed at first, then more confidently in the new tongue, though the spelling remained woefully uncertain.

One legacy the Establishment had bequeathed even the humble: in preparing them for confirmation it had made them literate, and not a few proudly recollected they stood first in Bible reading or response in catechism. Olof Hanson told his pastor, surprised the Mormons were literate, that "that was what helped me to accept the Gospel, the fact that I could read well; that I had read both the Old and New Testaments several times." John Nielsen remembered going to school every alternate day, as was the custom in his village, from the age of seven to fourteen.[102]

Converts who could not read or write were admonished to learn. English above all was "the language in which it had pleased the Almighty to manifest His will in this last dispensation"; it was the language of the *Book of Mormon* and of latter-day prophets.[103] Association with missionaries from America, the regular visits of church authorities from England, and the wealth of Mormon literature not yet translated and challenging the curious made English a living interest long before emigration. It was an inherent part of the new gospel, and the desire to learn it was another evidence of how completely Mormonism produced a break with the convert's past, separating him from mother church, fatherland, and native tongue, the transition begun even before he left. It was a striking contrast to the congregations Lutheranism transplanted to New Scandinavia, which kept the old tongue alive as the one vital link with the homeland.

Not only English was important to salvation; so was soap. "It is not enough for a person to believe, be converted, and be baptized for forgiveness of sins. The gospel promotes a reformation in every respect where many customs and habits inherited from the fathers are not in harmony with the gospel." Cleanliness was paramount. The Holy Spirit did not dwell in unclean tabernacles. "The first step in this so important reformation is to wash the whole body at least once a week and change linen as often. Thus may health be preserved, peace and good cheer, and sickness and death kept at bay." Such directives were as frequent as they were frank: "The Saints will forgive our speaking so freely, but it is necessary to speak clearly for your benefit."[104]

It would have been good doctrine for rural America at the time, and it anticipated Mormonism's catechism in Zion's frontier settlements when church wardens would visit the homes monthly and ask, "Sister Anderson, do you scrub your floors and wash your windows every Saturday that your home may be in order for the Sabbath? Do you see that your family bathe and put on clean clothing for the Sabbath? Do you pay back the things you borrow and hunt for the owner of things you find?" And "Brother Anderson, have you cut hay where you had no right to, or turned your animals into another's grain or field without his knowledge and consent? Have you taken water to irrigate when it belonged to another person at the time you used it? Do you preside over your household as a servant of God and is your family subject to you? Have you fulfilled your promises in paying your debts, or run into debt without prospect of paying? Have you labored diligently and earned faithfully the wages paid you by your employer?"[105]

Among the Mormons in Scandinavia the same inclusive morality prevailed, the training as intense and diligent. The doctrine on soap formed but part of the "general reformation" which would have the converts, human beings by birth, become Saints by adoption, legalizing their common-law marriages, ceasing card playing, abstaining from tobacco and strong drink, and paying their debts. The Lord wanted not only a clean folk but an honest one. Converts emigrating without settling old obligations damaged the cause. False promises, gossip, and backbiting were sources of grievance and unbecoming to a people who should be united. The ideal of social and religious harmony was arduously pursued; the number who fell by the wayside, often over trivial matters, only indicated how serious a commitment membership was and how far the converts had to go. In all respects they were expected to be an example to an already critical world.

Returning good for evil had its effects—at times it won over estranged members of the family, suspicious neighbors, and angry employers; it gained the respect of wary officials; it changed the face of a divided village and even erased national prejudices, for among the members themselves identity as Danes or Swedes or Norwegians was lost in their association as Latter-day Saints. To farm hand Hans Christensen, the calmness with which his brother Lars Peter met their father's drunken abuse when Lars joined the Mormons had "a convincing influence" upon Hans that Lars was "in the right." The way accused Mormons in Norway handled themselves in court led foundryman Carl Fjeld to seek them out and join them. Woodworker Nils C. Flygare of Lund was told he had to choose between Mormonism or his job: "If I keep you longer," his distressed employer confided, "all my workers will become Mormons," and paradoxically he discharged Nils but praised his honesty and skill.[106]

James Jensen remembered that half a dozen men owned the farms in Haugerup village, with the social distance between proprietors and tenants as wide as it had been in the Middle Ages; but more than half of Haugerup joined the Mormons, among them some of the landlords.

"From that time on a new relationship sprang up. . . . The spirit of equality and brotherly love which the new message had brought to them led to more intimate relations among all of the members of the Church in that little village." Nels Nelson was such a man and consecrated his wealth to aid his new brethren; he employed James and proved the family's benefactor, making possible their emigration to Zion with their seven children, to which Nels himself removed and where they continued a lifelong and grateful friendship.[107]

In Copenhagen master tailor Ola N. Liljenquist, the only burgher of the city among the converts, stood passport security for so many of his fellow religionists in 1852 that the officials summoned him to the city hall to belabor him for his audacity. He could be imprisoned for signing beyond his capacity. "I know these people and I am willing to take all risks on their behalf," he told them. For four more years, until his own emigration, he staked his reputation on hundreds of emigrants. The magistrate issued the same warnings, but the officers at the emigration office became more friendly. The busy tailor not only secured passports for emigrants, but offered security for converts who came to Copenhagen from other parts of Scandinavia because, as Mormons, they had lost their jobs and looked to the parent congregation for help. The law required a pass, a temporary address, and evidence of sufficient means of support, or, without the means, security lest they be sent back to their native town at its expense. Liljenquist never hesitated to guarantee them and their families, at first to the astonishment and dismay of the city fathers, like the passport officials, but they were pleased to tell him on the eve of his own departure for America in 1857 that they would rather accept his endorsement than that of many wealthier men, because the Mormons took care of their poor and the city had never had the slightest difficulty with anyone he had underwritten. On one occasion, after completing some nine hundred Mormon passes, Counsel Gendrup, who had often come to Liljenquist's aid when he was in difficulty, said to him: "Mr. Liljenquist, should you arrive in a better heaven than I, will you not think of me?"[108]

The master tailor was but one of an unexpected number of enterprising converts of refinement and substance who served as a leaven in every congregation powerfully working for self-improvement. The country crudities of some converts would furnish Zion itself with the comic figure of the "Sanpete farmer" and his household, earthy and unsanitary as a scene from Breughel, and they offended fastidious converts whose idealism had not anticipated such a lowly brotherhood and who did not stay long in such company. But those with tougher sensibilities remained to lift up their fellows and provide an effective native leadership. The convert-emigrants who returned from Zion on missions also served as living models of what the gospel and the new life could do. They attracted their kind and strengthened the work of reformation.

The fruit of all this husbandry in Eden's nursery was the formation of a people more than ever set apart from their unbelieving countrymen, suffering at once the consequences of that estrangement and enjoying the compensations of their new-found fellowship and place in the sun. Indoctrination for Zion was essentially indoctrination for America, but with a significant difference amounting to a paradox. Whatever the attraction of America and whatever the desire of the convert to be identified with it, he was brought to the painful realization that in joining the Mormons he joined a sect which America itself repudiated. Taught by doctrine and by circumstance to regard himself in the world but not of it, he learned early that he must shun gentile America as much as Babylon Europe.

The centripetal forces of persecution and ostracism in both America and Scandinavia intensified the feeling. The faithful accepted the world's stigma as a seal of their apartness and rejoiced in their union with a peculiar people in whose destiny they believed. In Scandinavia the apartness meant self-preservation as a valiant minority. In America it could easily become oppression as an illiberal majority, a barrier against inroads by outsiders. The indoctrination begun in some little community of believers in Scandinavia was reflected years later in a deliberation of Mt. Pleasant's lay priesthood, a mixed Anglo-Scandinavian-Yankee brotherhood, with an immigrant secretary keeping the minutes:

Prest. Jacob Christensen spoke of the High Priest Quorum having a Party between Chrismas and New Year Said no tea or coffee would be furnished. Spoke of inviting women (with their Husbands) who had married to men not in the Church. Levi B Reynolds spoke on union as L.D.S., Said Records was Kept of all our doings, said we should meet often together to enjoy ourselves without nationality, for we are all one Family and should be as Brethren. Spoke of inviting those who are outside of the Church, who married Mormon girls Geo Farnworth asked the privelege to say a few words, Said he did not consider it proper to invite outsiders into our partys because some had married outside of the Church (in fact a good number had done so) considered that our Girls who had married our Boys in the Church had more right to be invited, that to take such a course would be encouraging others to follow there example. Stated the instructions of the Presidency of the Church from Brigham Young, John Taylor, & Wilford Woodruff was that those in the Church in all their partys, Danceing &tc. that they keep themselves together, And let the outsiders associate together. Stated that he was opposed to so much mixing up.[109]

The doctrine of apartness was both a strength and a weakness. Inevitably what was a shield was also the target against which Zion's attackers from without and the disgruntled from within broke their lances. At length even many of the veteran converts would feel its weight and work themselves free of it, Mt. Pleasant itself becoming the scene of a major defection which made way for a sectarian academy in one of Mormonism's strongholds.

Akin to this apartness, so vital in forming the convert mind, was their total acceptance of the authority of the new church, the habit of putting church before country, priesthood before government. To believers, the word of church leaders was the Word of the Lord. Obedience to priesthood authority was the touchstone of good standing, whether it concerned spiritual or temporal affairs, whether – as it did often in Zion – it meant a call to go on a mission, advice to take another wife, or an order to stop trading with the gentiles. It brought converts the security of implicit trust in a higher management of their affairs, but more than anything else, such unquestioning obeisance gave the impression of slavishness and ignorance. It was an aspect of their indoctrination which bred serious difficulties, a source, like their apartness, of both inspiration and irritation and of a good deal of misunderstanding by outsiders, who generally believed the converts to be subjugated by "the ambitious aims of the . . . leading Priesthood."

Actually it was not so much subjugation as voluntary submission, a fact a few liberals did acknowledge: "If slaves at all, they are . . . slaves to their idealisms. . . . the docility and obedience of the people is the result of an attempt to be consistent with the religious assumptions upon which their faith is founded; and from which course, from their standpoint, they cannot depart without throwing off their faith altogether."[110] And it had to be remembered that "nearly every one of these supposed slavish Mormon people has . . . broken away from some popular and established church and joined his present one in the face of ministerial authority. . . . rendered sacred by tradition and habit. Men in this temper . . . would not be likely to feel very slavish." [111]

Products of a conversion that shook most of them to the roots, objects of a thoroughgoing reformation in their manner of living, welded together by doctrine and tried by experience, the proselytes found themselves impatient to "go up to Zion."

Israel, Israel, God is calling,
  Calling thee from lands of woe,
Babylon the great is falling,
  God shall all her towers o'erthrow.[112]

"Intentions are secret; who can discover them?" they might have asked with John White's *Planter's Plea*; and they found their motivation as mixed as the reasons for the migration of America's realistic first settlers, who believed "Nothing sorts better with piety than competency." [113] The temporal and the spiritual were inextricably mingled for a people who believed that a God who noted every sparrow's fall and numbered the hairs of a man's head would also concern himself with farms and merchandise and the daily transactions of the Saints. Was not the "all-seeing eye of the Lord" painted over the doorway of every shop in Zion?

In a letter to "Fisherman Carl Nielsen" saluting "brother-in-law, brothers and sister, son, relatives, friends, old neighbors and acquaintances, and everyone who might be interested to hear from us," Christian Nielsen, Danish miller three years in Utah, voiced the multiple causation: "We own our own house and land, animals and equipment to ride and till the soil . . . about twenty acres of plowland . . . two town lots. . . . About 300 Danish families live in this town and seven English miles north of us there are about as many. . . . In everything there is freedom; here is freedom of trade; here anyone may organize in whatever manner he wishes and follow as many trades as he desires. . . ." Grieving that a son, Niels Emmanuel, had chosen to remain in Denmark, the father urged:

He could have the fat of everything here. . . . He could work for himself. and not have to slave for another his whole life without ever having the pleasure of gaining something he could call his own. . . .

Niels is now at an age when he will become a soldier. He stands alone . . . and Europe is involved in a great conflict. . . . I strongly beseech you to advise and help him to travel from Denmark with the next departure of emigrants. . . . If the Constitution is still in effect they cannot forbid him to leave. . . .

And finally Nielsen struck the chord of religion so common in the letters of the converts: "The gospel moves steadily forward. . . . I pray you to greet my wife's brother, Peter Hansen, for us; we wish we could have him here, however much he was against us; that we forgive. . . . There are missionaries; listen to them."[114]

Even had the material and spiritual magnet of Zion been less powerful, the expulsive forces of their precarious situation in Scandinavia made the converts long for their deliverance. The eagerness to leave Europe's poverty, the incessant wars of kings, and futures barren for growing children easily outran the readiness. Sometimes in their distress the converts sold cheaply what they possessed and presented themselves at Copenhagen without previous arrangement, hoping for early passage, or for temporary respite from local storms. But the flight from Babylon, for all its sense of urgency and earnestness, was not a stampede. "Prepare not in haste, but in wisdom and order. . . . Let all that can, gather up their effects and set their faces as a flint to go Zionward."[115] Raising means to go to America became the great preoccupation of the faithful. There was no magic carpet. They could win their redemption only by lifting themselves up by their bootstraps.

II. EMIGRANT

CHAPTER 6

Bootstrap Redemption

"EVERYWHERE AMONG THE SAINTS THE NEXT YEAR'S EMIGRATION IS ALMOST THEIR EVERY THOUGHT. THIS CIRCUMSCRIBES THEIR PRAYERS, THEIR ANXIETIES, AND THEIR EXERTIONS."[1]

ALTHOUGH in Mormon thinking emigration was practically synonymous with conversion, it was fully a year and a half after the founding of the Scandinavian mission before the first proselytes set out for Zion. The delay was deliberate. Apostle Erastus Snow, for a while fearful of banishment, wanted local congregations strong enough to advance "the work of the Lord" unaided should his fears be realized. Headlong emigration would have weakened the young churches and deprived Snow of able and energetic converts who now comprised an effective native ministry, multiplying the efforts of the handful of American missionaries. Eager as the proselytes were to gather, they had to be restrained until the membership could stand the drain.

By January 1852, with his following nearly six hundred and growing daily, Snow ventured to send out some doves from the ark: twenty-eight of his people made hurried preparations to join a company of British Saints embarking from Liverpool in February on the *Ellen Maria*. They missed connections, and it was March 11 before they boarded the *Italy*; Snow himself caught up with them four months later in Kanesville, Iowa, from where he escorted them to the Salt Lake Valley, his "little flock of Danish Saints," as they became known, "All well and in good spirits."[2] They were the beginning trickle of what would swell into a stream before it subsided into a trickle again by the end of the century.

Meanwhile, before his own departure, Snow at a mission conference in Copenhagen in February had officially opened the door of the gathering: after August, he said, the Saints in Scandinavia would be permitted to emigrate, "with the exception of those who are needed to labor in the ministry." He polled district leaders to see how many of their members could be counted on to make up a large company in the fall, and he proposed the establishment of a fund "for the emigration of the Poor, on the principle of the Fund in America and England," a proposal which was "promptly and spiritedly responded to": subscriptions amounting to 450 rigsdaler ($225) laid the foundation of a *Vedvarende Emigrationsfond* or revolving fund for the mission, designed to be a branch of the churchwide Perpetual Emigrating Fund, and the conference was instructed to commence similar funds in each congregation.[3]

John E. Forsgren, temporarily in charge of the mission after Snow's farewell, pressed the Fund and preparations for the coming emigration at another mission conference in August, when membership stood at 924. Urging that only the faithful Saints emigrate and noting that "in far-off Utah" farmers, common laborers, stonecutters, ironmongers, blacksmiths, carpenters, "and all such" were needed in the settlements, he called for reports from the districts on how many would be ready by fall: Christian Christiansen from Aalborg Conference said most of the Saints there had good prospects, provided those who had means would "do their duty." Christian J. Larsen of Fredericia said his people had "great desires," but those who had property to sell could not find buyers. Johan Svendsen from the Lolland-Falster district echoed him. Hans F. Petersen from west Sjaelland (Zealand) had to report that a number of Saints were ready, but the means were lacking. Fred C. Sorensen from northwest Sjaelland said the desire to emigrate was general among the few Saints there; the poor had faith in the Lord they would soon have opportunity. Jens Hansen had to confess that on Fyen and the smaller islands the results were "little."[4]

By September, Willard Snow, who succeeded his brother Erastus as mission leader, could see that translating the doctrine of the gathering into Danish rigsdaler and Swedish kronor spelled formidable difficulties. "We have abandoned the idea of any of the Saints emigrating this fall," he wrote Liverpool. "Those who were ready, we have sent into the vineyard to labour until winter, when brother Forssgren [*sic*] will take charge of the whole company and lead them through to Zion."[5] In the succeeding months until January 16 of the new year, when the Forsgren company finally sailed, Willard was wholly absorbed in its preparations, at length finding what would prove to be the best channel for the whole emigration thereafter.

Scandinavia could profit from a dozen years of Mormon experience in transporting Saints from England, and from a longer apprenticeship on the frontier during movements of the church from New York to Ohio, Missouri, Illinois, and finally to Utah. The Mormons were old hands at chartering ships, organizing emigrants into self-governing, self-helping communities on board, securing train or steamboat connections in the States, and, before the transcontinental railroad, assembling wagons, oxen, mules, flour, and tents at river and railroad terminals. The Mormons even produced their own emigrant guides – William Clayton's *The Latter-day Saints' Emigrants' Guide*, published in St. Louis in 1848, for plains travel, and James Linforth's handsome folio *Route from Liverpool to Great Salt Lake Valley*, published in England in 1855 and grandly illustrated by Frederick Piercy's engravings, now a rare piece of Americana.[6]

Willard, who had shared much of this experience, kept in constant touch with British headquarters. On September 24 he inquired whether a ship could be sent to him from Liverpool. Eager brethren in Copenhagen almost thwarted his plan: he discovered they had circulated a subscription to buy their own ship, for which they had advertised in Norwegian papers. Willard told Forsgren he considered the arrangement premature and breathed thanks his name had not been signed to the notice.[7] Liverpool seemed willing to lend money and give drafts on Salt Lake for the "removal of the poor and paying the bill in stock," and wanted to know how many Saints from Scandinavia were ready to emigrate.[8] Brother Erastus meanwhile sent word from the Elkhorn warning that the emigration should go by way of New Orleans early enough to reach the frontiers by the end of April, with "Br. Forsgren or another experienced man to lead them . . . that they shall not be offended by officials as others have been in some instances."[9] His letter was published in *Skandinaviens Stjerne*, part of the emigration matter that after the February conference filled its columns. Willard Snow's epistles formed a canon of instructions for prospective emigrants and a chronicle of the preparations as they proceeded.

In the middle of October the brethren in Copenhagen received what seemed a workable proposition: an agent for Morris & Co. of Hamburg offered to carry emigrants from Hamburg to New Orleans via Hull and Liverpool for 46 rigsdaler steerage, 60 rigsdaler third cabin, and 80 rigsdaler second cabin, with children from one to twelve years 8 rigsdaler less. Mr. Morris himself, happening to be in Copenhagen, bettered the proposal: he would take the emigrants from Copenhagen itself to New Orleans via Liverpool for 52 rigsdaler, each passenger to be allowed 200 pounds of baggage. On November 16 the brethren closed the contract, "drawn up in Danish," with a down payment of 5000 rigsdaler. It provided for 300 to 350 converts to leave between December 15 and 20.[10]

The Forsgren company was beginning to look like a reality, but three days later Snow heard the disturbing news that "Bro. Thomson was disappointed in the sale of his property which left about 60 persons who had intended to emigrate to Zion with his help; this number had been counted in the contract. . . ." Upset at the number who had sold their effects and depended upon Thomson for their passage money, and fearful that more would be disappointed, Snow decided "to look more closely into Bro. Forsgren's arrangements for somehow he was apt to overreach himself."[11] The remaining emigrants meanwhile, through the district supervisors, deposited their money at the mission office in Copenhagen, which served Scandinavia as Liverpool served Britain and the Continent – as broker and clearinghouse transacting all the business between the convert-emigrants on the one hand and the shipping firm on the other. Bookkeeping became an important aspect of "going up to Zion." The emigration ledgers with their columns showing the names of families, age, occupation, and place of origin, and scrupulously recording amounts for ocean passage, railroad fare, tents, handcarts, and ox teams were altogether a living record of communities on the move.[12]

On December 20, when 294 Saints who had gathered in Copenhagen boarded the *Obotrit* for Kiel on the first leg of their long journey, Willard Snow could record with relief that "We paid off Mr. Morris, which in all amounted to about 13,700 rigsdaler." With a Mr. Requis he had exchanged 23,444 Danish rigsdaler for $12,456, "at a percent of 6 *skilling* to the dollar more than we might have done with Mr. Morris," a loss of 778 rigsdaler which Willard lamented. He sent $8240 on to Elder Isaac C. Haight in St. Louis to purchase cattle, horses, wagons, and provisions for the company, "to be delivered on the frontiers." Of the total amount, $662 came from contributions to the mission's Perpetual Emigrating Fund, and $970 from mission tithing.[13] It took more than a shoestring to get 300 Saints off to Zion.

For Morris & Co. the Mormon emigration was a windfall, and they treated it with respect and consideration, Mr. Morris himself playing host to Willard Snow and several of the brethren when they accompanied the Forsgren emigrants to England.[14] The relationship so cordially begun lasted until 1869, when Guion Company's steamships succeeded the sailing vessels Morris had regularly procured. Mormon contracts were gilt-edged – other brokers eyed them with envy. Shipping firms, not unselfishly perhaps, defended the Mormons when everybody else defamed them, but it was a fact that the Mormons met their obligations. Even Hr. Balin, a rival Copenhagen shipping agent, who was bitter that he did not get the contract to ferry the emigrants from Copenhagen to Liverpool and resorted to bribes and threats, overcame his malice. He doffed his hat politely to the brethren when he encountered them on the street, and was glad to arrange passage for the converts going independently or in little bands of a dozen or two which the mission office sent him.[15]

The organizing and financing of the Forsgren company, a bold venture fraught with risk, marked only the beginning of the Scandinavian phase of what for years was Mormonism's foremost enterprise. It was an operation oddly compounded of business sagacity and religious benevolence, a cooperative program making the most of experienced leadership, strenuous self-help, and timely assistance. By the end of the century the Scandinavian Mission had organized over a hundred similar companies involving a total expenditure of nearly $2 million.[16] The planning in Copenhagen, which took advantage of the tried Liverpool route and the experience of the English Mormons, lessened the sense of uprooting so universal among other emigrants and meant for the Scandinavian converts instead a tended transplanting, a shepherded migration.

The ordinary emigrant from Europe soon discovered, as handbooks warned him, that "he must look out for himself, choose the right route, buy the right ticket, get into the right car, and so on through the journey, without waiting for specific directions." [17] The Mormon emigrant, on the other hand, was relieved of these anxieties. Setting out for a strange country was at best a trying experience, but he found himself escorted by men he knew, in the company of fellow converts, and with the assurance of a welcome which would direct his settlement at journey's end. Every detail of outfitting, lodging, feeding, and transporting was prearranged.

In economic terms these operations were a kind of consumer cooperative, a pooling of the emigrants' meager resources into the hands of church agents which, together with support from those already in Utah, gave them bargaining power. It meant cheaper travel for those who paid their own way, and it created a carrier for those who could not – the "Lord's poor" for whom Brigham Young pleaded ceaselessly but who, given labor and opportunity in Zion, could soon repay their passage.

The heart of the system, pumping the needed credit into it, was called the Perpetual Emigrating Fund (P.E.F.).[18] Incorporated in 1850 by an enabling act of the territorial government, the Fund had actually been founded the year before at the fall conference of the church in Salt Lake City through outright contributions amounting to $5000 in teams, wheat, and California gold, provided at a time when the young settlement in Utah was itself struggling for existence.[19] The sacrifice grew out of pledges the Mormons had made during the Missouri and Illinois troubles to assist each other to the utmost and never to desert "the poor who are worthy" in moving beyond reach of their enemies. The spirit of this covenant and the program it had called into being were extended to Europe for the "redemption of the Saints." "The few thousands [of dollars] we send out by our agent at this time," wrote Brigham Young to Apostle Orson Hyde at Kanesville, Iowa, in 1849, "is like a grain of mustard seed in the earth. . . . we expect it will grow and flourish, and spread in a few years to cover England, cast its shadow in Europe and in the process of time compass the whole earth."[20]

An air of dedication marked this activity. Mormon representatives at ports of departure and arrival and at outfitting stations on the frontier considered their work "missions." Even teamsters were "called" from season to season to haul immigrants to the valley. James Brown in New Orleans not only secured provisions wholesale for a company of three hundred Scandinavian Saints arriving on the *Jesse Munn* in 1854, but, going aboard, he also "laid hands on their sick and felt to rejoice that I was where I could do good to the people of God." When they raised "their hands to heaven" and in their broken language exclaimed, "Our brother has come from the land of Zion to help us," his heart was "overflowing."[21]

To be sure, at times Mormon agents were accused of profiting from ship and railroad passenger rebates "per head" and fleecing the emigrant at every step, even down to dishonest weighing of baggage to collect excess charges. But the soul of the movement was altruism, not "profits for the priesthood," as embittered apostates sometimes alleged.[22] The usual 5 per cent brokerage discounts, "profits on exchange, commissions, etc.," as the financial summaries for each company described them, were promptly turned back into the system, making welcome cash available to emigrants with marginal resources. The statement of the *S.S. Wyoming* company in 1879, for example, showed £122.3 profit, £23 of it as 5 per cent discount on Guion Company's bill, £71 of it as exchanges, the rest as railroad fare rebates.[23]

Church assistance was businesslike, but in the interest of the emigrant himself: all future help depended on keeping the P.E.F. alive as a revolving fund; outgoing aid was not a gift, but a loan. Whether for the entire passage or for emergency aid along the way, he signed a promissory note. At Florence, Nebraska Territory, in 1860, for example, Johan Storström and Christian Christensen "having received the benefit of three hand cart shares" promised to pay "on demand" the sum of $39.60. Margaret Dening received $9.91 worth of provisions which she signed for, agreeing to pay "as soon after my arrival in Great Salt Lake City as possible." Anders Jensen, evidently in return for some service, received a voucher issued by the "Emigration Office" at Florence in 1863 drawing on the "Warehouse" for "four dollars in rations."[24]

Books kept at the central Tithing Office of the church in Salt Lake City suggest careful accounting. Receipts in a rare ledger for 1857 to 1863 show P.E.F. deposits or repayments, often in installments and in kind, by Scandinavians totaling $1287.81, in amounts ranging from $3.50 (representing 3½ bushels of wheat) to $356.48 (a joint receipt issued to "sundry persons" from Ft. Ephraim – better known at the time as "Little Denmark"). These payments applied on passage assistance received as far back as 1854. Peter Nielsen, for example, on May 29, 1861, paid $75.50 "for P. P. Thompson." Hans Larsen was credited on November 3 with $7.35 "on account indebtedness." S. C. Hansen on December 2, 1862, paid thirty-three bushels of wheat for a credit of $33.00 "account Anna Moritzen." The Ft. Ephraim entries for March

7, 1861, included nearly a hundred bushels of wheat at $1.00 a bushel, several yearling heifers at $10 each, steers at $20, a yoke at $10, and a horse at $100, this last munificent donation from Frederick Olsen on behalf of Neils Neilsen. On February 5, 1862, a receipt was made out for $33.80 to "Prest. Brigham Young for Caroline Neilson." [25]

These repayments were primarily for help extended at the frontier. P.E.F. cash for loans paying the whole passage was actually exhausted by 1857, although the benefits of P.E.F. purchasing and organization remained. Most of the 1810 Europeans brought over entirely at P.E.F. expense were English converts. Total Scandinavian P.E.F. cash disbursements between 1852 and 1887 did not exceed £1144, largely to those who had the ocean passage but not the little more needed to get them from Copenhagen to Liverpool, or from New York to the frontier.

P.E.F. aid to the Scandinavians in the form of church wagon trains assumed significant proportions. Of 10,843 Scandinavian converts setting out for Zion by 1869, before the completion of the transcontinental railroad, at least 6810 were transported from the frontier to the Salt Lake Valley in church wagons, signing I.O.U.'s for $36 for a share of the wagon as one of eight passengers – though they more often walked. This was wholly in the 1860s; in the 1850s 1032 went through by handcarts, which they could either purchase outright or sign for at $18 a share, four shares to the handcart. The rest, or about 3000, went all the way as "independents," having been able to buy their own equipment and provisions.[26]

Emigrants paying their own way received a contract in Copenhagen or Liverpool for the Atlantic passage. Those assisted signed a stipulation that "on our arrival in Utah we will hold ourselves, our time, and our labour, subject to the appropriation of the Perpetual Emigrating Fund Company, until the full cost of our emigration is paid, with interest if required." [27] A pledge so unmistakable and binding has led some historians to believe that emigrants became "practically indentured servants" in "the church clutches, from which they could not escape." [28] Folklore abroad accused the church of grinding the faces of the immigrant poor, not only exacting of each of them the expected donation of "a tithe of his time and toil" but also exploiting his labor while he worked out his debt. "Rumors in Denmark say that slavery exists here and that we are not free when we come here," wrote Jørgen

Christensen to his father and sister in Denmark as early as 1853, "but I say there is freedom here as nowhere else on earth." [29]

Jedediah M. Grant, unabashed counselor to Brigham Young, did propose indenture at one time when he recommended that "individuals who have friends in England, Denmark, Germany . . . and want a gardener, or a farmer . . . deposit the means, and we will send over through the P.E. Fund and get the family, and that family will assist you . . . until they pay for their being brought here." He "reckoned" that "six or eight thousand in Utah could act upon this principle" and hurry the territory along to statehood.[30] Whatever such individual contracts may have led to, official practice as well as policy was to have newcomers establish themselves wherever settlements were growing or being founded and they could find work. ". . . labor will be furnished to such as wish on the public works, and good pay; and as fast as they can procure the necessaries of life, and a surplus, that surplus will be applied to liquidating their debt, and thereby increasing the perpetual fund." [31]

The frequent blasts against slackers in paying their obligations, from Brigham Young's day down to 1887 when the P.E.F. Company was dissolved,[32] refute the notion that the church held the immigrant in an economic vise and, incidentally, reveal a good deal about human nature. There were differing opinions of what constituted a surplus. Brigham Young had little use for those who, having acquired a farm, felt they had to fence it first, increase their cow to a dairy, build a fine home, acquire a carriage, and hoard surplus grain for speculation before they paid up their passage. Occasionally someone would "run off to California" without paying his debt, even taking P.E.F. "wagons and bake kettles, frying pans, tents, and wagon covers" to boot. Bishops were told to hunt up P.E.F. debtors, collect, or set them to work "that the Fund may increase, and the poor be delivered from oppression. . . . If any men or women refuse to pay their passage to this place when they are in circumstances to do it, let them be cut off from the church, and then sue them at law." [33]

The bark was worse than the bite. Threats, complaints, and pleadings rang down the years, but the P.E.F. agreement remained a merciful instrument. In 1877, at Brigham Young's death, the Fund's accounts receivable ran to over a million dollars, without interest. John Taylor, who succeeded Young as trustee in trust for the church, at once made a conscientious effort to collect: he published the names of 19,000 debtors – 3489, or 18 per cent, of them Scandinavians – in a booklet sent to bishops throughout the church who once more were asked to undertake collection, but it was to be "consistent with the ability of the debtors to pay, without distressing the poor, the widow, the aged, or the infirm."[34] The deceased and the apostate were to be reported, survivors who could pay sought out, sons and daughters and in-laws encouraged to assist their parents, and husbands exhorted to take pride in promptly paying the debts of their wives contracted before marriage. Finally, debtors were to make every effort to pay their debts "IN CASH, as nothing but cash will gather Israel, but where it cannot be raised, such available products as horned stock, sheep, grain and the like will be received at local cash rates." To facilitate this business, bishops were authorized to use the telegraph line whenever they deemed it necessary.[35] In 1880, however, on the fiftieth anniversary of Mormonism's beginning, the church in a jubilee gesture reminiscent of ancient Israel forgave half the debt; bishops selected the "worthy poor" and their names were published in the *Deseret News* as having discharged their obligation.[36]

The directive of 1877 had noted that "thousands of poor Saints – many of them aged – are in Europe praying and begging for deliverance from Babylon." To "aid in saving scattered Israel" was the program's *raison d'être*. Contributions from church members both at home and abroad, advance deposits from intending emigrants, and prepayment of passage money by those sending for friends and relatives made up the working capital of the P.E.F., augmented by occasional investments, (there were "P.E.F. herds" and "P.E.F. farms" in Utah), but it was not known from one year to the next how much assistance could be made available. Raising means to go to America became the great preoccupation of the faithful in Scandinavia. "Everywhere among the Saints," wrote Christian A. Madsen in 1862, "the next year's emigration is almost their every thought. This circumscribes their prayers, their anxieties, and their exertions."[37]

Their "prayers, anxieties, and exertions" grappled with the hard reality of travel costs: it required only from $75 to $100 (150 to 200 rigsdaler in their own money) to get all the way from Copenhagen to Salt Lake City, but to families who had to multiply these figures several times over, it seemed a small fortune. The ocean fares remained essentially what they had been for the Forsgren emigrants: steerage cost $26 for adults, $23 for children under 14 or 12 or 8 (it varied), and $4 for infants; it never rose above $28 or fell below $21.50 (for the Hamburg caravan, which avoided the Liverpool expense), until steamship days, when it averaged $30. Train fare from New York or Philadelphia to the frontier cost $12 or $14; river boat passage from New Orleans up the Mississippi and the Missouri rivers was somewhat less, but the route was abandoned early because of killing diseases. Ox-team outfits cost about $225, fluctuating radically with the supply and demand, in some years far out of reach. In 1867, for example, a team cost $340.[38] The emigrants often shared the costs, eight to an outfit. If they went by handcart or church wagon their I.O.U.'s cushioned their immediate expenses. The completion of the railroad brought no great increase in fares, but it worked a greater hardship because the emigrants lost the advantage of this help at the frontier and had to have ready cash for the whole journey.

To meet these costs through the years, they helped themselves and they helped each other. For those few who possessed property and salable goods, the proceeds were often enough to carry them through. Anna Widtsoe, widow of a schoolmaster in Trondhjem, Norway, auctioned the family library in 1883; Hans Zobell, weaver, sold his Danish cottage for 400 kroner ($100) in 1869; and Andrew M. Israelsen, as a boy of seven, remembered the heavy red box of silver coins his parents received when they sold their little farm in Norway.

Martin Petersen Kuhre "went down to Soren's" on January 3, 1862, to learn Soren had sold his place "and was very glad to have the privilege to go up to Zion in the spring. . . ." Kuhre showed some buyers Niels Johansen's place a few days later, resulting in a sale, and Niels gratefully offered Kuhre money "to go clear up [to Utah] by agreeing to pay them again when I could." Kuhre received 270 rigsdaler of his own as his family inheritance, and 30 more as a loan from his nonconvert mother, who grudgingly mortgaged her house to pay him off when he refused to relinquish his claims. With an additional loan of 50 rigsdaler from his uncle Anders ("God bless him for it"), and 250 from Niels Johansen, Kuhre was better off than most. Not until he got to Florence, Nebraska, that June did he make out a note to Johansen calling for "132 dollars American money at 4% interest annually until the same shall be paid." Kuhre could not know his debt would never be paid; in 1865 he and his wife were killed in an Indian attack as they were working in the fields outside Fort Ephraim.[39]

Some early converts proved surprisingly affluent. "Only give the Saints the means," wrote John Van Cott. "And I am happy to inform you that many have been blessed with that. . . ."[40] The five hundred farmers, shoemakers, smiths, masons, tailors, and weavers and their families who made ready to leave on the sailship *James Nesmith* in January 1855 footed their own bill, some 3813 English pounds, of which 1638 pounds was sent to the frontiers in advance as "cattle and waggon money." In 1862 Soren Larsen Berstrup, a fifty-two-year-old farmer from northern Jutland, deposited 1815 rigsdaler at Mormon mission headquarters in Copenhagen as one of over fifteen hundred converts, all financially independent, preparing for spring departure from Hamburg in a special caravan of four ships. His deposit was disbursed as follows: 215 rigsdaler for the ocean passage for his family of six, 540 for a team, 90 for two cows, 150 for fifty sheep, 80 for four heifers, and 740 in exchange for $392, leaving a balance of "5 skilling, 8 penny," the whole breakdown an interesting revelation of advance preparations by a man who could afford a team where others pushed handcarts or had to be content to remain in "the States" till further assistance or self-help was possible.

Few could equal the treasure of farmer A. P. Kjersgaard Olsen, thirty-five, of Rakkeby, who in 1867 deposited 7000 rigsdaler, which, after disbursements for passage, plains equipment, and advances to various persons, left him a comfortable $1050 in exchange. By far the greater number, to judge from the ledger entries, had little or nothing to spare after paying their passage. Widow Sophie Catrina Wilhelmina Peterson, only thirty-one years of age but with five children to care for, had, so an 1856 entry soberly records, a balance of exactly one rigsdaler. The *Monarch of the Sea* company in 1864 exchanged native money for £1969, and the *Emerald Isle* in 1868 exchanged "drafts for $26,777.25 greenbacks, $1000 gold" in New York; in both instances the sums were over and above ocean passage costs and represented large deposits on the part of a few, but, spread among the total passengers and expended for railroad fares and provisions, they did not leave the companies flush.[41]

Those with ampler means assisted their less fortunate brethren, who often pooled their savings to enable some of their number to go who could send help later. As already noted, in 1853 contributions amounting to $662 went to aid the Forsgren emigrants. On March 1, as the company sailed up the Mississippi, they took counsel to see what should be done with those too poor to continue the journey. "There had been some doubt among the Saints as to their money," says an unknown diarist, "so it was explained to them, and several stood up and declared their willingness to offer their money and what extras they had to Elder Forsgren to handle as he saw best." J. C. Nielsen, writing from St. Louis in 1855, urged prospective emigrants not to take so many heavy chests with clothing enough for ten years. Last year's emigrants, he said, had to leave all their big chests at Mormon Grove. It was far better to use that money to pay the passage for another soul. The emigrants would need more patience than baggage, he added.[42]

The "Remarks" in the emigration records reveal some sources of help and speak, incidentally, of minor tragedies. Ane C. Hansen, a widow, forty-four, with three children, had deposited 200 rigsdaler in 1864 but "Backed out. Paid her money back to the secretary for the Society for the relief of distressed foreigners." Karen Pedersen, seventeen, from Fyen, was described as "Christensens sweetheart. Emigration will be settled for in England." Another widow, Dorthea Christensen, twenty-seven, with two children, withdrew because of "lack of funds." Painter H. Gyllenskog, thirty-five, and his family of five, had deposited 40 rigsdaler in 1857, but was crossed out with the note, "Shall not emigrate of want for means [*sic*]." Johan Erik Petersen, thirty-six, was booked to New York in 1877: "Says Staines [the church emigration agent] has for him 172 kroner [$43]." C. T. Jensen and Josephine J. Christiansen also headed for New York to get the "balance from Bro. Staines." Carpenter Niels Michael Jacobsen "goes as steward," it was noted in 1879, enabling him to earn his passage to America. Elders who had performed their labors satisfactorily returned home at the expense of the mission.[43]

The memoirs of the emigrants unfailingly record who helped them to Zion. Niels Wilhelmsen, emigrant of 1861, reminisced in 1883 that he had received various loans, among them 200 rigsdaler from "Peter Andersen of Gundsölille," who at the time was not yet a Mormon, "but whom many have cause to remember with gratitude today." A deliverer who like Moses never set his own feet on the promised land was Jens Andersen of Veddern, Aalborg, who had assisted no fewer than sixty of his fellows to emigrate; he met death on the North Sea in 1862 soon after leaving Cuxhaven.

Almost as dolorous was the history of another benefactor, Hans Rasmussen of Ammendrup: before he emigrated in 1856, he paid the church a tithe amounting to 700 rigsdaler, contributed 1400 rigsdaler to the mission's emigration fund, and paid, besides, the emigration fare for thirty fellow converts; he lost everything except his life and his family in the snowstorms that overtook his company in the mountains, and he arrived in Salt Lake Valley destitute; settled in Sanpete Valley, he sustained successive losses from Indian wars, droughts, and grasshoppers, to die at seventy-two, a severely tried Saint. Andrew Eliason, well-to-do Swedish landowner, sold his estate and enabled a hundred coreligionists to start out for Zion. Bent Nielsen was so free in outfitting his brethren and prepaying their passage to Zion that he was warned some might accept his money and then apostatize. To hymn writer Jacob Johannes M. Bohn he said: "You need never repay me because you labor for God's kingdom."

Hans Zobell observed in 1869 that "a great many of the young women emigrants would make a promise to become the second or third wife of a man if he would pay their passage to Zion." On the eve of his own departure from Copenhagen in July 1869, he noticed a "young sister" particularly who "bothered a rich farmer to pay her way over. He was stubborn, but at the last moment he gave in and she came along." Zobell had cause to be grateful, for he himself wooed the "young sister" aboard the *Minnesota*, but before the betrothal he made very sure that she had not bound herself in any way to the farmer.[44]

"Well do I remember the day," John Nielsen recalled, "when the missionaries brought us the welcome news that my parents had been hoping and praying for, for eleven years." John's father was sitting in the house making baskets and humming a tune when they came. "You must be in good humor," they said. "Yes, I guess it is of no use to cry." The father picked up an unfinished basket and began to work again. John, then eight years old, noticed that the visitors glanced at each other with a smile. "It is possible that you will emigrate to Zion this year," they said. John never forgot the look on his father's face: "That will surely please me." They told him that rich Brother Gregersen had sold out and was going to Zion and had offered to help others. One of the elders took a notebook out of his pocket to enter the names of the family. John, seeing his mother return from the bakery, ran to meet her with the good news. "She uttered the word 'Really?' and with a loud and joyous scream ran to the house. I say ran, if I would say flew it would be nearer right. I remember how surprised I was to see my mother run so fast, she was 44 years old and carrying a 12-pound loaf of rye bread." It was one time John did not begrudge the missionaries' staying to dinner—they were so poor it had often meant short rations for him. The family was told to get ready at once. "But despite our joy there was a little shadow cast over it." There was not enough money for all to go, and Niels, twenty, John's oldest brother, had to stay behind. "But as he was nearly grown and used to work out for a living it was not taken so hard."[45]

The redeemed did not always repay with kindness. A plaintive notice in the Danish-language *Utah Posten* (Salt Lake City) on August 8, 1874, stated that "Brother Lars Larsen Yderby, Oddens Sogn, Denmark," in 1866 had loaned emigration money to many brothers and sisters who still had not repaid him. Lars had become totally blind, and his son was now advertising for collection of the debts in the hope the publicity would shame some into revealing their whereabouts. On the plains in 1858, Knud Svendsen had to call a meeting to settle a dispute over 100 rigsdaler which Mikel Christensen had lent C. A. Madsen. The council decided in favor of Christensen. In Utah, Hans Jensen Hals, learning in 1869 that the "Scandinavian president" owed "bro. Arnoldus" of Moroni 6000 rigsdaler, interceded for him with the First Presidency of the church, who allowed Arnoldus a $2000 credit on his tithing, gave him $200 in produce, $750 in stock, and retained the rest "for the poor Immigrants journey from Denmark."[46]

Brigham Young constantly reminded the emigrants to secure receipts for their private loans. Gifts were another matter. It grieved the editor of *Morgenstjernen*, Danish monthly in Salt Lake City, that year after year many remained indifferent to their obligation: "Have you forgotten how eagerly you seized every means which would make your emigration possible?" By forgetting their promises they were preventing faithful members of the church in Scandinavia from coming to Zion. Even those "whose views of the latter-day work have changed" should nevertheless feel bound to pay their emigration debt. "Those who forsake their duty in this respect are therefore responsible for the distress of their brothers and sisters. . . . It is the sure road to apostasy."[47]

But there was remembering as well as forgetting. Knud Svendsen, arriving in the Salt Lake Valley on July 9, 1858, took stock of his possessions – his genealogy record, his diary, the clothes on his back. He owed 80 rigsdaler in tithing, $10 to Rasmus Olesen, $5 to Karen Jensen. He had $4 coming from Lars Jorgensen. He thanked the Lord he had been charitable in dividing his property in Denmark. By August 11, after various odd jobs, he went to Camp Floyd to make adobes for $1 a 100, earning $90.62 by September 12 with which he promptly paid his debts and now made some loans of his own.[48]

Significant far beyond meeting or failing to meet private debts were the individual and concerted efforts in the settlements to send help. After the general conference of October 1867, the church at large circulated subscription lists in the territory to "help home as many thousands of the Saints as possible," a campaign which raised $70,000 during 1868 for the general European emigration, besides 500 church teams sent to the railroad terminus at Cheyenne. In Scandinavia itself, whenever it was learned church team assistance would be available, the news was telegraphed to all the conferences, making for general rejoicing and hurried preparations to take advantage of the good fortune, though sometimes, as in England, it became a duty "to throw a little cold water upon the wildfire," because Saints in Zion "have sent word to their relatives here to sell off their furniture and propose to leave, without forwarding a cent to aid them, but with the startling information that every Saint would be gathered from Europe this season."[49]

Nevertheless, one third of the means for the 567 emigrants leaving Scandinavia in 1869 was sent from Utah. Work on the approaching railroad proved a boon because it was the one type of labor for which cash was paid, cash which could be sent to waiting relatives in the Old Country. Hans Zobell, unable to trade his wheat and molasses for a ticket to bring his mother-in-law from Copenhagen to Salt Lake, saved enough from a single winter's work on the railroad to send for her. At the same time that Scandinavians in Utah contributed twenty-five cents a month to a missionary fund, they organized local emigrant-aid societies whose contributions showed up on the emigration ledgers in Copenhagen as the "Moroni Fund," the "Ephraim Fund," the "Provo Fund." The renowned Scandinavian Choir in Salt Lake City held benefit concerts advertised as having choice programs and a worthy purpose. The predominantly Danish town of Ephraim, which by 1872 expected to have an emigrant fund of almost $2000, held a more singular benefit: Sarah Ann Peterson of the Women's Relief Society urged her sisters to donate all Sunday eggs to the fund, and other settlements followed suit. The hens, everyone swore, laid more eggs on Sunday than on any other day.[50]

The year 1872 marked the twenty-fifth anniversary of the arrival of the Mormons in the Great Salt Lake Valley, "this land of freedom," and it seemed fitting "we should remember our poor and suffering brethren in the Old Country" through extra exertions to deliver them. Old war horses like Hans Jensen Hals, bishop of Manti in the heart of the heavily Scandinavian Sanpete Valley, stumped the settlements, preaching emigrant assistance "in Danish and English." "Br. A. Fredriksen," speaking in Danish, encouraged the lay priesthood in Mt. Pleasant "to be willing to do what they was called upon to do especially for the gathering of the poor." W. W. Cluff, just returned from a mission to Scandinavia, toured the state "arousing interest in raising means to help the poor emigrate." As the result of these exhortations friends and relatives in Utah sent $10,000 to Scandinavia in the pioneer jubilee year, and in another single year, 1883, they sent $30,000 more to Sweden alone, enabling so many to emigrate that the mission could scarcely function.[51]

Such aid continued. In 1888, the year after the P.E.F. Company was dissolved, and "in spite of the ungodly clamor against the Saints," the people seemed "all the more determined to redeem their brethren from Babylon." Brigham City talked about "freeing scattered Israel . . . with much warmth."[52] Magnanimous assistance from the settlements was reflected in the columns of the emigration ledgers in the 1870s and 1880s: 14,463 rigsdaler in drafts and 5369 rigsdaler in emigration funds went to the aid of the 872 Scandinavian converts embarking on the *S.S. Wisconsin* in July 1873—amounting to roughly $10,000 of the company's total travel costs of $52,000. In July 1882, nearly ten years later, drafts from Utah provided 83,814 kroner, or $20,953, of the $43,935 expended by the *S.S. Nevada*'s 694 Scandinavian emigrants.[53]

Prepaid tickets were among the forms of assistance from Utah. J. A. Petersen, steamship passenger agent in Salt Lake, advertised regularly in the Scandinavian weeklies that his tickets were good for a year and those who wished could travel "with the Latter-day Saint emigration." He guaranteed his drafts to be valid "on all Scandinavian banks and post offices."[54] *Skandinaviens Stjerne* at times expressed distrust of help from some private sources: Saints had friends who sent them steamship tickets, but, it editorialized, they were often apostates who would lead young men and women from the truth; Saints should hold fast to the faith.[55]

Help from Zion was not an unmixed blessing. It multiplied the work of mission headquarters in Copenhagen and bred distrust when members inquired about tickets and exchanges supposedly sent by their friends and relatives. Positive such help had come, they often accused the office of withholding it. Nonmembers using Mormon channels often went to the police when the office could not fill unkept promises made by their friends in America. Headquarters pleaded with the Saints in Utah to be careful not to raise false expectations. It continually warned converts not to leave home for Copenhagen without notification: those for whom the office received drafts from Utah would be duly advised. Above all, the Saints must understand that deposits for emigration were consecrated funds, earmarked for one use only; those who knew that friends had sent money via P.E.F. or other channels were not to attempt to draw it for other purposes—a temptation particularly great during times of unemployment in Scandinavia.[56]

Generosity from Zion was matched by thrift and enterprise in the mission. Speaking of the branch of the P.E.F. established at the Copenhagen general conference in 1852, Erastus Snow was careful to explain that no member had special rights to the Fund's use, but "every brother, sister, or family might with diligence and economy strive to help themselves and by a saintly walk make themselves worthy to receive assistance. . . ." The Fredericia Conference established a branch of the P.E.F. in April, and Aalborg established one in May of the same year, "the Saints showing great liberality in their donations toward it." Skane Conference in southern Sweden with only 120 members organized its P.E.F. in June 1853, with a subscription of 108 rigsdaler. In these districts, treasurers were appointed to receive monthly contributions and record the names of donors; they were charged to give faithful accounting quarterly to church headquarters. It was expected that the poor who were assisted from the Fund would repay "as soon as they were able."[57]

Peder Nielsen, Danish shoemaker who spent more time working for the new movement than he did at his bench, journalized: "I was set apart to visit the Saints and collect voluntary contributions from them for three funds, namely, the Temple Offering, the Perpetual Emigrating Fund, and the General Fund of the branch [in Copenhagen]."[58] Those who had pledged donations had to be exhorted to be "as bountiful toward the Lord as he is toward them, and do not allow newspaper rumors or any other devil's work to weaken their zeal for the advancement of God's kingdom in these latter days."[59]

The Fund, a constant sermon subject, was untiringly promoted. And so were other means. After 1860 tithes, whose payment was an expected obligation, went largely for the emigration of the poor. Private saving was encouraged and savings plans, quite apart from the P.E.F., were inaugurated. Copenhagen headquarters received deposits to individual accounts which led to a regular savings system in a bank called significantly *Bikûben*, "Beehive," emblem of Utah. Carl Widerborg reported in 1859 that the year's deposits amounted to 3029 rigsdaler. By 1872 the congregation at Stockholm had an emigration fund of its own for loan purposes and was helping individuals with sums from 20 to 1000 kronor ($5 to $250). Copenhagen's *Emigrations Sparefonds Bog*, or Emigration Savings Fund Book, from 1876 to 1885 recorded 268 individual accounts, 138 of them in the names of women converts, totaling 32,566 kroner ($8141), of which 4833 kroner ($1208) was in the form of drafts and money orders from America with detailed directions for their use on behalf of specified persons. Some savings accounts ran several years, with deposits as small as 50 örer (about 12 cents) or as large as several hundred kroner (a Danish crown worth about 25 cents).[60] The *Regenskabs Bog*, the account book, was as important to Mormon migration from Scandinavia as the *Book of Mormon* itself.

It required long years for some to save enough from their pittance to accumulate even the few dollars needed for passage. "The great question among the Saints is 'How shall we get to Zion?'" wrote Niels C. Flygare in 1878. "Many have been in the church for fifteen or twenty-five years and grown old, but they are not tired of assisting in the good cause. . . ."[61] Mission leaders rationalized that the Saints should not desire to leave "without trials and opposition. . . . Experience has shown that the steadfast eventually find Zion, and having been tried here prove faithful. Others who leave too soon, prove not so faithful." More realistically, they pointed out that some were more thrifty in household affairs than others. The young, unmarried folk, who were unburdened and earning a living, should regularly set aside some of their earnings: ten örer (2½¢) daily would amount to 300 kroner ($75) in ten years. "If everyone did this, it would not be necessary for so many of our brethren and sisters to be left behind year after year." [62] It was slow, painful saving, but it brought them one by one, family by family, ever closer to the great day when they could go "home to Zion."

CHAPTER 7

Journey to Zion

"THOUGH WE HAD OUR TROUBLES ON THE JOURNEY, NOW EVERY HEART SWELLED WITH JOY TO SEE THE SNOW-COVERED MOUNTAINS AND BEAUTIFUL VALLEY. . . ."[1]

ONLY good news came back from the handful of emigrants who had left Copenhagen early in 1852. The *Italy* had brought the "little flock" from Liverpool to New Orleans by May 10, "all well in body and spirit." They had proceeded up the Mississippi and Missouri rivers to Kanesville, Iowa, where they had joined a large encampment of Saints getting ready to cross the plains. In July Erastus Snow had caught up with them and, as part of Captain Eli B. Kelsey's ox train of one hundred fifty wagons, had led them into the Salt Lake Valley on October 16. "They are all alive and well satisfied," *Stjerne* could tell its anxious readers, "and they urge their friends to follow them."[2]

Their letters dissolved the worst fears about the hazards of the long journey and silenced the skeptics distrustful of conditions in *Mormonlandet*, the rumor-ridden land of the Mormons. A few of the emigrants had already bought places to live and turned the first soil; Niels Jensen and his nephew Frederik Petersen were getting ready to build a pottery in the Second Ward, a parish soon to be known as "Little Denmark"; clerk Conrad Svanevelt's wife had a new baby, a girl they called Josephine Brighamine in honor of the prophets; the Rasmus Petersens were staying temporarily with Erastus Snow, turnabout for the time he had made his home with them in Denmark; tailor Wilhelm Knudsen looked forward to the arrival of his father's family with the Forsgren company and went north to the settlement at Box Elder to get ready for them; midwife Augusta Dorius married Henry Stevens and went south to Sanpete Valley, where Cecilia Jörgensen followed to become in time the plural wife of Hans Jensen Hals. It was a sad day when *Stjerne* had to report Svanevelt's defection, removal to California, and final return to Denmark, but a happy one when it could announce his reunion with the Saints.[3] So ran the news about the five families, six bachelors, and four spinsters who were the forerunners of the hosts to come. They were never out of mind, though it was not until death that some of them figured again in the news from Zion: the obituary always remembered they were "one of the first twenty-eight," and that paid them the highest respect.

An even greater watchfulness followed the adventures of the Forsgren company, which sailed from Liverpool on January 16, 1853, aboard the *Forest Monarch*, the *Mayflower* of the Mormon migration from Scandinavia. More characteristic of the future emigration in numbers and organization than the first group, the Forsgren pilgrims provided a more genuine test of the ability of Saints from the European mainland to make their way to Zion and establish themselves as equal citizens of the Kingdom. It was a long nine months before they could record in their journals: "September 30, 1853. This day we entered the Valley and camped in the center of the city." And it was a long way from Copenhagen, where in the previous December they had assembled to make preparations for the journey.[4]

Some had to travel far to get to headquarters. As early as the first of August, Lars Poulsen and his family of six, who had sacrificed their farm at half its 5000 rigsdaler value, left their native island of Jegendø in an open boat to make their way down Lim Fjorden to Aalborg, only to find cholera raging, and they had to put up in a simple hut on the outskirts of the city. It was November before they reached Copenhagen, but in time to assist a number of hopeful converts to join the company. Christian Ipsen Munk, a cooper from the island of Bornholm, came to Ronne and crossed over to Copenhagen with his family weeks early to lodge with eight other emigrant families in the same house "in perfect harmony," a friendship that would keep several of them close neighbors in the settlements.

At noon on December 20, the emigrants – 199 adults and 95 children under twelve – boarded the steamer *Obotrit* amid "songs of praise and thanksgiving" from friends and jeers from the idle gathered on the wharf at Copenhagen. A stormy night forced the vessel into a Falster harbor for forty-eight hours, and it did not reach Kiel in Holstein until the evening of the 22nd. Kiel was but three hours by train to Hamburg, where the emigrants aroused "great curiosity" the next morning as they marched through the streets to their quarters, a large hall on the banks of the Elbe just outside the city. They found their fare a "palatable and well-cooked meal, tea and bread and butter," though they had to sleep on straw and chairs scattered the length of the building. Willard Snow, John Forsgren, and Daniel Garn, Mormon missionary in Hamburg, had dinner with Mr. Morris of the shipping firm, who spread "a good table." Morris & Co. furnished the emigrants their breakfast on the morning of the 24th and, after their customary songs and prayers, saw them aboard the English ship *Lion* bound for Hull. A newspaper account picturing the emigrants as "driven out of Scandinavia" and making it appear an "act of humanity" on Hamburg's part to permit them to land and re-embark, angered Snow as "insult" and "pretense," because "Mr. Morris had paid $20 for the privilege of landing the steamer," and "the Senate and police authorities had been trying for a long time to drive Bro. Garn out of the country."

The company, reluctantly leaving an ailing "Sister Knudsen" behind, sailed down the Elbe in good spirits, rode out a fogbound Christmas Eve in Cuxhaven, and, buffeted by violent storms which strewed the North Sea with wrecks, finally dragged into Hull on the 28th. They crossed England the next day to Liverpool, where they were housed in a comfortable hotel, served a warm meal "immediately," and "taken good care of" until on December 31 they boarded the *Forest Monarch*, a "splendid sailing vessel" which had not carried passengers before; carpenters, in fact, were still installing the berths. "And thus," journalized Herman Julius Christensen, one of the emigrants, "the year 1852 ended with all its remarkable events. God be praised for the many blessings which he has bestowed upon his people."

On New Year's Day two tenders towed the frigate out into the River Mersey, but it was another fifteen days before favoring winds took it out to sea, a layover which brought "murmurings and complaints" but which gave the company a chance to regulate its housekeeping: two were named to help in the galley, and three to deliver foodstuffs to it; thirteen "captains" were to distribute daily provisions and seven more to ration the water; and two were to supervise cleaning the quarters.

Daily prayers and almost daily meetings permitted airing of feelings, provided inspiration and instruction, and established a pattern of general consent for conducting the emigrants' affairs: everything was ordered by vote. On January 11, when "the brethren and sisters raised their hands in agreement to live in harmony with each other," Willard Snow, who had settled with the Liverpool office, felt satisfied and returned to Copenhagen, leaving with the ship's officers a testimonial of his pleasure at the arrangements. Meanwhile, on January 7 and 8, the *Forest Monarch* received visitors newly arrived from Zion, among them Hans Peter Olson, on his way to fill a mission in Scandinavia, who "gave us good tidings of Zion, which caused us great joy." Dancing and games in the evening celebrated the occasion.

At last, on January 16, with the weather fair, the *Forest Monarch* set out to sea and headed for New Orleans. The Saints observed the event by taking communion. Five marriages, two births, and three deaths had seen life come full cycle while they were still in port; and Jeppe Bentzen, bitten by a dog in Hamburg, had to be left behind in Liverpool with a badly infected leg.[5] It was not many days before foul weather tested the improvised berths, which creaked fearfully, some even tumbling down. Brother Hans Larsen fell and knocked an arm out of joint, the first in an epidemic of bad hurts and bruises as land legs failed to hold the unpredictable deck. Though seasickness was universal, on the whole the weather was calm, particularly as they approached the southern latitudes, and the Atlantic crossing pleasant.

Within four weeks they glimpsed the West Indies and it became too warm to hear daily discourses on the millennium, the resurrection, and the gathering of Israel, though not too warm for Christian Christiansen's violin. But Brother Holzhansen stayed away from meetings altogether, and gave himself to levity; it was proposed, seconded, and unanimously agreed that he should be cut off from the church for having turned "to worldly ways." And Brother Andersen and his wife, it came out, were not united. The Andersens asked forgiveness and hoped to be remembered in the prayers of the congregation. But by the time the *Forest Monarch* reached New Orleans on March 17, matters between them had gone from bad to worse, and they left the company. A greater loss was the five who died within sight of the promised land and were buried in port.

At New Orleans, where customs officers mistook the emigrants for Irish laborers,[6] they bought fresh bread, but Elder Forsgren had to warn them not to go into the city, for the people were most ungodly.

They gave Forsgren a vote of confidence and, pooling their means to enable everyone to go on, moved by steamboat upriver to St. Louis, marveling at the panorama of life along the Mississippi—the extensive forests, here and there being burned over for a clearing, the pleasant towns, the spring song of birds, the orchards in fairest bloom, the slaves working in the fields, where Negro women rode the ox-pulled plows and children waved from the banks with wide handkerchiefs. "Everything looked full of life and very good."

In St. Louis, where Mormon emigrants were already familiar figures and the congregation numbered over three thousand, they found enough empty houses for a month's stay and worked at odd jobs while waiting for the "sickly season" along the river to pass, Forsgren meanwhile keeping them close together through frequent meetings, communion, and counseling, for the temptations in St. Louis were great. During April three more couples were married, five of the company died, two children were born, and a Sister Mathiesen was refused fellowship because she "had not made a true acknowledgment and could not be received into the Church without having the fruits of repentance." Thankful their troubles were no greater, half the company left on April 21, for Keokuk, Iowa, twenty-four hours away and not far from storied Nauvoo. The rest followed ten days later.

At Keokuk, where they became part of a great encampment of Welsh and English Saints, they found that Elder Haight, the church agent, had been diligent in obtaining their outfits for the plains. The "Danish camp," as they became known, pitched in a flowered prairie grove in a setting of oak trees and wild grape, was a lively place as they learned the mysteries of the yoke and whip in handling oxen and got used to living in tents and wagons, "as good as a house."

In conference on May 17, the camp members put their accounts in order and renewed their covenants; they unanimously agreed to sustain Brigham Young, his counselors, and the apostles, approved Elder Forsgren's leadership, voted to travel under four captains, ten wagons to a company, and agreed that "anyone found drunk in the Danish camp would be cut off from the Church." Elder Christian Christiansen read a letter from Copenhagen reporting that the membership in Scandinavia had risen to 1400, that the brethren in Norway had been released from prison, and that several persons had been baptized in Sweden. It was a day of "enlightenment and instruction"; the captains "expressed their feelings in a spirit of humility"; and the conference closed on a note of general satisfaction. The camp was ready for the plains.

Christian Nielsen, one of the emigrants with an eye for memorable detail, found the crossing "not wearisome at all." Going barefoot to save his shoes, he walked by the side of his two yoke of oxen and his heavily loaded wagon "of excellent quality and solid, far surpassing the Danish." Besides his family, he carried "a widow from Bornholm and her two children." He grew sunburned and let his beard grow. "Many of us look formidable," a sight for the begging and thieving Indians: "they have no beard." The oxen fattened on the fine grass; wood and water were plentiful.

The worst hardship, besides the constant hazard of falling from the wagons or being run over by the stock, was the weather, the sudden storms that broke over Iowa and Nebraska frightening beyond anything known in the Old Country: the ominous thunder and the flaming sky, with lightning striking terror among the tents, cloudbursts drenching them, and winds whirling them over, left the emigrants cowering and helpless. A quieter grandeur was the sight of the buffalo herds, the thousands of deer and antelope, the far-stretching, uninhabited country itself with its great rivers to ferry.

By June 25, they camped at Kanesville near Council Bluffs to rest for a week, only to have their peace seriously disturbed when the Niels Pedersens, the Jørgen Nielsens, and Frederikke Frederiksen withdrew declaring they would go no farther. "Jørgen Nielsen said there were liars and slanderers among us, and that it was not better among us than any other place in the world." He brought the law from the city to force the return of certain oxen to him, but H. J. Christensen had driven them off, and Jørgen hauled him into town and made him pay an eleven-dollar fine. To the rest of the company Jørgen seemed "possessed of an evil spirt," and he and his disaffected fellows were excommunicated; they were the beginning of an apostate element in Council Bluffs and later Omaha that would grow with each emigration, in time augmented by backtrailers from Zion itself, who gave western Iowa and eastern Nebraska their earliest Scandinavian settlers.

George P. Dykes, familiar to many of the Forsgren emigrants as Erastus Snow's early companion in Scandinavia, happened to be in Council Bluffs and counseled them "against talking with any of the people of the town, as there was no place where the Devil had more power than right here, and the people would do all they could to keep the Saints here." But old Father Christiansen, the choirmaster, destined shortly to lay down his weary bones in the mountains, voiced the general feeling when he said that he would not remain there, no matter how much he was offered; he could just as well have remained in Denmark, but he wished with all his heart to come to Zion. Elder Forsgren said "everything which would delight the soul" would be found in Zion, but he also warned them not to be dismayed if, when they "came home to the Valley," they found some ungodliness.

There was no more defection, only the tedium of creeping along sixteen to twenty miles a day in mud and sand and dealing with unruly stock that tried tempers and brought out "imperfections" to be repented daily. They crossed creeks with colorful names like Wolf and Rattlesnake and Crab, and joined the English Saints in building bridges; they fed curious Indians – a band of sixty once – and were strictly forbidden to take any Indian ponies on pain of being cast out of camp. Resting only on the Sabbath, they passed one by one the historic landmarks of the Oregon and California trail – Scotts Bluff, Laramie, Bridger.

To Christian Nielsen the way presented an amazing litter of dead animals, strewn wagon parts, clothing, and equipment, the shambles left by the goldseekers stripping for the race to the coast. Emigrants who could not bear to see such waste overloaded their wagons each day with their finds – the "beautiful" brass kettles, pans, and wheel rims – only to be forced to abandon them all again before nightfall. It was all very comical. Reflecting on the rivalry of the goldseekers, Christian was impressed that in Mormon wagon trains the emigrants helped each other: if one lost an ox, the others came to his aid; if something broke, the whole company waited until it was mended – the smith set up his forge and in a moment made repairs. No one was left behind, though he observed that the selfish ones were the first to call for help.

"At last we neared the valley." On September 30, in the evening, they entered Great Salt Lake City, to be met by their old familiar, Erastus Snow, who re-baptized them all the next day to wash them of the sins of the journey and renew their covenants. It was a visible token they had come out of the world; they were in Zion, and what was past for them was merely prologue.

Some of the immigrants found a temporary home with the first twenty-eight, who had already given their neighborhood a distinctly Danish character. Some followed John Forsgren north to Fort Box Elder, where his wife was living with her father, Bishop William Davis, founder of the settlement. With John went his brother Peter, the weaver, and wife, and his sister Erika, who would become the bishop's plural wife. Most of the company, on Brigham Young's advice, went south within a few days to the high country of Sanpete Valley to strengthen Father Isaac Morley's colony.

"One would imagine we were tired of traveling," but Christian Nielsen went the 150 miles with them to Spring Town, soon better known as New Denmark. The people along the way were good to them, "overloading" them with "all kinds of articles"; in Provo someone killed an ox for them. But the farther south they traveled the more it looked like war, until they came to mute evidence in the form of two wagon boxes tipped over, their wheat and broken chests spilled on the ground in a skirmish that had seen eight Indians and four townsmen killed. They found Spring Town practically deserted: "It was a wretched fort; the walls were miserably built, the houses in unlivable condition, and we had to be armed constantly; there was good grassland here and they could become fine fields, but we were too weak to resist the Indians." In November Christian took his family to nearby Manti, where his services were needed to build a grist mill, which "with God's help" he built "after the Danish fashion." Before winter all of the company were called in from Spring Town to Manti. Within a year the larger emigration even then forming in Copenhagen would reinforce them and secure what for the moment seemed a precarious stake in Zion.

The Forsgren company left a golden track in Mormon history. Their casualties in death and apostasy had been providentially light. They had provided a model of self-help, cooperation, and democratic leadership, with authority and humility alternately exercised in crisis with good results, and they had settled in strategic areas which would influence the colonization of the emigrants to come. An ounce of their success was worth a pound of propaganda in Scandinavia, and a hundred companies confidently followed in their wake, their adventures continually renewing the twice-told tale of the first voyagers and pioneers. They gave the migration of Scandinavian Mormons a distinctive pattern.

In the Old Country, many of the converts had never been farther from home than the nearest market town. For them the *Skandinaviens*

Stjerne became an emigrant guide, its minute instructions encompassing every detail of preparation and departure; and the presiding elders in the conferences were their faithful shepherds, guiding them through the legal maze of obtaining passports, assisting them in the disposal of their goods, and even bending to the task of packing.

Farmer Hans Jensen Hals, emigrant of 1854 who had settled in Manti, the husband of three wives and able counselor to Apostle Orson Hyde in handling Danish affairs in the settlements, was back in Scandinavia on a mission in 1865, to find his experience at a premium and his time absorbed with emigration matters:

> I went with N. Nielsen to the Poor Commission in Nortranders School and received a promise of 200 dollars for him to travel on. . . . Held two meetings in Aalborg. The Emigrants were upbuilt and counseled in their preparation. A blessed day. . . . Received 4,000 *rigsdaler* Emigration money from C. Christensen and Jens Olesen from Thylan. . . . Bought material for tents and sleeping bags for the emigrants and put the tailors to work sewing them. . . . Came to Copenhagen and delivered to Pres. Widerborg 6,196 Emigration money. The accounting was correct. . . . Rented P. Larsen's hall for the emigrants from Vendsyssel. . . . Passed out certificates and passports, and held a meeting in the hall. Fourteen Brethren gave their farewell talks. . . . Received a letter from Christansen in Zion, and there read about the travels of the Emigrants. . . .[7]

In April 1868 he was told he would lead the next company of 627 to Zion, a stewardship which kept him constantly preoccupied and which was not discharged until his arrival in Salt Lake on September 25, when at Brigham Young's invitation he made his report from the stand in the Tabernacle. And even then he could not rest: he went to "Brigham's office to find out if the families could get the money back for them that had died on the way," and he took some of them with him to Manti. "Now I could go home with my family and attend to my duties." And he was proud to bring with him five instruments – a tenor tuba, two tenor horns, an alto horn, and a flute – which he had bought in Copenhagen for his town's brass band.

Before 1869 and the completion of the transcontinental railroad, instructions warned the proselyte that the journey would take from six to nine months: leaving in midwinter and arriving on the frontier in spring or early summer, the emigrants should have clothes for both extremes of weather, and shoes to last the journey. It was not true, they were told, that they had to take along enough clothing to last ten years, nor need they be concerned about differences in standards of dress as they prevailed in the Old Country – in the New World such things did not matter. They were advised to part with the heavy chests "inherited from the fathers since time immemorial" and to take light trunks and suitcases which they could readily carry on board ship and load easily into "prairie wagons." They should not take over a hundred pounds in freight per person because few could afford to pay excess weight charges, which on the plains alone, in pre-railroad days, amounted to $24 a hundredweight.

Those who expected to go all the way to "the Valley" should have at least 150 to 200 rigsdaler, and be prepared against "robbers and false brethren who will appear friendly as long as your money lasts." They would have to take their own bedding and cooking and eating utensils, preferably tinware, items advertised for purchase at cheapest rates at Mormon headquarters in Liverpool. Emigrants must have food for five days while en route to Liverpool. Those who had valuables would do better to convert them into cash and plan to acquire a good cow that would give milk "to their children on the plains . . . and it will be no sin to have a few dollars left for homemaking in the Valley." Artisans who desired to take the tools and models of their trade should choose the lightest and most valuable.[8]

After 1869, when steam and rail made for swifter passage, the instructions were still as detailed and full of oft-repeated precautions: lash your luggage well; mark baggage "Utah, U.S.A." with lampblack; use leather tags, not paper; don't wrap luggage with sail cloth, for it prevents rapid opening at the customs; in coming to Copenhagen, don't leave baggage on various railroad platforms en route; the office force at Copenhagen will meet anyone who sends notice of train or steamboat arrival; you must furnish your own food to Liverpool, costing about 10 kroner ($2.50). Adults will be allowed 135 pounds of freight on their ticket, children half as much; be prepared to pay excess freight charges, either in Copenhagen before setting out or to the Mormon agent in New York; take all the bed clothing you can; your food basket or box should be long and low allowing it to slide under the seat on the train; don't forget hand towels, comb, and soap for each person; be prepared to pay lodgings, drayage, and other expenses incurred in Copenhagen.[9] This attention to small expenditures suggests how closely the voyage was budgeted for the majority: any unforeseen outlay, however small, spelled disaster.

The instructions reflected the times: in 1872 heads of families with insufficient means to see them through to Utah were discouraged from believing that, if they could only reach the eastern states, they would find "lots of work" to enable them to return or send for their families. "Experience has taught us this is not so easy." In 1885, when conditions were equally bad, but happily offset by lower rates, Saints were reminded to keep faith with proved church methods: other agents might offer even cheaper passage but were not as responsible or as interested in the welfare of their clients. "Do not go without a shepherd."[10]

The *Stjerne* was an emigrant guide with a difference: instructions were invariably accompanied by a moral rider. They began with dollars and concluded with dogmas, a portrait of Mormonism anxious to give no offense to an already critical world. Let the Saints honor every debt incurred en route and leave a good name behind, free from blame. Let them conduct themselves according to the laws of the land in all respects that they might be "justified before man and God." Let them be prayerful, repentant, seeking knowledge "by study and by faith." Let them honor cleanliness as a heavenly principle, doing everything essential for health, for "an unclean body is not fit temple for the holy spirit that dwells there." Again and again the difficulties of the journey were rehearsed, the necessity for spiritual preparation underlined. The Saints must go with "singleness of purpose." Those without faith had better not go at all, for they would never withstand "the hate of persecutors or the power of the Destroyer."[11]

In sailing-vessel days the Saints were frankly told that the risks were great, sickness and death constant companions of the voyage over the water and the trek across the plains. Especially was the toll high among children. "Very few ever get through with them all," the father and mother of four small children were told.[12] Scandinavians seemed particularly susceptible to measles; common killers were cholera and dysentery. Companies after 1869, traveling the entire distance by steam and rail, suffered no losses at all, but earlier they buried normally 10 per cent of their number before journey's end. Most tragic were the parties which left in January 1854 aboard the *Jesse Munn* and the *Benjamin Adams*; 200 out of 678 lost their lives, most of them of cholera while in camp at Westport, Missouri.[13] The only comfort was that they died "in the Lord."

There was also comfort in the record of safety at sea. Ships were dedicated before departure, and they were pictured as "flying like a cloud towards the promised land" with a special providence controlling the winds and the waves. Captains were impressed: said the skipper of the *S.S. Idaho* with 703 Scandinavian Saints on board in 1874, "I have conveyed Mormons safely across the Atlantic for eighteen years and have never heard that any ship went under with them on board." To be sure, there were other reactions to Mormon praying and singing: the mate of the *John J. Boyd*, carrying 437 Scandinavian Mormons in 1855, grew superstitious because of a prolonged passage and declared that ships with preachers on board were always sure of trouble.[14]

Going to America involved more than stepping aboard a vessel on one side of the Atlantic and disembarking on the other. It was a whole series of journeys. The proselytes first had to make their way to Copenhagen, main assembly point. Unless they lived on Zealand itself, that meant crossing the straits from Jutland or one of the Danish islands, and the Sound from Sweden – short laps but adventurous to many who were seeing the face of their country for the first time. Swedish Saints funneled through Malmo. Subsidiary assembly points in Jutland were Aalborg in the north, Aarhus in the middle, and Fredericia in the south, all along the east coast. The same little steamer picked up waiting emigrants in succession on its way to Copenhagen or, when groups were large enough, took them directly to Kiel or Lübeck on the German portion of the peninsula, where the Copenhagen detachment joined them. The journey was continued by rail to Altona, within walking distance of Hamburg, or to Glückstadt, a little farther down the Elbe. Except for the years 1862, 1865, and 1866, when parties went directly from Hamburg to America, the emigrants moved across the North Sea to Grimsby or Hull and entrained for Liverpool along with whatever Norwegian Saints had come directly from Christiania or Stavanger.

The North Sea passage was often the roughest part of the whole journey: accounts describe the horrible retching in the holds of the vessels, sometimes little better than cattle boats, the hold thickly layered with sand in which the sea-green sick buried their vomit or burrowed for miserable sleep. Shelter at various stages of the journey certainly had none of the comforts of home; a sensitive Norwegian woman found the "poor Saints" packed into a large hall in Copenhagen, given beds on straw in a loft in Hamburg with no segregation of men and women, quartered in a "kind of stable" in Grimsby, and sheltered in "a rude shed" in Liverpool. But the converts, mostly farmers, artisans, and laborers, were on the whole less squeamish and, rejoicing in their new-found fellowship, expressed their gratitude for these way-station accommodations: time and again their journals speak their relief at finding good food and adequate shelter waiting for them.[15]

From Scandinavia to England was but a foretaste of interminable changes, endless distances. After the Atlantic there stretched a continent to cross. Until 1855 Mormon emigrants traveled the New Orleans route, utilizing the waterways to get as far inland as possible – Keokuk or Quincy on the Mississippi, Atchison or St. Joseph on the Missouri. To avoid the murderous climate of the lower Mississippi, all emigration after 1855 passed through eastern ports. The route in the states was determined by the best contract Mormon representatives were able to make. In 1866 the 684 converts aboard the *Kenilworth* arriving in New York from Hamburg found that the church agent had gone to some lengths. He sent them by coastal steamer to New Haven, thence by rail to Montreal in "dirty cattle cars," along the north bank of the St. Lawrence and lakes Ontario and Erie to the St. Clair River, where they were ferried over to Port Huron, Michigan, to continue by rail to Quincy, Illinois, via Chicago; there they were ferried across the Mississippi and entrained for St. Joseph, continuing by steamboat up the Missouri to the town of Wyoming, Nebraska, where they were met by church teams waiting to trundle them to Salt Lake.[16]

The tortuous itinerary did not disturb the Saints as they prepared to leave the Old Country, for there was too much excitement at departure. A Dane remembered the scene in Copenhagen in 1869: with his mother and sister he stayed with four hundred other emigrants, the greater part Mormons and "mostly farm folk," at the Bolles Hotel. The sitting room was in constant motion. Some people went about in the crowd begging to be taken along. "It was a sight to behold" – four hundred people marching from the hotel to the dock, lugging their worldly goods to the clanging of loose tinware and singing "Think not when you gather to Zion your trials and troubles are o'er. . . ." At the dock he remembered vividly how a mother gave her three small girls a last embrace before turning them over to a young woman to be taken to Zion.[17]

Crowds of the curious were always on hand, scornful of their countrymen who were foolish and disloyal enough to leave home as victims of the double delusion of America and Mormonism. Sometimes there were scenes. At the boat landing in Copenhagen in 1857 an indignant crowd tried to snatch the children away from one convert couple: let the elders be damned, but it was too bad the young should face a shameful upbringing in the Mormon kingdom. In 1868 the leaders of a company of 627 proselytes were arrested just as they were embarking and hauled before the magistrate, only to be cleared when nothing could be found against them.[18]

Times changed. When the *S.S. Otto* left Copenhagen for Lübeck in 1872 with 397 proselytes aboard, *Stjerne* gave thanks to "our agent, Hr. Duhrsen, his assistants, the police, the militia, and the captain for their humaneness, forehandedness, and willingness to serve with which each in his place assisted us and our friends in accomplishing the departure." No one drank a toast of farewell schnapps; there were no "depressing pipes, cigars, or nauseous quids," but only "friendliness, unity, helpfulness, and patience." And there was a noticeable absence of the usual emigrant weeping; instead, "joy and thanksgiving reigned for the chance to go to Zion."[19]

In Liverpool, once aboard the ship which would carry them across the Atlantic, the converts found themselves members of a well-ordered community. A select committee of the House of Commons on emigrant ships for 1854, after examining the Mormon agent in Liverpool, concluded that "no ship under the provision of the Passenger Act could be depended upon for comfort and security in the same degree as those under his administration. The Mormon ship is a family under strong and accepted discipline, with every provision for comfort, decorum, and internal peace."[20] Under a general presidency – for the shipboard company was of mixed nationality – the Scandinavians had their own supervisors responsible for things temporal and spiritual: cleaning and galley details, morning and evening devotionals, recreation and morale.

It was customary to berth families amidships, separating the single men from the unmarried women. Watchmen maintained vigil during the night. In 1861, after six days at sea, the realistic president of the company aboard the *Monarch of the Sea* suggested it would help the crowded condition of the vessel if betrothed couples got married at once; thirty unions were forthwith solemnized.[21] Hans Jensen Hals found the crew of the *Emerald Isle* ugly: they molested the young women and threatened the brethren with physical violence when they interfered. Hals as president of the company remonstrated with the captain, who only rattled the irons he had used, he said, on former insubordinate passengers. Such bad treatment was rare, but lustful sailors were a common enough source of trouble.[22]

Life went full circle: births, deaths, and marriages. For the children there was semblance of school, for the adults frequent lectures, generally by returning missionaries recounting things to expect in the new home. Everyone diligently studied English, or they sewed the tents and wagon covers they would need on the plains. If in no other way, the passing of the days could be noted by the menu, which might be "sweet soup" on Sunday, pea soup on Monday, rice on Tuesday and Wednesday, pea soup on Thursday, barley mush on Friday, and herring and potatoes on Saturday. In addition to the food requirements of the British Passenger Act, the Saints were supplied with two and a half pounds of sago, three pounds of butter, two pounds of cheese, and one pint of vinegar for each statute adult, and half the amount for children between one and fourteen; one pound of beef or pork weekly for each adult was substituted for its equivalent in oatmeal, provisions which enabled many of them to live "more bountifully" than they had lived in their native countries.[23]

Arrived at the Battery in New York and delivered to Castle Garden, the Mormon companies received the same special care. An able man like William C. Staines, for years (1869–81) the church immigration agent in the port city, wrought a swift and practiced order out of the confusion of inspection, securing lodgings, and expediting the transfer to the trains, which usually saw the converts through to the frontiers without change of cars or mixing with other passengers. On one occasion Staines dispatched a company of eleven hundred immigrants in eight hours.

Newspaper reporters, eager to give a curious public a glimpse of each new shipload of Mormons – particularly during the antipolygamy crusade of the 1870s and 1880s, when it was alleged that foreign converts were recruited from "the dregs of society" for immoral purposes in Utah – observed their quiet conduct as they passed through customs, evidently under some "controlling influence," and were surprised to find them "as fully intelligent as the ordinary immigrants." They had come voluntarily; most of them had paid their own way; there were as many males as females, old as well as young; and there were no paupers. A New York *Times* correspondent found the 723 converts arriving on the *S.S. Wisconsin* on June 7, 1877, "not without a share of youth and beauty, although the beauty was high in the cheek bones and too rugged for New-York belles." Another reporter found the men in an earlier company "strong, healthy fellows, averaging thirty years of age and divided about equally in occupations as farm laborers and mechanics." Another, in 1882, concluded that "the immigrants in the party were thrifty people who would probably do well in Utah." [24]

Some observers were prejudiced by the circular which Secretary of State William M. Evarts in 1879 sent to United States diplomatic and consular officers in Europe seeking the aid of foreign governments in preventing the departure of Mormon proselytes, "prospective lawbreakers" and "misguided men and women" lured by "agents . . . operating beyond the reach of the law of the United States." [25] The *Times* described the first group to arrive after the Evarts communiqué as "an unintelligent-looking crowd, but . . . fairly clean as compared with other batches of their brethren who preceded them in Castle Garden." [26]

In 1880 the *Times* reported an incident: the *Nevada* had discharged 338 Mormons; as usual, representatives of the New York Bible Society and the Protestant Emigrant Aid Society moved among the throng distributing New Testaments printed in the converts' native language, but the Mormons seemed indifferent to this proselyting. A missionary of the Emigrant Aid Society, Blossett by name, emboldened by the Evarts circular, attempted to convince the Mormons of their enormity in believing in polygamy. When he asked who instituted polygamy, he was told "Almighty God." "No," ventured the missionary, "it was Cain after he murdered his brother Abel." Whereupon, says the account, "one of the elders seized the venerable man of God and flung him violently aside," and Garden attendants had to come to his aid.[27] But such episodes were rare. Despite popular antipathy, government hostility, and increasingly rigid inspections reflecting more stringent immigration laws, Mormon companies moved through customs with remarkably few delays or detentions.

On the frontier new experiences awaited the converts by way of camp life and the handling of oxen, an accomplishment most of the autobiographies dwell on, not a few confessing how disastrous it was when greenhorns tried to substitute harness "Danish style" for the yoke or "Yankee manner." A full outfit before railroad days consisted of a wagon, two yoke of oxen, two cows, and a tent to each ten individuals; and the emigrants found the provisions, stockpiled in advance, abundant: flour, sugar, bacon, rice, beans, dried apples and peaches, tea, vinegar, salt, and soap. There were modifications – the system was not flush every year.

A tragic chapter in the migration was that of the *Thornton* company, which left Liverpool May 3, 1856, with 764 Saints on board, 163 of them Scandinavians. They arrived on the frontier late, encountered delays in outfitting, and set out with handcarts, only to be caught in the highlands of Wyoming by storms and freezing weather, with rations low and strength failing. They were in pitiful condition when help arrived from the Salt Lake Valley, but not before some sixty had lost their lives.[28] Yet between 1856 and 1860 a thousand pushed hickory carts the thousand miles from Florence, Nebraska, to Utah. C. C. A. Christensen proudly recorded that he entered the Salt Lake Valley with the Danish flag flying from his cart, his trousers flapping in tatters about his legs.[29]

James Jensen, a sixteen-year-old member of Christensen's company, remembered some of their experiences, their distresses more typical than the extreme privations of the year before.[30] In the negotiations for handcarts at Iowa City, eagerness led to imprudent haste. The two-wheeled carts were crudely constructed, with wooden axles and bottoms made of strips of wood covered with canvas. In these a family could take along only the barest necessities. They had to leave many Old World treasures behind in their camp grove three or four miles outside the city. They hoped these would be kept by some friend, some brother or sister who would somehow or other forward them on to Zion. But they were disappointed; the goods were so commingled it was not easy to tell the owner. And often it was necessary for needy emigrants who came after to use what was nearest at hand. "We never heard any more about the things we left behind us."

James remembered that four mule teams had been assigned the handcart emigrants to haul provisions and the sick, but the wagons, driven by unfeeling teamsters from the Valley, were often too far ahead to give support. The emigrants finally took up a collection among themselves and from a passing farmer bought an ox team they could control. This became their hospital, at times carrying as many as twenty persons.

At Florence, Nebraska, where the Mormons maintained a re-equipping station that season, the emigrants reorganized. Some were unwilling to go on under existing unhappy conditions. Dissatisfied with their Scotch leader, they wanted one who knew their language and customs, who could have their confidence. He came along in the person of Christian Christiansen, veteran of the Forsgren company who had been sent out from Utah to look after the Scandinavian Saints in the Burlington area. He was hailed with delight when Mormon agent James A. Little put him in charge. The company, numbering 544 with 68 handcarts, 3 wagons, 10 mules, and a cow under four Scandinavian group captains, moved forward with renewed zeal. The Jensen family took up stations like so many other families: father and son James were the wheel team; younger brother and sister Karen were the leaders; the mother pushed; one youngster of seven trudged alongside, an infant under two rode. Sick sister Sophia died along the way.

After inspection at the first camp those thought unable to make it were sent back, among them a Swede, Hulberg, who had a feeble wife. But the disappointment was more than he could bear and, loading his wife into his cart, he made his way far in the rear of the company until it was too late to turn back. At Loup Fork, where Indians guided the emigrants across, the women clung on behind the naked braves on horseback. Little children in the carts remembered the terror when the water rose so high there was barely breathing room between the current and the cart cover.

James remembered some things vividly: the prickly pears his bare feet inevitably ran into; Niels Sorensen's wife appearing one morning with a new infant in her arms, born in the brush unknown to the rest of the company; the man who could not smell who killed a skunk and who, without change of clothes, had to stay behind at Deer Creek; the injured ox the commissary of Johnston's Army gave them on the Sweetwater. It was welcome beef; the emigrants did not kill any buffalo for fear of a stampede.

On the eastern plateau the company were met by flour teams from Salt Lake Valley and gave their handcart equipment in security for 9200 pounds of flour. They did not begrudge the obligation – it meant that repayment would make possible similar help to those who came after. Within thirty miles of Salt Lake they were met by teams bringing bread, cake, and fruit, the fruit a special delicacy for the sick and worn-out. "On the 13th of September, a Sunday, we marched with feelings of thankfulness and grand expectations into the city of the Saints. One out of every ten of our number had died on the journey."

Not all emigrants had the means to go on to Utah. Handcart companies like Jensen's in the late 1850s and the practice during the 1860s of sending out wagon trains from the settlements in the territory to meet the emigrants at the advancing railroad terminal enabled several thousand to cross the plains and mountains whose journey would otherwise have come to a temporary, but disappointing, end.[31] A. W. Winberg, for example, in charge of a party of 557 Scandinavians who left Hamburg on the sailship *B. S. Kimball* in 1865, wrote that nine wagons were put at his disposal by P.E.F. representatives at Fort Kearney to help 150 "independents" faced with a stopover. He added an interesting bit for readers of the *Stjerne* in the Old Country: "Lybert's mother, who is eighty years old, is determined to go on foot all the way from Wyoming [town in Nebraska]." [32]

John Nielsen remembered the apprehension in his company in 1866, "whether we would have to cross the plains with hand carts or whether the church would have their wagons up on the bench waiting for us." The emigrants had just taken their luggage off the boat near Florence on the Missouri and were "huddled together on the river bottoms . . . talking about it." John saw Niels Nielsen, the presiding elder, leave the company, climb the banks, pause a moment at the top, look around, and disappear. In an hour he came down the hill again. "He approached us with a smile, bidding us prepare to carry our luggage up on the bank. That the church wagons were there to take us to Utah. . . . There sure was joy. We felt like one who had wandered among strangers and had at last reached home sweet home and friends." The outfits, sent out from Sanpete County under Abner Lowry, had been waiting weeks for the tardy *Cavour* company.

The joy was turned to grief when cholera, which had already taken a toll of the emigrants aboard ship and en route from New York, broke out again, leaving hardly a family intact and not abating till they reached the mountains. The deaths, John Nielsen remembered, ran "far past the hundred mark, and in history it has gone down as the cholera train." He remembered the heartbreak at St. Joseph when an early victim could barely shake hands with his weeping wife and children, who had to be dragged from his side when they had to leave him to die among strangers.[33]

Sometimes the emigrants sought employment in eastern cities or in the country around the westernmost terminal. C. O. Folkmann wrote from Iowa City in 1858 that ten of his company had bought thirty acres to till for a season since jobs were scarce. "We are now American farmers." Elders Haight and Hoier had received them and rented a house with seven rooms for them with all the accommodations for cooking and washing, but "best of all" it was a place where they enjoyed peace and could hold services and they organized themselves into a branch of the Iowa City congregation. The young and unmarried men in their company had gone on to the Valley – these were the uncertain days of the occupation by Johnston's Army – while the families and sisters remained behind. Folkmann found Iowa so friendly he was convinced the Lord had prepared it as a temporary haven for them.[34] Sometimes the emigrants served as teamsters for the merchant trains which formed at the outfitting centers and moved on to Salt Lake; or they worked on the railroad. In 1868, Valley-bound emigrants encountered friends from the Old Country working on the railroad, "already long before we reached Echo Canyon. . . . among them Bishop Johannessen." [35]

Congregations of Scandinavian Mormons flourished at different times in Chicago, Burlington, Alton, St. Louis, and particularly Omaha, in the main composed of those forced to tarry. The church in Utah, concerned lest they stray from the fold, usually sent an experienced countryman to look after them. A conference in St. Louis in 1857 advised the Scandinavian Saints stopping temporarily in the States, to move to Omaha and Florence, Nebraska, places "being built up with great energy," where the brethren could find work and "come west." By 1860 most of them had moved, Jens Peter Christensen, who had spent five years in the States and presided over the Danish congregation in Alton, leading a company of 123 into the Valley in September.[36]

In June 1867 the first company of Scandinavian converts crossed the Atlantic by steam; two years later, in July 1869, the first company made the entire overland journey by rail. The total travel time was reduced to twenty-seven days, and hardships and hazards were practically eliminated. There was less need for housekeeping and organization aboard the modern ships of the Guion Line, but the Saints maintained their identity as a community, berthing apart from other emigrants and conducting their devotionals and dances as before.

The cross-country route was less of a steeplechase, though there had been charms in days of less rigid schedules such as the time an obliging railroad conductor in 1863 stopped the train at Palmyra, New York, and over six hundred Saints fresh from the *John J. Boyd* poured out to see the sacred Hill Cumorah and the fabled grove where Joseph Smith had seen his first vision, and "to pluck a flower or blade of grass from the locality as a memento." [37] In 1886 C. F. Olsen found Mr. P. Jurgensen, agent and interpreter for the Baltimore and Ohio Railroad, "exceedingly alert, courteous, and friendly, doing all in his power to make the trip pleasant." The agent had met Olsen's company in Baltimore and accompanied them all the way to Chicago, reserving first-class cars and seeing that in Chicago they had a smooth transfer with only half an hour's delay.[38]

If real dangers were fewer, the number of predatory merchants seemed to increase. Leaders telegraphed ahead for wholesale quantities of bread, but the emigrants always had numerous private purchases to make and only the threat of boycott by the company spokesman made honest men of most vendors. The brethren were zealous in shepherding their people through the league of "thieves, pickpockets, and apostates." Disillusioned Mormons from former emigrations, drifting back to centers like Omaha, tried during stopovers to dissuade their countrymen from continuing on to Utah, particularly the young women. Strangers offered them "care and protection" if they would remain.[39]

Anthon H. Lund, in charge of 397 emigrants crossing the continent in July 1872, found conditions so bad in Chicago that he preferred to use freight cars when he was threatened with a long delay because of a coach shortage. The curious found their way barred as they sought entry into the cars. A Swedish traveler in 1884 reported that one could move through a train at will until he came to the "Mormon cars," which were locked.[40] Vigilance aboard the trains, as at the hatchways aboard ship while in port, gave rise to the belief that Mormons attempted to insulate their charges from outside contact lest they learn something of their deception. But the proselytes could hardly hear worse reports than they had already weathered in the Old Country, and their freedom in moving about at layovers, some even remaining behind, discredits the notion.

There was more solidarity than insularity. Cars made up entirely of Mormon emigrants had the same social intimacy of shipboard organization, so much so that the piety of new converts was sometimes shocked. "The Norwegians and Danish were in their own coaches," a Mrs. Olsen told Pastor Andreas Mortensen, who won her back to Lutheranism, "and when it became dark in the evening, the returning president of the Scandinavian Mission came in and carried on shamefully with the young girls; they danced and shuffled the whole evening." [41] Some converts were not prepared for the hoedowns and Virginia reels they were to witness in the settlements.

The actual arrival in the valley of the Great Salt Lake was for the convert-emigrants the high point of their lives, surpassing even the day they set foot on America's shore. "One day as we were traveling I noticed the head team stop and the next and so on till an irregular circle was formed. I learned that we had just crossed the line into Utah and the company all bared and bowed their heads, and Niels Nielsen the Presiding Elder, offered up a prayer of thanksgiving after which we proceeded on our journey." [42] The mood, the particular expectation at the moment of arrival, a trivial incident pleasant or unpleasant, often conditioned their future joy or disappointment in the spiritual claims and material promise of Zion. "As we came out of Parley's canyon, the Saints met us in droves, bringing fruit and edibles in abundance, and though we had our troubles on the journey, now every heart swelled with joy to see the snow-covered mountains and beautiful valley where the fields and meadows were still partly green and many trees full of fruit. . . ." [43] So wrote a Dane whose heart was light because of the Norwegian girl he had married en route, and because of the "small, neat dwelling" where, in 1865, they found themselves happy. A widow found Zion on a bright, sunlit day in 1883, and fell in love with mountains which reminded her of her native Norway. A bitter winter, three weeks on wheat "shorts," and years of toil at dressmaking failed to dampen the new attachment.[44]

It was not to be expected that Saints should see miracles on first viewing the valley, that the lame should run, the blind see, and the sick be made whole, as some said they had been "solemnly assured" they would. On the contrary, as the bitter Miss Ingerøe discovered in 1864, "the nearer we drew, the more sorrowful and exhausted the immigrants became." Hans Zobell had his disappointments. Arriving at the railroad terminal in Ogden in August 1869 with a party of nearly six hundred Scandinavians – the first to come all the way overland by rail – he was moved to exclaim: "So this is really 'Zion' indeed, but what a reception. No shelter, no brethren, none of the pure in heart to bid us welcome; but on the other hand we learn that there are a lot of untrustworthy people right here." Rustling their own food and camping on the banks of the Weber River for three days while waiting for wagons to take them on to Salt Lake, they consoled themselves with the thought that there things would be better. But when church wagons eventually brought them to the capital, they were "dumped out in the tithing yard" and made their bed "on the ground with high heaven for a roof." No one paid "the least bit of attention" to them until an old man next morning distributed a "big basket of green corn and cucumbers" among the immigrants. Zobell's faith, however, was more surely grounded than that of some of his fellows. Though he stood "with empty hands," he felt "an assurance that if God had given me the call to come here, He would not leave me here to starve and to be without shelter." [45]

There were mismanaged occasions (magnified by the hypersensitivity of the new arrivals), but on the whole, the same order and organization which had found them in their native villages and transported them across ocean and continent were marshaled to receive them at journey's end. Helping hands reached out from the Valley long before the immigrants arrived: supply trains loaded with flour and produce, and extra wagons to give the weary a lift, and experienced help to guide the difficult oxen down canyon roads often met them deep in the mountains when strength was lowest and discouragement great. Forerunners among their countrymen in these trains were a joy to see, and occasionally old familiars, Americans who had filled missions in Denmark. Erastus Snow himself encountered Peder Nielsen in camp at Big Mountain two days out from Salt Lake, and Brother Knudsen, who hitched two of his oxen to Peder's wagon and drove it himself "for which I am very thankful as P. Hansen who generally drives it is not a good driver." [46]

Before railroad days they emerged from Emigration or Parley's canyons, drove along dusty Emigration Road, and camped on Emigration

Square, the names descriptive of Zion's foremost activity.[47] Church wagons went several blocks farther to the "emigrant sheds" built against the walls of the church office enclosure or "Tithing Yard." If the immigrants had traveled in "P.E.F. wagons," they could live in them until they found something of their own or were taken home by relatives and friends who converged on the city for the occasion. Church teams were equipment loaned for the frontier-to-Salt Lake mission, and their drivers were usually eager to get back to the settlements.

The arrival of an immigrant company was always a festive event in the life of pre-railroad Utah. A band and procession met the first party to be entirely assisted by the Perpetual Emigrating Fund, a mark of honor to the poor. For the survivors of the handcart ordeal in 1856, Brigham Young's text in one Sunday sermon showed special solicitude: "When those persons arrive . . . I want them distributed in this city among the families that have good, comfortable homes; and I wish the sisters now before me, and all who know how and can, to nurse and wait upon the newcomers, and prudently administer medicine and food to them."[48]

A few years after Hans Zobell's trying experience, when the railroad was serving Salt Lake, the Scandinavians themselves were providing their countrymen the warm welcome Hans had so sorely missed. Reported the *Deseret Evening News* on September 26, 1872: "The Scandinavian brethren and sisters of this city have appointed a committee, of which A. W. Winberg is chairman, whose duty it is to prepare a hearty reception in the shape of a bounteous collation, at Ballo's Hall, for the emigrants who are expected to arrive tonight." Some six hundred strong, the arrivals were conducted from the depot to the hall, where a band "discoursed sweet music" during supper. Brigham Young and other church dignitaries, moreover, had met them midway from Ogden to tour the coaches and greet their "strange brothers and sisters from across the sea," a flattering attention.[49]

Succeeding newcomers were often banqueted by resident Scandinavians in the Tithing Yard, where countryman Niels Jensen was on hand as an attendant. It remained the center of interest all during the immigration period. In the early years particularly, the chests and boxes from abroad and from "the States" usually meant added comforts for the community. One Norwegian's window lights and keg of nails were especially sought after.

Miss Ingerøe, resenting the eyes of the curious, felt that the "old Mormons from the city" were looking over the women as a butcher would livestock. The pickings in her company were slim, she observed; there were no "usable women, girls, or laborers" because most of the young people had become engaged or been married en route. When a married Dane offered her temporary shelter in his tiny adobe cottage, she accepted with some trepidation but decided he was more interested in her cow than in her. Jonas Stadling in 1885, making what he called "a forbidden visit" within the enclosure, found a Swedish girl weeping, and insinuated that it was because she faced a life of servitude.[50] It must have been a rare immigrant indeed who did not shed tears at some time.

In their attention to both temporal and spiritual matters the instructions the immigrants received on arrival were reminiscent of their indoctrination before departure. An English traveler was impressed by Brigham Young's practical counsel to an early band:

> You are faint and weary from your march. Rest, then, for a day, for a second day, should you need it; then rise up, and see how you will live. . . . Be of good cheer. Look about this valley into which you have been called. Your first duty is to learn how to grow a cabbage . . . then how to feed a pig, to build a house, to plant a garden, to rear cattle, and to bake bread; in one word, your first duty is to live. The next duty—for those who, being Danes, French, and Swiss, cannot speak it now—is to learn English; the language of God, the language of the *Book of Mormon*, the language of these Latter Days. These things you must do first; the rest will be added to you in proper seasons. God bless you; and the peace of our Lord Jesus Christ be with you.[51]

Franklin D. Richards, familiar to many immigrants as the church agent in Liverpool, whose name appeared on their passage contracts, sermonized while in Salt Lake City between missions: "If you look about you and see the Saints who have been here some years, and the choice locations taken up by them . . . do not fret your souls; remember that those brethren made the roads to this place . . . made the bridges, opened the canyons. . . ." He knew it was natural for the Saints who came from abroad to be "very diligent in inspecting God's people, to see if they are as righteous as they ought to be." New arrivals stood at the forks, he said. "If you wish to travel downward, the great depot of that route is California; if upward, the great depot on that is this city."[52]

And Jedediah M. Grant told those who came expecting a heaven how to get it: "If you have brought a small one with you, keep it, and keep adding to it. . . . If you do not have means enough to buy a farm, go to work and make one. . . . If you have around you the garb of sectarianism you must calculate that the Mormon plow will turn that under." [53]

In the life ahead of them, most of the Scandinavian immigrants learned how to handle the "Mormon plow," as their flourishing settlements in Zion would testify; but some inevitably were tempted by the fleshpots of California or were overcome by longing for the old home or, for causes profound and trivial, backtrailed to Nebraska and Iowa to join those who had fallen by the way. Anti-Mormons were fond of asserting that "at least two thirds" of the emigrants would return to their native lands if they could, but "alas! the Church has no emigration fund *from* Utah." [54] During the 1850s, 2989 converts left Denmark, but the 1860 census counted only 1824 Danes in Utah, evidence, with due allowance for deaths, that not all reached their destination or, having reached it, stayed. Some of these may have come on later: at least 1396 converts, both British and Scandinavian, who emigrated between July 1857 and June 1860, remained in the States, but the church had "good cause to presume . . . a good number of these have gone through to Utah without settling on the way." [55]

According to one backtrailer's story to the New York *Times*, at least half of the large emigration of 1854 – which numbered 678 when it left Copenhagen – left for California the following spring. But such guesses were wild, and usually garnished with hearsay tales about Danites given orders to pursue the apostate emigrants in the disguise of Indians to steal their cattle and murder the emigrants themselves. "Those in authority curse the emigrant trains which pass through on their way to the Pacific, as they afford means for the dissatisfied persons to escape," said the New York *Times*, reporting in 1857 that 200 persons were on their way from Utah to the States. "They bore the appearance of persons who had seen much trouble and privation – being reduced in body and dejected in mind. . . . They rejoiced that they had at last reached a land where they could once more live at ease." [56]

Departures of the disillusioned from Zion were common enough for *Biküben*, Danish-language newspaper in Salt Lake City, to run a facetious advertisement: "In case someone in Utah becomes tired of living among the Mormons, here is an opportunity which you will seldom find . . ." and it went on to describe the offer of someone in Nebraska ready to "sell or trade" an eighty-acre farm for property in Utah.[57]

Some converts, overwhelmed at the train of calamities that beset their coming to Zion – the deaths, the deprivations – felt these to be God's judgments upon them for having forsaken their homeland against the advice of friends and their broken families. They went back beaten or defiant, hoping to make restitution or at best peace with themselves. The gentile Bourkersson, after three years in the territory and embittered by the loss of his Mormon wife to someone else, left in 1867 with an eastward-bound company of about fifty wagons "filled with estranged Mormons." To his astonishment, he found among them "many" Swedish families with whom he had journeyed to Utah. They seemed to experience an even greater camaraderie now on leaving together. In his testament published after returning to Sweden, he pleaded with his countrymen to remain in the fatherland, but if they insisted on migrating to America, then not to go farther west before they had looked at Wisconsin, Illinois, Iowa, or Minnesota, where they would find fruitful earth for a reasonable price, a healthful climate, and Swedish Lutheran churches and societies.[58]

Frue Ingerøe, with sensibilities too delicate for the rigors of pioneer life, found her journey to Utah and her stay there an unrelieved nightmare and after a year hastened back to Norway, a Stanley back from darkest Africa, to lecture on the benighted Mormons.[59] Christian Michelsen, back in Denmark after a miserable absence of four years during which he could not feel the glories of an adobe and sagebrush Zion, contrasted the loveliness of the Old World with the hardness of the New. On his return, the sight of Ireland first refreshed him: the ruins of the monasteries, the little towns nestling in the hills "all bore the stamp of antiquity"; England's trim wheat fields witnessed that "here . . . no land is wasted," and crossing the Channel, he soon heard "that dear Danish speech from every mouth"; hurrying to his native Odense, he shrived himself of his Mormon associations in "a long talk" with his old pastor.[60]

A startling exodus occurred in May 1863, when Brigadier General Patrick E. Connor's California Volunteers escorted about 160 "seceders from the Mormon Church" from their sanctuary at Fort Douglas in Salt Lake City to Soda Springs, Idaho Territory, where they were allowed building lots and shelters near the new post being established on the trail to Oregon and the Bannock mines. When Connor at the same time sent an empty train to Carson for quartermaster's stores, he furnished transportation there for 150 more of the seceders. These were all Morrisites, nearly half of them Scandinavians, followers of the ill-fated Welsh convert Joseph Morris, whose revelations expressing dissatisfaction with Brigham Young's management of Zion and predicting an immediate Second Coming had drawn many disillusioned Saints after him until his violent death and the disruption of his colony in the summer of 1862. It was a tragic scattering, a cruel inversion of the hope that had originally gathered them home to Zion.[61]

The dissatisfied beat the widest trail back to western Iowa and eastern Nebraska. In Council Bluffs and Omaha and Fremont, and in Douglas, Washington, and Dodge counties, Nebraska, it was well known that the oldest Danish settlers were or had been Mormons. "They would not, to be sure, admit it," confided an old Dane in Omaha, "but one knew it well enough." [62] Zion lost a pair of famous future sculptors when wood carver James Borglum from Jutland, father of Gutzon and Solon Hannibal, turned back in 1868 from Ogden to St. Louis to become a doctor and finally establish a practice in Fremont, Nebraska, with a 6000-acre ranch for his sons to manage. The sons would one day carve a national monument on Mt. Rushmore.[63] Johan Ahmanson, former Swedish Baptist, brilliant but headstrong, who had filled a distinguished mission in Norway before emigration, suffered the misfortunes of the luckless handcart company of 1856, which he later described as if it were the whole emigrant experience; moreover, he did not find the leading brethren in Zion spiritual enough, which may have meant that he did not find his advancement in church councils rapid enough to suit him, and he fled to Omaha to write an embittered book and in time become well known as "Dr." Ahmanson.[64]

Knud Svendsen, on his way to Utah in 1858, encountered Old Country convert-acquaintances in the vicinity of Omaha and Florence: "Jacob of Nojstjert and wife, and Jens Godtfredsen, and Christen Smed of Vreiler, and Christen from Brensen, and many Danes besides, easily 100. There is much weakness among them; the Devil has great power here." [65] And Peter O. Thomassen grieved in 1872 that he saw "many a familiar face that once was one with us, but our feelings were no longer one. Many expressed remorse at their folly and lacked only the means to journey to Zion, while others vented their bitterness in harmless spite." It was with a sense of relief W. W. Cluff could report that "to a man" his company got through all right, despite the temptations of apostates along the way.[66]

The church expected the mortality – it was used to apostasy in the mission, desertions en route, and disaffection in Zion itself. It was severe with the weak, quick to turn them over to "the buffetings of Satan." Far from grieving over defections by the way, it rationalized that they saved Zion a good deal of trouble. It could not brook ingratitude. "Though nineteen kindnesses may have been extended to them, because the twentieth did not come in the form in which they thought it should, they overlook the nineteen and find fault."[67] P. C. Geertsen was ashamed of some of his countrymen: "Many of those who clamored most loudly to be freed from Babylon, once in Zion have no time for sacrament, but go to the mines to worship the God they love, the almighty dollar."[68]

The ill at ease at first preferred to leave Zion, but in time they asserted their claim to a stake in the new country on other than church terms and remained, often fair game for sectarians anxious to make inroads among Zion's elect. As backtrailers they turned up in a surprising number of places in the United States, where the little eddies of their lives were lost in the general stream of history. But those content to take Zion as they found it became Mormon villagers, distinctive as the adobe bricks and irrigation ditches which now became their daily concern.

III. SETTLER

CHAPTER 8

Mormon Villagers

"BRO. C. HANSEN, TEACHER, REPORTED THAT HE FOUND A GOOD SPIRIT WHEREVER HE WENT AND HE WISHED TO CARRY OUT THE BISHOP'S COUNSEL AS TO GOOD FENCING."[1]

THE first thing we did," Anders Thomsen remembered, when he arrived in Spring Town in mid-October 1853 with a number of the Forsgren immigrants, "was to go down to the river bottom and cut some frozen grass. We had some ox teams which had to be cared for. When we had done this we had to build a fort wall against the Indians."[2] Because the colonists were almost out of provisions, they divided into two parties, one to stay home and build the walls while the other went to the older settlements in Utah County fifty miles away to work for food. Anders, almost twenty-two, went with the work party, earning enough to fill his wagon with potatoes which he shared equally with the man who had built his section of the wall.

Anders and his countrymen were ready now to make their homes in Spring Town, but Brigham Young did not consider the little community safe for the winter and instructed them to fall back on neighboring Manti, now four years old, where Father Isaac Morley and his English converts put them up. "The people here were liberal and kindhearted and gave us rooms." Early in the spring of 1854 Anders joined a company of fourteen that moved out to Ephraim Creek, seven miles north, where once again they built a fort, the rock laboriously quarried and hauled from above town. They built a corral to keep the cattle from thieving Indians, grubbed brush with poor tools, and at last began to farm. They put in "a little crop" and dug ditches to water it, but by then it was late in the season and frosts destroyed most of the grain. In the spring they put in another crop, but the grasshoppers ate all of it. "This left a kind of dark picture before us," particularly since most of the new arrivals from Scandinavia the previous fall had come on to

Ephraim. Most of them lived on potatoes, though Anders and a few others went down to Cedar City after wheat. "This was about the end of the second year. After that we raised crops and did a little better."

It was a characteristic beginning, familiar to nearly every early immigrant, whose arrival spelled both an asset and a liability in Zion's hazardous economy – a liability as one more mouth to feed from resources always marginal, an asset as another squatter to secure Mormon title to the domain, another strong back to fulfill prophecy and make the desert blossom.

When the Jensen family arrived from Denmark with a handcart company in 1857, Anders found himself a wife in their daughter Christiana. They made their first home in a one-room hut in the fort, where two children were born, Christiana never forgetting how she made her first baby's layette from her husband's handkerchief and an old shirt. When the town was laid out in 1860, they built a three-room adobe cottage on the lot they had drawn and farmed "the old twenty" as their tract outside town would be remembered by their descendants. Christiana worked alongside Anders, at noon climbing on the old horse to ride home and nurse her baby. They sowed grain by hand, cut hay with a scythe and the grain with a cradle, binding the bundles by hand and hauling them home by ox team where they flailed it and fanned out the chaff. By 1864 the children numbered four. "Ten years had now passed since the beginning of Ephraim and everything was moving along pretty well."

In the fall the church called Anders and his family to establish a settlement farther south, in Circle Valley, Piute County, where they built a log cabin with chinks so wide the wind sifted the manure in from the community corral, covering the bed and the big box used for a table as well as storage. Yet it was a place where Anders thought they could "nestle down for the winter" and get ready for another siege of pioneering. But the Black Hawk Indian war broke out, bringing disastrous loss of livestock and constant threat to the handful of settlers, whom Brigham Young now released from their colonizing mission. With Christiana so weak from childbirth she had to sit on a chair to pack the family belongings, the Thomsens made their way back to Ephraim, where they could start all over again – this time for good, with fruit trees and a hop vine on the backyard fence for beauty as well as homemade beer marking the change in their fortunes.

A traveler passing through Ephraim one Sunday evening twenty years after its unpromising start, found it one of the loveliest villages he had seen, "with its neat cottages, and streets shaded by long lines of trees, with not a sound to break the stillness of the air but that of the running roadside streams, and the setting sun gilding the snowy mountains in the background. . . . the herd boys driving in their cows . . . a few people leaning listlessly over the fences." [3] It was a pastoral in "dreamy repose," belying its hard past.

In 1849, when Mormon missionaries first set out for Copenhagen, Zion was the provisional State of Deseret, a regional empire bounded by the Rocky Mountains and the Sierras, the Oregon country and Mexico, with a corridor opening to the Pacific for an eventual port of entry for immigrants expected to come the water route round the Horn.[4] By the time Anders Thomsen and the first proselytes from Scandinavia reached the Valley, Deseret had been reduced to the Territory of Utah, boxed in by arbitrary parallels and meridians, to be further trimmed as surrounding territories were created. But what was left still challenged the imagination. "Utah" meant "the tops of the mountains," and it was in the tops of the mountains Isaiah had predicted the House of the Lord would be established and all nations flow unto it. Brigham Young sent out exploring parties to discover every habitable valley and pre-empt the Kingdom – here was a land where the Mormons at last could be the original settlers, keeping the outsider in the decided minority. By his death in 1877, Young had founded 358 communities, including outposts in California, Arizona, Nevada, Idaho, Wyoming, and Colorado.[5] If arable land was scarce and water the price of blood, the limitation proved an advantage: noting ruefully that the Mormons "have not only settled but have filled all of tillable Utah," a federal commission in 1888 concluded that "those who hold the valleys and appropriate and own the waters capable of use for irrigation, own and hold Utah, and nature has fortified their position more strongly than it could be done by any Chinese wall or artificial defense." [6]

It was a commonwealth making no distinction between temporal and spiritual affairs under the strong central direction of the great colonizer as president of the church – and for ten years as governor of the territory as well – with apostles serving as regional administrators over the presidents of stakes (dioceses) and the bishops of wards (parishes). Quarterly church conferences by regions and semi-annual conferences of the whole church in Salt Lake City gave isolated settlements the sense of a wider community, while the interlocking local and church-wide jurisdictions united the energies of Utah villages and European missions to build the Kingdom, a tremendous pooling of resources which put manpower and wealth at the disposition of the authorities whether for an exchange of grain between settlements, the founding of a cooperative store, the building of a local railroad or telegraph, the erection of temples, or the founding of new settlements. Brigham Young's own regular visitations magnetized the commonwealth, his voice and his handshake a living experience as he made his progress through the settlements. He was the president of the High Priesthood but also always "Brother Brigham," who knew his people intimately and their need of his homely advice.

Colonizing the drouth-ridden, scattered valleys of Deseret demanded cooperation both far-flung and intimate, with every new settlement part of the larger design and every settler a responsive part of the community in a life at once determined by desert conditions and overcoming them: the fort wall raised for defense against Indians, the big field for planting enclosed by united labor to keep out the livestock, the unfenced lands grazed and the wild hay gathered in common, the ditches dug and the dams erected by the whole community to share and control the precious water, the roads built into the canyons for timber, the home sites in town determined by lot for church-centered living, the outlying farm lands parceled into minute holdings for intensive cultivation.

The communal forms expressed vital functions. More than that, the Mormon farm-village, in which the Scandinavians found themselves mingling with Americans and other Europeans in a unifying religious brotherhood, expressed an ideal. It was the Kingdom in small, patterned after the Prophet Joseph Smith's blueprint for the City of Zion, which he intended as early as 1833 to become the model of holy communities in time to cover the earth.[7] The dynamics of this idea, and the design – actually carried out in Nauvoo – inspired Brigham Young. Great Salt Lake City itself, with its ten-acre blocks divided into 1¼-acre lots, its streets wide enough to permit an ox-team's full turn, its Temple Square and ward meetinghouses, its civic Council House, its centered shops, and its surrounding farms served as prototype for every settlement in the territory. Isolation, Indians, irrigation, and a New England town tradition were merely immediate causes of what already had a final cause in the heavenly model.

The idea of the Kingdom, however mundanely expressed in Utah's humble villages, nevertheless animated the life in them: "Br A Fredriksen spoke in Danish and stated that we vas not com her to this Walley for to bild os self op only but for to help the poor & work for the opbilding of the Kingdom of God also incorech the Brethren to help Br Svend Larsen to put in his Krop and said we will not loos anything by doing so." [8] The earth was the Lord's and the Saints considered their stake in the village an "inheritance." It seemed to Brother Larsen ridiculous and an evil for the brethren to go to law in a water dispute, employing gentile lawyers "for to giv us right in the Kingdom of God" instead of seeking "redres for rongs amonst ourselfs." [9]

When Bishop Ola N. Liljenquist advised "every man when the day for voting comes to go and deposit our votes before going to our labors and prove by our actions that we will sustain the Holy Priesthood," [10] it was without a sense of church interference with the state. It was the democratic way of supporting the goals already set for the Kingdom; political union was another form of cooperation, and it seemed no more prescriptive than uniting to dig a ditch or build a meetinghouse. Society here was a counterpart, however imperfect, of the exalted community in the world to come, when the same bishops and presidents who presided over the affairs of the Saints now would judge them. In such a view, church and civic affairs became virtually one and, for the believer, wonderfully coherent, making him ready to answer a variety of calls—to pioneer new settlements, serve a foreign mission, send a wagon to the frontier to fetch poor immigrants, serve as bishop or ward teacher, give a tithe of his increase to the common storehouse, a tithe of his labor to building meetinghouses and temples, and consecrate, if need be, everything he had as the Lord's steward.

The Scandinavian convert-settlers, spiritually citizens of the Kingdom before they even arrived, were readily absorbed into the corporate Zion. Its intimate life was strongly reminiscent of the Old World village, even to the dominance of the church in daily affairs, with the notable difference that here they were themselves clothed with the priesthood and vested with the authority of marshal, school trustee, selectman, justice of the peace, watermaster, and fence-viewer. Besides, they rubbed shoulders with Americans who were veterans of other frontiers, the tried survivors of the Nauvoo and Missouri persecutions, and as the newcomers heard their experiences in Sunday meeting and worked side by side with them in church and community affairs, the immigrants obtained a vitalizing sense of a living tradition, a divinely unfolding history, and of their own important function in it.

So motivated, the arrivals from Scandinavia were welcome additions for carrying out Zion's great dreams. Most of the first company went to Sanpete Valley; a few went to Box Elder; a number, principally skilled workmen, remained in Great Salt Lake City. To these centers later immigration naturally gravitated, Sanpete and Sevier counties in the south, Salt Lake County roughly in the middle, and Box Elder and Cache in the north becoming early, and remaining, the strongholds of Scandinavian population. The Scandinavians soon made Cache and Sanpete valleys known as the granaries of Utah and by 1884 they were being described in the gazetteers as "exceedingly well to do."[11] Before long they were to be found in most of the settlements which, like beads on an unclasped string, lay in the arable valleys and along the footings of the Wasatch range running down the center of the state. "The people are like bees; when they fill up one place, they swarm out and build up a new one. . . . About three hundred Danish families live in this town," wrote Christian Nielsen from Manti in 1856, "and about seven English miles north of us there are about as many."[12] *Morgenstjernen*, a Danish monthly, in 1884 had eighty-three agents in as many settlements, suggesting a widespread concentration.

Scandinavian Mormons colonized Idaho and Nevada in the 1860s and Wyoming, Arizona, New Mexico, and Colorado in the 1870s; some joined refugee colonies of polygamists in Mexico and Canada in the late 1880s; a few followed Mormon entrepreneurs to Oregon in the 1890s to carry on lumbering operations. Scandinavians participated in two of Mormonism's most heartbreaking colonizing expeditions, the Muddy River mission in 1868–71, consistently wiped out by floods, and the San Juan mission in 1880 in the badlands of southeastern Utah, which they had to reach by way of Hole-in-the-Rock, a treacherous cleft in the sheer wall of the Colorado down which they blasted a trail and a history. Jens Nielsen, already a veteran of four settlements, survived the ordeal to become bishop of Bluff,[13] one of the seasoned colonizers who led what might be called the second wave of Mormon pioneering which sought to build up "the waste places of Zion" and extend its borders, a vigorous and far-flung program after the death of Brigham Young.

Bishop Hans Jensen Hals of Manti wrote in 1878 that he had been called to go to the San Luis Valley in southern Colorado to found "a home for thousands of Latter-day Saints," because "Utah is becoming too crowded for us. . . . Because our poor brethren and sisters who come to these tightly populated towns in Utah have no chance to get land to cultivate for themselves, the Lord has led our brethren the apostles to take this step for Zion's outspreading." He was going ahead in a few days with a company of experienced elders to lay out the towns and be on hand to help "my countrymen" when they came the next year.[14] One of his countrymen was Hans Christensen Heiselt, who had been called successively to Pleasant Grove, Fountain Green, Castle Valley, and finally San Luis, where he eventually became bishop of Sanford, living to a ripe ninety-one years. As late as 1900 seven companies of Mormon colonists from southern Idaho and northern Utah set out from Ogden for the Big Horn Basin, Wyoming, with Bishop N. P. Larson of Thomas Fork and other Scandinavians among them.[15]

The Scandinavians gave their names to some places: Jensen, for Lars Jensen, who built the ferry on Green River in 1885; Axtell in Sanpete County, after Axel Einersen; Anderson in Washington County, after Peter Anderson's orchard in 1869; Peterson in Morgan County, for Charles Shreeve Peterson, its bishop; Elsinore in Sevier County, founded in 1874, after the Danish town where Hamlet once stalked a ghost, though it is doubtful any of the immigrants had ever heard of him; Widtsoe in Garfield County, for John A. Widtsoe, Norwegian dry farm scientist; Lockerby in San Juan, after an early resident; Yost in Box Elder County, after Charles Yost in 1880; Swedish Knoll in Sanpete because Niels Anderson herded sheep there; Christianson Canyon in Tooele County, for an early Swedish settler along Deep Creek; Borgeson Canyon, for Anders Borgeson, who built the first molasses mill in Santaquin.[16] There were, besides, nicknames like Little Copenhagen for Mantua, a hamlet of Danish families in Little Valley; and Little Denmark for half a dozen towns. Rural communities dominantly Scandinavian invariably had a Danish Ditch, a Danish Field, a Danish Bench, and a Danish Woods, suggestive that out of language needs in the early days it was convenient to divide up the commons in this way.

In a number of communities Scandinavians outnumbered all other foreign-born, and their second generation formed the greater part of the native-born. But there were no exclusively Scandinavian colonies, which would have been contrary to the idea of the Kingdom, whose fellowship overrode ethnic distinctions. Salt Lake City by 1885 did have a "Swede Town," but it was a suburban development promoted by businessmen eager to profit from the great influx of Swedes into the capital in the 1880s. The Scandinavian Building Society in Salt Lake in 1889 was simply an urban expression, through united cash, of what once could be done through united labor in the settlements.[17]

The "Little Denmark" of Salt Lake City's Second Ward, begun by the first handful of immigrants in 1852 and steadily augmented, was not exclusive: though twenty-nine of its fifty-eight households in 1860 were Scandinavian, they lived side by side with their American, English, and Scotch neighbors in a community as mixed as the country settlements.[18] Not that relations were always amicable. Charles L. Walker noted in his journal on Sunday, October 23, 1859, after complaining of the cold and "a pain in my bowels," that he had "calculated to go to the Tabernacle but a Danish Brother came for me to settle a difficulty between him and a scotch man both parties were near to fighting point neither would yeild nor could I get them to see the thing in the right light both wanted to have the thing fixd their own. but after laboring with them for about 2 hours I got them to see as I saw and before I left I had all made straight and the parties shook hands and felt pretty well toward each other considering how they felt previous to my coming to them." The point is that Dane and Scotchman could take their trouble to an Englishman, their fellow ward member, and resolve it.

A few days earlier Walker had recorded another typical service: "At night I went down to the 5th Ward to get a Danish man that could speak English. I took him with me to two Danish Families that had come in this season and we encouraged them in their faith religion and temporal welfare." And a year later he could note "at night I went to the ward meeting the time was half took up in reconfirming about 30 of the Brethren and Sisters that came in this fall from England Denmark and some from Africa. . . ."[19] After 1860 the Second Ward became less the Scandinavian center, the immigrants scattering freely throughout the city, where their friends and relatives following after were naturally attracted to them and soon gave other neighborhoods a Scandinavian complexion. Scandinavian domestics, moreover, served in numerous non-Scandinavian families.

Scandinavians, as Mormons and farmers, shunned gentile establishments like Corinne, a railroad boomtown, and Silver Reef, a briefly prosperous mining community; but they did not hesitate to sell their produce to the unbelievers at a profit, the cash from soldiers, miners, and railroad workers often the only money they saw in their early barter economy. "We benefited much from the soldiers," noted Hans Jensen Hals, speaking of Colonel Johnston's occupation forces at Camp Floyd; "when they bought our vegetables, butter, eggs, and pork and other things we charged them high prices."[20] The full-scale development of the famous copper mine in Bingham after 1890, and its accompanying smelters and refineries, appealed particularly to the populous Swedes of Salt Lake and Grantsville who found employment there.

Along with the continued emigration of English converts during the half century the Scandinavians brought Utah's rate of population increase to 253.89 per cent by 1860 (when it was 35.58 per cent for the United States as a whole and 246.15 per cent for states in the Western Division) and kept it high during the 1860s and 1870s – 115.49 per cent as contrasted with a rapid decline to 60.02 per cent for the Western Division generally. By 1880, however, Utah's rate of increase, 65.88 per cent, was below that for the Western Division's 78.46 per cent. By 1910 more Greeks (657) than Scandinavians (479) were giving Utah as their destination at American ports, reflecting the changed fortunes of Mormon proselyting.[21]

Meanwhile, the Scandinavians contributed heavily toward giving Utah a high proportion of foreign-born: from 1850 to 1890 Utah was consistently ahead of the United States as a whole and of the Western Division in the percentage of foreign-born. In 1870, when Mormon Territory counted nearly twice as many Scandinavians as Nebraska, 68 per cent of Utah's population was of foreign stock (persons having one or both parents foreign-born) and 35.3 per cent was foreign-born. In 1890, 66.28 per cent of Utah's population was of foreign stock. Only North Dakota with 78.98 per cent and Minnesota with 75.42 per cent exceeded it. The United States average was 33.02 per cent. In 1900 Scandinavians in Utah formed 34 per cent of the state's foreign-born, their highest figure, which they would not again equal; and Scandinavian stock that year formed 16 per cent of a total population which was

41.8 per cent of foreign or mixed parentage. Throughout the half century, the Scandinavians formed the largest immigrant group in Utah next to the British, who in the 1860s comprised 74.4 per cent of the state's foreign-born, gradually diminishing to 47.7 per cent by 1900, when the Scandinavians most nearly approached them.[22]

In 1902 Anthon H. Lund, Danish immigrant of 1862, could tell a big reunion of Scandinavians in Brigham City, "We are now 45,000 and are a great power in our state." [23] His own appointment the year before to the high office of counselor in the First Presidency of the Mormon Church was itself a signal recognition of that power, an official acknowledgment of the role his countrymen were playing in Utah's affairs.

For him as for his people it marked a rise from humble beginnings. An English settler described how the newcomers struck root:

> I have seen many Scandinavian families come into Manti in pioneer days with no means of support. Most of them had small trunks that contained all their earthly wealth, a few clothes and some bedding. Some walked from Salt Lake City to Sanpete County. Former countrymen would take them into their homes for a few weeks. Then the new immigrant would acquire a lot, build himself a small adobe home, surround it with a willow woven fence. Soon a few acres of ground were added to his accumulations, every foot of which was utilized. Mother and father and every child in the Scandinavian home worked. None of the wheat they raised was wasted and after it was threshed with the flail, the Scandinavians cleaned their wheat with hand-turned mills. They chopped their animal feed with a hand chopper so that it would go farther, and provide better animal food. There was no waste. I am an Englishman, but I have always said that the Scandinavian was thrifty, honest and God fearing, and set us a worthy example.[24]

For those unprepared for the crudities of frontier living, the dugouts, lean-tos, and adobe houses of young settlements were a source of dismay. One woman, who could see only poverty and hardship in the one-room dwellings, wept at the sight of a clean tablecloth and a tea service from the Old Country, fragile refinement resisting the desert.[25] Yet another knew that if Scripture had promised deserts blossoming as the rose, the settler had to help a little. "In this letter I send you five dollars," wrote Anna Widtsoe in 1885 to a sister about to leave Norway; ". . . if you can, buy and bring with you . . . two myrtles with strong roots, several bulbs of Mrs. Rian's white lilies, as many bulbs as you can secure of Jacob's lilies. . . ." [26]

The immediate urgency for the new arrivals, of course, was how to survive from one day to the next, how to make a living. Some historians have the converts "parceled out" among paternalistic bishops throughout the territory, suggesting a passive dependence on the part of the immigrant and an autocratic management on the part of the church. But the Kingdom was no welfare state. In the early years it had too many "starving times" to offer any guarantees. It looked, in fact, to the strength and sinew of the immigrants themselves to aid it. It extended helping hands and provided a pattern for survival, but the immigrants had to live by their own sweat and make their own decisions. They were only too glad to receive direction, like Niels Wilhelmsen, who in 1861 took Brigham Young's personal advice (the meeting was a great moment in Wilhelmsen's life: "He knew my name well") to go to Weber Valley, where he bartered his frock coat for a log cabin in newly founded Morgan and his "best Danish suit" for five hundred pounds of flour. "We are twelve Danish families here, but live in the midst of many English. Here are unity and peace."[27] Wilhelmsen was the kind of responsive clay Heber C. Kimball had in mind when he said "You have got to be subject to the master potter. I am a potter and brother Brigham is a potter, and we understand the business."[28]

Among the Scandinavians, their own energy and initiative informed the clay. Stonemason Gustave Anderson, an early resident of the Second Ward, was officially assigned during the 1850s to greet his countrymen as they arrived at the Eighth Ward Square, site of Salt Lake's present city and county building and once better known as Washington or Emigration Square.[29] Besides the informal welcome of friends and relatives come in from the outlying settlements to escort the newcomers back with them, and the welcome of leading churchmen – often Brigham Young himself – the greeting was but the beginning of the lifesaving, soul-saving concern of the church for the immigrants in which the immigrants themselves, as soon as they gained experience, became the shepherds – another demonstration of the self-help that had marked their missionary service as converts while yet in Scandinavia. Brigham Young sent Canute Peterson, for example, to Ephraim in 1863 as bishop,[30] a strong hand to settle differences among the local Scandinavians. He eventually presided over all the settlements in Sanpete County as stake president, his long experience as frontiersman and foreign missionary bringing the region needed strength and stability and winning for his people so much respect the church built a temple in Manti, the county seat, even before the great shrine in Salt Lake was completed, to serve as their spiritual center. Brigham Young appointed Canute its construction superintendent and it was built largely by skilled Scandinavian hands, dedicated tithing labor, even to the murals of its ceremonial halls.

In every settlement a "Scandinavian Meeting" or "Scandinavian Organization" auxiliary to the regular Mormon congregation – and only auxiliary, for the Scandinavians did not form autonomous churches any more than they formed exclusive colonies – proved an effective instrument of adjustment in the mother tongue while at the same time the immigrant converts were learning to participate in the life and leadership of their respective wards. Farmer Hans Jensen Hals presided over the "Danish Organization" in Manti in the 1850s and 1860s while an elder in the Manti Ward and later its bishop; carpenter Hans Lorentz Dastrup looked after the Danes in Big Cottonwood in the 1860s; and James Anderson became "the mouthpiece of the bishop to his countrymen" in Spanish Fork in the 1870s.[31]

Scandinavians, moreover, served as special "ward teachers" and "home missionaries" to their countrymen, again supplementing the customary work of the local wards: brushmaker Jacob B. Jacobsen was such a teacher in Salt Lake's Eleventh Ward in the 1890s, later becoming bishop of the Manti South Ward, and the Swede Charles E. Forsberg was a home missionary among the Scandinavians in the Salt Lake Stake in 1901, one of a corps of twelve directed to visit and assist the newly arrived, the widows, the orphans, and the backsliders, and to conduct "cottage meetings" in their own tongue,[32] a move long needed in the city, which had lost the sympathies and compulsions of pioneer days.

Another care was to send missionaries who had been prominent in Scandinavia, both native and American, on tour through the settlements encouraging their fellows. "Traveling patriarch" Ola N. Liljenquist, former mission presidents like W. W. Cluff, Jesse N. Smith, John Van Cott, and apostle Erastus Snow himself kept in touch with their one-time converts, often addressing them, if somewhat rustily, in their own tongue.[33] Chief patriarch John Smith, who had filled a mission to Scandinavia in the 1860s, was frequently on circuit, and kept busy as an interpreter. Christian D. Fjeldsted, a foundryman in Denmark and known for his amusing anecdotes, was called in 1872 to take up a labor with the Scandinavians in northern Utah and was constantly on the move among them.[34] In 1884 he was elevated to the Council of Seventy, next ranking body to the Council of Twelve, to which the Danish photographer Anthon H. Lund and after him the Norwegian chemist John A. Widtsoe were named, giving the Scandinavians strategic representation in the leading quorums of the church to continue the pastoral concern for the immigrants that for so many years was Mormonism's preoccupation, inseparable from its program of colonization. It was an effort, in N. Christian Edlefson's phrase, to keep them "Saints" and not merely "Mormons"; the former, he said, built up Zion; the latter only themselves.[35] And it was a demonstration of how completely the Scandinavians had become part of the Kingdom.

All the solicitude was a sign that getting started was difficult at best and not without its casualties. The private journals, once crowded with the experiences of conversion in the Old World, dwell on the events of the first day, the first season. Hans Jensen Hals, 25-year-old farmer, camping on Union Square in October 1854 with nearly six hundred Scandinavians, rejoiced in the ox the townspeople had provided for company meat. The next day, after hearing Brigham Young and the Twelve preach in the Old Tabernacle, he "chose to go to Sanpete Valley," where in Manti he looked up Niels P. Domgaard from his native village in Denmark who had arrived the year before with the Forsgren company. "I bought there a little house for 16 dollars in work and began to work for others to earn wheat. I got two bushels a day. Later got potatoes for part and earned well." Soon he could say "My property was well to do, with bed, work clothes, one ox and 2 cows. I built a little shed for the animals, cut hay and earned some provisions." Before long he was head of the Danish Field to regulate its fencing and ditching, a municipal councilor, county claim adjuster, a Seventy in the lay priesthood, captain of ten in the militia, and husband of three wives, building a "comfortable" house in which each of them "had it just the same towards the street, and I had a room for myself."[36]

Jens Jensen, sixteen, who arrived with a handcart company in 1857, remembered how kindly Bishop Taft of the Ninth Ward counseled his father's family, turning over to them a five-acre piece of land to cultivate and teaching them how to haul wood from the canyon with his ox team. The father on his first trial put the yoke on upside down.

Mother and sister gleaned wheat and turned part of their two-room cottage into a wheat bin. They lived the winter on bread and molasses and squash butter. Jens himself, who lived in the tiny place till he was twenty-five, hired out to Bishop Pettigrew, hauling logs on shares from City Creek Canyon to Brigham Young's sawmill, where Young once showed Jens how to unload his logs.

At length Jens could buy his own yoke of cattle and he felt himself "now a capitalist." He put his team willingly at the disposal of the bishop in 1862 for hauling emigrants from the frontier – losing one ox by it – and the next year himself drove a four-yoke team to the frontier, getting a taste of both the "ugly and testy dispositions of some emigrants" who were hard for the wagon captains to manage, and of the reckless indifference of some of the teamsters, excessive in their coarse jests. By 1865 he was a thriving enough teamster to have two yoke of cattle, a span of horses, and a building lot, and to have married Petrina Sorenson, a Danish pilot's daughter and recent immigrant. Petrina made their clothing, wove carpets from sheep's wool, and framed pictures cut from magazines to adorn their one-room house. Jens was sowing wheat on Brigham Young's "Forest Farm" one day when a neighbor shouted over the fence that he had been called on a mission. He let out his crops, sold his team, moved his young wife in with her parents, and departed, completing a cycle begun when missionaries had found his own parents in their Danish village and beginning a similar one for the converts he would find in his thirty-nine months abroad.[87]

Karen Nielsen Christensen, widowed on the plains when her husband Christian was shot to death in a hunting accident, was thrown on the mercy of a fellow Dane who owned half the family's ox-team outfit – the wagon was partitioned and she occupied the rear half. He treated her badly the rest of the journey until a fellow immigrant "pulled his whiskers some." But arrived in the Valley, the partner dumped the pregnant Karen, her two small children, and her few belongings out on the ground at the Eighth Ward Square, tied her old black and white one-horned cow to a trunk and "away went that robber of a widow and we never saw or heard of him anymore."

Blacksmith Johan Otterstrom, who had come to the city from Ephraim for iron, witnessed the little drama, unloaded his mule-drawn wagon, and headed back to Ephraim with the widow and her family instead. On the way they were trapped by heavy snow at Fountain Green, where the townspeople put them up in the log schoolhouse, provided them with wood and provisions, and looked after the old cow. In a few days Niels Clemmensen came to the rescue with oxen and barrow and delivered them in Ephraim's "Old Fort," where they took up quarters in one of the many cellars measuring some 14 by 14 feet, 8 feet deep, with a two-foot wall around the edge and two small window-lights in the south wall and a chimney in the north dugout wall. They had bread made of half-grown wheat – "Growing seasons were very short in early days" – and potatoes "cooked in many ways and dipped in salt." The birth of a calf in the spring made the family "extremely happy." Karen had given birth to a girl in December, making three orphans, but in February she married the good Samaritan Niels Clemmensen and moved into a small adobe house on the city lot. By this marriage she would have four children only to lose them all and another child within twenty-one days of "putrid sore throat" in the fall of 1868, when diphtheria took the lives of seventeen children in Ephraim. "We were also encumbered with the Black Hawk Indian War," a son remembered. "It was terrible from 1865 till 1872."[38]

John Nielsen's childhood recollections were less grim: as an eight-year-old in 1866, he and his sister of sixteen peddled for cash or trade their father's baskets about the neighborhood in Big Cottonwood, where an Old Country friend had given him a start. When all the neighbors were supplied the children would occasionally walk to Camp Douglas, some eight miles away, and from there to Salt Lake City, three miles more, and home again in one day, more than a twenty-mile circuit. "I imagine that I can still feel how tired that I would get in carrying what to me was an unduly heavy load." They were afraid to go into the more pretentious buildings in Salt Lake – Brigham Young might live there.

When the family moved to Bear River City ("I can't see why they called it a city, for it just consisted of a few log houses built together in a fort . . .") John remembered one day how the residents came back from the driving of the Golden Spike at Promontory, waving their hats and shouting "Hurrah for the railroad." John's father had helped build the Weber Canyon stretch of it, and now it meant a measure of prosperity, for the railroad town of Corinne near Bear River City bought the settlers' wood, butter and eggs, and wild hay for cash.

And there were times when Bear River was gay, dancing in the light of a sagebrush fire to the music of a Dane and his three-stringed violin. And when Niels Nielsen organized a Boys' Meeting in 1869 "It was not long until the girls made themselves at home there, and we sure had some good meetings." Beneath this gaiety it was all the more heartbreaking for the settlers to discover one day that their land was being ruined, alkalied by the waters of the Malad River which had seemed at first their life. In the general exodus from what had been a hopeful Scandinavian settlement, the Nielsens went back to Big Cottonwood, worse off than when they had left it three years before.[39]

In 1861, shoemaker Peder Nielsen, pleased that Erastus Snow himself had visited the immigrant camp, remembered the many friends who met them. With his wife and son he went home with J. Svendson, "who received us very well," for a first day's visit, returning that night to their wagon to sleep. Peder had "many offers to go to people" but he decided to stay in Salt Lake for the time being, though there was a shortage of houses. He found one near Brother Svendson's store, bought some leather from Erastus Snow, and by the fifth day after his arrival was at work at his shoemaker trade to find it went "pretty good according to the circumstances," for he had not worked at it for the eight years he had served his mission in Scandinavia. He stayed the winter in the city, attending meetings in the Bowery on Temple Square, calling on Brigham Young with Erastus Snow, enjoying a dance "for the first time among the Danes in Zion," and marrying as his plural wife Hulda Larsen, whom he had converted in Scandinavia and who had traveled to Zion with his family.

In the spring of 1862 he went to Weber Valley to work for Bishop C. S. Peterson, who soon appointed him his counselor. When he found his cow dead one morning, it seemed to him Lucifer was trying him most severely, all the more so when the man who had lent him money for emigration demanded his wagon as part payment and would not be persuaded to wait till fall, though his creditor already had a good wagon. But Peder yielded, feeling it better to be wronged than to do wrong, and managed to pay $15 on his debt besides. So great were the demands of making a living in the new settlement that Peder noted with alarm some of the people were even working "temporally" on Sunday.[40]

Martin P. Kuhre, no matter how hard-pressed, was never so profane.

Regularly every seventh day he wrote the one word "Sabbath" in his diary, bringing brief respite to otherwise endless labors:

We dug potatoes up for Bro. Sorensen. . . . I bought a city lot for my steer. . . . I sold 16 panes of glass and got a lamb. . . . I chopped wood for cooper Hansen. . . . I am at David Thompson's working with the threshing machine. . . . We clipped our sheep. . . . I planted trees. . . . I made a chicken house. . . . I plowed for Peter Anderson while he fixed my wheel. . . . I loaned my wagon to the city. . . . I was with old Ole in the Denmark woods to bring posts. . . . I planted melons and made a pig pen. . . . Jens Andersen assisted me in making adobes. . . . I fixed the floor joists. . . . I laid up the uprights and filled in. . . . I commenced to cut on Bro. Hansen's hay lot. . . . I butchered for Andrew Thompson. . . . I bound wheat for Niels Petersen. . . . Whitewashed the room in the new house.[41]

The entries, so laconic and matter-of-fact, compress a whole history, like Hans Christensen's long labors as he moved, with numerous reversals, from indigence toward security.[42]

A farmhand twenty-two years old when he arrived with a church wagon train in 1862, Hans went north twenty-five miles to Kaysville, where his brother had rented a blacksmith shop from Bishop Christopher Layton. His first concern was to pay the church the $50 he owed it for his plains transportation. His next was to go down to Pleasant Grove at Christmas time to "Sister Poulsen's from Weibye," who had traveled in the same emigrant company, to marry one of her daughters. The girl had been ill crossing the plains and lost her hair, "which didn't improve her looks any" but she was "a true Latter-day Saint." Packing her earthly possessions in a bushel basket they hitched a ride to Salt Lake City with a neighbor and put up at her uncle's, Jens Weibye the tailor, hoping to find a way to Morgan County to make their home somewhere on the Weber. "I went up in town every day for a week or more, looking for a chance to go, but found none. It must be remembered that we did not own a cent. All we had in the world was our clothes, with the exception of a small frying pan which my wife's mother had given her, to start housekeeping with."

At the Tithing Yard one day Hans heard of a man from Morgan with a load of wood. "I hunted him up and told him our situation. He said that he had no other wagon but a pair of running gears, but if we could hang on to them we were welcome to go with him." They took the chance because, although they were welcome at Uncle Jens', "they had also just arrived in the country and consequently was not extra well provided." They tied their basket to the running gears and clung on, walking a good deal to keep warm, for it was winter with snow on the ground. They spent the first night with Old Country friends in Farmington. The next day they made their way up Weber Canyon and arrived at the settlement of Milton late at night. "And thus ended our wedding trip."

They stayed with Lars Peter, the blacksmith brother, Hans working in the shop the rest of the winter, the wife boarding about with other people to lighten the burden. Hans bought a town lot, but had no means to build. He hired out to a Swede, L. P. Edholm, who was to pay him a yoke of oxen and a pair of pants for four months' work. "Nearly everybody in the place were poor, the place had just been settled and most of the settlers was emigrants."

At the end of the four months Hans had his yoke of oxen, but nothing to feed them. He worked another month to get feed for the winter. Now he had feed and cattle, but no wagon. He hired one for labor and went into the canyon after logs, dug a cellar, covered it with willows and dirt, and moved into it the last of October. "Although my wife had been raised in a good home, she was very thankful for this, although it was indeed a poor excuse for a home, but it was our own." Their furniture consisted of a bedstead made from poles, a small clothes box which also served as a table, a borrowed skillet, one or two three-legged stools. His wife, who soon gave birth here to "a fine boy," could get "a little spinning or knitting" from some of the neighbors with "a little piece of meat, a bit of butter, or a little milk" in pay. Themselves taken care of, "in the spirit of a true danishman, I went to work and fixed a comfortable shelter for my Oxen."

In mid-winter Hans took the chance to haul four thousand shingles down to Farmington for $2 a thousand. He hired a cart, built a rack for it, shod his oxen, and loaded the shingles, making his way through three and four feet of snow, crossing the half-frozen Weber River several times. It was very cold "but we were sadly in need of the few dollars to be gained." Halfway down the icy canyon the cart slipped over the bank of the dugway, dragging the oxen after it, and tipped over. Hans managed to get the oxen loose, but stood helpless before the upside-down cart and the shingles tied down with chains which he could neither loosen or break. He had no choice but to go back for help. He reached home by midnight and the next day with his brother and a neighbor returned to the wreck, uprighted it, and at length reached Farmington twenty miles away without further trouble and received his pay. "That was the first cash I earned in Utah, and it was dearly paid for."

In the spring of 1864 he rented a small farm, his half share of the crop amounting to seventy-five bushels of wheat and the same of oats. Wheat was high that fall with the opening of the mines to the north. In Salt Lake attending the annual church conference, he sold it for $8 a bushel in merchandise which enabled him to buy "a few necessities." What grain he used he threshed with a flail on the frozen ground. Some of it he donated to the Weber Canyon road project: "Means was wanted for the purpose, and promises of great profits, and sometimes almost threats of perdition was used to obtain it, so after some persuasion I turned over fifty bushels of my small crop of oats to help it along, which cut us very short of means for another year."

The next year he rented the same farm, added a little more, bought an old wagon in Salt Lake, paying for it with grain, and on the way home bought a cow for five bushels of wheat and ten bushels of potatoes. Up to that time he had been renting the cow "Sister Kjer" had brought from Florence, Nebraska, paying her in butter yearly. "I only mention these instances to show how we had to struggle with poverty, in order to make us a home, and in all these privations my wife bore a noble part, always industrious, and understood how to make the most out of little."

In the summer of 1865, and for seven years thereafter, the grasshoppers destroyed most of the crops. Hans, like so many other desperate farmers, worked for the railroad, finding the pay good but provisions and horse feed high. By 1870 "I was getting tired of these grasshopper wars . . . and concluded to try my luck somewhere else. . . . My crop was gone, there was nothing to lose." In 1873, after a brief trial in Huntsville in Ogden Valley, where he had been offered a farm cheap, he took his family of five south to Sevier Valley, neighbor to Sanpete, now that the Indian wars were over, living in C. Poulsen's barn until he got out logs to build house and stable. He planted a small crop, "enough to bread us for the season." The new home seemed promising, permanent, and he celebrated the occasion by traveling to the First District Court in Provo to get his naturalization papers.

The next year the Saints in Richfield, as in all the settlements, were instructed by the church to form a United Order,[43] "to join their temporal interests together, elect from among their number their most experienced and suitable men to direct their affairs, and by a united and disinterested action . . . prevent class distinction from growing up . . . on account of some accumulating wealth, while others were kept in poverty." To Hans "this proposition came like a trial."

I had labored hard to get a comfortable Home for my Family, and was now in a fair way to accomplish this. I had House and Lot in town, a Farm consisting of twenty-five acres of good farming and Hay land, a good team and necessary farming Implements, and a few Head of cattle, and I felt that I was well capable of running my own affairs as anyone else. After the meeting was closed I felt a spirit of despondency take possesion of me to some extent. I went home, talked it over with my wife, we prayed about it, talked about it, and came to the conclusion that we had embraced the Gospel, and gathered with the Saints, not for the sake of obtaining Wealth, but to obtain salvation, and we also understood that the only sure way to obtain that, was by yielding cheerful obedience to the requirements of the Lord, through his appointed and authorized servants. We joined the Order, subscribed to its rules, and labored in it faithfully and cheerfully four years, until it was dissolved, according to the council of the Priesthood, which took place in the winter of 1878.

In the spring Hans found himself "again in possession of my Farm . . . and I made a start again on my own hook." His family was growing larger – he had married another wife two years before and rented a place for her to live until he bought her a house and lot on the outskirts of town; but the loss of the three youngest children, who died of the croup, was "a hard trial, especially to their mothers."

In rapid succession Hans, now an established citizen of Richfield, head of a family of fifteen, was appointed clerk of the First Ward, a High Priest in the Sevier Stake and member of its High Council, a home missionary, a member of the board of directors of the Richfield Cooperative Institution, and school trustee for the district. In 1884 he was called to serve a mission in Scandinavia and given only a few days to get ready, but he "set about to raise the necessary means." He found himself somewhat in debt because in his effort to keep his growing sons "around home as much as possible. . . . away from mining camps and other places of loose morals," he had bought more land for them to work; and he was in the middle of building additions to his homes. It was not easy to sell property for cash; besides, six other elders from Richfield had been called on missions at the same time and were also trying to sell their property like Hans. He sold his young livestock and managed to dispose of his shares in the cooperative and fifteen acres of farming land at a "considerable sacrifice." Friends and neighbors contributed fifty dollars and saw him off for Scandinavia.

Ill health cut his mission down to nine months and he returned, only to face arrest and imprisonment as a polygamist in the crusade that turned Utah into a vast underground. But his prison term gave him the leisure "more than have [has] ever been the case during my life before" to write his memoirs in the small, red, stiff-backed notebook that became a cherished family possession, with its humble yet proud preface: "I have conceived the idea of writing down a short sketch of my own life, thinking, that although not of much importance to anyone else it may be of some interest to my children or their descendants at some future time. Being serving a sentence of imprisonment in the Utah Penitentiary for the serious crime of having treated my wives, as wives, against the peace and dignity of the Laws of the United States. . . ."

The Hans Christensens, the Martin Kuhres, the Peder Nielsens, and the Jens Jensens built the Kingdom. More than numbers and endurance, they brought to it Old Country skills which often spelled the difference in a community between want and prosperity. They had much to learn in the new environment, but they had much to give. It was the parable of the talents, each turning his ability to good account. In unexpected ways their hands benefited the community. Sanpete Scandinavians might be accused of going to bed with the pigs and the chickens, but nowhere were the animals better housed in winter or the stock better cared for, and the butter improved as a result. A Yankee might raise flax for linseed oil and not know what to do with the straw, but his Danish neighbor, a flaxman, could construct a simple instrument for shredding and preparing it for the loom. A midwife, graduate of Copenhagen's Royal Hospital, lived out her days in tiny Elsinore and Pleasant Grove, serving the surrounding settlements in her calling and achieving a wider influence through her "Letters to the Young Women of Zion" on hygiene and her sorely needed classes in obstetrics, though she felt it necessary to excuse "my poor language" because "I was fifty years before I started to speak the first English word" and "My heart has been filled with sorrow and grief, too, much of the time, and checked my interest."

In a country where building materials were scarce, the thatched roof and the half-timbered house of the Skane countryside were welcome importations, and the blue doors and bright-colored trim of the houses and the woven willow fences surrounding the yards also became characteristic of the New World communities. A Danish farmer began Utah's first dairy cooperative, rounding up four hundred cows from his fellow townsmen in Brigham City to pasture and tend them on shares. A Swedish choir leader and monument worker cut the drinking fountain for Temple Square, the capstone for the Brigham Young monument, and the onyx casket in which the *Book of Mormon* was presented to King Oscar II. A Norwegian soil chemist, witness as an immigrant boy to the life-and-death struggle of his people to conquer the arid West, fittingly became one of the foremost irrigation and dry-farming experts in the United States. And the state's land-grant college was from the beginning heavily staffed by Scandinavians and their offspring seeking ways to conserve the land their fathers had dearly bought.[44]

Although nearly everyone, regardless of his former occupation, had to turn to farming at first, the town system made it possible for some to follow familiar trades. Skilled workers were usually at a premium: "Of artisans, masons surpass all others," wrote Christian Nielsen from Manti in 1856; "they earn three dollars a day, but agriculture is more important."[45] Logan, with a population of 1400 by 1874, had a business directory in which, among the Scandinavians, were listed a sewing machine agent, four blacksmiths, two boot and shoemakers, two cabinet makers, a druggist, two doctors, a furniture dealer, a pearl barley miller, a planing mill owner, a ropemaker, a tailor, and a "general dealer."

Salt Lake City at about the same time boasted a Scandinavian compositor, blacksmith, clerk, sawyer, hairdresser, plasterer, weaver, tinsmith, photographer, potter, wood turner, gunsmith, watchmaker, stonemason, painter, miller, cabinetmaker, machinist, wagonmaker, clerk, upholsterer, artist, logger, physician and surgeon, glovemaker, jeweler, moulder, carpenter, bricklayer, shoemaker, and tailor.[46] Advertisements in *Biküben*, the Danish paper founded in 1876, and *Svenska Härolden*, serving the Swedes by 1885, suggest it was possible for the Scandinavians to have every need from midwife to undertaker attended to by countrymen or by firms where at least one employee spoke the old tongue. *Vi taler Dansk og Norsk, Vi säga Svensk* ran like a refrain through the announcements. Imposing temples in Logan, St. George, and Manti, built during the 1870s and 1880s, provided employment for many Scandinavian craftsmen, as did the temple in Salt Lake City itself, which was forty years in building, the greatest of the church "public works."

In the early years the church maintained a works program in the city both to help the immigrants themselves and to benefit from immigrant skill in building projects like the Council House, the old Tabernacle, the Social Hall, the Endowment House, the Bath House, the Tithing Store, the Beehive House and the Lion House (Brigham Young's residences), and the Church Office during the 1850s; the Salt Lake Theater and the new Tabernacle in the 1860s; the Assembly Hall in the 1870s, with the Salt Lake Temple under construction until 1893. At one time or another Temple Square operated carpenter, paint, stonecutting, blacksmith, and machine shops, a lime kiln and an adobe yard nearby, a foundry, a pottery, and sugar, paper, nail, button, and bucket factories.[47] "I work on the Tabernacle," wrote carriage maker Christoffer J. Kempe to Denmark in 1865; "my wages are 5 dollars so that in 2 days I can earn all we need in a whole week and in 14 days I can provide for the whole winter. But," he could not refrain from adding, "the good times which we enjoy here have brought not a few Gentiles into the valley who would enrich themselves at the expense of the people."[48]

Purely "to keep the English and Danes at work," and to set a good example for the other settlements, Brigham Young ordered six miles of stone wall erected around Salt Lake City in the winter of 1853–54. Other more functional walls went up around the Deseret University lands, and Temple Square.[49] Public hands, incidentally, were honored as "Zion's Workmen," who marched as a group in parades and processions under their own banner and were honored several times a year at special picnics and balls. The construction of the Salt Lake Theater in 1861–62, where Scandinavian dramatic companies would later perform, was a church project, made possible by the sale of surplus materials when federal troops evacuated and by the use of European skills. In August 1861, for example, sixteen stonemasons, eight stonecutters, sixteen diggers, three millwrights, and fifteen carpenters were at work on the building.[50] The Dane C. C. A. Christensen and the Norwegian

Dan Weggeland helped decorate it and paint its scenery, as they did the temples, giving them the best days in lives usually denied artistic expression.[51] Scandinavian laborers and craftsmen from the country were often called on missions of from a few months to sometimes several years to work on the temples, the local priesthood fraternity supporting them with cash and produce.[52]

Though Salt Lake City with its shade trees and gardens and running water in the streets seemed only a Mormon village on a larger scale, and rural enough in 1870 for many of its residents still to be listed as farmers, it was a thriving commercial mart: it was the great reception center of the converts from Europe, the thoroughfare since the days of the forty-niners of immigrants on their way to California, the wintering place for miners, the rendezvous of the soldiers from nearby army camps, and the great gathering place of the Saints at general conference time come to hear the prophets, to visit with each other, and to see what the latest merchant trains had brought in from the East.

With a population of 25,000 by 1869, and about to boom with the railroad at its gates, Salt Lake City seemed cosmopolitan and tempted new arrivals to remain, sometimes to their social and economic detriment. "Our young sisters" employed as domestic servants in the city gave some concern: they were abusing the freedom and equality which they enjoyed "in America, in Utah in particular." Treated as members of the family, they ate at the table "with their superiors" and were permitted to visit friends and attend meetings. "But that seems to be too much for the one-time enslaved, oppressed servant. She becomes a 'high-hat' and at length believes that an employer has no right to put some limits on his servants. . . . Our Scandinavian sisters adopt the world's frivolous morals and customs. Their wages won't stretch to buy all they desire, so they seek employment in hotels, saloons, and boardinghouses." It was the open door to destruction. "Do not forget, sisters, for what you came to Zion. . . . Avoid the world's taint and fashion's corruption." Salvation lay in finding employment with a "good and faithful family" until they could establish their own homes.[53]

The flurry of railroad construction and the rise of business houses on East Temple Street (inevitably to become Main Street) and palatial residences of mining magnates along Brigham Street provided the newcomers with work for a while; but by 1873 the boom was over, a casualty of the countrywide financial panic, worsened by numbers of miners who had drifted in from shutdowns and turned to former occupations and by farm laborers "metamorphosed" overnight into craftsmen, as one newspaper complained, making it difficult for immigrants with bona fide skills to find work.

A Danish correspondent from Ephraim in 1874 noted the "hard times, unemployment, and little opportunity" in Salt Lake and recommended the advantages of the country: "In the past year only a small number of immigrating Scandinavians have come down to the southern settlements, although it is a good location and the prospects are good for both artisans and farmers."[54] Sevier Valley, 130 miles south of Salt Lake and neighbor to the "Little Denmark" of Sanpete Valley, was crying, "Come and use me, rejoice with me; I will feed and clothe you, work and earn for you; come soon and redeem me from my idle state!" Already seven settlements had a population of 427 families, "of which two thirds are Scandinavians. . . . All that is needed is a couple of hundred energetic people [in each place] not afraid of work."[55]

The *Deseret News*, church organ, complained in 1878 that "times have been dull here for a considerable period" and urged newcomers to "Get away as quickly as possible into the newly settled districts. . . . Never mind about inexperience of country life. You can learn as others have done." It was "very pleasant to settle in a place like Salt Lake City, with its varied attractions and the opportunities it affords of instructions from the general authorities of the Church," but people would have to make up their minds to live there "from hand to mouth for some time to come." If they pushed out into the country, however, they could win independence. "Harvest is approaching, hands will be wanted to gather it in; with the gathering of the crops come demands for improvements of various kinds which furnish work for the mechanic as well as the common laborer, and notwithstanding the change in our affairs in this Territory, it will be found that those who scatter abroad into the growing villages and towns of Utah, will have no need to complain like the stickers. . . ."[56]

The theme was the same six years later in a *Morgenstjernen* editorial which found many newly arrived Scandinavians without work in the city. They were encouraged to "spread out," to establish farms in areas still not claimed. "Don't be afraid of the country, even though your whole life has been spent in Europe's cities."[57] Jacob Christensen of Deseret, seconding the motion, said his town, though having irrigation troubles, could at that moment use a smith, a shoemaker, a mason "and other artisans."[58] Country fears were minor but real: an inexperienced arrival like Hermina Thuesen was given a chicken for dinner but she had to take it to Norwegian friend Anna Kempe to be shown what to do with it. Carl Madsen, a carriage maker, on his arrival in 1881 went home with Bishop Barton to Kaysville: "The next morning I was handed a bucket and directed to go to the barn. I caught the idea I was to milk the cows, a thing I had never done before."[59]

Such correspondence reflects the changing character of the immigration as well as of the local scene. The new arrivals were now principally urban, a large proportion laborers without the country knowledge of the first comers. It was no longer necessary to turn "willingly because one had to" to farming. Yet numbers did try their fortunes on the land, taking up homesteads under the more liberal provisions of the Desert Lands Act, for example, and came to know, like their forerunners, the life of the village that was after all most characteristic of Scandinavian experience in Utah.

As pioneers, whether early or late, Scandinavian Mormons differed little, perhaps, from their countrymen building homes in Dakota or Nebraska or Minnesota. But as yeomen developing Zion they were significantly different. Desperate private struggle and lifesaving cooperation were common enough on the American frontier, but on the Mormon frontier the idea of the Kingdom encouraged survival when lesser hopes failed, and the conditions of life "under the ditch" promoted cooperation not merely occasional like a house-raising or a harvesting bee but daily and endemic to the society. The history of Hyrum, typical of communities which Scandinavians helped to build "from the stump up," can be understood in no other terms. Their commitment to Zion's larger purposes was all that sustained the settlers through successive adversities – that and the inspiring leadership of Ola Nilsson Liljenquist, the Swedish tailor remembered as the one burgher in the Copenhagen congregation and mainstay of the Saints needing security for passage to Zion.[60]

In 1862, back from a mission to Scandinavia in charge of nearly 600 emigrants, Ola, at Brigham Young's urging, took some of them with him to northern Utah to pioneer new country. "Follow the high-water mark," Young told him; "never mind what is in your way." In mountain-ringed Cache Valley, once the rendezvous of fur traders, some Scandinavians under Yankee leadership had already founded Hyrum, named after the martyred patriarch brother of the Prophet Joseph Smith. It was little more than a rude fort crowding fifty-eight American, Scotch, English, and Scandinavian families together in close quarters. Dirt-floored log cabins with greased paper serving as windows faced each other across the enclosure. Fear of the Bannocks, often on the prowl for horses and food, kept the settlers living within the stockade and sent them armed each day to the outlying fields. But to Swedish eyes the valley was beautiful, and, with ample water for irrigation, and winds from the canyon to sweep the air clear of early frost, the place had possibilities.

Ola, well known to most of the settlers before he even arrived, was gladly received when in a few months he was named their bishop. As bishop, Ola was both spiritual pastor and temporal steward of his flock, for until Hyrum was formally incorporated as a town in 1870, the church was the only government. When he was also elected the town's first mayor, it was hard to tell where one office left off and the other began. The Sunday sermon dealt as often with potatoes as with prayer, for the practice of religion was a matter of everyday survival in a community where things big and little had to be shared – from irrigation water to a shovelful of hot ashes from a neighbor's fire on a cold morning, or a "start" of his homemade yeast.

Bishop Liljenquist's program for the settlement was both immediate and far-reaching: conciliate the Indians; extend the town beyond the confines of the fort; develop the resources of the surrounding country. Following a well-established Mormon pattern, he laid out a new site of ten-acre blocks, checkerboard fashion, with streets six rods wide, and reserved a central block as the public square. A town lot, twenty acres of outlying farm land, common grazing, a stake in the irrigation ditch, and timber from the hills were every resident's inheritance.

Dwellings were still humble, but not uncomfortable. Built of logs, they could usually boast a floor of rough boards, curtains at a solitary window, and a huge fireplace flanked by high-backed wooden settees which more than likely took up one end entirely; into its built-in side oven went the once-a-week baking. Pots swung on their hooks from a crane over the hearth. Candles, made by dipping cotton strings in hot, melted tallow, stood on the mantel. A spinning wheel, a dash churn, a hand loom, a big board table scrubbed clean every day, a corner cupboard holding all the family dishes, a box of wool in one corner and a box of linsey-woolsey from the loom in another – these were the furnishings, relieved perhaps by a string of dried apples or peaches hung along the wall. Each family had a dugout cellar for milk, vegetables, and meat, and each lot had its kitchen garden and at the rear a shed for the family cow.

Soon the *Deseret News*, pioneer newspaper in Salt Lake City, could report "the little settlement of Hyrum" as "flourishing . . . and all faithfully laboring to make their location a place delightful to the eye. . . . Bishop Liljenquist is making strenuous efforts to have good orchards planted out, in which the brethren are aiding him." But Hyrum also had "a large crop of free-sown grasshoppers."

The grasshoppers and the price of peace with the Indians, whom it was cheaper to feed than to fight, kept the settlers living from hand to mouth. It was a bishop's duty, as Ola discovered, to wait upon the Indians at their pleasure. Chief Pocatello and his begging tribe could usually be appeased with gifts of flour and beef. But the grasshoppers, like a biblical plague, descended season after season and ravaged everything. The settlers fought them with birch drags, drove them into heaps and gunny sack traps and burned them, into pits and buried them, into water and drowned them, and, under Bishop Liljenquist, planted a field in common to winter wheat which ripened before the summer scourge. Still things were so bad in 1867 and 1868 that men abandoned the land and went to work on the railroad then approaching Utah.

By 1873 it was apparent that the town badly needed new economic opportunity. Bishop-Mayor Liljenquist felt persuaded that salvation was to be found in their own backyard. For ten years he had been told it was next to impossible to open up Blacksmith's Fork Canyon: it was "national work," he was told, not to be undertaken by a handful of people, and besides, it "wouldn't pay." But in a series of town meetings he won support for his plan to build a toll road which would pick the lock to the grazing and timber regions he knew lay at the head of the canyon. The people formed a road company, subscribed 128 shares at $40 each, payable in labor, and in six months, by August 1873, with pick and shovel and axe, sweated their way through fourteen steep and tree-covered miles. There were times when they were discouraged and returned to their chores at home, but invariably Ola, as road superintendent, would come down from the mountain declaring he felt "strong as a lion and good for another week" and call for the drones to come out of the hive. Every able-bodied man and boy earned shares in the road with his labor, which were eventually redeemed in kind from the other cooperatives which soon followed.

Within a month, with Mayor Liljenquist its elected president and over half of Hyrum's families as shareholders, a steam sawmill company began operation in the stands of red and white pine the road made accessible. Out of it grew also a shingle and lath mill, a lumberyard, and a second sawmill, powered by water and specializing in railroad ties. Cash was scarce, but in exchange for labor, the mills furnished material for houses, barns, and fences in town to take the place of dugouts and old sheds and willow fences. They did more than that. They gave Hyrum a marketable commodity, and people could pay their taxes and afford luxuries like factory-made shoes and a newspaper. Hyrum's prosperity soon doubled its population.

Well before spring of the next year, the town organized a dairy cooperative; through a subscription of 351 shares at $5 each, eighty-eight families – nearly all of Hyrum – scraped enough cash together to send east for dairy machinery. In the newly opened herd grounds twenty-one miles from town they built cellars and houses for making butter and cheese and sheds for the herd. They advertised for cows to be "rented" during the summer, the owners to receive half the cheese each cow produced. People all over the valley responded, and sent their animals to Hyrum's summer pasture.

It was the beginning of an annual ritual; the big pole corral east of town became the scene of great excitement spring and fall, times when for the young people especially life was at high tide. It was like the Old Country's migration *til säters*, to the mountain pastures. Girls from town stayed the summer to do the milking and their singing could be heard of an evening far down the canyon. The boys did the chores, made deliveries and carried back supplies.

Butter and cheese were not the only products of the summer pasture: it was the scene of matchmaking, the place where Niels Hartvigsen fell in love with Lula Brown, and Robert MacFarland courted Christina Jenson. Young Hyrum crossed international borders and chose themselves life partners. And Bishop Liljenquist, smiling, was not sure which was the greater profit for the town.

At higher altitudes the sheep of still another town cooperative ranged under Rasmus Larsen's care. Surplus mutton found its way to the cooperative slaughter pen, and wool to a central wool-carding machine. Hyrum eventually became the state's wool-shipping center and breeding grounds for fine strains of sheep.

A general store in town, dealing in everything from thread to horse collars, had already been operating as a cooperative since 1869. Hyrum's enterprises might properly have read: "The people of Hyrum, proprietors and workers, producers and consumers." In 1875 all the cooperatives – the store, the road, the mills, the dairy, the sheep herd – were combined into "The United Order of Hyrum" with a board of directors made up of names like Allen, Christianson, McBride, Williams, and Petersen under the former Swedish tailor as president. Everyone in town who had held stock in one or the other enterprise now found himself holding stock in all. But the conversion seemed natural. It breathed the spirit of Ola's philosophy: "Any cooperative movement that takes the people along on the high road to prosperity and makes them feel that they are acting their part in the great missionary labors committed to them from on high has a right to be welcomed and supported by all."

In 1881, when Hyrum's population had grown to 1400, mostly Scandinavians, the *Deseret News* saw moral as well as economic benefits deriving from this home industry. It gave work to surplus labor and to the youth of the town, and since cooperative employees were paid in "one third cash, one third merchandise, and one third material" and were thus "unable to spend their earnings abroad or to squander them in extravagance, they have used their means to beautify and build up the town." A townsman like Gustave Anderson embodied the spirit of the place. Swedish handcart pioneer of 1857 who came to Hyrum in 1866, he was known for his skill as a master stonemason and for his fastidious dress. He took great pride in his work and in his person. In neither could he ever excuse any carelessness. He was careful to make the well-tailored clothes brought from the Old Country last as long as possible. As soon as he came home from meeting, he would take off his Sunday best and required his family to do the same. Whenever the children walked with him to church, they had to walk either well behind or in front of him lest they kick dust on his polished boots. With walking cane, white shirt, and vest and gloves, he seemed the aristocrat. He set a standard for the town. He extended his desire for neatness and order into a public duty and built a snow plow which he drove himself to clear Hyrum's paths after a storm. With him it was not vanity but joy in fine things, a determination to bring refinement to a pioneer community. At church conference time he would lend the bishop his own best suit of broadcloth to be worn on the stand; he took pride in having his bishop as dignified as any of the visiting brethren.

The town knew other refinements: "Bishop Liljenquist is doing all in his power to encourage education and music. By his advice the Female Relief Society are about to purchase a library for the use of our schools." "H. Monson, esq." was teaching instrumental music; H. H. Peterson, vocal music, and "with success." Hyrum in the 1880s seemed too good to be true: "Everybody is busy, no loafers to be found in our streets; peace and good order prevail."

It was a far cry from the dark days of the 1860s when grasshoppers for seven years running had destroyed the crops and very nearly the confidence of the young community. The prosperity came from sound principles: the good bishop held that a union of interests promoted a union of the people; if one undertaking met with hard times, the others could carry it along like good Samaritans; and since practically every family in town had shares in the United Order, they would tend the welfare of the community as a mother her nursing child. "The brethren who organize a cooperative will endure almost every hardship that their offspring may live." And down the years the report was always, "We need not tell you that Bishop Liljenquist is alive to the interest of Hyrum, and he is sustained by the faith and good works of the people." One of his "natural laws" was the principle of free choice and mutual consent, which had to operate, he said, in cooperatives as in marriage. It was possible to tell a dissatisfied shareholder, "Our contract is for twenty-five years; at the end of that time you may call," or to say to a wife, "Our contract is for life and you must grin and bear it," but he preferred to mediate. As the husband of three wives he might have mused – and he could be humorous – that a polygamist had to learn cooperation.

Hyrum's good name endured. In 1928, a generation after Bishop Liljenquist's death, the American Farming Publishing Company of Chicago awarded "the cooperative city" a silver loving cup as the rural community "scoring highest in the state in contributing happiness, comfort, and well-being to its people."

Cooperation, formally expressed in Hyrum's enterprises, was ingrained in Scandinavian Mormon experience. Born of necessity, it took numerous forms, sometimes amounting to a ritual, like Ephraim's harvesting of the wild hay from the common meadow. No one was to cut hay until after midnight of July 25, the day after the annual holiday commemorating the arrival of the Mormon pioneers. The harvesters, each one eager to get to the best hay first, would attend a community dance until the stroke of twelve, when all would yoke up their oxen and shout them on to the hayfield. There each man, without assistance, cut a swath with a scythe around the hay he wanted, but he was not to encircle more than he could cut, singlehanded, in one day. Any left standing at the close of the day fell to any comer. After the first day there were no restrictions. Because the meadow lay equidistant from three settlements, intercommunity rights had to be established. One of the apostles decided which area should belong to each community. In time the hay lands, like the farm lands, were allotted to individuals in the three towns, each man receiving a frontage of three rods.[61]

The erection of Mt. Pleasant's fort wall in 1859 fell to four companies, each company divided into tens with their captains, and four general overseers, one for each side of the wall. The "first ten, north line" were English, Yankee, and Scotch. The "second ten, north line" were all Scandinavians under Andrew Madsen, captain, as were the "third ten, south line." All other tens were mixed, but dominantly Scandinavian: 69 out of the 117 who built the wall, the names familiar as those appearing only recently on the passenger manifests of emigrant vessels where they had first learned to work together under "captains of ten" in shipboard affairs. The wall, 26 by 26 rods, 12 feet high, 4 feet thick, tapering to two at the top, was completed in eighteen and a half days, with each man's labor scrupulously recorded for his own time and "team time" and "wagon time" if he had used them. Boys were credited with half a man's time.[62]

Ditches, like walls, were cooperative. Bear River, where Scandinavians began as a "cellar city," in 1868 dug an irrigation canal from the Malad River to the "Big Field" with shovels, wooden plows, and the "Mormon scraper" – the old tongue scraper. The raising of the flag at seven one morning was the community signal that the water was ready to be turned in, and every man assembled at the center of the fort. Under Presiding Elder Niels Nielsen, with shovel and spade over their shoulders and knapsacks on their backs, they marched like soldiers to the field to dig the network of irrigation ditches that had been surveyed. They did not know they were letting an enemy into their gates: the alkali waters of the Malad in a few years would render their land worthless and send them away dejected to try again elsewhere, while some in desperation stayed to turn their plows into the sagebrush, plant grain, and to their surprise obtain a fair yield, thereby introducing the practice of dry farming into the valley.[63]

Meanwhile, looking to a future they believed in, they ran a cooperative farm of four survey sections where most of the young people in the community sooner or later served a valuable apprenticeship, their wages fifty cents to a dollar a day, paid partly in tithing scrip and partly in cooperative store coupons. The community bought a bull to improve their herds and in a unique insurance program agreed to contribute toward reimbursing any man who lost livestock on the range.

As a community they signed a contract with the railroad to put the men to work during the winter of 1868–69. They agreed among themselves to share the pay equally, except a few who objected to the partnership and demanded a daily wage. Presiding Elder Nielsen obliged them with another contract. When the work was finished and the settlement made, the laborers on shares averaged $10 a day while the day laborers received only $5. They were dissatisfied, but Nielsen maintained that a bargain was a bargain. The controversy rose to such a pitch that only a town meeting could decide the question. When the settlement was still in favor of the cooperators, the dissatisfied heckled the chairman from their seats: "Give us a Yankee, give us a Yankee for Bishop." Perhaps with this episode in mind, stake authorities sent William Neeley the following year to take over as presiding elder, with Lars C. Christensen and Frederick Sorensen as counselors. Not every Scandinavian had Bishop Liljenquist's gift for conciliating his own countrymen. Yet Lars Johnson, a later bishop of Bear River, served so well for fifteen years the congregation was unwilling to accept his release when it came. In three quarters of a century, Bear River had only one bishop who was not Scandinavian.[64]

Sending wagons to the advancing railroad terminals in Nebraska and Wyoming after dependent immigrants during the 1860s was another form of cooperation born of necessity and brotherhood. Every settlement provided a quota of teams, and the Scandinavians, remembering the assistance they had themselves received, ungrudgingly donated manpower and equipment in answer to the annual call: "Pres. Coats urged us to assist the Bishop and respond to every call and more especially how to assist in raising Quota of teams for the Emigration of the poor and all who spoke urged and in their feelings seemed to respond to this call believing it to be Dictated by the Holy Spirit." [65] "December 1, 1861, selected to go east the following spring to gather the poor: Peter Frederiksen, Hans Poulsen, Soren Rasmussen, Niels Waldemarson." Six wagons, twenty-six yoke of cattle, six teamsters, and one horseman, "well equipped for a long journey" accordingly left on April 16, to return on October 5 "with a number of emigrants who desired to locate at Mt. Pleasant." When the teamsters came back from the frontier in 1866 with survivors of the "cholera train," Mt. Pleasant took in fifty-three orphans who were "distributed among the Saints in the city who applied for them." [66]

Another community task incumbent upon the villager, the citizen of his country as much as the Kingdom, was militia duty, particularly urgent during Indian dangers. Sanpete's veterans of the Schleswig-Holstein war formed the Silver Grays. Mt. Pleasant held a party in August 1865, "in honor of the boys who had just returned from their hard and dangerous expedition to Green River in pursuit of Indians," an escapade in the Black Hawk conflict. The following day the "standing army" left equipped for an Indian campaign, taking up temporary stations in the hay fields to be ready in a moment's notice "and at the same time have an opportunity of cutting their hay." [67] Mendon in Cache Valley held its three days' muster in Logan Island in September 1869: "As usual a good time was had and much appreciated. There was some of the brethren who was careless and did not turn out to those drills, but it was as much a duty to muster the drill and have guns and ammunition as it was to attend Meetings and pay Tithing or attend to any other duty." The whole valley worked out a system of flag signals: white meant danger, red actual hostilities. The liberty pole was removed from the public square in Logan to the bench some ninety feet higher, where it could be seen by most of the valley settlements. More distant places were warned by courier.[68]

An informal cooperative activity born not of danger but of equally pressing economic need was freighting produce from village farms to "the City" – which was of course Salt Lake City – or to the more profitable mining camps. Money was scarce and needed for taxes, "wedding stakes," and emergencies. "There was a whole summer in which I did not see a dollar in money," remembered John Dorius of Ephraim; "consequently every man with a good team and wagon tried to do a little freighting to the mines."[69] Teen-age boys turned teamsters, many sons of immigrants buying farm land from the original pioneers with money earned in this way. Sanpete, rich in grain and dairy products but poor in cash, developed a thriving trade with both Salt Lake City and the mines. Farmers brought their surplus products to the cooperative store in Ephraim or to Peter Christensen's place in Manti, where the freighters loaded up for the market. Because butter came in from Scandinavian farms in all sizes and grades, it was dumped into a large mixing vat where girls worked it together into one color and flavor, molded it into one-pound squares, and packed it in thick wooden boxes. It kept cool in the bottom of the wagon underneath sacks of flour in turn covered with grain. Eggs were packed in oats, 125 dozen eggs to a box.

The journey to market was slow and hazardous – ten days' round trip to Salt Lake City, a month to southern Nevada, two weeks to Silver Reef or Frisco in southern Utah – but the pay from the mines was in gold, and welcome. Teamsters traveled together for protection against highwaymen. "We were paid $1.00 per hundred pounds to Frisco and 75 cents to the other camps regardless of distance. Those were the happy days of freighting!"[70] In Salt Lake City the butter was sold on market-row, where retailers were glad to get Sanpete's product. On one trip John Dorius, who took turns with three other Scandinavians from Ephraim in marketing the cooperative's produce, had five hundred pounds of butter to dispose of but found that its price had dropped below what he had paid for it at home. He retailed it himself and made his profit. Besides butter and grain from the farms, the freighters took woolen goods the women knitted – sweaters, sox, and comforters – which sold well at the mines, a windfall slight but significant to many Scandinavian families.[71]

In an unusual home industry requiring the attention of the whole family, Christine Forsgren of Brigham City made 130 yards of silk during the 1880s, using a loom her weaver husband, Peter Forsgren – Mormonism's first convert in Scandinavia – made for her. They produced the eggs, raised the worms, spun and colored the silk, and wove it, all at home. Besides underwear, satin vesting, neckties, and other dress goods, she made herself a "genuine silk dress," which won considerable fame throughout the territory.[72]

In every village, as the years passed – and frontier conditions along with them – times got better, bringing more material comforts but also more debts, and a decline in the distinctive features of Mormon cooperation. "Credit was largely indulged in, not by everyone but by the greater part of the people who allowed themselves to be entrapped," lamented George Sorensen, Mendon's recorder, in 1891.

> What book agents failed to lay before the people to induce them to either give their note or promise, the farm implement agent would not be slow to make up, and what he left, the organ dealer would supply and carriage and buggy agents carts, spring wagons and too many other articles to be here made mention of to say nothing of the merchant who of them all dealt the heaviest blow, where heretofore men had been reluctant to go into debt 5–10–15 dollars, they would many of them go into hundreds in this one branch of family and farm necessities, or thought to be necessities.[73]

His indictment was reminiscent of President Thurber's warning in Sevier Stake in 1876: "Counseled the Saints not to patronize doctors, lawyers, or sewing machine agents, remarking that he would rather die than have a doctor kill him, and considered it a ruinous policy to have too much machinery." [74] "Drummers are here in swarms," cried the Ephraim *Enterprise* on June 8, 1892. And it noted regretfully that ". . . boys and girls raised on farms are not content to remain at home and work. . . . So they drift to the cities; a few of them succeed, the masses fail, and not a few go straight to moral and physical ruin." [75] It was a jeremiad for the Mormon village.

A dedication reminiscent of early days returned in 1893 when "the main topic was for all church members to be reconciled" as "the Great Temple in Salt Lake City" neared completion. Congregations met "to forgive and be forgiven. . . . many good times was witnessed in many places." [76] There was a sense of a history closed a few years later, at the great pioneer jubilee of 1897, when Mendon's heaviest donation was $106 to the Brigham Young Monument Fund, the monument presiding over Main Street in Salt Lake City, looking out over a commonwealth in which the Scandinavians had had so intimate a part.

It was precisely their complete identification with the Kingdom, their ready absorption into a predetermined program, that was distinctive about Scandinavian settlement in Utah. The immigrants were "Pagtens Folk," a covenant people, and their Old Testament imagery led many of them even beyond the common forms of cooperation endemic in Mormon society and into practices as extreme as consecration, the United Order, and polygamy. Abraham could claim them as his own.

CHAPTER 9

Seed of Abraham

"INCREASE WILL MARK YOUR WAY . . . WIVES & SONS & DAUGHTERS . . . THE FAT OF THE HILLS, AND THE FLOWR OF THE VALLEY WILL ALL MINISTER TO YOU HORSES & CATTLE TOGETHER WITH RICHES OF HEAVEN & EARTH."[1]

WE SHALL be called to account for every blessing we receive," Erastus Snow told the quarterly conference of the Sanpete Stake in 1878. With their own Canute Peterson presiding, the Scandinavians, who formed a large part of the audience, heard the apostle with respect. He had first brought them the gospel in the Old Country and now it was always good to hear him talk about the affairs of the Kingdom in his regular visitations. His advice, as usual, was practical: some of the brethren thought there were not births enough reported, but he thought there were not marriages enough; the young men should take the daughters of Israel as wives, and not wait until some scalawag ran off with them. The Seventies should wake up to their duties and when called, not let the first thought be to send an excuse. He wished the sisters to keep at the business of silk raising until the brethren woke up to the importance of the enterprise. And the Saints should not let cooperative institutions flag, or build up opposition establishments in their midst. Apostle Orson Hyde followed with advice to swarm out and open up settlements in other localities because their numbers were rapidly increasing and the supply of water was limited.[2]

The concerns were familiar, and out of them would come new calls, with every call another test of faithfulness. The Scandinavians remembered Orson Hyde's bluntness at an earlier conference: in the Father's house were many mansions – there was the parlor, the kitchen, the back kitchen, and then again the outhouse. If they wanted the highest glory, they had better obey *all* the commandments, from ceasing to curse their teams in the canyons to taking more wives that "those Spirits that were never in the flesh might be tried to find out if they were worthy of an inheritance among the sons and daughters of God." [3] The Mormon village was a state of mind framed by the Old Testament, with daily affairs constantly seen in the light of eternity.

The minutes of the High Priests' Quorum in Mt. Pleasant, one of the congregations in the Sanpete conference, mirror that state of mind. The ranking body of the lay priesthood, the quorum from 1859 to 1915 consisted of 97 Scandinavians out of a membership of 160. Of these, 69 came from Denmark, 23 from Sweden, 6 from Norway, 10 from England, 1 from France, 2 from Canada, 6 from Switzerland, 3 from Germany, and 24 from the United States – New York, Pennsylvania, Missouri, Illinois, Iowa, Indiana, and Utah. In 1883, of 48 current members, 30 were Scandinavian.[4] Mt. Pleasant Ward, seat of the quorum, had a Yankee bishop in William S. Seeley, with Scandinavians Peter Jorgen Jensen and Jacob Christensen as his counselors, and eventually a Danish bishop in Christian N. Lund.

The High Priests were a body sufficiently mixed so that discussions were often bilingual, with interpretation from Danish to English, English to Danish, particularly on important matters "so that the Brethren would know wot the [they] vas woting on." A Scandinavian member was often glad "he could speak a little English so that his brethren could discern his spirit and feelings." "The Danish Brethren was incorage to expres ther feelings in ther own Language if the [they] var unable to speak in english" was a common notation, written, as the phonetic spelling suggests, by an immigrant secretary. Svend Larsen, former skipper of *Zions Löve*, which had plied between Scandinavian ports with the Mormon missionaries, received his appointment as clerk of the quorum in 1870 with humility, stating that "he was willing to do anything he could to sustain this Work & for the opbilding of the Kingdom of God but as he is a poor Speller in the English Language he felt to giv pleas [place] for a better educated man when such one should be at hand." [5]

The lay priesthood was a patriarchal town meeting in small, a democratic council of the Kingdom where the participants never thought to distinguish between their roles as Saints and citizens but easily discussed taxes and tithing together. Believing that the "Government of God as a theocracy was superior to democracy or any of the institutions of man,"[6] they nevertheless worked out their civic and religious problems by common consent – by motion, discussion, and vote – whether it was to put down card playing, to take an assignment to the "cotton mission," or to expel a member for sending his children to a gentile school. It was expected the outcome would always conform to the ideals of the Kingdom and uphold the hands of "those in authority" in whose inspiration they believed. The combination of local initiative and strong central direction was irresistible. Whoever was not content to exercise his influence always within the determined pattern, soon found himself numbered among the apostates. There was no room for a loyal opposition. Who was not for the Kingdom was against it. The archetype lay in heaven itself, which had cast out the rebel angels.

The very intimacy of the brotherhood, a source of strength, was also a cause of friction, and much energy went toward keeping harmony. The soul was frequently on trial in the quorum, where free expression, whether as criticism or confession, proved a powerful chastener, and sometimes the Abrahams cast out an Ishmael, or an Esau left his birthright. Jens C. Thomasen, back in the quorum after a long absence "caused by circumstance and not by dislove to the brethren," questioned Brigham Young's fitness to lead "this people." "The Priesthood," he said in Danish, "is one ting & the mand [man] that bear et is another. . . ." Which caused Brother Davidsen, translating, to exhort Brother Thomasen not to talk evil of the authority in the Kingdom of God. But Petter Pettersen Tybo was of Thomasen's mind; he had faced the Devil before and was not afraid of facing him again: "When President Young was a poor man, he was honest, but after he is getting rich he keks [kicks] up lick [like] a fat Horse & that he has not got his riches honestly." Tybo felt like helping to build the temple if he had anything to do it with, but he could not.

The quorum was glad to have the brethren speak their opinion freely, but it was the language of unbelievers and boded ill. Bishop Seeley, declaring it was their duty to pay their tithing without asking where it went, warned that the people were about to be purified.[7] Thomasen, in fact, left the church soon after to become one of the first elders in the Reverend James D. McMillan's newly established Presbyterian congregation.[8]

Jens Godfreysen, on the other hand, did not feel himself "too smart to take counsel." He "felt well this day in the Kingdom of God," though at times he confessed he had "more life in Denmark than he had now" and prayed night and morning to overcome the evil power, and if he had done wrong openly to be rebuked openly but if privately to be rebuked privately.[9] It was a common humility, expressing the intense striving of the brotherhood as they kept "uppermost in Mind day and Night to do right and Keep their Covenant sacred" that "the blessings of peace and union" might dwell among them. With the zeal of Puritan beadles they brought the whole life of the community under surveilance: Was there "a lying spirit" abroad? The brethren were exhorted to check it. Did Willis Petersen have trouble in his family? He called for help from the quorum, a plea Christian Hansen interpreted from the Danish. Did Brother Mills owe Father Riste $9.60? Brother Mills was refused fellowship in the quorum until the debt was paid, a dispute tried by the quorum presidency and the visiting teachers: "all in vain consequently those Brethren was disfellowdshipd from the Quorum ontil it was setlet between themselv," which was not until from June of one year to February of the next.[10]

Did Brother James Ivie assault and abuse Brother Alvin Strickland for punishing the Ivie child at school? Ivie was reprimanded and the schoolmaster relieved of his post. Did the incorrigible Father Ivie go after hay before the appointed time, standing against his brethren "with his eyes wide open"? He was dropped from the quorum until he improved his manners, only to get into trouble again for going to the canyon on the Sabbath day. Brother Yessen had to explain all these vagaries to his countrymen in Danish.[11] Did Brother Sanders in an "unwise prayer" curse the parties who had removed his fence unlawfully set on the sidewalk? He was forgiven by a special council on confession of his folly.[12] Did Brother John Young and his wife exhibit "un-Christianlike conduct and inhumanity unbecoming a Saint"? They were cut off, and bound over to the civil court on trial of cruelty to their child. Did Caleb Hartley race horses and gamble with the Indians? He was cut off and should he seek to return would have to pay $15 to the Perpetual Emigrating Fund as a fine.[13] Did anyone refuse to pay his proper tithing in kind, hoarding his grain for high prices instead of making it available to the Lord's storehouse or applying it to the Perpetual Emigrating Fund or the Missionary Fund or *Deseret News* indebtedness, he was "handled" for his fellowship.[14]

Did the City Council wish to alter the streets on the north side and encountered opposition from the south side? The quorum went on record urging the people to be careful of each other's feelings and to respect each other's rights. Did the Saints use tobacco? Brother Larsen spoke to an uneasy brotherhood in both Danish and English about the Word of Wisdom to give them "a good and clear understanding . . . of that principle." Did Brother Peter Andersen absent himself from quorum meetings? The teachers called on him to encourage him in his duties as an elder in Israel. Were the Saints drawn from the right track by the whiskey saloon, the dance hall, or the Presbyterian Church and its school? Let parents keep themselves and their children away from such places. Did Brother Lake refuse to take his children out of the Presbyterian school? He was disfellowshiped.[15]

Was there excitement about "the water question"? Let the teachers be warned that if there was bloodshed in the matter, they had not done their duty, the "sin of negelection" would rest upon them, an "instruction" Brother Davidsen took pains to interpret into Danish. Did the people trade with apostates and gentiles? They were called to account for the injury they were doing themselves. Was anyone tempted to capitulate to the Edmunds Bill, renouncing his plural wives? Congress itself could not ruin the Kingdom of God; the First Presidency had prayed that the Lord would frustrate the work of the bill, a prayer "answered immediately."[16]

The record was not all strenuous admonishment: "Bros. Assmussen, Miller, Widergren, Iversen and Jensen all spoke and felt well & thankful for the privilege of the gospel in their old age and decline of life."[17]

With equal energy, inspired by the same ideology of the Kingdom, which lent peculiar significance and relation to every activity small or great, the priesthood engaged in a variety of practical labors. They sent teams to the frontier for immigrant poor at the same time they sent Christian Widergren, Jeppe Iversen, Jorgen T. Sandberg, Andrew Jensen, Peter Iversen, Oka Sandberg, and Niels Widergren to the cotton district, Utah's Dixie, as "colonization missionaries." They provided a widow and her family with butter, wheat, flour, potatoes, wood, carrots, and molasses, the list of contributors as international as the membership. They subscribed their share of Mt. Pleasant's $4000 in labor tithing toward building the Spanish Fork Canyon road, with $1000 petitioned from the county to be added to a legislative appropriation for the same purpose. They held a caucus to elect a representative to the county convention to name delegates to the constitutional convention in Salt Lake City—a meeting embellished by "singing by the Danish brethren" and "full of instruction."

They contributed provisions to feed the Indians. They subscribed to a public building to be called the Social Hall, at $20 a share, to which not more than thirty-two couples would be invited at any one time by the head teachers in the respective wards, with one bushel of wheat the pay for the evening's entertainment, cripples and widows free, and no beer to be drunk in the hall. John L. Ivie and Rasmus Frandsen were named the committee for the house to act as floor managers, furnish music and candles, and supervise the cleaning.[18]

At one roll call the clerk marked the condition of every man's portion of fence "as to quality and quantity." The brethren took Brigham Young's advice to store enough grain for a two years' supply. They recommended the *Deseret News* to heads of families "as peculiarly the organ of the Church."[19] Every man over eighteen donated $10 in labor to build the new meetinghouse, under James Hansen and Nils Rosenlöf as contractors, only to have the work discontinued when Brigham Young saw it, with the walls partly up, saying it was too small. They sent John Ivie, Paul Stark, Peder Nielsen, C. P. Larsen, James C. Haubro, George Merrick, Bendt Hansen, Morten Rasmussen, Sören Jacobsen, and Hyrum Winters to settle the Muddy, and they donated $507.66 to support stonecutter Kresten Nilsen, a member of the quorum, called to labor in the quarry for the Salt Lake Temple.[20]

They appointed Erasmus J. Yorgensen, Morton Rasmussen, and Andrus Yonnsen to erect a Liberty Pole and took subscriptions to buy the national flag, a sign the Kingdom was after all American. Mt. Pleasant, in fact, following the fortunes of the Civil War in 1861, wished orders had been sent "for our teams to have freighted the Union out here, we could have preserved it so well in this salt country."[21] It was not uncommon for Bishop Seeley to counsel the brethren "who had not got their Citisenpaper to get it so as to vote in the August elecktion."[22]

Mt. Pleasant's dedication to the social, economic, and religious ideals of the Kingdom, with an occasional dissenter the price of union in a closed society, was typical of the Mormon community. Only in such an atmosphere could practices like cooperatives, consecration, the United Order, and polygamy be introduced.

The rise of cooperative stores in the late 1860s was a churchwide development, a move to preserve social unity as well as local resources. Threatened by the growing strength of the gentile merchants and jealous of the wealth they were taking out of the territory, Brigham Young in 1868 decided to make the people themselves their own merchants. Z.C.M.I., Zion's Cooperative Mercantile Institution, was founded as the parent wholesaler, with retail branches in the settlements. Independent Mormon merchants were given notice they were expected to close out their stocks and merge with the church cooperative, taking shares in it in return.[23] Supporting Z.C.M.I. became a new test of faithfulness. Trading with the gentiles was considered bad behavior. Fellowship depended on it. One thrifty Scandinavian woman in Bear River City, getting a better bargain in stoves in gentile Corinne nearby, was called publicly to repentance by her Scandinavian bishop, but she refused to make confession or to take back her buy and stalked out of the meetinghouse, not to return.[24]

Wherever Scandinavians were dominant, however, the cooperative merchandising idea seemed to flourish, expanding into a union of shareholding enterprises, as in Hyrum under Ola Nilsson Liljenquist, and in Brigham City, where by 1879 twenty-four of the sixty members of the United Order Council were Scandinavian, among them some of the very earliest immigrants, like the weaver Peter Forsgren and the iron founder Hans Peter Jensen. The council were "those most influential in the community, selected on account of their integrity, faithfulness, and willingness to labor and assist in promoting the cause of union and brotherhood."[25]

Brigham City's 1600 inhabitants, one third of them foreign-born, were spending three kinds of currency in their homemade prosperity: merchandise orders, as good as Greenbacks at the cooperative store; checks, good for home products, paid in one-sixth merchandise to the employees; and "Home D," called by the Scandinavians "Home D—d," good only when accompanied by one-fourth store order or cash, and then only in homemade goods. It was reported that "St. Clair, the lecturer" once took "Home D" for tickets, and some wags palmed off big bills on him, taking their change in cash; "but then it was a 'bilk' all round, so they were square, and the wags are happy."[26]

Down in Manti, Bishop Hans Jensen Hals noted in his diary on January 1, 1869, "We began our united business," and by the end of the year could report they had an inventory of $20,000 with shares standing at $10 which, within four months, had paid $4 interest. The little community of Mendon, "desirous of not being behind her sister settlements in the great work introduced for the benefit of all Saints," organized a store on April 1, 1869, capitalized at $900, took stock in nine months, and cleared 143 per cent. "We have turned our capital nine times, purchasing and paying for nearly $10,000 worth of goods," a business making possible purchase of "a first class Threshing Machine" which they used cooperatively to keep the toll grain once paid out to other settlements. ". . . and we intend to continue, and by the blessings of Israel's God, never to rest in the good work commenced, until factory after factory be reared, strengthened and consolidated in the great cooperative work." Two years later Mendon dedicated a new cooperative store during the same week the cars of the Utah Northern Railway ran into town for the first time, when the children were given a ride, all the road employees a banquet, and the town feted itself to a grand all-night ball.[27]

Zion's Cooperative Mercantile Institution was as much the Lord's as the temple. His all-seeing eye, universal in Mormon iconography, appeared over the portals of its headquarters and its branch stores. Anything bearing its mark was considered good. In a day when the drummer was suspect because usually a gentile, Z.C.M.I.'s salesmen enjoyed special favor. In Ephraim one festive night the Scandinavian bishop stalked onto the dance floor to cry, "Stop the music! Stop the music! They iss drummers in our midst." In the hush that followed he was seen to have a hurried conference with two strangers, only to emerge from it beaming, "It's all right; they iss drummers from Z.C.M.I.!"[28]

The cooperatives, with all their religious implications, were only a prelude to the more sweeping economic reforms attempted in 1874, when the hard times following the panic of 1873 complicated Utah's effort to remain economically self-sufficient despite the railroad and its influence. The United Order, primarily a shareholding union of home enterprises in Hyrum and Brigham City, initially envisioned a more far-reaching communitarianism – a return to the Order of Enoch, as it was sometimes called, when the purified Saints held all things in common. It was an ideal long cherished in Mormonism, going back to the days of Joseph Smith, for a time attempted and in one form known as "consecration and stewardship."[29] The middle 1850s had seen a consecration movement in Utah, part of the reformation of 1857, a major revival when the Saints at the approach of Johnston's Army were rebaptized and exhorted to dedicate their lives anew to the Lord. Scandinavians like Peder Rasmusson of Manti City, nourished as proselytes on ideal visions of Zion, readily deeded their property to the church, to receive it again as stewards.[30] It was an effort to stiffen Mormon resistance against the temptation to sell their land to outsiders, to provide, in fact, a legal instrument making it impossible. But consecration was only momentary, subsiding with the revival.

A great many converts, however, preferred its total commitment. Over a hundred Scandinavians in 1862, finding Zion not communitarian enough, followed Joseph Morris, a Welshman who founded a communal settlement on the Weber in anticipation of the imminent Second Coming, only to have it broken up by a dispute over the ownership of a wagon when a dissenter tried to reclaim it. The sheriff, called in to retrieve the property, declared war on the hapless Morrisites, shot the prophet down, and dispersed the colony. Some of the Scandinavian enthusiasts worked their way back to Denmark, to prove a thorn in the side of the orthodox missionaries.[31]

In 1874, with the United Order officially launched, the zealous could push cooperation to the limit, forming within regular congregations special fellowships in which their goods, their time, and their talents were pooled and placed at the absolute disposal of the local order. The United Order became yet another test of faithfulness, splitting some communities in two as some Saints joined, others did not. Members were baptized into it and sometimes went off to establish an ideal settlement of their own, like Orderville, more completely communitarian than any other, in which a number of Scandinavians participated, Goudy Hogan of early Sugar Creek fame, among them.[32] Zion's latest economic plan caused a tremendous stirring throughout Utah as the Saints debated its merits and the apostles traveled up and down promoting it.

In Salt Lake City on May 16, 1874, "At a meeting of the Scandinavians in the Seventies' Hall, they voted themselves into Enoch," but in the city the Order was hardly more than a paper organization and did not survive the month.[33] In Mt. Pleasant the priesthood argued it: Brother Fredriksen and M. Christensen said they were willing to join it and do what was requested because they understood it was the will of God, but Niels C. Nielsen said he couldn't see it in that light, though he would strive to obtain knowledge about it.[34]

By November 1874 Soren Jacobsen could write that as one of the United Order brethren his time was no longer his own. Artisans were working at their own trade as far as possible; each man was responsible still for his own plot, though they worked together during the summer in the canyons and in the fields; they harvested the hay and stacked it into two big stacks, one north and one south of town; and they established a storehouse where everyone in town could secure his necessities. They had a steam sawmill going in Cedar Creek Canyon and had to delay threshing a week while they built a road to it before the snow fell. It was "heavy work," and only "such a society" could undertake it. "We meet each morning at our different work places, where the best unity and understanding reign. All goes, on the whole, beyond all expectation. The Order is organized in all the towns of San Pete, but only Mt. Pleasant and North Bend have till now taken hold and begun work in it."[35]

Mendon was instructed in the United Order when Apostle Snow called a meeting of representatives from all the Cache Valley settlements. When Bishop Forster said Bishop Hughes was away on a mission and he didn't think Mendon could make a start until his return, Snow wanted to know if the Kingdom had to stop in Mendon because of that. "This saying," Isaac Sorensen recorded, "was enough as the people of Mendon was a law-abiding and obedient people."[36] About one third of the community joined the Order, consecrating their property in good faith, never thinking to own it again. Members of the Order went to work ploughing together, organized into companies of ten, with a superintendent over all work. It was a novel sight, Sorensen recalled, to witness from ten to twenty teams coming into town from their work at noon and night; each man attended to the watering of the farm he had turned over and he also kept his own cows, sheep, and horses for his family's use. They credited each day's work, and when the harvest was over and threshing done, they shared the produce according to the labor. "The man with twenty-five acres fared the same as the man with five acres, or the man with none at all."[37]

There was no loss of fellowship by those who did not join the Order, except that those in it thought those outside were perhaps weak in the faith. Yet Mendon could not help feeling it "a peculiar change . . .

with some in the Order and some out and all as members of the church." It was said often enough that the Order would break up, some declaring that when Bishop Hughes returned he would "break the Golden calf in pieces." Yet "the brethren worked with a will and all united, although it was soon evident that the time had not come for the establishment of the United Order," and when the bishop returned, he told the people of his dream: "The tide was not yet high enough to float the ship." [38]

Almost everywhere human failures forced the Orders to be abandoned after a season's trial. In Richfield, where Hans Christensen so painfully committed himself, the Order lasted longer – from 1874 to 1878 – than any other except the one in Orderville, though at the end it too, like the others, had to undergo a difficult redivision of property, when Hans lamented that most of his equipment, though now returned to him, was worn out.[39] The history of the Orders was brief but remarkable. And they left some remarkable documents in their articles of agreement, like those of the Oak Creek United Order on the edge of the Millard desert, where fifty of the one hundred fifteen signatories were Scandinavian, with the Danes Peter Anderson as treasurer and George Finlinson as appraiser and clerk. As the congregation heard Bishop Edward Partridge read the Preamble aloud at the organization meeting on Sunday morning, May 3, 1874, they must have felt the weight of his warning that they would have more need now of living their religion than they had ever had:

REALIZING by the spirit and signs of the times and from the results of our past experience the necessity of closer union and combination of our labors for the promotion of our common welfare and,
WHEREAS, we have learned of the struggle between capital and labor resulting in strikes of the workmen with their consequent distress and also the oppression of monied monopolies, and,
WHEREAS, there is a growing distrust and faithlessness among men in the political and business relations of life as well as a spirit for extravagant speculation over reaching the legitimate bounds of the credit system resulting in financial panics and bankruptcy paralyzing industry thereby making many of the necessities and conveniences of life precarious and uncertain, and,
WHEREAS, our past experience has proven that to be the friends of God we must become the friends and helpers of each other in a common bond of brotherhood, and,
WHEREAS, to accomplish such a desirable end and become truly pros-

perous we must be self-sustaining, encouraging home manufacture, producing cotton, wool and other raw materials, and not only supply our own wants with manufactured goods but also have some to spare for exportation and by these means create a fund for a sure basis upon which to do all our business, and,
WHEREAS, we believe that by proper classification of our labors and energies with a due regard to the laws of life and health we will not only increase in earthly possessions at a more rapid rate but will also have more leisure time to devote to the cultivation and training of our minds and those of our children in the arts and sciences, and,
WHEREAS, at the present time we rely too much upon foreign importation for a large share of our clothing and other necessaries, and also bring from abroad many articles of luxury and of but little value for which we pay our money, most of which articles could be dispensed with, and
WHEREAS, we believe that the beauty of our garments should be the workmanship of our own hands and that we should practice more diligently economy, temperance, frugality and the simple grandeur of manners that belong to the pure in heart, and,
WHEREAS, we are desirous of avoiding the difficulties and evils above alluded to and feel the necessity of becoming a self-sustaining community, fully realizing that we live in perilous times socially, morally, politically, and commercially
THEREFORE BE IT RESOLVED, That we the undersigned being residents of the places set opposite our respective names do hereby of our own free will and choice and without mental reservation or purpose of evasion and also without any undue influence constraint or coercion having been used by any party whatsoever to direct and guide us in this action mutually agree with the others and with our associates and successors to enter into and form a Copartnership.[40]

Though Oak Creek's experiment did not outlive the year, with the communitarian idea meanwhile dissolving into more workable joint-stock enterprises, it had been a searching apprenticeship in total cooperation and a grilling moral reformation when more than once the brethren had been asked to keep from grumbling and been told that "the man that will not do a day's work is a dishonest man and he will deny the work and go to hell." [41]

A form of cooperation peculiar to Mormon society was, of course, the plural household. Polygamous families, miniature communes, had to learn how to get along together. As doctrine, polygamy assured the Saints they were providing earthly homes among the righteous for pre-existent spirits who otherwise were condemned to be born into ungodly environments. A man's family here would be his in the world to come. If he desired eternal increase, a progeny as numerous as Abraham's with which, like God, he would one day people an earth of his own, he could make a realistic beginning in polygamy. The parable of the talents meant "plurality of wives," so Brother Davidsen of the Mt. Pleasant High Priests maintained, and though Brother Yessen stated this was not "according to his feeling," he was willing to be corrected when Brother Troscot said "it was just so important to obey that Prinsiple [*sic*] as to be baptized for the Remission of their Sins."[42]

The same zealous commitment which led Scandinavians to join the United Order led them into polygamy. But only some. "All do not strive equally for heavenly glory," President John Taylor told a Swedish journalist in 1883.[43] Hans Zobell's wife certainly did not. When Hans once broached the subject to her, he found at dinner time one day only two potted geraniums on the table, one young and full of swelling buds, the other a plant nearly bloomed out which had been about the house a long time. "Which of these will you keep?" she wanted to know. "Study them, take your time, then tell me what you decide." Hans understood and no second wife ever crossed the threshold. And young Knud Svendsen, just arrived in 1857, far from contemplating polygamy, would take not even one wife until he heard from Matte Pedersen, the sweetheart he left behind in Denmark, though he found his friends marrying all around him, urging him to follow suit, and insistent Ellen Kartrine even lent him a copy of *Celestiale Aegteskab*, a translation of Orson Pratt's persuasive defense of "celestial marriage."[44]

On the other hand, Jens Hansen's blessings outran those the Lord gave Father Jacob: his family numbered thirty-seven, but his house was a house of order. At dinner time a Danish editor in 1877 found him sitting at the head of the table, his eldest wife at his left followed by seven others in order of marriage. At his right sat his eldest son, other sons descending by age like steps to the youngest. The daughters sat at the foot of the table. "The enemies of polygamy," commented the editor, "have said that this system weakens the race," but, according to him, Patriarch Hansen seemed to refute the notion. Congress ought to do something to encourage others to follow the patriarch's example, he thought: give a man forty acres of land for every woman he married and ten acres for every child; and every man who reached his twenty-fifth birthday and was still unmarried ought to pay the government $250 and thereafter $100 annually as long as he remained single. What about the antibigamy enactment of 1862? Why, as soon as the law-makers sobered and became "unprejudiced by carpetbaggers and the kind of men who would gladly profit from their neighbor's possessions," that law would be annulled.[45]

Patriarch Hansen, one of Mormonism's earliest converts in Denmark, wearer of the cross Dannebrog for bravery in the war with Germany, and now leading citizen of Spanish Fork, increased his wives to fourteen before his death, an unchallenged distinction among his countrymen. He had lost his first wife in 1854 in crossing the plains. When his brother died in the same emigrant company, Jens had married the widow, honoring the Mosaic law to raise up seed to his brother; and shortly he married a Danish emigrant to raise his "own family."[46]

But most of the Scandinavian polygamists contented themselves with two wives, though Soren Jensen, Danish carpenter who joined the arches supporting the great Tabernacle in Salt Lake, had five, and James Joranson, Swedish bishop of Fountain Green, had six, and still managed two missions to Sweden. C. C. N. Dorius of Ephraim, a Danish farmer aged fifty, had five, one of them, Mary Williams, aged twenty, listed in the census schedule in 1880 with her father's family but with the notation: "Generally known and acknowledged as wife of C. C. N. Dorius, and living at his home."[47] Polygamy must have presented a problem to the census taker, who usually described the first wife's occupation as "Keeping House," and that of the remaining wives "Assists in House." Much-married elders like these gave the impression that the Scandinavians took to polygamy more readily than other converts. John Codman, who believed that chastity was a rare virtue in the Scandinavian countries, "from which the Mormon supply is derived," felt it needless to waste sympathy on the "poor female slaves of Utah" (the quotation marks are his). They preferred polygamy to "ordinary house servitude."[48] Commentators like Codman were deceived by polygamy's notoriety, unaware that while it played a prominent role as doctrine it was practiced only reluctantly and by a small minority. Mormon society was overwhelmingly monogamous.[49]

Scandinavian polygamists, too, were in the decided minority among their countrymen. Spanish Fork, where Jens Hansen maintained his patriarchal menage of eight wives, showed but four other Scandinavian polygamous households in 1870 as against eleven non-Scandinavian. Three of these had two wives each, and one had three. Scandinavian women shown as plural wives of Scandinavian males in the town numbered seventeen, and one as the wife of a non-Scandinavian.[50] In Ephraim, Utah's most exclusively Scandinavian community, where Dorius and his five wives lived, out of 240 Scandinavian heads of families in 1880, 24, or 10 per cent, were polygamous, involving 52 plural wives. By nationalities, of 181 Danish heads of families, 15 were polygamists, involving 33 Scandinavian women; of 34 Norwegian heads of families, 4 were polygamists, involving 8 Scandinavian women; of 25 Swedish heads of families, 5 were polygamists, involving 11 Scandinavian women. The average plural household had two wives. Polygamists of other nationalities in Ephraim were only three, and two of these had married Scandinavians. Fifteen families in the census schedule were headed by women who could be plural wives rather than widows.[51]

Of 722 men in W. H. Lever's *History of Sanpete and Emery Counties*, Scandinavian centers, 12.6 per cent were polygamists. Of 522 Scandinavian men in Esshom's *Pioneers and Prominent Men of Utah*, 147, or 29 per cent, were polygamists, involving 325 Scandinavian women and 40 non-Scandinavian women; besides, 101 Scandinavian women were married as plural wives to men of other nationalities. Most of these polygamists – 102 of them – each had two wives; 32 had 3 wives; 7 had 4, and 6 had 5 or more, the Scandinavians in numbers, as in age, following the typical pattern of polygamous unions. The list shows a higher percentage than the Ephraim census because it names leaders and prominent men, who set the example. Plural marriages were even higher among the Yankee leadership: 38 per cent of the 1220 American men named in Esshom; among the English, 28 per cent. The average for the foreign-born was 27 per cent, putting Scandinavian plural marriages slightly higher. Altogether some 15–20 per cent of the 6000 families noted in Esshom appear to have been polygamous.[52] It is suggestive that the ratio of women to men was higher among the foreign-born in Utah than among the native-born; that Sanpete County, so heavily Scandinavian, was the one county in the state with more women; and that Logan, strongly Scandinavian, to sample another class, was the one city of 2500 and over with more women.[53]

Another way to estimate the incidence of polygamy among the Scandinavians as compared with the rest of the Mormon membership, is to look at the arrests and convictions recorded during the years the national government pressed its prosecution of the antibigamy law. Of 462 convictions for polygamy in the Territory of Utah in the 1880s, 83, or 18 per cent, were Scandinavian.[54] There were more arrests than actual convictions for "unlawful cohabitation," the definition which finally enabled the courts to secure indictments. Ole L. Hansen appeared before Judge Charles S. Zane and an anti-Mormon jury on the charge of *ölagligt samlif* as *Nordstjernan* described it, only to be given his freedom – to everyone's amazement. *Nordstjernan* editorialized that it was "the official's high regard for Scandinavian integrity which let him free."[55] But by 1888 the Scandinavians were by no means being exempted – of 219 "co-habs" in the Utah Penitentiary that year 61, or 28 per cent, were Scandinavian.[56]

The prison record, so unusual for Scandinavians, was not a stigma but an honor. Mt. Pleasant turned out the brass band to welcome Bishop N. P. Madsen on his release on February 2, 1888, after "108 days' service under Warden Brown."[57] Speaking of the general situation, Isaac Sorensen noted in 1886 that "so many had went to prison that it seemed as if it had become more popular, and there was not so much excitement when a person was arrested. . . . A man would rather suffer than have his family brought before these courts to testify and often asked indecent questions. Yet to the praise of the Heroes they stood it in nearly all cases bravely, a few recanted, but their numbers were small."[58] The "co-habs" were "Prisoners for Conscience' Sake," as the Dane Andrew Jenson, himself one of them, called his manuscript compilation of "brethren and sisters" imprisoned in the Utah, Yuma, and Detroit penitentiaries from 1884 to 1892. Compiled from prison files and private journals, the 883 names include 216 (nearly one fourth) that are recognizably Scandinavian, memorializing the charge, the judge, the fine, and the prison sentence – withal a most curious Book of Martyrs.[59]

Mads Christensen, like so many of his fellows, kept an autograph album during his term in prison, a mirror of the sentiments which brought him there and sustained him during his weary months.[60] He began it on February 12, 1888:

> Go litle book thy distined course pursue,
> Colect memorials of the just and true,
> And call on evry frend, far of, or near,
> For a token of remembrans dear.

"You are confined for doing the works of Abraham," wrote William Willie of Mendon, "whom God by himself sware Saying, Surely blessing I will bless you, and multiplying I will multiply thee." And John L. Anderson spelled out as best he could, "in three Monts I am here fore I leved viht my own wifes, that is wad Edmons beall [Edmunds Bill] the spiys cexty maill [miles] from home the [they] brot me here, and loket me ope insid airon bars." Aaron Hardy of Moroni looked to the day

> When honest men can own their wives,
> And wives can love the men
> Who'er not afraid to honor them
> By going to the "Pen."

Mads renewed old friendships, encountering some of his original fellow emigrants and former missionary companions, like C. H. Monson, now of Richmond, and C. C. N. Dorius of Ephraim, who recalled the event in verse:

> Thirty years in Utah spent
> Since you and I with handcart went
> Together puled acros the plains
> Two hundred, remember not their names.
> The gospel cleansed us free from stain
> Obedience bro't us to this pen.

They formed a goodly fellowship, an elite, signing themselves "Yours in the Covenant." They were able later to write an absorbing chapter into their memoirs, even becoming the subjects of stories stranger than fiction, like Hans Sorensen of Sevier, whose disguises to elude the "federals" were so complete with pipe and beard and miner's togs that only the family dog recognized him.[61]

"The greatest trouble the people experienced," Mendon's Scandinavian recorder complained, "was the continual raid of the Marshals, some of them far from being Gentlemen, often insulting people where they made their visits." However, it was "a most singular yet pleasing fact to state, that in all these times of trouble and persecution . . . no rows of any kind occurred, there was an Overruling providence in it all notwithstanding the hatred of many of the Marshals." The hardest fact of all was that "The spotters generally were apostates, as also many of the Marshals."[62]

One or two of the Scandinavians became the center of momentous polygamy trials. In September 1888 Hans Nielson was tried and convicted on two counts on the same day for the same offense – one indictment under the Edmunds Act for unlawful cohabitation and one under the Edmunds-Tucker Act for adultery with his alleged plural wife. After serving his sentence for the first charge he was denied his petition of habeas corpus at his arrest on the second, and his case was taken to the Supreme Court of the United States, which understood it to be a test case and advanced it upon the calendar, arguing it within a month after Nielson's arrest. The Supreme Court ruled that multiplication of punishments was not the policy of the law. To proceed upon the principal of "segregation," which held a polygamist guilty of a new offense every time he stepped into his plural wife's house, would require centuries of time to discharge. Nielson's release freed several others convicted in like fashion.[63]

Hans Jesperson of Goshen, arrested a year later on the testimony of his second wife, who confessed under oath that she had come to Utah the previous November and married Jesperson in the Manti temple and later at the Endowment House in Salt Lake City, gave the church some embarrassment because President Wilford Woodruff had stated the church was refusing to give recommendations for plural marriages. It was "incredible," he said, and he was looking into the matter. It was prelude to his manifesto of 1890 which called on the church to obey the law of the land.[64]

Quite apart from celestial glory – though that was the theological heart of the matter which infused the "prisoners for conscience' sake" with a martyr spirit – polygamy worked some immediate and practical results. It sought to eliminate prostitution and adultery and to ensure every woman a worthy husband. Salvation was slim for an old maid or a woman married to a gentile. Better to have part of a good man than none at all, or than all of a bad one. Providing for the widow or spinster immigrant was a community obligation. It was a good bishop who saw that no woman went without a husband – even, so folklore had it, to offering to take her under his own roof. If the woman received no offer, it was not considered immodest for her to take the initiative. Hyrum's Swedish bishop sent Caroline Swensen to stonemason Gustave Anderson's to make her home, and she became his fourth wife. Hans Jensen Hals took his late neighbor's widow as his plural wife to give her a home and, like Jens Hansen, who married his brother's widow, to raise up seed to the departed.[65] A strong-minded woman like Anna Karine Widtsoe, widow of a Norwegian schoolmaster and immigrant to Cache Valley in 1883, resisted all advances, devoting herself instead to her two sons to bring one of them eventually to the presidency of a state university and the other to the chairmanship of its English department. And a woman like Hannah Sorensen, uprooted in a tragic separation from her family in Denmark, served out her days alone as a midwife in Sanpete, writing letters to the "daughters of Zion" on hygiene and conducting needed courses in obstetrics.[66]

It was not unusual for the fruitful wife of a polygamous household to give one of her children at birth to a barren wife of her husband. In May 1866 shoemaker Peder Nielsen recorded that his wife Hulda gave birth to another son; in September he noted with satisfaction that "Hulda gave him to my wife Marie that she might have him as her son, as if she herself had given birth to him. . . . This made Marie rejoice very much; may the Lord bless this act and all my family and everything under my care. . . ." Emma Anderson recalled that she was given to "Grandma Anderson," her father's first wife, by Maren Haroldson, the third wife, to be raised as her own.[67] The term "Aunt," by which the children in polygamous households knew the "other mothers," had special significance in Mormon communities.

With the divine purpose and the practical point of view eliminating romantic love, no situation proved too awkward to handle: Goudy Hogan courted one of Knud Nelson's girls when the family arrived in Bountiful in 1853 as part of the famous Forsgren company. He had his eye on Bergetta, the younger, but when they got ready to go to the Endowment House, Christiana, the eldest sister, persuaded Goudy to take her along as chaperone, and once there persuaded him to make her his wife too—and as the eldest she became the "first wife." Erastus Snow performed the double ceremony, in Danish, for the benefit of the new arrivals. Goudy later married a third sister, Anna.[68] Hans Christian Hansen, about to leave on a mission to Scandinavia, by chance encountered a new arrival at a friend's home in Salt Lake. The spirit whispered that Mary Jensen was to be his plural wife. How to get word to Hedvig the first wife miles away in Plain City? The spirit had told her too and she had been prompted to come to Salt Lake, where she herself attended the ceremony and escorted the new wife back home while Hans went off on his mission, the new wife, strong and capable, proving a godsend in the farm work.[69]

Polygamy made for an intimate cooperation uniting not only the family but the whole society with patriarchal bonds. Intermarriage was common and broke down ethnic barriers both among the Scandinavians themselves and between them and other nationalities. Some families were decidedly international. The Dane John T. Dorcheus married Danish, English, and Scotch wives to beget seventeen children. His Danish wife, incidentally, was 21 when he married her at 23; his English wife was 26 when he married her at 26; and his Scotch wife was 19 when he married her at 40, following the typical age pattern in polygamous unions. Englishman Alonzo L. Farnsworth married American, Danish, and Swedish wives. Twelve per cent of the wives of 147 Scandinavian polygamists listed in Esshom's *Pioneers and Prominent Men of Utah* were non-Scandinavian; besides, as already noted, 101 Scandinavian women were married as plural wives to men of other nationalities.[70]

Some of these women were married to leading churchmen, a sign of acceptance by the high priesthood that Scandinavian blood was considered worthy of begetting a celestial progeny, a practical demonstration of the doctrine that "God hath made of one blood all nations." The mayor of Salt Lake City, the commander of the state militia, several of the apostles and the first presidents of Seventy, and a counselor to Brigham Young all had Scandinavian plural wives. Erastus Snow married one of his early Swedish converts, Anna Beckstrom, after her emigration and the death of her husband. Snow kept her in Salt Lake City while he colonized southern Utah with his four other wives, who, family tradition says, would not accept the widow Beckstrom because she had pestered the apostle into marrying her.[71] John Van Cott, who had been to Scandinavia twice as mission president, married a Danish girl of seventeen. Heber C. Kimball, counselor to Brigham Young, married Norwegian sisters from the Fox River colony in Illinois. Mayor A. O. Smoot married Anna Mauritzen of Norway as his fifth wife, who became the mother of Reed Smoot, long-term apostle and United States senator from Utah. Apostle Lorenzo Snow, enterprising leader of Brigham City cooperatives, and one day to become president of the church, took to wife Minnie Jensen, daughter of iron founder Hans Peter Jensen, early stalwart from Aalborg, and his wife Sarah Josephine, who had translated the revelation on plural marriage when it reached Denmark in 1853.[72]

Brigham Young himself did not make a Scandinavian one of his twenty-seven wives, but his eldest son John W. married Christena Domske, who as Tena had gone to help in the home but soon became the fifth in a household of four other wives who were American and English.[73] Brigham Young did employ Scandinavian domestics, as did many others. Scandinavian girls showed up as early as the 1860 census as housekeepers and Scandinavian youths as laborers in over a score of Anglo-American households in Salt Lake City. Some of the young Scandinavians were undoubtedly orphans from the tragic handcart company of 1856, when the Saints threw open their homes to the survivors.[74]

Plural marriages were not promiscuous. They had to be contracted with permission of the first wife and approved by the president of the church, the ceremony performed by the priesthood in the Endowment House in Salt Lake City. "Dear Brother," Brigham Young wrote Bishop Seeley of Mt. Pleasant, "You are at liberty to baptize James Christensen, and if you can recommend him as a good man, he can have Anna Christine Jensen sealed to him."[75] Away on missions, husbands might find converts they wished to marry, but the ceremony could not take place until they returned, though sometimes in their impatience they made promises, and it proved a trial to the wife at home to discover that the husband had already made his selection. Anders Nielsen, who had left two wives at home, on his way down to Sanpete after his mission stopped in the Endowment House to marry two more, but one of his wives in Manti went out the back door as he came in, taking her children with her, not to return.[76]

Canute Peterson had better fortune. Already married to Sarah Ann Nelson, daughter of one of the famous Sloop Norwegians, he lived with the Rolfson family in Osterrisor on his mission to Norway and on their emigration in 1857 he married Gertrude Maria. When Charlotte Ekstrom, daughter of a Swedish stonemason Peterson had known in Christiania, emigrated in 1866 and stopped at the Peterson house in Lehi on her way to Provo, she was asked if she could weave, and she remained, the next year to become Canute's third wife. By Sarah Ann he had nine children, by Gertrude Maria six, and by Charlotte five. The Ephraim census of 1870 showed him 46 years of age, his wives 43,

40, and 21 respectively, with his real property valued at $7000 and his personal at $2500.[77]

Some hearts were broken. Maria Krause, separated from her family as a girl of eight and taken to America by the Madsens, who gave her a home, felt obligated to marry their son Peter, though she really loved someone else. The plural marriage proved unhappy. She had herself at length installed on a new homestead, to which she obtained the deed when her husband in a weak moment, beset by deputy marshals during the antipolgamy raids, thought to protect his property. When he had served his "co-hab" sentence he tried to retrieve the title, but Maria refused. Madsen made a trip to the farm to carry off the animals and equipment, but neighbors came to Maria's aid and drove him off at gunpoint. The bitterness did not dissolve even on his deathbed, when he refused to call for her. Maria, never denying the gospel, filled her days with good works, a familiar figure in the Mt. Pleasant countryside as she drove about in her buckboard gathering donations for the poor on behalf of the Relief Society.[78]

Peter Hansen of Hyrum noted with sorrow that against his will he had been brought to *saegn a Devors* (sign a divorce) for his third wife, Stine Marie, by whom he had three children, leaving him two wives and sixteen children.[79] For those who took their role as Abraham seriously it was a distinct loss.

Unremitting as the demands of the Kingdom seemed to be, the immigrants were not forever pitched in a sober key. There were times when, as Elder Christian Larsen urged, they gave up "the cares of the harvest and hay field."[80] In their own tongue they enjoyed a considerable life of the spirit, as indispensable to their well-being as their lands and increase and the water they had learned to bring down from the hills.

CHAPTER 10

Mother Tongue

"THEN DANISH SPEECH FALLS ON THE EAR,
THE SWEETEST SOUND A SOUL CAN HEAR."[1]

FOR the Mormon immigrant, the break with the Old World was a compound fracture, a break with the old church and with the old country, often with family and friends who disowned him and made him glad to leave the past behind. Besides, Europe was Babylon; Utah was Zion. The new church was an American church interested in unifying the brotherhood, not in perpetuating backward-glancing cultural differences. English was the Lord's favored language in which he had spoken his will in this last dispensation. The old tongue was tolerated only as an expedient mediator, a means of teaching the gospel and informing the immigrant of the affairs of the Kingdom in a language he could understand until he learned English.[2] In the many mixed marriages among the Scandinavians themselves, moreover, English often became the compromise speech. It is not surprising that in Utah the mother tongue died out quickly, a costly loss for the church itself, as it turned out, when it discovered that the second-generation Scandinavians sent abroad on missions had to take valuable time to learn the old language.[3] Elsewhere in the United States, in communities of Scandinavian and German Lutherans, for example, the church as part of the old Establishment performed an exactly opposite function: it strengthened ties with the homeland; it was a flame keeping warm the old language, the old faith, and the old customs through religious services and newspapers and denominational schools in the mother tongue.

Not that Zion belittled immigrant speech. The *Deseret News* scolded those who made fun of the foreign converts: "In time the Lord will restore a pure language, and then who will have reason to boast that he can talk an impure language better than his neighbor?"[4] Admittedly

English, whatever its divine favor, was difficult, as the unorthodox spelling of immigrant diaries testifies: "The Law pearseguasion was kap op," wrote Bishop Hans Jensen Hals of Manti, who had been in America thirty years, "and maney af the Leding man was arastet and put in the pennetancery for Coabetesion om Some Lef for Mexsico and Some for Uropa," by which he meant that "The law persecution was kept up and many of the leading men were arrested and put in the penitentiary for cohabitation and some left for Mexico and some for Europe."[5] On his forty-first birthday in 1868, after ten years in Zion, Knud Svendsen concluded the second volume of his daybook and bravely resolved to write the next in English and to pray more in English: "May God bless my efforts."[6] Most journals unconsciously moved from the old tongue to a bastard English, a rare and often humorous mixture of both languages, like Hals' "Jeg kjobtte en 6te Part i en Stem Saw Mill" when he talks "om Busnissin."[7]

Edward Anderson observed the same confusion in the oral speech: ". . . one may hear the various changes in Danish from North Jutland to Copenhagen, and listen to Norwegian as spoken in Christiania, Trondhjem and in the mixed-German Bergen, also to the worst Skane or southern Swedish, and to the best as spoken in Goteborg and Stockholm, or hear the different varieties of Swedish from Upsala to Ystad, and yet not hear anything quite like the mixture which is called Danish, Norwegian and Swedish in Utah."[8] Sanpete Valley in the early days boasted an even greater curiosity: The Scandinavians encountered Indians more often than they did Americans, Christian Nielsen of Manti said, and were learning Indian more readily than English.[9] Not unlikely some Indians learned to speak English with a Scandinavian accent!

The church sympathized with the immigrants in their language difficulties, and Brigham Young as governor of a territory getting ready to receive thousands of proselytes from abroad made spelling reform a matter of state. As early as 1853 he asked why, in an age of steam and science and the "dissemination of Letters and principles," the way could not be "paved for the easier acquisition of the English language, combining as it does, great extension, and varied expression, with beauty, simplicity, and power, and being unquestionably the most useful, and beautiful in the world?" He hoped the "correction of its orthography, upon some principle of having characters to represent the sounds which we use" would make it less abused, more easily acquired. "I am happy to learn that the Regency are deeply engaged in investigating this interesting subject. . . ."[10] The Board of Regents of the newly created University of Deseret had been assigned in October to work out a system and prepare a school book in the reformed spelling.

On January 19, 1854, the *Deseret News* announced the "New Alphabet," thirty-eight phonetic characters having a double advantage: "By this means, strangers cannot only acquire a knowledge of our language much more readily, but a practiced reporter can also report a strange tongue so that the strange language when spoken can be legible by one conversant with the tongue. . . ."[11] The church expected the Deseret Alphabet, as it was christened, to prove "highly beneficial in acquiring the English language to foreigners as well as the youth of our country. We recommend it to the favorable consideration of the people, and desire that all of our teachers and instructors will introduce it in their schools and to their classes."[12]

By the time *The Deseret First Book* appeared in 1868, however, after many delays in securing a satisfactory font of type, enthusiasm for the reform had almost died, and the books themselves finished it: the stiff and ugly alphabet was deadly. Though the Regents spent $20,000 in appropriations – an educational fortune for the times – to print 20,000 copies of first and second readers, 8000 copies of part of the *Book of Mormon*, and 500 copies of the whole work in the phonetic transcript, the experiment never caught on. Outsiders mistook the Deseret Alphabet for a cabalistic language, designed to put the immigrant more than ever at the mercy of the church. But its only damage was to give a few luckless students a lifelong spelling handicap. It was another ill-fated expression of the yearning for a more perfect society.[13]

The mother tongue itself proved a better instrument of adjustment than the artificial spelling reform. It was at least alive. "Dumb Swede" or "simple Dane" might have been folk images of the foreigner in Utah, but in their own language the "dumb Swede" and the "simple Dane" were articulate enough. The church was hospitable to their need to express themselves in the only way they could. The immigrants did not form autonomous congregations for worship in their own tongue; but for their instruction and welfare the church did foster a Scandinavian Meeting in every community large enough to support one, with presiding officers drawn from the three countries. It was strictly aux-

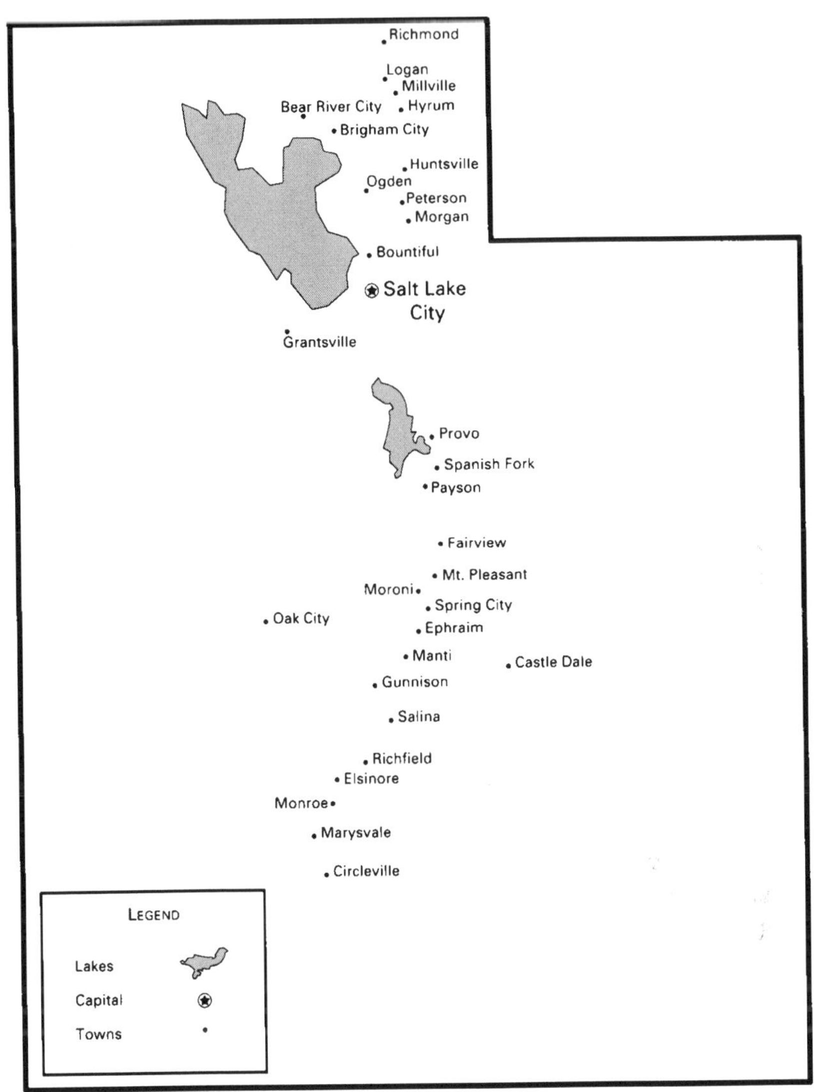

Map 3. Chief centers of Scandinavian settlement in Utah, 1852–1905.

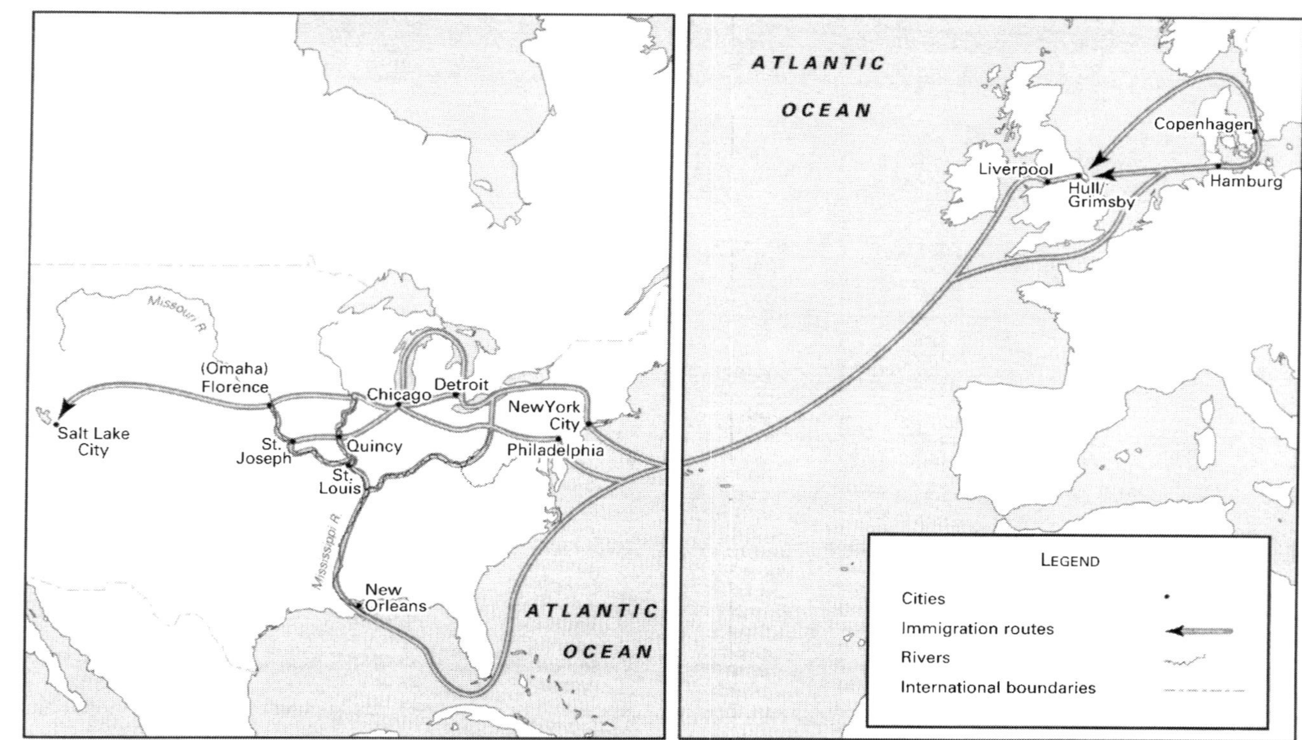

Map 4. Primary routes of LDS Scandinavian immigrants to Zion, 1852–69.

Figure 8. *Reunion of Scandinavian converts, June 15, 1900.* Scandinavian immigrants frequently held reunions. This photograph was taken at the Saltair Pavilion on the Great Salt Lake. Among those pictured are Anthon H. Lund (first row, second from right) and his wife Sarah Ann Peterson (first row, second from left), Anna Widtsoe (second row, third from left), and Andrew Jenson (third row from front, far right) and his wife Emma (second row from front, far right). Courtesy LDS Church Archives.

Figure 9. *Sarah "Sani" Ann Peterson Lund, 1909.* Sarah was the daughter of Canute Peterson of Norway. She married Anthon H. Lund, of Denmark, in Utah. Courtesy LDS Church Archives.

Figure 10. *Grave marker of Ola Nilsson Liljenquist, 1916.* Liljenquist, a Swedish convert-emigrant and a master tailor, stood passport security for hundreds of fellow members before emigrating himself in 1857. Brigham Young called Liljenquist to be a bishop on a colonizing mission to northern Utah, where he later organized a successful dairy cooperative in Cache County. Courtesy LDS Church Archives.

Figure 11. *Missionaries in the Scandinavian Mission, July 15, 1866.* The back row includes A. Paulsen, Jonas Johansen, John Larsen, Johan Andersen, Lars Hansen, and Peder Nielsen. The middle row includes Knud Haroldsen, Peter Nielsen, Peder Andersen, Anthon L. Skanchy, Ole Hansen, and Barre Jensen. The front row includes C. C. Falkmann, Svend Larsen, C. C. A. Christensen, N. Wilhelmsen, Frederick C. Andersen, and Tholl Samuelsen. C. C. A. Christensen became a well-known artist and poet in Utah. Courtesy LDS Church Archives.

Figure 12. *Hans A. Hansen house in Ephraim, Utah, ca. 1890.* Built of adobe and plastered with scoring to simulate evenly coursed ashlar stone masonry, the house is an example of vernacular architecture. In the central passageway, a circular staircase built of pine and finished to resemble oak illustrates expert carpentry. It is on the National Registry of Historic Places Inventory. Hansen was a farmer and, on occasion, freighted for Brigham Young. Courtesy Utah State Historical Society.

Skandinaviens Stjerne.

Organ for de Sidste Dages Hellige.

Sandheden, Kundskaben, Dyden og Troen ere forenede.

1. Aarg. Nr. 1. Den 1. October 1851. Priis: 24 ß Qvart.

Om Kirkens Organisation.

Udtaget af „Etoile du Deseret", udgivet i Paris af John Taylor, een af de tolv Apostler.

Man har ofte gjort os det Spørgsmaal siden vi ankom til Frankrig: Hvorledes er Eders Kirke organiseret? For at tilfredsstille dette Spørgsmaal, ville vi meddele følgende Underretning.

I det lille Skrift, som vi allerede have omtalt, have vi omtalt Kirkens Oprindelse, en Engels Sendelse til Joseph Smith, Opdagelsen og Oversættelsen af ældgamle Annaler. Vi have beskrevet Kirkens første Organisation, som er en Gjenindførelse af den oprindelige Christendom, dens Præstedømme, dens Lære, dens Anordninger, dens Gaver, dens Velsignelser, dens Kraft og Indsættelsen i forskjellige Betjeninger. Men vi ere endnu ikke komne til de enkelte Omstændigheder ved vor Kirkes særdeles Organisation, og hvad vi nu have isinde at gjøre.

Medens Joseph Smith levede var han Kirkens Præsident. Han havde antaget to Raadgivere, der bleve erkjendte af Kirken, hvilken altid har Stemme i alle Ting og Ret til at antage eller afslaae. Efter hans Død blev Brigham Young indsat til Præsident, paa Grund af hans Stilling som Præsident over de tolv Apostler, hvilke have ubetinget Myndighed efter Præsidenten. Han har to Raadsherrer, der ere udvalgte iblandt de Tolv (Heber C. Kimball og Willard Richards), der alle blive fremstillede for Folket og antaget af det. Præsidentskabet udøver Myndighed over alt hvad der staaer under Kirken.

Efter Præsidentskabet kommer de tolv Apostler, hvis Embede bestaaer i at prædike Evangeliet og at vaage over Kirkens Anliggender og hvad der bliver prædiket iblandt alle Folk. De have den samme Myndighed som udøves af Præsidentskabet i Zion, i alle de Verdensdele, hvor de opholde sig, hvor de Hellige forsamle sig, og disse ere under dette Præsidentskabs umiddelbare Styrelse. De ere kaldte ifølge Aabenbaring og anerkjendte af Folket. — De Tolv have en Præsident; for Tiden er det Orson Hyde der har erholdt denne Myndighed ifølge sin Alder og lange Tjeneste.

Der er en Embedsclasse ved Navn de Halvfjerdsindstyve, hvoraf der er tre og tredive «Quorum», hver paa halvfjerdsindstyve. Deres Forretning er at prædike Evangeliet eller at lade det blive prædiket over al Jorden. Der er en Præsident over hvert Quorum. Der er desuden en Forening af syv Præsidenter, som have en Præsident i deres Spidse, hvilke atter have Præsidiet over alle Præsidenterne i hvert Quorum iblandt de Halvfjerdsindstyve, og de staae alle under de Tolv.

Derpaa følge de Ældste, som ere meget talrige. Deres Bestilling er at prædike Evangeliet, hvor de opholde sig og efter Omstændighederne. Men det fordres ikke

Figure 13. Skandinaviens, *1851.* This LDS periodical, published in Denmark for Mormon converts, contained sermons, stories, and news from the Scandinavian settlements in Utah. *Skandinaviens* has had a continuous existence since its beginning in 1851. In 1877 a similar periodical, *Nordstjärnan,* began in Sweden. Courtesy Special Collections and Manuscripts, Harold B. Lee Library, Brigham Young University.

iliary to the regular congregation in which the Scandinavians found themselves worshiping side by side with their Yankee and English neighbors under a bishopric often of mixed nationality. The Scandinavian Meeting, or Organization as it was sometimes called, in turn sponsored choirs, amateur theatricals, and outings and reunions on Old World holidays and mission anniversaries, when life was at high tide for the newcomers. Such lay activities growing up around the church kept it the center of the immigrants' intellectual life and went a long way toward preserving church loyalties when they were threatened in the 1870s by the arrival of Presbyterian and Methodist mission schools which tried to make an appeal through services in Scandinavian.[14]

Whatever the church promoted was always inclusively Scandinavian, making no distinction among Danes, Swedes, and Norwegians – an ideal inherent in their new fellowship as Saints and a union paralleling the organization of the mission in Scandinavia itself, which until 1905 was administered as a single unit. In the face of history, which had seen the three countries often at odds, the church urged harmony. "I recognize no nationality," wrote Peter O. Thomassen in 1887, who, himself a Norwegian, had edited both Danish and Swedish periodicals in Salt Lake City. "He is my countryman who acts justly, whoever ennobles mankind. . . . We are all sprung from one Father, who in his wisdom has scattered us over the whole world. . . . Those who are called know his voice and gather from all nations to one place in order to do his will."[15] Scandinavian unity seemed so complete in 1890 that "the young people in Zion do not know there are three nations in Scandinavia."[16] The turn of the century, however, saw the idyl rudely disturbed when a Swedish editor attacked the "Skandinavisme" that was making mere "Swedish Scandinavians" out of his people, or worse, changing them into "Danish Scandinavians."[17]

Otto Rydman, talented and somewhat histrionic editor of *Utah Korrespondenten*, had little use for Scandinavian union, which he felt made for a bastard culture at best, and at worst a Danish imposition on the less numerous Swedes and Norwegians. The Danes, it seemed to him – and he echoed a widespread sentiment in Salt Lake City's rapidly growing Swedish colony – the Danes, with Anthon H. Lund in a powerful position as apostle and finally a counselor in the First Presidency of the church, governed the *nordiska falangen* as in Queen Margareta's time. In his paper, founded in 1890 at first to serve the church, only later to antagonize it, he stumped for unadulterated Swedish culture and called for separate Swedish meetings. He accused the church of starving the Swedes spiritually as the result of Danish supremacy in the Scandinavian Meeting.[18]

It was one thing to promote Swedish cultural autonomy in nonreligious activities, but quite another to advocate Swedish separatism within the church. Besides, Rydman's invective angered church authorities and they rebuked him. When in 1901 he tried to observe *Julottan* in a ward meetinghouse on Christmas morning – a service which in Mormon eyes was too reminiscent of Lutheranism – he found the doors closed against him.

He retaliated by vilifying the leaders of the Scandinavian Meeting and the editors of the rival and conservative *Utah Posten*, who had him tried before a church court and excommunicated for "publishing false and malicious cartoons and articles" and for "ridiculing and criticizing men holding official positions in the Church, thereby causing dissension and bitter feelings among the Swedish Saints." [19] But Rydman, an accomplished performer with Thalia, the Swedish dramatic society, and an engaging satirist in his column signed "Tomte" or Robin Goodfellow, was personally popular and eighteen hundred petitioners from all over the state protested his dismissal, appealed to the First Presidency for a rehearing, and endorsed his plea for a Swedish auxiliary within the church separate from the Scandinavian. When their petition was denied they staged a mass meeting, a dramatic episode in what the American papers called "The Swedish Uprising." [20]

After a silence of some months, during which it studied conditions in every place where Scandinavian meetings were held and determined the status of every petitioner, the church answered the malcontents in an epistle from the First Presidency: "To the Swedish Saints: Instructions in Regard to the Holding of Meetings, Amusements, Social Gatherings, etc." [21] Making it clear that the church court no more than a civil court was to be influenced by "popular clamor in mass meetings, or by protests, however numerously signed," and noting that hundreds of the petitioners had no standing in the church and that a number belonged to other nationalities and even other denominations who could hardly claim a right to be heard in matters of church discipline, the epistle reaffirmed an established policy: "The counsel of the Church to all Saints of foreign birth who come here is that they should learn to speak English as soon as possible, adopt the manners and customs of the American people, fit themselves to become good and loyal citizens of this country, and by their good works show that they are true and faithful Latter-day Saints." National antagonisms had been almost unknown in the stakes outside Salt Lake City. At the jubilee of the church in 1880 twenty-five different nationalities were represented, who "under the unifying force of the Gospel and the peaceful influence of the Holy Spirit, have blended together and become one."

Statistically the declaration punctured the insurrectionists' balloon. It could see no partiality shown to Danish or Norwegian Saints. The Scandinavian Meeting in Salt Lake City was actually presided over by a Swede, with a Dane and a Norwegian for counselors. Though the Swedes in Utah in 1900 numbered 14,180 as against 29,312 Danes and Norwegians, Swedish brethren had presided over the mission in Scandinavia more terms then Danes and Norwegians together. Moreover, Swedes held responsible positions in all the orders of the priesthood wherever they resided. "These brethren do not hold these positions because they are Swedes, but because they are men of God. . . . We consider the catering of politicians to nationalities wrong, and we do not believe in doing it in Church matters. Let the man of merit be placed in position of trust, whatsoever may be his nationality." The petitioners everywhere, said the epistle, when asked "Do you want separate Swedish meetings in your locality?" answered, with few exceptions, "We would rather continue to hold our meetings as we do at present; but if the Swedish Saints in Salt Lake City desire separate meetings, we think they ought to have the privilege."

The epistle reviewed the situation in the Salt Lake Stake, Rydman's home diocese: out of 521 names on the Salt Lake City petition, but 311 were members of the church, and most of these withdrew their names. The Swedish Saints there, it appeared, were not being neglected. Swedish home missionaries paid constant visits and conducted frequent cottage meetings. The Scandinavian Meeting, under the direction of a presidency in which all three nationalities were represented, regularly heard Swedish speakers and Swedish singing. Swedish gatherings were actually being held in the Fourteenth Ward twice a month. The joint social gatherings were always agreeable. Scandinavians the year before had contributed $4000 toward the meetinghouse in Copenhagen and for missionaries and various benevolent objects, without counting contributions for ward and general church purposes. Such liberality was a proof of harmony.

The official declaration advanced other telling arguments: a great many of the Scandinavians were intermarried; it would be absurd to separate husband and wife in meetings, social gatherings, excursions, and conferences. There was no objection to separate meetings where the numbers in each nationality justified them. But the Scandinavians did not have many talented speakers and could ill afford to divide their forces. And why should they deny themselves the privilege of listening to able speakers in other tongues? "The inconvenience of the difference in the languages is smaller than the inconveniences of that division which has been advocated by a few extremists." Eighty per cent of the signers of the petition, the epistle noted, could speak and understand English: let these attend the regular meetings in their own wards and leave the foreign-language meetings primarily for the aged and the recently arrived.

As to amusements and their conduct: the declaration reminded the Saints that the Scandinavian Meeting was a church auxiliary, and all auxiliaries were subject to the control of stake presidencies or bishops who should direct all public entertainment. Let Scandinavian committees consult with the proper authorities before planning beyond their jurisdiction.

"God is no respector of persons," the declaration concluded. "We deprecate the attempt to build walls of separation between Saints from different countries, and fanning into flame the dying embers of former national hatreds. . . . We warn the Saints against following the lead of men who with mistaken zeal are sowing seeds of discord and discontent, and are using national sentiment to make that an offence which was not so intended."

Rydman was not convinced. For another dozen years his paper remained a bitter and sarcastic voice decrying the evils of "Skandinavisme," only to be sold out at last, with its dwindled subscription list of three or four hundred, to *Utah Posten*, the rival he had once slandered.[22] Swedish Mormons in time came to celebrate their *Julottan* with church approval, but church-sponsored outings and reunions remained "Scandinavian," with proper care taken to see that each nationality was duly represented on the program. In 1905, when Norway and Sweden dissolved their political union, the mission in Scandinavia created a separate Norwegian Mission, the moves supporting separate auxiliary activity within the church in Utah.[23]

Long before Rydman's dramatic bid for Swedish meetings within the church, societies – literary, musical, mercantile, political – independent of the church were serving national interests, supplementing in a far less objectionable fashion the limited mother-tongue activities of the church and providing a welcome relief from its strenuous didacticism. Occasionally these societies tried to be inclusively Scandinavian, but secular union quickly fell apart. Salt Lake City attempted a literary Scandinavian Association in 1869 which "went along smoothly" for a time. Joint effort assembled a "right good library" and stocked a reading room with weekly periodicals from Copenhagen, Stockholm, and Christiania.[24] And during its short life it welcomed the great violinist Ole Bull and his company when they came to Salt Lake. But "it was soon evident that the foreign-minded elements could not work long in fellowship." It was an old story, lamented the editor of *Utah Posten*: "A lack of the spirit of unity is one of the Norseman's weak characteristics. . . . We acknowledge this truth with sorrow, especially as applied to our three brotherfolk. Every one of the three nationalities has its own particular objections to anything Scandinavian." The Norwegian "Norske Klub," following in the wake of the late Association, looked more promising.[25]

Altogether, whether inside the church or out, there was considerably more life of the spirit in the mother tongue than outsiders, imagining the Mormon immigrant ignorant and depraved, were aware. N. Bourkersson, who after three years had enough of the culturally arid West, headed one chapter in his book about the Mormons in 1867 "Arts and Sciences," but he left the page blank except for the quotation, "Out of nothing comes nothing."[26] He might have been one of the scoffers "Arbeidsbi," Worker Bee, had in mind when, describing Ephraim's homemade culture in 1876, he mocked, "Can any good come from Nazareth, or good butter from Sanpete?"[27] A great many of "our foremost towns" held low opinions of "us poor creatures in Sanpete," where it was supposed the cats and pigs licked the milk pans, the hens laid their eggs in bed, and the dust was mixed with the butter.

Arbeidsbi wished to turn loose *Bikūben*'s whole swarm on such ignorant impressions. To be sure, "since about two thirds of the total population in Sanpete is Danish, Swedish, or Norwegian, it naturally follows that many of our national peculiarities survive here—some good, others less good." But things were improving: "Even our social enjoyments are undergoing a thorough reform." Card playing, drinking, riotous feasting, fighting, and using tobacco were now rarities. Ephraim had built a little theater and the last winter had seen several dramatic productions and concerts "of an instructive character." A small company of Scandinavians had produced the Norwegian comedy *Til Saeters*. Most of the settlements had their local dramatic group or at least a good choir; several even had a brass band.

In Manti there was "a real doctor" whose counsel was to be followed in preference to "quacks, stargazers, and similar charlatans whom a few simple-minded people and superstitious families have visited in necessity." A wise Dane, Christensen by name, more generally called "Taenkeren," The Thinker, who for some years had played doctor, fortuneteller, and astrologer, had disappeared altogether, but another, called "The Little Witch," had taken his place. Arbeidsbi hoped that the Scandinavians would be ashamed of themselves for permitting such "miracle makers" to thrive in these enlightened times. "Information is certainly on the increase among us." [28] Ephraim's Polysophical Society in 1891, with its lectures on physiography, its sketches from Scandinavian history, and its songs and recitations in Scandinavian as regular fare, would have made him happy, though what would he have thought of the Ephraim Dramatic Company, an almost all-Scandinavian cast, performing an Irish play, *Shamrock and Rose*, in Peterson's Hall? [29]

Nearly every settlement could match Ephraim's zeal, though an artist like C. C. A. Christensen complained resignedly that poetry would have to wait at the moment, while hard work could not. He had to meet the demands of the practical present.[30] Neighboring Manti in 1871 had a brass band which played "lively melodies, in part Scandinavian." M. Pedersen's Scandinavian Choir in Provo, for which he transcribed all the music, and his evening class in English grammar gave him "little spare time." [31] The Scandinavian Choir in Salt Lake was considered in 1878 "the best we have had in many years." [32] In 1891 the city's Scandinavian Dramatic Club, which sometimes performed in the famous Salt Lake Theater, as did the Swedish society Thalia, gave fifteen performances in southern Utah, typical of its road-show activity for the benefit of countrymen in the settlements.[33] Danske Klub, another amateur group of actors, had done the same in the 1880s.

The 1890s saw a Scandinavian Mercantile Association and a Scandinavian Democratic Club. In the same decade the Swedes formed Norden Society, Svenska Gleeklubben, Harmonien, and Svea, and after the turn of the century those most estranged from the church joined less indigenous associations like Vasa Orden, just as the Danes formed lodges of the Danske Broderskap.[34] English classes, insurance brotherhoods, emigration fund societies, and sport clubs multiplied – altogether a rank growth representing a profusion of causes and interests. In their patriotic eagerness to celebrate Old World holidays, the national orders often ran competition with the church-sponsored organizations. Both Vasa Orden and the Swedish Mormons celebrated *Midsommarfest* at the same resort on the same afternoon, sharpening the rivalry. But seven hundred Scandinavians joined hands in Salt Lake City on New Year's Eve in 1901–2 in a ball, concert, and supper at Christensen's Hall when Governor Heber Wells addressed them.[35]

As immigration dwindled and the first generation disappeared, activities that were once necessities died off, or, perpetuated for sentimental reasons, lacked vitality. A natural association, antecedent to the formal organizations and never losing its vitality, was the informal evening over the coffee cups in each other's homes when the guests, as Emma Anderson remembered, in the early days brought their own lump sugar in their pockets.[36] The church frowned on infractions of the "Word of Wisdom," the brethren bearing down on the use of tea, coffee, tobacco, and strong drink; but the Scandinavians believed they had a special dispensation to drink coffee and their homemade beer. With at least one Dane it was a particular mark of devotion to go without coffee on Sunday.[37] God-fearing and obedient, the Scandinavians were, if anything, more indulgent in their entertainments, their eating and drinking, than the converts from Old or New England. The past, too recently left behind, broke through the discipline of the new faith especially on festive occasions. It was then the old stories were remembered and new ones told born of unique situations in the Mormon community. Ephraim in time came to be known as "the town that laughs at itself."[38]

The immigrants were articulate not only in this fashion. They wrote. Scandinavian literacy, the product, says Sigrid Undset, of much reading on long winter nights, made Mormon immigrants a select group. Besides, with theirs a religious migration, a response to a call, an appointed gathering, they felt a particular motivation to record their part in a divinely ordered history. Seeing the hand of the Lord in everything, they recorded his wonder-working providences with the soul-searching of the Puritan diarists, a frame of mind which explains the pious and didactic spirit of their journals and letters. Like other immigrants, they wrote and reminisced because, of all people, they had something to write about. Although they were ordinary persons, theirs was not an ordinary experience. They saw new scenes and felt the emotions these scenes awakened. Every decision became momentous, every act of great consequence. Theirs was experience heightened by constant comparison: all life became a double scene, having a vital and immediate interest in the new, a lingering attachment to the old, despite their rude break with the past. Theirs was all anticipation, all recollection, with the experience of the particular moment weighed in the balance. Often unable to communicate what needed saying in the new tongue, they turned with special relief to their journals or their letters home which became their confessional, their compensation. Yet the dominant impression, despite the introspection, is that the wounds of trouble and doubt healed quickly—the flesh was sound, the faith triumphant. It is as if the strong-faced portraits that used to hang on parlor walls should speak.

It was twenty years before Utah Scandinavians issued an organ in their own tongue, but meanwhile they contributed letters and amateur verses to *Skandinaviens Stjerne*, the mission periodical published in Copenhagen which they had come to know so well as converts and which many continued to read in the settlements. *Stjerne* made isolated inlanders surprisingly well read in international affairs, but it could not satisfy their provincial and immediate needs.

At last on December 20, 1873, pricked on by the threat of denominational proselyting among the immigrants, the Danish-Norwegian *Utah Posten* made its appearance: "Scandinavians in this Territory have for many years felt the necessity of an organ whose language they could fully understand, and through it receive the spiritual and intellectual food for which their religious faith creates a desire." Many countrymen, it said, living in settlements mainly Scandinavian, had had little opportunity to learn English. "We wish to make *Utah Posten* a modest means of assistance during our present period of development. . . . We encourage all our friends among the Norwegians, Swedish, and

Danish in Utah to act as father to the newcomer . . . and to nourish it to health and strength in the form of 'Greenbacks.'"[39]

The first foreign-language publication in Utah, the weekly seemed lusty enough at birth, but it was destined to live only thirty-six issues, a victim of hard times in the panic of 1873 – the "Greenbacks" had not been forthcoming, even though the paper had arranged with Sven Lovendahl at his Traveler's Rest in South Cottonwood to accept produce at current prices in payment for subscriptions. C. C. A. Christensen sent the editor a rhyme with assurance that money would one day follow:

Oh, then the farmer will happy be
And wear those modern "collars,"
And I will send the *Posten* three
Of the very newest dollars.

To which the editor, not to be outdone, replied:

Then write with your pen as you fully intend
If others but write with their pennies, my friend.[40]

The editor capable of such humor under trying circumstances was Peter Olaff Thomassen of Drammen, Norway, immigrant of 1863, who had served a seven-year apprenticeship as translator and editor of *Skandinaviens Stjerne*. In Copenhagen he had also conducted the church choir and composed a number of hymns. A good churchman, he slanted *Utah Posten* for the Scandinavian Saints, to bring them "the addresses of the Presidency and the doctrine of the Church in a language which reaches the heart. . . . It will not concern itself with politics, that is to say, with partisanships." But Thomassen had a genuine concern lest the Liberals, who opposed the church, should win immigrant support. His early numbers showed the direction: he reprinted a speech by Brigham Young and reproduced the People's party – or church – ticket in the municipal election.

He appointed agents in Sanpete and Sevier and Box Elder counties, in Cottonwood and Bear Lake Valley, and made Nils Grahn a representative at large to tour the settlements on behalf of the paper. The "Korrespondence" column printed Grahn's reports. He could rejoice in a large circulation, though subscription was small: the paper, popular enough, went from hand to hand. Three dollars was a good deal of ready money. Importation of a special Danish font would have to wait better financial conditions. There was now and again someone who did not sympathize with the new venture at all: at Spanish Fork, Grahn heard "the remarkable claim of some fellow countrymen that they would never permit a Danish paper or book to come into their home. Their mother tongue should be locked up. All should be English! (Which, I think, they never learn.) But, the Lord be praised, all are not of the same mind. In contrast I would mention Summit and Goshen, where the brethren received me heartily and personally recommended my errand."[41]

News was really a minor interest in *Utah Posten*. It was, more importantly, a journal of expression and opinion. For the Scandinavians it was a kind of circular letter. For the first time they could be addressed as a whole: through its pages, Erastus Snow, the honored "Apostle to Scandinavia," could address "The Scandinavians in Utah."[42] They were now more than ever communicants, with each other, with their church, with the world around them.

The biographies and sketches they gave of themselves in the "Korrespondence" column were more fascinating than the *feuilleton*, the serials like Hugo's *Lucretia Borgia* which followed every fourteen days. Verse found a place on the front page. Reviews of the activities of the Norkse Klub, the Skandinaviens Literaire Forening, emigrant benefit groups, and the plays in the Salt Lake Theater were regular features. Himself something of a poet, with literary taste and training, Thomassen gave his paper exceptional tone. By every rule, *Utah Posten* should have lived.

On October 22, 1874, a month after the death of *Utah Posten*, a liberal organ, the *Utah Skandinav*, printed in Swedish, Danish, and English, made its appearance. Intended to advocate "equal political rights for all citizens; to encourage a liberal education and to urge the establishment of free schools; to advise our countrymen to become naturalized, and then exercise their rights as citizens of this great Republic; to encourage home industry . . . to incite our young men to study and become useful workers in other and different avocations, besides those which require only manual labor,"[43] *Skandinav* seemed enlightened enough, but the paper's libelous methods were offensive, on one occasion earning the editor a caning on Salt Lake streets. In church eyes it was "apostate," a "plague," especially since the Scandinavian faithful were at the moment without an organ to defend themselves against its weekly attacks.

To Anders W. Winberg, president of the Scandinavian Meeting in Salt Lake, it seemed a duty to do something to counteract *Skandinav*'s poison. On August 1, 1876, he issued *Biküben*, "The Beehive," which tilted with *Skandinav* on every occasion and after a year could quip: "*Utah Skandinav* says that there are nine Scandinavian Mormons in Utah for every Liberal. It shows that its three-year activity has borne the expected fruits."[44] With *Skandinav*'s suspension, *Biküben*, with two exceptions, had the Danish-Norwegian field to itself for more than half a century.

Winberg, a Swedish blacksmith turned merchant, who before his death at seventy-nine became Patriarch Winberg, confessed his inexperience, but the paper's modest claims, its familiar tone, and its picturesque title found favor with readers. They never tired of hoping "lille Biküben," the little Beehive, would be filled with honey, or of signing themselves in their correspondence as "Bees." As the editor made his tours of the settlements drumming for subscriptions, he wrote accounts of his visits, and readers came to look forward to his homely gossip; he was their informant, and *Biküben* their grapevine. Soon Winberg was able to report that out of ninety Scandinavian families in Pleasant Grove, for example, thirty subscribed to *Biküben*.[45] *Biküben* carried no fiction during its first year and but little verse. Its pulse beat in the correspondence column and its editorials. In later years, it established a *Bibliotek*, a library of selected books, mostly religious, issued from its own press after they had been serialized in the paper as *udklip* chapters – sections so printed that they could be clipped out, folded, and formed into book sections consecutively paged. The slim shelf of Scandinavian books produced in Utah was largely the product of the *udklip* idea, which every Scandinavian paper as it came along adopted.

In 1885, after nearly a decade, *Biküben*'s greatest crisis came from an unexpected source. A fellow churchman of Winberg's, the Dane Andrew Jenson, was dissatisfied with *Biküben*'s unprepossessing literary style. In 1878 he had tried to organize a firm with Winberg and John A. Bruun when Winberg's struggles to keep the paper alive nearly worsted him, but the three could reach no agreement. The matter came to the attention of John Taylor, president of the church, who declared, said Jenson, "in the name of the Lord that if we didn't overcome our antagonistic attitude toward each other and continue to publish *Biküben* together, we would, sooner or later, have occasion to regret it."[46] They submitted their misunderstanding to a committee of arbitrators: Winberg resumed control and ownership; Jenson and Bruun were paid for their brief services. But Jenson's influence had made itself felt: the paper began to publish a column called "Kunst og Literatur." President Taylor had hinted at *Biküben*'s shortcomings when he encouraged "brethren and sisters from Scandinavia of literary ability" to contribute "occasional articles to strengthen and enliven and diversify the contents. . . ."[47] But Jenson had continued to criticize *Biküben* and finally, in January 1885, decided to launch his own Danish-language newspaper, calling it *Utah Posten* with Peter Thomassen's permission. He offered subscribers his historical monthly, *Morgenstjernen*, as a premium. The new venture was a formidable threat to "the little *Biküben*," and there ensued some lively verbal scuffling.

In almost jubilant tone Winberg announced on January 15, 1885, two weeks after the first appearance of the new *Posten*, that he had secured the services of "an old journalist," none other than Peter O. Thomassen himself, who only a week before had written Jenson a letter congratulating him on the continued use of the old name and expressing the hope *Utah Posten* would become the leading newspaper among Scandinavians in all America.[48] Winberg nonchalantly continued to run on his masthead: "*Biküben* is the only Scandinavian newspaper published in the Rocky Mountains." He held out until February 12, when he modified the statement to "*Biküben* is the *best* Scandinavian paper. . . ." Winberg was not to be cowed by Jenson's assertion that *Utah Posten* had the "consent and recommendation of the Church authorities." He made it clear that neither on request nor under compulsion would he withdraw from the field. *Biküben* had its faults, he said, but to bring it to its present status, to keep it alive during eight years, a period which had seen many Danish-American papers elsewhere rise and fall, had required "something more than wind." And "Since Brother Andrew Jenson invites 'all intelligent Scandinavians' in Utah to subscribe to *Utah Posten*, we will invite all the remaining Scandinavians to subscribe to *Biküben*. . . ."[49]

By April 16, 1885, *Biküben* was again "the only Scandinavian paper published in the Rocky Mountains." The rivals had joined forces; Jenson yielded to church advice to grant *Biküben* its priority. For a year Jenson helped Winberg, at length to turn his energies to compiling and writing history. Winberg, a polygamist, meanwhile had his personal troubles: on December 9, 1886, he editorialized on being hailed to court on five cohabitation counts. It was the era of antipolygamy prosecution under the Edmunds Act. In 1891, after fifteen years of active management, he sold out to Thomassen and became superintendent of the Norden Mercantile Company, catering to Scandinavian tastes in "norsk fetsill, getöst, mysöst, schweizeröst, and rokt öl." [50]

When Thomassen died suddenly, a number of leading Scandinavians in Salt Lake called together by Anthon H. Lund of the church presidency took *Bikūben* under their wing as the Bikūben Publishing Company. In 1895 it became church property, with Jenson called to manage it, though he "would rather have gone on another foreign mission than receive this appointment"; but he stuck doggedly to his task for fifteen years.[51] By the time *Bikūben* was suspended in 1935, it had, despite its crises, enjoyed an unbroken life of fifty-nine years. It had had its lapses: an apocryphal tale relates that it once went to press with a page of jumbled type and the note "This page was pied by the printer"; and there was the time Winberg reprinted a whole page from a previous issue because he had not had enough help to hand set all the new copy; and as late as 1913 a sentimental editor in collusion with typesetter and printer decided to abandon the usual Christmas issue and "celebrate the whole holiday in quiet with our dear ones around the family hearth." [52] *Bikūben* never lost the common touch.

Andrew Jenson, who, in spite of everything, found himself editing *Bikūben* for so many years, produced Utah's first book in a foreign language, a life of Joseph Smith, the Mormon prophet, in Danish, which appeared in 1879 with J. A. Bruun as collaborator.[53] Jenson visited every settlement for subscriptions for the work, since it was printed sixteen pages at a time and sent out semimonthly. It was the beginning of a productive career in church historical writing for the one-time farmer and railroad worker, emigrant from Hjorring Amt in 1866. He had filled a mission to Denmark from 1873 to 1875, working on the *Stjerne* in Copenhagen, training ground for so many editors of Utah's Scandinavian press.

In 1882 he founded *Morgenstjernen*, a Danish monthly devoted to a history of the Scandinavian Mission, biographies of leading Scandinavians in Utah, excerpts from daybooks and immigrant journals, European news items, and occasionally important sermons by church leaders. It was deemed valuable enough to be continued, after four years, as the *Historical Record* in English, a source book of church information which ran to nine volumes. Jenson became assistant church historian, an indefatigable collector and classifier, a chronologer and encyclopedist in his chosen field. He was annalist rather than historian, but during his life he assembled the sources from which future church historians could work. From 1895 to 1897, on behalf of the church, he toured its missions the world over, collating, copying, abridging, preserving church records in every congregation he visited, packing many of them off to Salt Lake for safekeeping at the church historian's office. Because so much of his early work was in Danish, he has not yet been fully appreciated.[54]

One of the measures advanced in 1885 to settle the *Bikūben–Utah Posten* controversy was the Scandinavian Publishing Company, to be founded "for the purpose of promoting Scandinavian literature in Utah," but it did not materialize.[55] In the same year, the Swedish accomplished what their Danish-Norwegian brethren could not: on June 4, 1885, the Swedish Publishing Company at Salt Lake brought out *Svenska Härolden*, the first publication in Utah entirely in the Swedish language, and, judging from its self-laudatory editorial, something of a national triumph – it pleased the elated publishers to be able to demonstrate that the Swedish were a distinct people. The first issue carried a two-edged congratulation from P. O. Thomassen – a jibe at popular notions concerning Scandinavia, and an admonition addressed to the Swedes themselves: "Several educated Americans wonder why we are to have a Swedish newspaper when we already have a Danish. These gentlemen do not know that Swedish and Danish are two different languages. . . . God who gave the American his language also gave the Swede and Dane theirs. He did not give it to us to be thrown away at some future time or to feel ashamed of. . . . It would please me very much to see German, French, Irish, and Welsh newspapers published here in Utah. . . ."

Svenska Härolden paid a good deal of attention to religious and political affairs as they affected the Saints. An editorial on October 17, 1889, refuted the Salt Lake *Tribune*'s assertion that half the Scandinavians in Salt Lake had left the Mormon Church and joined the Liberal party. The truth, said *Härolden*, is that there are fifty Scandinavians in the People's party to every five in the Liberal. Its preoccupation with saving the souls of its readers may have been *Härolden*'s undoing. Begun as a paper varied in content, with an accent on literature and the industrial activities of the Swedish people, who were mostly townfolk (there was not the correspondence from the settlements that characterized the Danish-Norwegian papers), it labored toward the end under the heavy hand of theology and homiletics and political harangue. Its constant appeal was for unity among the Scandinavians, but it meant perhaps "church unity" or "political unity" rather than the cultural unity which would permit diversity of opinion. It did not live beyond 1892, no more than two years after a livelier paper, *Korrespondenten*, was begun.

Getting wind of the new venture, *Svenska Härolden* had felt hurt: it had broken the path under difficulties; the Swedish people could not support two papers; the Saints could not have two different goals; they had one aim and needed but one medium to express that aim.[56] Luckily for *Härolden*, perhaps, fire destroyed its equipment and abruptly halted its career, leaving the field to Otto Rydman and his campaign for Swedish culture, already described.

Korrespondenten was challenged in turn by a new *Utah Posten*, this time in Swedish, which appeared in 1900. Rydman took delight in pointing out that the officers of the Scandinavian Publishing Company, backers of the new venture, were anything but Swedish: three of its officers were Norwegian, two were Danish, and its two Swedes were really "Swedish Scandinavians." Rydman could not suppress his mirth when he quoted this group as expressing the wish, in *Posten*'s first issue, that the paper would be received "as a welcome guest in Swedish homes in Utah as well as other parts of our great land where a little affection is still found for the language *we* learned at *our* mother's knee." [57] Rydman suspected that a Swedish paper maintained by "Norwegian, Danish, and Swedish Scandinavians" was a bid for Scandinavian support in the coming elections.

He did not have to guess. *Posten* frankly announced itself as a political organ, supporting the Democratic ticket, and it kept its price to one dollar a year to come within the reach of all who had not accumulated any "Republican wealth." But the new paper also ran Esaias Tegner's "Song to the Sun" in English translation to demonstrate to Americans that the north was not a land of gloom and perpetual darkness; and it ran a full page of fiction and a column of "Reflektioner" and miscellanies from current American magazines like *Harper's*. It showed conviction without *Svenska Härolden*'s heavyhandedness, and lightness and wit without *Korrespondenten*'s impudence. When a Republican victory dashed its political hopes, it settled down to cultural effort and a goal of five thousand subscribers by January 1902. It was too ambitious an undertaking, for the 1900 census showed only 7025 Swedish-born living in Utah. In two years the paper sold out to the church, for whom it became "a reliable and able advocate," in time joining *Bikūben*, *Beobachter*, and the *Utah Nederlander* as one of the Associated Newspapers which the church subsidized until 1935.

More than an aspect of culture in the mother tongue, the Scandinavian papers were also an instrument promoting all its other forms – its musical and literary and dramatic societies, the social evenings, the reunions. The papers advertised them, previewed them, described and reviewed them, stirring up friendly rivalry between communities, establishing standards of performance, effecting communication where before had been only association. Reviewers could sometimes say that "national songs in quartet as well as in choir fell from happy lips," that "a couple of excellent violinists did their best to heighten the gay atmosphere," or that "everyone was especially pleased to hear old Lumbye's 'Drommebilleder' recited in a most appropriate manner." [58] They could watch *Store Bededags Aften* and as their eyes ran over the heading of the red handbill let their thoughts go back to *Kongens Kjobenhavn* and be reminded how in times long past they took a walk on the ramparts to hear the bells ring and then went down to drink tea and eat warm *Hvedetvebakker*, or wheat cakes. But they could also deplore that Miss Hansen sang her dressmaker song without opening her mouth wide enough, or that Mr. Ertman portraying a simple baker should be so affected and mouth his inflections and talk about something he had "putted i en box," or that Hr. Jespersen's song "Den lille Ole" was more suitable for school children. It was too bad to look forward to the charming *Til Saeters* only to be thrown into confusion when the mountains reminded one of Norway, the wide student caps of Sweden, and the talk of Aalborg.[59]

An unfailing delight, however, were the contributions from immigrant writers who through the papers reached their widest audience. In them the mother tongue had its sweetest triumph, at times aspiring to literature, an indigenous literature though in a foreign language. There was not a professional among them. Even the editors had to supplement their income at other tasks. Their reward was small except in the affection and esteem of the people for whom they wrote. Jacob Johannes Martinus Bohn, for example, immigrant of 1853, whose verse frequently appeared in *Utah Posten* and *Biküben*, and who had written most of the hymns in the first edition of the Danish Latter-day Saint psalmody, labored "from April conference till past Christmas" on a new edition of the hymnbook "without compensation or thanks, and no one gave me so much as a honeycomb or a copy of the completed book as a small acknowledgment for all my hardships, but took from me, as from everyone else, three marks for the book." To Bohn it was a small trial: in Aalborg he had seen his home destroyed by a mob but had praised God when among the ruins he found his journal and its sixty precious poems undamaged. "If my inconsiderable poems can help to gladden my brethren and sisters and glorify the name of the Lord, then God alone shall have the honor." [60]

C. C. A. Christensen of Ephraim – C. C. A. as he was universally known – enjoyed a popularity among his people seldom won by prophets in their own country. "There are guests in the parlor, but what's in the pot?" asks a dismayed housewife in one of his sketches. For sixty years, from the time he wrote his first hymn in Copenhagen in 1851 until his death in Salt Lake City in 1912 at the age of eighty-one, C. C. A. kept his amateur literary pot boiling and never disappointed his guests. His Danish verse was something of an institution among them. They sang his hymns from the little pocket *Salmer for de Sidste Dages Hellige*, heard his reunion pieces, and read his rhymed letters and humorous sketches in *Biküben* and *Skandinaviens Stjerne*. In 1921 a major literary event among them was the appearance of *Digte og Afhandlinger*, memorial edition of his collected verse, representative articles, and a short biography gleaned from his journals.

Danish convert to Mormonism, three times missionary to Norway, immigrant, handcart pioneer of 1857, and by turns bricklayer, scene painter, artist, and farmer, who had known a boyhood of abject poverty made bright by six winters of instruction in the Royal Art Academy at Copenhagen because a woman of means once took notice of his skillful bird and animal silhouettes – C. C. A. had a background that enabled him to say in his verse the right, if not necessarily the final, word about the experiences of his people common to their odyssey of conversion, migration, and settlement in a new country.

Man kalder mig Digter – jeg er kun Maler
Og Dansk er det Sprog, jeg daglig taler. . . .[61]

"They call me a poet," he recited at a *Skandinavernes Folkefest* in Logan in 1892, "but I'm only a painter, and Danish is my daily speech." However slightingly he may have regarded his avocation as a writer of familiar verse as compared with his professional interest in brush and canvas, his ear served him as well as his eye and he recorded the interests of his people in authentic accents. To the familiar, the cherished, the sentimental, and the comical in their lives he gave dignified or witty or gently satirical expression as the occasion demanded. Sometimes the expression was felicitous enough to become memorable and part of the oral tradition of Danish, Norwegian, and Swedish Saints alike, for all read him. "Den søde Lotte" was often sung to an old-world tune, "Den lille Ole":

I know a maid and she is fair,
But she is hard to please, I swear;
When her caprices rule her mind
She's still becoming, but less kind. . . .

She passes lightly in the dance
And easily from Ole to Hans,
Who must confess like Samson old
That men are weak and women bold.[62]

"Jo, jo," heads would nod: "Yes, yes, C. C. A. has said it." He could move them with his hymns of simple faith or as surely rouse them to laughter at any spectacle of themselves he chose to hold up to their view.

Anyone who ever read it at all remembered "Et Gilde paa Landet," the description of a Christmas party at the home of Hans the tilemaker and his good wife Martha. It originally appeared in 1874 in *Utah Posten*, to which C. C. A. was a frequent contributor.[63]

Pass the word, there's a party as well as a dance,
And we've been invited by Tilemaker Hans;
Hans is a man of respect and no fool,
Though at home, it is said, his wife Martha would rule;
On that they're agreed, thus all things go well,
So Hans isn't dumb on that score, you can tell.
Now it was Christmas: all things were in order
In kitchen and cellar and in the fat larder;

The grain had been threshed, the pigs had been fed,
And Hans felt secure, for under his bed,
Down deep in his strongbox lay hidden his wealth,
While to a stout sock in the mattress, by stealth
He added recruits as a handy reserve:
The jingling coin seemed to steady his nerve.
For Hans was forehanded and thought in the main,
"With money there's nothing a man can't obtain."

The poet relates how he prepares himself for the affair, selecting a roomy vest and his widest pair of pants:

For when Hans gave a party I was sure of one thing:
His barrels were quite like a bottomless spring.
I thought I would do him what honor I could
And readied myself as a grateful man should.
"At three o'clock sharp," had been Hans's request,
And he stood at the door to welcome his guests.
They came, frock and frockcoat, the lads and the lasses,
The old and the staid and a few upper classes:
A German who barbered, an Englishman cold,
A French hairdresser and a Norman from Molde.
In color and cloth all the fashions paraded,
Balloon skirts and bonnets not a little were aided
By sparkling eyes and by lips with a smile,
Each seeking the favor of others the while.
Some wore brooches and rings, and were gaily attired,
And as fitted their station were duly admired.

The preliminaries over, the company is seated:

The bishop sat first at the head of the table,
A likable man and every whit able.
Next came the Maeren [64] — but oh what a name
To fix to our honorable *Byfoged* [65] Ravn.
We honor the title and hold in respect
The position deserved by our mayor-elect,
For here in America, above all in San Pete,
Is little of rank and less of elite.
Here one can't afford to put on any airs,
The judge makes the pants that the criminal wears;
If not as a tailor, as the old saying goes,
Then the judge as our barber "takes us all by the nose."
Our major in peace may be seen with his sheep
While the adjutant probably clerks for his keep.
The priest may not preach as well as he plows,

And the sexton himself doubtless weaves his own clothes.
With them, if a man is as good as his word,
He's the equal of all, and at times may be heard.

Other people present include Kristoffer the marshal, storekeeper Hans, Soren the tailor, Morten the cooper, and Peter the smith:

Next to Peter the smith sat a helmsman from Norway
Who as a nightwatchman now sleeps all the day.
He steers a safe course on the land, doughty sailor,
And keeps himself far from the dangerous water,
Touching nothing but wine as the best kind of drink
While his eye seeks his girl with a weatherwise wink;
And when the effects of the wine have begun
He dreams, to be sure, that they two become one.

The company is rounded out by a baker, a builder, and an editor who is also a printer. All are impatient to begin, when Hans rises to make a speech:

"Friends, my countrymen, and womenfolk too,"
Hans stuttered and coughed, and his face became red,
But Martha took over and cried, "That will do;
Away with the speeching. We'll tell you instead,
We thank you for coming. Now eat all you can."
And as if at a signal, the music began.

All fall to and make short work of Martha's excellent cooking. Following the dessert of tarts and cake, the men retire into the corner where the wine barrel has been installed; the women content themselves with coffee. The evening turns to "drinking and dancing, and dancing and drinking." Toasts follow in rapid succession; the poet recites a well-received verse and is rewarded with another glass, but he has already had too much and finds he needs help:

The helmsman, quite ready to give me a hand,
Had seen many wonders in faraway lands;
He knew what dis-eased me, and coolly began,
"This sickness, my friends, I have witnessed before;
It's a common contagion in Bearn I swear,
But how it could strike in our midst this poor man –"
"I fear it's the plague straight from Poland," one cried;
"We'll be dead before morning, it can't be denied."

In the panic that ensues, all attempt to find their wraps at once and head for home, but in their foggy state they only manage to create wild confusion. The din is so great the musicians stop playing. The helmsman, meanwhile, enjoys the scene, until at last he explains what he meant:

> The panic subsided; as it came, so it went;
> The bibulous helmsman, when his laughter was spent,
> Roared out his confession: he cried, "Don't you know,
> It's the wine made in Bearn, the plague you would flee
> Is locked up in this barrel; but here's the worst blow –
> The barrel is empty, a real tragedy."

But the host trundles another cask into the corner, the music starts up again, and the gay company resumes its alternate drinking and dancing until the rooster crows. As the party breaks up, the poet takes his unsteady leave of Martha and Hans, and, amid cries of "Glaedelig Jul," finds his way home, next day to send off his description of "the party in the country" to *Utah Posten.*

C. C. A.'s verse commentaries on the times and his description of the local scene and the characters he knew provided perennial entertainment: the formula varied little, but the observations and witticisms were timely. In 1895 he wrote a *Rimbrev*, or letter in rhyme, to *Bikūben* describing life in Ephraim during a cold February: to keep warm in the evenings the young people waltzed to the music of a rather imposing assemblage of instruments – three violins, two flutes and a dulcimer, a bass viol, a clarinet, guitar, mandolin, and five harmonicas "which the boys can play." There were also a silver cornet, trumpet, bassoon, harp, organ, and piano. The town was currently doing well with a homemade remedy for sick folk that sold at a very high price "because what is expensive is considered good," and people bought it up at a great rate. The fact, said C. C. A., that the concoction contained a generous quantity of brandy may have had something to do with its success. To be sure, one had to have a doctor's prescription, but it was easy to develop symptoms which miraculously disappeared on purchasing the "medicine."

> The newest Kurikurium
> Brings into town a tidy sum,
> All this without, let me repeat,
> Without our practicing deceit.

So the *Apotheket*, where the jars bore Latin titles "to hide from common folk what was in them," was doing a thriving business; it was the drugstore where all kinds of goods were sold – brushes, coffee, tobacco, oil, lacquer – and where moreover, in one corner, was found the post office, on Fridays the rendezvous for people from all around as they waited the arrival of *Bikuben*:

> Then Danish speech falls on the ear,
> The sweetest sound a soul can hear.[66]

C. C. A. loved *det Danske Sprog* and took every opportunity to make the immigrant feel proud of it. He had only scorn for those who hid all Old World books and bric-a-brac and tried to conceal their foreignness. He was willing to hope the Adamic tongue had been a form of Scandinavian, and in several allegorical poems in which the scene is laid in the hereafter, he peoples the spirit world with his *søskende*, has them speak their own Danish, Norwegian, or Swedish, and organizes the Mormons among them into a Scandinavian Stake! [67]

Sometimes in his homely way he turned his attention to the politics and economics of the day, but without lampooning individuals: he was too kind for that. In 1893 the country had been hearing many plans to bring back dollar prosperity; at a Scandinavian entertainment in Manti, in rhyme, as usual, he summed up the panaceas of gold and silver and antitrust laws and tariffs, and then presented his economic dream for Sanpete, guaranteed to give every family a new carriage, an organ in the parlor, perhaps even a pianoforte, and new clothes for the womenfolk from head to toe. His plan, he said, was simpler than any that had been proposed: let the chickens lay twice a day and see that eggs sell for a dollar a dozen, wheat for three dollars a bushel; let the cows give milk in rivers that never run dry, and the churns always yield premium butter; and when it rains, let it rain cabbages and potatoes.[68]

In Ephraim the next year he sounded the economic theme again, but without mischief. Tone and proposal were alike serious: away with greed, drunkenness, and disunity; put a spinning wheel back into every home, dignify weaving, and make homespun fashionable, a popular trademark of beauty and quality; let thrift have its reward; let every man eat honest bread, and industry and brotherhood will bring back good times.[69]

C. C. A. was fond of "homespun" – it stood for quality: he might have welcomed the word as a judgment of his verse. In the poem "For og Nu" (Then and Now), read at an Old Folks' gathering in Ephraim in 1909, he satirized the attitude of the younger "enlightened" generation in their belittling of everything associated with the past. Grandfather's shirt, he said, was always white; it was made of the best linen spun at home by grandmother's devout hands. It was paid for with an honest kiss, and lasted many a year, not like the cheap dyed cloth one bought from modern merchants and tailors who were seldom honest.[70] C. C. A. was old-fashioned in things he thought counted.

C. C. A., who once sold his watch on the streets of Fredrikstad that he might eat, who on several occasions as a Mormon missionary had suffered imprisonment and been given a diet of bread and water for five days together, and who had sacrificed his professional talent as an artist that he might make the adjustment called for by life in the settlements[71] – that C. C. A. did not have tongue in cheek when he spoke about matters of principle. In this he was most like his people. He kept a balance between the serious and the comic. He could praise the Lord or poke fun at Scandinavian foibles. He knew their nearness to sentiment and tears, but he knew also their capacity for laughter. C. C. A. was a salutary influence among his people then, as he is a delightful memory among them today. The mother tongue could have wished no better singer.

CHAPTER 11

Inroads: Conflict and Crusade

"EVERYBODY'S TALKING ABOUT UTAH."[1]

IT IS ironic that Mormonism, as native to the United States as Indian corn, once seemed notoriously un-American. To the Christian Convention gathered in Salt Lake City in 1888 to review "the situation in Utah," it seemed, in fact, anti-American. Rev. A. S. Bailey, addressing all the denominational workers in the territory, believed that a traveler visiting Utah would find not simply "more that is European than American," but "a spirit foreign to the spirit of Americans . . . a system indigenous indeed, but hostile to American ideas."[2]

His charges were familiar: Mormonism restrained trade in forbidding the Saints to do business with the gentiles; it controlled the People's party, invoking a religious test for political office; it taxed property in the form of tithing; it indoctrinated the schools; it mocked the American home with its oriental abomination, polygamy; it was a Kingdom bent on overthrowing the government. "With missionaries in every State in the Union, with a strong lobby at the national capital, and with recruits being brought in by hundreds from the Old World, this plague cannot be easily quarantined."[3]

To Christian patriots determined to make an end of polygamy and theocratic rule in Utah, the flow of proselytes from abroad was a particular vexation. It was all too true that Mormonism, as a British reviewer observed, owed its survival and continuing growth to "persecution, martyrdom, and immigration."[4] Immigration fed all the other iniquities: it replenished polygamy, it strengthened the hand of the priesthood, it supplied subservient colonizers to extend the "American Turkey" and docile voters to spread its subversive influence. Rev. J. M. Coyner imagined the annual trainloads of foreign converts "scattered over the great mountain regions of the West" and shuddered to think Mormonism might eventually command sixteen western senators and dozens of congressmen.[5] "It is clear," said *Harper's Magazine* in 1881, "that the Mormon Kingdom in Utah is composed of foreigners and the children of foreigners. . . . It is an institution so absolutely un-American in all its requirements that it would die of its own infamies within twenty years, except for the yearly infusion of fresh serf blood from abroad."[6]

Immigration, elsewhere considered so characteristically American, perversely stamped Utah as alien and seditious and kept it a vassal territory for nearly half a century. When the slanders of recreant federal officials induced President Buchanan in 1857 to send troops to Utah to depose Brigham Young, Stephen A. Douglas, who had once befriended the Mormons, applauded the action: "Nine-tenths of the inhabitants are aliens by birth who have refused to become naturalized, or to take the oath of allegiance." Should Johnston's Army fail to bring them to "a sense of duty," he was ready to repeal the organic law of the territory on the ground they were "alien enemies."[7] "Buchanan's Blunder" proved there was no Utah rebellion, but the "Mormon Question" persisted. In 1860 the first Pony Express brought rumors that a bill was being considered to remove the capital to Carson Valley and change the name of the territory to Nevada,[8] a bid to shift control into gentile hands that never materialized, though Utah, already drastically reduced from Deseret, continued to lose ribs in the creation of neighboring territories which soon outran it in achieving statehood.

After the Civil War, with the antibigamy statute of 1862 on the books, the Mormons became one of "those great pressing themes," as Samuel Bowles put it, along with the "Pacific Railroad and the Mines," to which the country turned its official attention. Spanning the continent with Speaker Schuyler Colfax in the summer of 1865 to measure "the national breadth," the editor of the Springfield (Mass.) *Republican* concluded that "The conflict of sects and civilization, growing up there in Utah, will soon solve the polygamous problem – rightly and without bloodshed – if the Government will make itself felt in it with a wise guardianship, a tender nursing, a firm principle."[9] The "Government," of course, meant the Republican party. "We mean to put that business of the Mormons through," a New Englander told a British traveler in 1866. "We have done a bigger job in the South; and we shall now fix things up in Salt Lake City."[10]

But it was twenty years before things were "fixed up." While the

Republicans tried to redeem the other half of their pledge to crush the "twin relics of barbarism, slavery and polygamy," the Mormons resolutely went on redeeming their own pledge to gather Israel and build the Kingdom.[11] It was campaign promises versus divine injunction; the Lord finally yielded to Uncle Sam, but only after Congress and the courts, the press and the pulpit, had been turned into a battleground. "Everybody's talking about Utah," wrote a Danish immigrant in 1880,[12] though not everyone was telling the same story.

Affairs were grossly exaggerated. The Honorable W. H. Hooper, Utah's delegate to Congress, found the Mormons "the most vigorously lied about of any people in the nation." They firmly believed that fifty million people were "calling loudly" for their extinction.[13] The extremists did in fact call for Sherman to march through Utah as he had marched through Georgia;[14] they wanted to dissolve the legislature and govern Utah by commission; and they clamored for enforceable legislation that would disfranchise polygamists and prohibit Mormon immigration. The same New Englanders whose emigrant societies had wrested Kansas from the slave interests were ready to overrun Utah – until they soberly reflected that the Mormons had already pre-empted all the arable land.[15] The moderates had more faith in education and the changes time and the railroad would bring. Moral force might "persuade Brigham to lie down with Bowles" and get "Boston and Salt Lake City . . . to shake hands as Boston and Charleston have already done."[16]

The cry went up to Christianize Utah. "If you really have the interests of Utah at heart," one gentile wrote his pastor in 1869, "just send here about twenty-five earnest Methodist preachers, that can sing and pray, and turn them loose; it would do more good than all the Cullom Bills Congress could pass."[17] Rev. M. T. Lamb, looking for a bright spot in "all the dark canvas" of Mormonism, found immigration itself a blessing in disguise. "Through the strange providence of God there have been thrust upon the Christian workers of our country 50,000 young people in Utah, who, if they can be brought under the influences of the truth . . . are worth ten times as much . . . as they could have been had their parents remained in the stagnant, uneventful life of the old country." But, he had to admit, "Filled from their infancy with bitter prejudice and even hatred of the Christianity represented by the Evangelical churches, they are very hard to reach."[18]

As early as 1865 a Danish convert wrote home that "a few of the world's preachers" had come to Utah "under guise of winning people back to 'true Christianity.'"[19] In Salt Lake City's Independence Hall, completed that year and destined to become a center of gentile activity, the Reverend Norman McLeod, Congregationalist minister and chaplain at nearby Fort Douglas, preached "civilized Christianity" to "a large and intelligent congregation," taught a Sunday school of some two hundred scholars, and lectured weekly on the evils of polygamy. The "work of God" seemed established "on a firm and enduring basis."[20]

Though the reverend himself shortly departed to lecture in eastern cities on the Mormon problem, scores of dedicated denominational workers after 1869 took up the great work of Utah's redemption, supported by the collections in eastern congregations and remembered in their prayers. In the deliberations of the missionary societies and the annual conferences of the churches, benighted Utah took priority over heathen Africa. Missionary reports coming from the small towns and villages especially had an air of martyrdom, of heroic effort for small gain. "Work in an exclusive Mormon town is necessarily very slow," recalled the Presbyterian S. L. Gillespie in 1876. "Apostates from the Mormons are cut off from business and society, as well as from their Church, and so have to seek homes elsewhere; and the few Gentiles attempting to live among the Mormons rarely stay more than one year; so that all our mission work among the Mormons is 'sowing seed upon waters,' requiring great patience and perseverance."[21] Nevertheless, by 1880 the Protestants had 22 ministers serving 24 churches, and 25 mission day schools with 54 teachers and 2250 pupils; by 1890, the high-water mark of their activity, they had 62 ministers serving 63 churches, and 64 schools with 323 teachers and 7007 pupils.[22]

Inevitably, with Scandinavian immigrants so numerous, the denominations sensed a special opportunity and were soon making urgent appeals to the home mission societies and boards for ministers and teachers who could speak the language. "If a Norwegian or Danish Lutheran priest should go to Sanpete County," wrote the renegade Andreas Mortensen in 1887 of Mormonism's Scandinavian stronghold, "he would have half the Mormons follow him."[23] He was scolding the lethargy of the Establishment in Scandinavia, whose missions had neglected Utah. Oddly enough, it was not the Lutherans but the Presbyterians, closely followed by the Methodist Episcopal Church and the Baptists, who first made inroads among the immigrants.

On March 3, 1875, the Reverend Duncan J. McMillan of Alton, Illinois, seeking a high, dry climate for his health, arrived in Mt. Pleasant, one of Sanpete Valley's dominantly Scandinavian towns with a population of 1346, nearly half of it first-generation immigrants. After spending a few nights on the counter of the post office, he found room and board and, on his first Sunday, received a dual invitation to speak: one from apostate Mormons to come in the afternoon to their unfinished Liberal Hall; the other from the Mormon bishop, W. S. Seeley, to speak to the Sunday school in the morning and a large congregation in the meetinghouse in the evening – a cordiality usually overlooked by partisans who remembered only a dramatic opposition which developed later. The Liberals offered him their building, subject to a $1500 mortgage, to begin a school which they would patronize, their tuition to be credited to the mortgage. And if McMillan desired to preach, they said, they would attend his services. The minister accepted, converted the hall into a Presbyterian chapel, and, fashioning his own desks from rough lumber, on April 20 opened his school with thirty-five students, the mayor of the town among them; the number was soon increased to over a hundred.

Though he had come as a perfect stranger, "not knowing even the name of anyone in town," McMillan's experiment, the first of any denomination, of carrying the gospel into an exclusive Mormon community, seemed promising enough at the end of the first year for the Board of Home Missions to commission him, appropriating a missionary salary but nothing for maintaining the school. "It was an individual enterprise on my part, and I received not a dollar of salary or support during the first year." Though a congregation filled the small house every Sunday with deepening interest, McMillan often felt alone "100 miles by stage from any Christian brother or Gentile friend." [24]

In July of the first year he weathered his worst storm when Brigham Young and several of the apostles came to Mt. Pleasant for a valley-wide conference. Among them was Erastus Snow, who twenty-five years before had first brought Mormonism to Scandinavia and was now concerned about his converts. The brethren came to promote the United Order and call for a renewal of Mormon covenants through rebaptism, a revival which seemed all the more urgent with McMillan in town. Brigham Young, never charitable toward apostates and harassed by signs of Mormon disunion all over Utah, was not loath to abuse McMillan: "There is a mischievous stranger, a Presbyterian minister, in this valley," he is reported to have said. "He has no business here. The Lord has given me these valleys, and to those whom I choose to have occupy them. . . . I am informed that Saints have gone to hear this man preach, and have sent their daughters to his school. The next thing you know he will send sorrow and distress to the hearts of the mothers of these girls." In terms that made sensational reporting in *Harper's* and the anti-Mormon Salt Lake *Tribune*, he threatened: "You must not be deceived by the fact that this man seems a gentleman and a moral man. . . . He is a wolf in sheep's clothing. What would you do were a wolf to enter the field where your sheep are? Why, you would shoot him down. . . ." Extremist accounts, reputedly drawn from McMillan's notebook, do not leave the inference in doubt, but have Brigham Young ordering the congregation of 2000 to attend to McMillan's destruction.[25]

There was no violence and McMillan stayed, though Canute Peterson, stalwart Norwegian of Fox River fame and now presiding over the Sanpete Stake, accosted him in the street soon after with "Are you that damned Presbyterian devil?"[26] Alleged ambuscades and stonings are as doubtful as the claim that McMillan preached with a Bible in one hand and a revolver in the other—a stereotyped portrayal of the denominational missionary in Utah designed to rouse the conscience of the East and loosen its purse strings. But Brigham Young's warnings clearly did frighten the people into keeping their children away from McMillan's school—at least until September, when he opened a Sunday school that soon recouped his losses, enrolling a membership of 200 that, it was proudly recorded, rivaled the flourishing St. Marks school in Salt Lake City.[27]

The local priesthood continued to admonish the "Fathers in Israel" not to patronize the Presbyterian school, the dance hall, and the whiskey saloon—the three were always named together. Ebbe Jessen believed it was "not so bad an injury to the church to get drunk as to send our children to the school." Attendance was made a matter of church loyalty. Those who did not comply were disfellowshiped, like Brother Lake, who insisted McMillan was a gentleman and said no one could force him to take his children out of the school. Svend Larsen thought his conduct unwise, for it would bring the Saints eventually "into bondage to one of the daughters of that great and abominable church"; Mikkel Rasmussen wished the brethren to be merciful to Brother Lake, and Jens Nilsen thought it wisdom to bear with him "yet a while," but after Brother Lake's statement had been interpreted into Danish "that the brethren may know what they was voting for," he was disfellowshiped by a vote of 16 to 7.[28]

McMillan, stoutly supported by such apostates, used his own funds, won credit, made a trip east to raise money, and appealed through his church papers for aid, though one of his own denomination responded: "Any fool that would attempt such a mission ought to starve or be driven out."[29] The town, as would prove true with denominational effort everywhere else in Utah, was more interested in the Presbyterian school than in the Presbyterian church. It was two years before McMillan received his first communicants, and these were two English women. Meanwhile, in November 1879 two Swedish evangelists of the Free Christian Church, the Reverend F. Franson and Mr. J. F. Fredrickson, arrived in town to make some thirty converts, and sixteen more in neighboring Ephraim.[30]

At length, in 1880, five years after McMillan's courageous beginnings, the organization of the Presbyterian Church was perfected with eleven members, the elected elders and deacons bearing names like C. A. Peterson, Jens C. Thompson, Nils Jacobsen, and Soren J. Neilson which once honored Mormon rolls in Scandinavia. Services were carried on in English, Danish, and Swedish, with hymnals ordered printed in all three languages. By 1893 the church had 73 members, with a Sunday school of 45 and a home for boarding girls where they could be under "Christian influence and receive practical instruction in housekeeping." The home was part of the Wasatch Academy, a major development out of McMillan's mission school. Still operating under the auspices of the Woman's Executive Committee of Home Missions, it was the forerunner of successful Presbyterian academies in other towns in Utah, among them the still flourishing Westminster College in Salt Lake City.[31]

In the first spring, McMillan extended his work to nearby Ephraim, a town of nearly 2000 and most flourishing of the Scandinavian settlements, where the people opened the South Ward schoolhouse to him. The Saints were courteous though frank to say, "We do not want you to teach our children." The Presbyterian Church was organized in 1880 with only twenty-four members, who had dwindled to twelve by 1895, when they became part of the Manti fold. Here as in Mt. Pleasant the Swedish evangels of the Free Christian Church followed in his wake and by 1879 were holding Gospel meetings in C. A. Larson's hall, developing "great interest despite earnest opposition." [32]

In Manti, smaller than Ephraim, but the county seat and about equally English and Scandinavian, the Reverend Mr. McMillan's brother, J. S. McMillan, and his wife opened a mission school in September 1877. The Reverend R. G. McNiece came down from Salt Lake City the next spring to preach in Fox's hall and organize the church with ten members. One of the ruling elders was Andrew Nelson, Presbyterianism's most spectacular conversion: as Anders Nielsen he had come to Utah in 1853 wtih the famous Forsgren company to settle in Spring Town; he had filled a Mormon mission to Scandinavia twelve years later, had married four wives, and as a prosperous farmer, stockholder and justice of the peace, was looked upon as a pillar of the community. Differences with his bishop over nothing more serious than card playing ripened him in disaffection, to be plucked by the Presbyterians and become their mainstay when they came to Manti. He lived with his third wife, but to travelers he seemed that curiosity, a Presbyterian polygamist.[33] Nelson sent his eighteen children to Manti's mission school, where attendance had ranged from 60 to 125 since its beginning in 1877, and which in 1881 was housed in a handsome building of native oölite – the same beautiful stone as the Mormon temple, the Presbyterians always added. Its pupils became public school teachers, one of them a county superintendent and another a city principal.[34]

After McMillan's brave undertaking in Sanpete Valley, the Presbyterians were emboldened to proselyte in other Scandinavian centers: Brigham City at the north end of Salt Lake Valley and in the settlements in Cache Valley. In April 1876 the Reverend S. L. Gillespie preached in the courthouse in Brigham City, or Box Elder as it was first known. In December 1881 the Board of Home Missions sent P. T. Brohback to Hyrum to work among the Scandinavians in Cache Valley. He gave his first sermon on Christmas day to an audience of fourteen. Carrie Nutting had opened the field with a mission school a month before. They soon had modest chapels there and in nearby Wellsville and Millville, the minister busy preaching twelve trilingual sermons a month and conducting nearly as many exhortations and prayer meetings. By 1895 the services were mostly in English and Swedish. In 1884 the day schools in the three towns were enrolling 107, the Sunday schools 130. Hyrum flourished with 101 in the day school in 1892, while Wellsville had to be given up and joined to Mendon.[35]

In Mendon, across the valley from Hyrum, a Miss McCracken "built up a good school notwithstanding the bitter opposition of the Mormon priesthood to all Christian work," but the Mormons treated her so badly in the spring of 1884 that she quit the field.[36] The Scandinavian keeper of the Mendon Ward Historical Record compared the Presbyterians to the Pharisees of old, particularly one "Camble [Campbell?] a very live man in his profession . . . he spared no means in working against the church and its members not hesitating to spread . . . falsehoods against the people of his own town where he had lived for years and never had been molested by anyone." He lectured in the East "and no lie however black was too great for him to swear to as being true." [37] But by 1895 the Presbyterians could claim for Mendon "a strong and rapidly growing sentiment in favor of higher Christian education, which is admitted to be one of the direct results of the Presbyterian mission school work." [38]

Two products of the mission schools not appreciated at home were Hans Freece and N. E. Clemensen of Mt. Pleasant, "The two shining lights . . . and the two biggest pumpkins" of Utah Presbyterianism, as a fellow townsman called them.[39] The "two reverend slanderers," sons of early Danish immigrants, joined the ministry, Clemensen to serve in Logan, Freece to attend Park College, take a law degree at Columbia, and become a special speaker on Mormonism for the Woman's Board of Home Missions. Objects of flattering interest in Presbyterian circles outside Utah, they offended their home town with testimonies which depicted themselves as once "poor, deluded, ignorant, blind pagan Mormons." Clemensen seemed a "very irrational, erratic 'blood and thunder' ingrate," and as late as 1905 in Mt. Pleasant itself, after an eastern tour attacking Mormon Senator Reed Smoot, did not hesitate to call the people of Utah "law breakers" and recommend a mission school in every town to overthrow Mormon treason. Freece, considered a "slippery, oily, slimy hypocrite," at the same time traveled in Europe trying to arouse foreign governments to what he was convinced was still a Mormon menace. His family in Utah felt driven to make public repudiation of his irresponsible carryings on.[40]

A happier memory was Mt. Pleasant's first public celebration of Christmas when many saw their first Christmas tree laden with presents from eastern missionary barrels and their first oranges, which children mistook for yellow apples. Arranged by Mr. McMillan, the event supplied the topic of conversation for days after. "And so, many modern customs were brought here through the medium of the church and school that have served both to entertain and instruct its patrons."[41] It was an example of the constructive services of the Presbyterians, services more popular and persuasive than their religion. To the orthodox, they were subtle schemes of the Adversary to lure the children. By 1885, before they even left Scandinavia, Mormon converts were being warned against the sectarian schools in Utah.[42]

The image of the gentile was fearsome. But the grateful students, beneficiaries of the kindly and cultured influence of so many of the denominational workers, knew better. The granddaughter of a Danish immigrant who was one of the founders of Ephraim remembered that "somewhere in the grades" her father decided "it would be wise to send us children to the Presbyterian school. It was a shock to our relatives and friends. . . ." But the teachers were Reverend and Mrs. G. W. Martin, "wonderful examples of people who stuck with their post," who, for all the minister's austerity – he never slipped out of his role as pastor – "made friends if not converts." They were interesting, different: they would hitch up the surrey and visit the southern canyons and bring home Indian relics and wonders of nature "that the local people did not value." Their home was the town's library and their Temperance Union sponsored a reading room, "warm, well lighted and furnished with tables and comfortable chairs," with plenty of good books, current magazines, and daily papers. Utah history owes Mr. Martin a debt: he kept the only complete file of the *Manti Messenger*.[43]

In the neighboring hamlet of Gunnison, Mrs. M. M. Green, missionary from New York, performed an even broader service. She arrived in 1884 with her daughter and started a school with thirty-five pupils. Since "the majority of the homes were Scandinavian and house-keeping, as we understand it, was unknown to them," they taught the girls sewing, "the lessons graded from first lessons with a needle to dressmaking and art embroidery," and, in the second year, "the Kitchengarden, taking Saturday morning for it; the occupation material, or outfit, was a gift from Dr. Hall's church in New York." Cooking school followed Kitchengarden, "in our own home, for the girls of our school and several Mormon girls were allowed to come by paying ten cents a week. . . ." After three years Mrs. Green saw "a wonderful change and transformation in the homes, neat, well-kept houses, and good food nicely prepared on their tables."

Since Gunnison had no minister, Mrs. Green read a sermon every Sunday evening and on Wednesdays a "popular lecture," or she staged a musical or debate or "an evening with some historical character and his times." A reading room open nightly supplemented these Wednesday evening "literary engagements." Besides these educational services, Mrs. Green "had much to do with the sick." Gunnison had no physician, the people knew "nothing of the laws of health," and Mrs. Green procured the Mormon meetinghouse to give a course of lectures. Whenever she attended the sick, she made it a special point to tell the family how to avoid the sickness thereafter, "till now the standard of health is much higher than when we first came, and the Mormon bishop told me not long ago that he had carefully marked the difference in the surrounding towns, giving me credit for teaching the people how to prevent sickness."[44] Service like this was an unheralded but far-reaching aspect of the "conflict of sects and civilization."

Other denominations followed in the wake of the Presbyterians, their experiences remarkably alike, if less extensive. The Congregationalists, despite their admirable New West Education Commission, which began an academy in Salt Lake in 1878 and by 1895 had schools in many towns with 200 teachers and 7000 students, and despite their Sunday schools and Temperance Bands and Loyal Leagues, their reading rooms and Benevolent Societies, "all devised for the purpose of elevating public sentiment and shaping character according to Christian models," paid no special attention to the Scandinavians.[45] The Methodists did, writing a whole chapter of "Scandinavian Methodist" activity into their Utah history.

The Scandinavian work began in 1882 when Bishop J. F. Hurst, following a decision of the annual meeting, appointed P. A. H. Franklin, a convert from Mormonism, the first special missionary. When the following year Franklin was transferred to the Sanpete Valley Circuit, Martinus Nelson, from Norway by way of Chicago, became pastor of a First Norwegian Church in Salt Lake and principal of a Norwegian school conducted in the home of Miss Emily L. Anderson. The Woman's Home Missionary Society that same year sent Lisa M. Sangstad as its first lady missionary to Utah. The Scandinavian Methodists in Salt Lake were few but strong enough to survive the burning out of their chapel in 1892 and to rebuild it. Rev. Francis Hermans, pastor in 1893, explained the small membership as "Owing much to the migratory state of the population, all being working people . . . when the last crisis came a good many returned East in hope to better their condition." The Sunday school, however, he said, was most encouraging.[46]

The Scandinavian Methodists had small congregations in at least a dozen communities besides Salt Lake, in the main where Presbyterians had already made a beginning, like Mt. Pleasant and Ephraim in Sanpete Valley and Hyrum in Cache Valley. "Our work here is uphill," "The work is hard, but is looking up," were familiar phrases in the reports. Often the Scandinavians shared the same facilities with the English Methodists, as in Brigham City, where the Scandinavian workers were confident "fruit will be gathered . . . for the garner on high." By 1897 the work in Mt. Pleasant among the English and the Scandinavians was consolidated under a single pastor, a common pattern by that time.

By 1893 the Methodists had eight preachers, one lady missionary, fourteen churches and "Mission Homes," valued at $50,000 and four parsonages at $2750. Missionary appropriations for general and school work among both English and Scandinavians during 1890 alone reached $24,000; the Board of Church Extension contributed another $10,000, and the Woman's Missionary Society $10,000 more. T. C. Iliff estimated that by 1895 the Methodist Episcopal Church had spent $500,000, the Presbyterians $880,000 on Utah.[47]

As with other denominations, it was a large outlay for little return: 23 probationers, 98 members, though the 11 Sunday schools with 17 teachers and 287 children, and the 11 day schools with 13 teachers and 495 children were the usual hopeful sign. The day schools provided instruction in "all the common English branches," and the girls were taught "domestic industries." All the day and Sunday schools were conducted in English, though the congregational singing employed Norwegian and Danish Methodist hymnals as well as the Epworth Hymnal and Gospel Hymns. Young people's societies and a few ladies' aid societies managed to raise $1000 for self-support and benevolence in 1892, and $690 for improvements and indebtedness. *Vidnesbyrdet*, the Norwegian and Danish weekly Methodist church paper, was "largely circulated in the Territory." In 1888 the work was organized into a district, with Martinus Nelson as presiding elder. In 1892, by which time one hundred traveling and local preachers had been employed, it was taken out of the Utah Mission to become part of the Western Norwegian and Danish Mission Conference.[48]

The Baptists had Swedish missionaries in Salt Lake by the end of 1884 – Anna B. Nilsson and Caroline Larson – and the following year, in response to "most urgent appeals" from the District Missionary of the American Baptist Home Mission Society and Baptist pastors in Utah, the board sent five – a considerable reinforcement – to Utah, two of them Scandinavians, since "there was great need." Miss Nilsson found the work in Utah "the hardest she had ever done." She was greatly moved by the poverty of the people and claimed to be feeding forty to sixty each month in Salt Lake City. Miss Larson wrote downheartedly that while there were many Scandinavians in Ogden, there were but three Baptists among them. Her greatest success came in the Industrial School in Ogden, in women's meetings, and in the homes. But she regretted there was no preacher to speak to them in a language they could understand. What the visits gained was lost because there was no duly organized Scandinavian Baptist church. She pleaded for Scandinavian preachers.[49] At length, in 1891, some Scandinavian brethren in Salt Lake City withdrew from the First Church to form the Swedish Baptist Church, with John B. Bloomfield acting as pastor. Four years later, however, it had only a dozen members.[50]

The Lutherans came late and their activity was largely urban. The earlier immigrants had little love for the Establishment and failed to kindle to it no matter what their eventual quarrel with Mormonism. The Augustana Synod had the Mormon proselytes in mind for ten years before actually sending two missionaries among them in 1882, but they found the discouragements great, the soil stony, and no missionary stayed long. In twenty-seven years, which saw long vacancies, the only fruits were seven congregations, with 294 communicants and six churches.

The yield for other Lutheran synods was equally barren.[51] A Swedish Lutheran congregation founded in Salt Lake in 1885 could boast only thirty members in three years.[52] In 1888 Frans August Linder, acting under sanction of the Evangelical Lutheran Augustana Synod of North America, held services in Ogden's Presbyterian Church after meetings had been held some months at the home of Hanna Lund. The Elim Swedish Lutheran Church was organized in 1888 with ten charter members, but by the time its chapel and parsonage were built in 1890 it changed its name to the Elim Lutheran Church and conducted services in English. The synod supported it with over $3000 from 1888 to 1891, and countrymen from Rock Island sent proceeds from a fair as a donation.[53] A Norwegian Home Missionary Society sent Pastor Skabo to Utah in 1891; Andrew Israelsen, a Mormon missionary in Norway, remembered the pastor's farewell, when Andreas Mortensen, apostate Mormon, spoke on "Joseph Smith, a False Prophet."[54] Like other baffled missionaries, Pastor Skabo would ascribe his indifferent success to the fact that apostate Mormons were lost altogether, becoming "infidels" and "free thinkers."

Danish Lutherans were tardiest of all, strange in view of the overwhelming proportion of Danes among Utah's Scandinavians, but it reflected perhaps the general indifference of Danish immigrants elsewhere in the United States to the home church. The Danish Mission Society at Neenah, Wisconsin, in time to become the strongly Grundtvigian Danish Lutheran Church in America, was not organized until 1872, when Danes numbered 30,000 in the United States. Norwegians had organized as early as 1850, when they numbered 12,000. Before 1872 there had not existed a single purely Danish congregation with a Danish minister. Not more than 5 per cent of the Danes in the country were in any way associated with the Lutheran church, a lukewarmness which may have resulted from the factional wrangles of the church in Denmark.[55]

Whatever the reasons, the Danes generally showed little concern for their countrymen lost to Mormonism. Though a society had been organized in Denmark in 1869 to do missionary work among the Danes in America, it was not until 1906 that the "Utah-Missionens Udvalg," conceived in Denmark, sent Pastor Harald Jensen to Salt Lake City to found a Danish Evangelical Lutheran congregation. Denmark paid for all but $2700 of the $17,000 to build the church Tabor, constructed in 1908. Jensen had been associated with *Kristeligt Dagblad* in Copenhagen and in 1899 had gone to Blair, Nebraska, for the diminutive

Danish Church Association, which in 1884 had been formed by congregations once belonging to the Norwegian-Danish conference.[56]

Hans Freece, Mt. Pleasant's notorious Presbyterian convert, described the "Indre Mission" as a refuge for those "who escape the Mormon fold and renew relations with the mother church in Denmark." The Danish consulate was to look after the welfare of Danes who, having been deceived by Mormonism, sought aid and advice. He described the reclaimed converts as coming from "the better element of the rank and file of the Mormon Church." He asserted Salt Lake had a strong Danish anti-Mormon committee whose secretary was touring America urging his Danish brothers to join them in saving the Danish girls from the grip of the Mormon octopus.[57] Freece was simply up to his old tricks. The Danish church in Salt Lake, in spite of all his claims, remained small.

To the extent they merely played upon prejudices and Old World ties that made their proselytes not only less Mormon but less American, the Lutherans were not the constructive force in community building that the other denominations, and certainly Mormonism itself, attempted to be. The aims were different: Mormonism, for example, planted the immigrant; Lutheranism attempted to unsettle him. Mormonism had him break with the past; Lutheranism turned him back nostalgically to the old tongue and the old church in futile longing. Lutheran congregations could hardly thrive when only a gnawing discontent instead of an illuminating faith formed the bond of fellowship.

If in numbers the result of denominational effort in Utah was small, in influence it was much greater. The missionaries and the malcontents dramatized their needs and difficulties, provoking a national crusade. Frances Willard wrote a preface to Jennie Froiseth's *Women of Mormondom* calculated to harrow up the soul of the nation.[58] Eliza Young's *Wife No. 19*, detailing the hard times of Brigham Young's divorced wife, was hardly another *Uncle Tom's Cabin*, but it drew tears from Harriet Beecher Stowe, who – daughter, wife, and mother of clergymen – felt an uncommon tenderness for the reports coming from the Christian martyrs in Utah. She gladly contributed to the Anti-Polygamy Society and its *Standard*.[59] The salvation of Utah was peculiarly a woman's work. "In thousands of church parlors throughout the nation . . . sober, dignified and purposeful, they sat on horse-hair sofas around tables covered with worn green baize and passed resolutions."[60] The

President and Congress could hardly turn a deaf ear to such notable and insistent busybodies, to voices so pure and convincing. Besides, the Liberal party in Utah, a union of anti-Mormons of whatever faith or political persuasion, had long been struggling for leadership and had maintained an effective lobby in Washington. Impatient with the slow reformation of the denominations, they looked to the law.

On a rising tide of public feeling against the Mormons, carpetbaggers and crusaders joined hands to pass one abortive bill after another seeking the formula that would at last throttle polygamy and its nourisher, Mormon immigration: in 1867 the Cragin bill, which sought the abolition of jury trials in polygamy cases; in 1869 the "iniquitous" Cullom bill, which would subject Utah to complete federal control, an attempt which stirred Mormondom to its center and occasioned a mammoth protest meeting in the Tabernacle in Salt Lake to petition the Senate not to pass it; in 1874 the Poland bill, which would have jury lists drawn by the clerk of the district courts to procure non-Mormon jurors; in 1876 the Christiancy bill, which would disqualify jurors who scrupled to convict polygamists; in 1882 the Edmunds Act, which at last made "cohabitation" a punishable offense, since polygamy was hard to prove, and which disqualified polygamist voters, brought United States marshals and their deputies and the days of the underground to Utah, and a commission to regulate its elections; in 1884 the Hoar bill, which would dissolve the Perpetual Emigrating Fund; and finally in 1887 the Edmunds-Tucker Act, which dissolved the Fund, disincorporated the Mormon Church itself, disfranchised the women, and led to the capitulation of the church in the official manifesto in 1890 abandoning polygamy. The addition of polygamists to the excluded classes in the federal immigration law in 1891 came as an anticlimax.[61]

Hardly a presidential message after the Civil War failed to allude to the "Mormon Question." President Grant, with Mormon-eaters like Vice-President Schuyler Colfax and Dr. John P. Newman, pastor of the Methodist Episcopal Church of Washington, advising him, dealt heavily, reversing Andrew Johnson's unobtrusive policy. "It is not with the religion of the self-styled Saints that we are now dealing," he told Congress in 1872, "but their practices. . . . they will not be permitted to violate laws under the cloak of religion." He had found territorial officers "willing to perform their duty in a spirit of equity and with a due sense of sustaining the majesty of the law."[62] The Saints in Scandinavia read his message in 1873 as the *Stjerne* reprinted it from the New York *Herald*'s account, "President Grant and the Mormons," and they may have had misgivings the year before when, at Brigham Young's arrest at his home in Salt Lake City, *Stjerne* queried, "Should the Saints Leave Utah?"[63] The threats only strengthened the resolve of the faithful to gather, which made the crusaders redouble their exertions. It was a vicious circle.

President Hayes, after a visit to Salt Lake City with General Sherman in 1880 during which the Liberals made sure he got only their point of view, expressed a sentiment stronger even than Grant's: "To the re-establishment of the interests and principles which polygamy and Mormonism have imperilled, and fully reopen to the intelligent and virtuous immigrants of all creeds, that part of our domain which has been in a great degree closed to general immigration by the immoral institution, it is recommended that the government of the Territory of Utah be reorganized."[64] President Garfield the next year charged that "The Mormon Church not only offends the moral sense of mankind . . . but prevents the administration of justice through the ordinary instrumentality of the law."[65] After Garfield's assassination, which in some quarters was laid to a Mormon fanatic, President Arthur felt convinced that the Utah problem could be solved only "by the exercise of absolute federal force."[66] Even President Cleveland, far less inclined to press the campaign—the Edmunds-Tucker bill in 1887 became law without his signature—was persuaded that immigration "reenforced the people upholding polygamy" and called upon Congress in 1883 to pass a law that would "prevent the importation of Mormons into the country."[67]

With immigration central to the whole problem, it was inevitable that the contest between the Mormons and the United States should move into the international arena. "I would thank you to keep your Mormons at home," President Buchanan told Lord Clarendon, secretary of foreign affairs for Great Britain. "The English Mormon is a strange article."[68] In 1879 Secretary of State William M. Evarts dispatched a lengthy circular to United States diplomatic and consular officers in Europe directing attention of the growth of Mormonism through recruitment abroad.[69] He instructed them to seek the aid of foreign governments in preventing the departure of "large numbers" of "prospective lawbreakers," and through the public press of the principal cities and ports of Europe to call attention to the subject and the "determined purpose" of the United States to eradicate polygamy.

The Supreme Court had that year upheld the constitutionality of the antibigamy enactment and had dispelled any doubt concerning the ability and intent of the government to enforce it. Friendly powers, Evarts felt, would not willingly permit the United States to become a "resort or refuge for the crowds of misguided men and women whose offenses against morality and decency would become intolerable" in their own land, and he asked them to take steps to check "these criminal enterprises by agents who are thus operating beyond the reach of the law of the United States."

> Under whatever specious guise the subject [of polygamy] may be presented by those engaged in instigating the European movement to swell the numbers of the law-defying Mormons of Utah, the bands and organizations which are got together in foreign lands as recruits cannot be regarded as otherwise than a deliberate and systematic attempt to bring persons to the United States with the intent of violating their laws and committing crimes expressly punishable under the statute as penitentiary offenses.[70]

What Evarts failed to envision was how any government was going to recognize potential lawbreakers and under what pretext they could be prosecuted before the fact. And if America nursed the serpent by permitting Mormon agents to go abroad in the first place, she could not expect the countries of Europe to kill it by cutting off its tail. The London *Times* ridiculed the whole idea, while the London *Examiner* could not refrain from commenting on the "plaintive appeal": "The morality of this circular is admirable; the logic is lamentable." The *Examiner*, convinced there was not injustice enough in England to punish the Mormons, was amazed: "The Great Republic has afforded a refuge to the visionaries of Europe. Into its bosom have been welcomed the professors of every faith and of no faith at all. Imperialist Princes and democratic Nihilists equally go through Garden Island unnoticed. . . . Why do they not prevent the landing of German Socialists, Russian Nihilists, and Irish Finians?"[71] Elder N. C. Flygare, in charge of a company of Mormon emigrants from Scandinavia arriving on the *S.S. Wyoming* a month after the Evarts communiqué, noted that the secretary's letter had been widely published abroad but few believed anything so absurd could be seriously fathered by the American government. The Mormons, he said, were not disturbed by it in the least.[72]

The Danish minister for foreign affairs felt that "joining the Mormon community can in no wise be likened to the resolution to contract polygamous alliances," and found it impossible "according to the principles generally admitted in penal law" to see in Mormon proselyting "an attempt to incite to a violation of the laws of the United States." [73] While he deplored the expatriation of Danish subjects, he did not see that Denmark was empowered to stop the abuse. The United Kingdoms of Norway and Sweden indicated that the government and public sentiment were "averse to having their population victimized and depleted by immoral and criminal means" and agreed to discourage Mormon activity as far as consistent with law.[74] All three countries promised a campaign of enlightenment through notices in the press against the "fallacious promises" and "the enticements of the emissaries of Mormonism." [75]

The official warnings sharpened anti-Mormon feeling. Prussia banished the American missionaries. In Copenhagen a sectarian convention could agree on no matter of business or doctrine until the subject of Mormonism came up, "when all immediately united in the sentiment 'The Mormons must go.' " [76] During the decade 1880 to 1890, however, the missionary force abroad actually more than doubled – not a few of the elders were refugee polygamists evading the Edmunds law – although conversions fell by some 2600; emigration declined less sharply, even increasing by several hundred in Sweden, since in the early 1880s many long-time members finally were enabled to go to Zion.[77]

Convert-emigrants from Scandinavia numbered fewer than one thousand annually during the 1880s, but Mormon immigration remained in the popular mind an alarming invasion capable of perverting the nation's morals. Reported the Omaha *Herald* in 1885: "The arrival in the United States of a few hundred Danes who have been brought here by the Mormon church is the signal for an outcry in the eastern press against their admission into the country, and calling on the government to stop this kind of immigration." The *Herald* defended a program which might be "a plain matter of business" in increasing the wealth of the territory and the church, but which "combines with it positive Christian charity." [78] The majority thought otherwise. In January 1882, alone, mass meetings were held in cities as scattered as Chicago, Portland (Maine), Rochester, St. Paul, and Pittsburg, where governors, congressmen, and clergy helped pass resolutions calling for enforcement of the antibigamy law and the prevention of statehood for Utah.[79]

At the Madison Avenue Congregational Church in New York, the Reverend Dr. Newman wailed that the locomotive which was supposed to sound the death knell of Mormonism instead had drawn to Utah "trains laden with converts . . . brought from across the seas." It pained him to see the country calmly permitting these foreigners to be clothed with all the rights of citizenship. "But one official diplomatic protest was ever made against such proceedings, and Mr. Evarts deserves all honor for making it."[80] Methodist ministers gathered in Philadelphia in February unanimously invited "the attention of the executive authorities at Washington to the relation of European emigration procured by Mormon emissaries to the continuance and enlargement of this great evil, and we suggest careful inquiry whether more effective measures may not be taken to anticipate and prevent this constant supply of this organized iniquity."[81] In Utah itself Governor Eli Murray in 1883 quaked a warning to the secretary of the interior "and through you the country" that they were beset by "another irrepressible conflict."[82] In vain did John T. Caine, delegate from Utah, in denouncing the Edmunds-Tucker bill in 1887, call attention to the fact that the last census had showed a more rapid decrease in foreign-born population in Utah than in twenty-nine states and the District of Columbia.[83]

The common image, like the editorials in the New York *Times*, pictured Utah's "defiant polygamists" being "reinforced by thousands of converts secured by their missionaries in the Southern States and in Europe." The *Arizona* had just landed 505 converts: "Four-fifths of these misguided persons came from the Scandinavian peninsula."[84] Even an observer like John Codman, whose *Mormon Country* had given an accurate and sympathetic description of the 1870s, now joined the alarm: "Most of the 'plural wives' of the present time," he wrote in 1881, "come from those Scandinavian lands where chastity is scarcely considered a virtue, but is readily yielded for earthly profit, to say nothing of celestial glory. There is a market for them in the small settlements and on ranches, where they prefer to be members of the family, even of the second or third grade, rather than to accept the position of servants." In his view, such women were criminals. On arriving at Castle Garden they should be warned of the consequences of violating the antibigamy statute, and if the government considered the abolition of polygamy of as much importance as cities regarded the suppression of houses of ill fame, "let it make similar periodical raids on the farm houses of Utah." He was sounder when he asked, "What more, in addition to carrying out the present laws, can be done to hasten the work which railroads, newspapers, and fashions are fast accomplishing?"[85]

In the anti-Mormon campaign, the common fallacy that the church brought the immigrant over at its own expense made its Perpetual Emigrating Fund the object of special attack. The Edmunds Law of 1882, "begotten by prejudice, conceived in ignorance, and brought forth in hate," as the Mormons felt,[86] did not lay the axe to the root of immigration. Territorial Governor Eli H. Murray in his annual report to the secretary of the interior in 1883 protested against the special legal privileges under which the P.E.F. Company operated. "By this act [of incorporation in 1851] the whole system of emigration is handed over by the legislature to a corporation under the control of the Church. No other system has by law been authorized or permitted in Utah, and this rich corporation continues as a part of the Church and State machinery to gather converts from all parts of the world."[87]

An amendment was consequently added to the Edmunds-Tucker bill, then before Congress, which would annul the laws that had created the P.E.F. Company. The act of 1887 did disincorporate it as part of a similar action against the church itself.[88] After bitter court proceedings the company was dissolved and a receiver appointed to assume charge of its assets. Its property consisted of "a safe, desk, records, account books, promissory notes, paper of various kinds, and $2.25 in defaced silver coins"; the company's statement as of November 10, 1887, showed total assets of $417,968.50, nearly all in the form of promissory notes, uncollectable and of no value.[89] The strength of the "rich corporation" had never lain in idle wealth but in constant use as a revolving fund. Its life, now over, had drained into the lives of the people it had assisted.

A further and local attack on Mormon recruiting was to deny the convert-immigrants citizenship on the grounds of allegiance to a church considered treasonable to the government. In 1857 Judge W. W. Drummond objected that "a certain tool of Gov. Young, named Appleby" as clerk of the supreme court "would occasionally go to the houses of those English Mormons, administer to them an oath, give them a sort of certificate, and pronounce them naturalized citizens." In this way, he charged, alien-born citizens, not legally naturalized according to the acts of Congress, cast the majority of votes and held many of the offices. "The laws of the Territory are nearly all void from the beginning in consequence of being passed and made by alien enemies of the country. . . . no man was voted for unless first nominated by Brigham Young." Judge Drummond asserted that "fifty a day of those poor, deluded and silly creatures were brought into Court as Jurors, and each for himself would swear that he was a 'naturalized Citizen,'" but examination of his papers showed that "this Ajax of the law Appleby" had administered the oath outside of court and "in the name of Israel's God" had pronounced him citizen.[90]

Twenty-five years later George Q. Cannon, English convert and perennial Mormon delegate to Congress, whose own naturalization was questioned, was meeting similar accusations: "He knows it is charged that the Mormon people consist principally of the very lowest classes of Europe, people who neither know nor care a whit about our form or system of government . . . that many of these are not bona fide citizens of the United States . . . that it is asserted that he has each time been returned as a Delegate to Congress by the votes of these alleged aliens."[91]

Associate Justice Thomas J. Drake, holding district court in Provo in 1866, ruled that the probate courts had no power to issue naturalization papers, and all that had been issued were illegal, null, and void. He refused papers to any man who defied the antipolygamy act of Congress. "We are proud to record," editorialized the New York *Times*, "that the Judges of this Territory are firm in the discharge of official duty. . . . The U.S. Courts in Utah are now considered an honor to the country."[92] District Attorney Charles Hempstead at the same time denied petitions for naturalization coming from those practicing polygamy. In 1870 Chief Justice James B. McKean, eager to make the Cullom bill law for Utah, went further: he denied naturalization to those who simply believed in the doctrine. When the judge asked John C. Sandberg, a Swede, and William Horsley, an Englishman, whether or not they regarded the act of 1862 as binding upon them, Sandberg replied he believed it right to obey the laws of God rather than of man, and Horsley declined to answer, whereupon McKean refused them citizenship, declaring they were "not of good moral character." [93]

To one sympathetic observer, the unrelenting efforts to deny Mormon immigrants the rights of citizenship were among the evils attendant on "Pro-Consular governments," enabling a man like McKean to "ride roughshod over Article 5 of the Amendments of the Constitution": "It was his wont, not only to anticipate indictment, trial, and conviction, by the sentence he imposed, but to compel men to testify against themselves when applying for naturalization, and then, upon the testimony thus tyrannically and unconstitutionally obtained, he uniformly refused to naturalize them." Ironically, the same men, "decayed politicians," who had enfranchised promiscuous and devil-worshipping Negroes in the South would disfranchise polygamous Mormons. "The reason for this decided preference for the idle, shiftless, thieving Negro, as an elector, over the industrious, thrifty Mormon, who believes in a religious delusion, does not readily appear to one not versed in American politics." The explanation was simply that the carpetbagger expected Negro votes "to keep himself and his friends forever *in*, while he knows that Mormon votes, intelligently cast, will keep himself and friends forever *out*, with no hope of handling Mormon money. . . ." [94]

The immigrant vote was, of course, of greatest importance to the church. "Get clothed at once with all the rights of an American citizen," Apostle George A. Smith urged the Saints in a sermon in 1874 in Richfield, Utah, in the heart of Scandinavian country. "You have a judge in this district who is a just and honorable man, and who does not consider himself a missionary sent here expressly to convert you. If you lived in Salt Lake City I would tell you to see Judge McKean and his whole 'ring' in perdition before taking the false oath he seeks to impose." They should not shirk their duty if drawn on a jury; they should not lie before God or man but convict anyone indicted for polygamy entered into since 1862 if it were proved. "We know that law is unconstitutional, and we can beat them in their own courts. Don't be nervous about it. Take a little valerian tea and put your trust in God." Unaware that events would prove him wrong and that it would take more than trust or tea to get the Saints out of their predicament, he urged them to show the world they were law-abiding. "We have stood a good deal, and we can stand it to the end." [95]

That same year an editorial on a recent municipal election in Salt Lake City at which "opposition to the 'regularly nominated' ticket was . . . the strongest ever pulled in Utah," expressed satisfaction that the Mormons were learning to exercise their citizenship as they pleased and still remain good men. "It should also teach those lobbyists at Washington who are working for proscriptive legislation, the very important fact that Utah is revolutionizing herself more effectively than can be done by Congressional interference supported by military or brute force."[96]

But the lobbyists didn't think so and pointed to Utah's giving the vote to women as a special act of contempt for the government. "Girls under age and alien women with the odor of the emigrant ship still upon their clothes, without ever having taken an oath of allegiance to the United States, without the slightest idea of the meaning of the act they are performing, or what is intended by it, cast their votes as they are instructed to in some tongue unknown to the ordinary American and go away dazed." Were it not for the steady influx of foreigners, "low, base-born foreigners, hereditary bondsmen," Mormonism's "two dreadful features," polygamy and the exalting of church over state, would "die out in America in two generations."[97]

The gentile *Circular* objected to citizenship being conferred upon alien women by their marriage with naturalized or native-born citizens. "If woman is equally a *femme sole* after as she is before marriage, by what subtle fiction can she be supposed to take upon herself the citizenship of her husband?"[98] And the *Circular* cited a maneuver during Logan's municipal election in 1874 as an illustration of the misuse of woman suffrage in Utah: there the liberal Mormons and non-Mormons joined forces and gave the church party "such a scare that at about noon, on the day of the election, the brethren feared their little union of church and state was in danger. So the bishops fell back on their old plan, and brought out the Female Relief Society in full force." Mormons who had not voted the church ticket were required to be rebaptized in penance, and a number of young men who refused were excommunicated. "No man can be a free, independent American citizen, and at the same time be a good citizen of the Kingdom of God."[99]

A late decision subscribing to that conviction, and still in the spirit of Judge Drummond's charges of 1857, was Judge Thomas J. Anderson's denial of citizenship to applicants in Salt Lake City in November

1889, because the religious covenants of the Endowment House, which an apostate Mormon divulged, gave highest allegiance to the Kingdom of God and were considered treasonable to the United States.[100] President Wilford Woodruff had the Endowment House razed forthwith, a dramatic preliminary to his manifesto the following year which discontinued polygamy itself. In his manifesto, President Woodruff cited the current accusations – blood atonement, the murder of apostates, the power of bishops' courts over civil courts, the dictation of the ballot and of temporal affairs, the treasonable nature of the endowment, the union of church and state – and refuted them. And he considered "all attempts to exclude aliens from naturalization and citizens from the exercise of elective franchise, solely because they are members of the Mormon Church," as "unpolitic, unrepublican, and dangerous encroachments upon civil and religious liberty." [101] That was evidence enough for Judge Charles S. Zane to rule in October 1890, that membership in the Mormon Church should no longer be a barrier to citizenship, though Judge Anderson, now in the second district at Beaver, had no faith in the manifesto and reaffirmed his former ruling.[102]

It had been patently true that the Saints were expected to support the People's party; to subscribe to the *Tribune*, Liberal organ, instead of the Mormon *Deseret News* was tantamount to apostasy. Mt. Pleasant, center of Mormon disaffection and already the seat of Presbyterian influence, was inevitably the most prominent Liberal municipality in central Utah, whereas neighboring Manti was strongly of the People's party. With division along national lines in 1891, Mt. Pleasant naturally went Republican – the crusading party which had solved the Mormon question as it had solved slavery – and Manti went Democratic. But in the final drive for statehood, now within sight, the church sent its emissaries throughout the territory advising people to abandon the old Mormon–anti-Mormon feud. If the Liberals simply became Republicans and the People's party all Democrats, the fight would continue. That had to be avoided at all costs, though in Salt Lake it looked very much as if the Scandinavian People's party Political Club simply converted itself into the Scandinavian Democratic Society. The brethren made some arbitrary assignments: in Panguitch, which had four eligible voters, they said, "Now you two be Republicans and you two stay with the Democrats." This they did, the two voting the Republican ticket so long they felt themselves real Republicans.[103] It could hardly be otherwise in towns where politics were still so intimate that oyster suppers at homes celebrated victories and losers wheeled winners down Main Street in a wheelbarrow.

Though it was not until the act of March 3, 1891, that the specification "polygamists" was added to the federal list of excluded classes, the popular and official agitation of the 1880s made things increasingly unpleasant for proselytes at ports of arrival, where previously they had experienced little trouble. To the anti-Mormons it seemed that more shiploads of converts arrived after the Evarts communiqué and the Edmunds Act than before. Since it was "assisted immigration," there were determined efforts to exclude the Mormons as paupers. Superintendent Jackson of Castle Garden detained twenty-five converts – four families – from Iceland in July 1886, because they could not show more than $25 all told. Mormon agent Hart, who was ready to supply them with tickets to Utah, argued that they would be provided with homes as soon as they arrived and there was no danger of their becoming public charges.[104]

In August, Immigration Commissioner Edward Stephenson detained 45 considered paupers out of a company of 301 Mormon immigrants arriving on the *S.S. Wyoming*. All went on eventually but a woman and three children, who were shipped back to England.[105] In September, Stephenson detained 44 in another company "by a strained application" of the pauper statute. Judge Andrews of the New York Supreme Court released them on writs of habeas corpus and they went on to Utah.[106] Every company that year witnessed some detentions. Never had the Mormon immigrants been subjected to such rigid questioning.

For Commissioner Stephenson the Mormons were a perplexity. On July 15, 1886, he wrote a letter to acting Secretary of the Treasury C. S. Fairchild, calling attention to the difficulty of enforcing the Act to Regulate Immigration of August 3, 1882. He considered the $500 bond for paupers invalid but he believed the commissioners were authorized by law to exclude the shiploads of Mormon converts, and asked that he and his associates be instructed to bar them. The *Nevada* had just landed 497 Mormons; two more shiploads of 700 were shortly expected; Stephenson urged shrilly that they should not be allowed to land.[107] The New York *Times* expressed its editorial sympathy with Stephenson's difficulty, but "while we are of the opinion that the nation suffers by the admission of these persons, we cannot see that the law provides for their exclusion." They could not be excluded merely as potential lawbreakers, and as for pauperism, the church "sees to it that no converts come in that condition." A possible loophole was that perhaps the immigration authorities need not accept Mormon promises to provide. Yet, it was too evident that there were no Mormons in almshouses.[108]

The detention of part of a company of 145 Saints, British and Scandinavian, who arrived at New York on the *S.S. Wisconsin* in the fall of 1888, received considerable notoriety. According to the press, they were mostly "young females, New Mormons, freshly recruited for immoral purposes."[109] The cry went up for their deportation. It developed, however, that the emigrant party consisted of 75 men, 60 women, the rest children, and that the individuals detained were three families and five boys and three girls under sixteen years of age without natural or legal guardian, though accompanied by missionaries. A Swiss family was held because of an inbecile son. A Mrs. Christine Patterson was "guilty of being 53 years of age and having with her two innocent grandchildren."[110] An investigation from Washington and assistance from the Guion Line—long patronized by the church—and Utah's delegate to Congress brought "obstructing officers to terms," and another "Mormon menace" passed into history.

In May 1890, the arrival of 140 Mormons, mostly Swedes and Danes, on the *S.S. Wyoming* led Inspector Mulholland to reflect on a visit to Utah the year before, when he learned that "the Mormons rely largely upon European converts to keep up their population, as their own children were apt to become Gentiles as soon as they grew up." He was ready to find "any reasonable pretext" for stopping the next shipload of immigrants and making "test cases" out of them.[111]

In 1891 members of a special commission appointed by the United States Treasury Department to conduct a general immigration inquiry visited Guion and Company's offices and Mormon headquarters in Liverpool, examined the records, secured "full information, and concluded the accusations against the Mormons respecting emigration from Europe were without foundation."[112]

But some crusaders were convinced that polygamy had simply gone underground in Utah after 1890 and, apparently never thinking to consult actual statistics, they declared that recruiting abroad for sinister purposes was being prosecuted with vigor. A pair of American alarmists, touring Europe on behalf of the Interdenominational Council of Women for Christian and Patriotic Service, tried as late as 1909 to rouse foreign governments to stop Mormon emigration. But in Denmark they were told they should look to their own reforms at home, and in England they found that "shipping interests opposed an anti-Mormon crusade."[113] A few years earlier the highly combustible Swedish "Föreningen Vaksamhet" or Vigilance Society urged government action against the Mormons, but it could produce only hearsay evidence of "white slavery."[114]

The agitation by this time was an anticlimax, a temporary violation of the gentleman's agreement of the 1890s that polygamy would be allowed to die a natural death. When the widely publicized Senate investigation of Reed Smoot, senator-elect from Utah in 1903, concluded without scandal, the conflict and crusade gave way to an era of good feeling and the Mormons became in time eminently respectable, so respectable, in fact, that diehards now accused the national government of subservience to Wall Street in dealing with the Mormons: it was good business to treat them well.[115]

The legislation aimed at drying up the main tributary to Utah's unorthodoxies had simply hastened what changing social and economic conditions were already accomplishing. Zion, once preached with so much intensity and conviction and expressed in a great program of immigration, was no longer a closed society. It had met successive reforms with enterprise and stiffened resistance – it had met the gentile merchants with Zion's Cooperative Mercantile Institution and the United Order, mission schools with church academies, worldly fashions with young people's retrenchment associations, polygamy raids with the underground, and all the legal attacks with petitions and mass meetings and an expenditure of eight million dollars in the courts.[116] But Zion realized at last that it had to accommodate itself to changing times. The gentile had come to Utah, and with him the world. Zion as an ideal expanded beyond the provincialities of Deseret and came to mean any place where the pure in heart dwell. Mormonism spiritualized its message and no longer frightened the nation as an *imperium in imperio*. Insisting less on building a literal Kingdom, it joined hands with eastern capital to build a greater Utah.

With the establishment of a state Bureau of Immigration in 1911, what had been almost exclusively a Mormon enterprise turned secular, and Commissioner H. T. Haines in a letter to T. V. Powderley could advertise Utah as "a splendid state for the best classes of immigrants," part of his effort to secure for Utah "a fair share of the admitted aliens to the United States" and induce them to leave the congested centers and come to the sparsely settled West.[117]

In Europe itself Mormonism's biblical millennium no longer appealed to a skeptical generation. And governments struggled resolutely to improve economic and social conditions to keep their populations at home. The turn of the century saw a National Society against Emigration in Sweden and a Society for the Restriction of Emigration in Norway which emphasized the development of domestic opportunities.[118] Life in Scandinavia had become more congenial and the Mormon Zion looked less attractive to emigrants who would have to undertake the journey at their own risk.

Although nearly seven hundred Mormon missionaries served in Scandinavia during the 1890s, they did not bind the stout sheaves of their predecessors; they were only gleaners. The decade saw no organized emigration; converts left independently or in small groups usually companioned by a returning missionary. They were now like travelers who happened to be bound for the same destination and no longer, as Copenhagen and Liverpool had come to know them so well, a community on the move. By the turn of the century, a whole year's emigration did not equal what had once been a single shipload. It was clear that for Mormonism in Scandinavia the harvest was over.

EPILOGUE

Fulfillment

ON THE weekend of July 26 and 27, 1902, Brigham City, seat of fruitful Box Elder County overlooking Salt Lake Valley from the north, swelled to over twice its size. The whole town turned inside out to accommodate the estimated four thousand visitors to the great Scandinavian reunion. They arrived by team from the surrounding towns and by special trains from the north and south. On Saturday night the Scandinavian Dramatic Association of Salt Lake got things under way at the Opera House with a performance of *The Fisherman from the North Sea.* On Sunday morning at nine, eighteen coaches full of Scandinavians from Salt Lake arrived to be met at the depot by the military band and, with carriages and wagons for the aged, be escorted to the Tabernacle for services at ten. Arches of evergreens, flags, and bunting festooned the sidewalks approaching the square, and over the entrance to the Tabernacle grounds huge letters spelled out "Velkommen."

Brigham City's own quiet Sunday was drowned in the babble of the reunion. The Sunday schools were dismissed and the meetinghouses of the First and Second Wards thrown open to the overflow crowds from the Tabernacle. In the school grove west of the Tabernacle the young ladies of the Mutual Improvement Association set up seats and tables and held immense quantities of sandwiches, coffee, cake, ice cream, and "summer drinks" in readiness for the picnic to follow. Amid the singing of the Scandinavian choir from Logan, the sacred concert in the afternoon by the military band, and the recital by "the best Scandinavian talent in the state" in the evening, the purpose of the reunion was almost lost.

Reunions were annual affairs, when it was good to be reminded, as Bishop Ole H. Berg told them now, that "We are not Swedes, or Danes, or Norwegians, but God's Saints." But this year was special. They had come to Brigham City to honor Peter A. Forsgren, the Swedish weaver who half a century before had been the first man to join the Mormons in Scandinavia. He had risen from his consumptive bed in Gefle to be baptized by his brother John, who in 1850 had accompanied Apostle Erastus Snow to found the mission. Peter and his sister Erika had come to Zion in 1853 with the first large company of Scandinavian Saints. En route he had married Christine Knudsen and with her had gone to live in Box Elder Fort under John's father-in-law, Bishop William Davis. They had made their home in Brigham City, as the fort was renamed, ever since. Not a few of the town's floors were carpeted with rugs from their loom. Now, with his gold-headed cane, token of his countrymen's esteem, and with a flowing mane like Walt Whitman's, he looked the founder and father of them all.

The reunion epitomized the history of the Scandinavian Mormons and their distinction among Scandinavian immigrants to the United States: their religious motivation as dissenters from the old Establishment and as converts to a new and American authority, the Kingdom of Zion; their union as Scandinavians overriding Danish, Swedish, and Norwegian divisions, a union which had characterized them as proselytes, as emigrants, and as settlers; their self-help under an American doctrine and program and an American leadership, effecting their transformation from despised ugly ducklings to respected Saints and citizens, members of a flourishing church and a prosperous community they themselves had helped to build.

It was not a bad record. "We are now 45,000," Anthon H. Lund told them, "and a great power in our state." They could be forgiven if they did not count the losses and the failures, the backtrailers, the disappointed, and the disaffected. At the moment nearly two hundred of their sons were in Scandinavia as missionaries preaching the old dream of Zion. They could sing the hymns of longing for Zion now, as they used to do while still in Babylon, and look out the Tabernacle windows upon the mountains of the Lord, their fields and villages. It was a time of thanksgiving and pride: for their record in church, with countrymen as bishops and stake presidents and patriarchs, and one of them in the leading Council of Seventy and another as apostle and a member of the First Presidency; for their record in the state, with countrymen as mayors and councilmen, solid farmers and directors of cooperatives, schoolteachers and professors, one of them the president of the Agricultural College, another the state superintendent of schools. Sunday night the excursionists could entrain for home feeling it had been a good conference.

Down in Ephraim, Canute Peterson, nursing his rheumatic hip with a cushion and too ill to go to Brigham City, read of the doings and thought about the promises old Patriarch John Smith had made him in Nauvoo nearly sixty years before – that he should have an inheritance in Zion and gather for it and raise up a posterity to keep his name in remembrance. It had all come to pass, not only for himself but for his people. In October he could die, "in the harness" as he had been determined to, content that the promises had been fulfilled. One by one, like him, the founders, once stripling disciples burning to build the Kingdom, were going home. Heaven, they must have felt, was but a greater Scandinavian Zion.

SOURCES AND NOTES
INDEX

Sources and Notes

HAVING a literal faith in the books out of which men shall be judged, the Mormons have been from the first a record-keeping people. The Prophet Joseph Smith, who himself kept a journal which formed the basis of a documentary history of his church, advised his elders to keep daily accounts: "For your journals will be sought after as history and scripture. That is the way the New Testament came, what we have of it, though much of the matter was written by the apostles from their memory of what had been done, because they were not prompt in keeping daily journals."

The footnotes below reflect the richness of the Mormon sources. With each chapter fully documented, it is needless to reproduce a formal bibliography here, except to call attention to principal archives. The Historian's Office at the headquarters of the Church of Jesus Christ of Latter-day Saints in Salt Lake City is the chief source of information on the history of Mormon activity in Scandinavia. Most of the mission and emigration records have been assembled there. The names of the Scandinavian converts may be followed from the mission membership book, with its notation "Emigrerede til Amerika," to the emigration ledgers kept in Copenhagen and Liverpool, to the log of the journey kept by the clerk appointed in every shipboard company, to the announcement of their arrival in the *Deseret News*, and finally to their entry as "members of record" in one of the congregations in Zion. Mormon shipping lists, a manuscript "Scandinavian Mission General History" in several fat loose-leaf folios extending from 1850 to 1926, a manuscript history of "Church Emigration" providing a description of each organized emigrant company to 1869, and the records of individual congregations are invaluable, as are the complete files of the mission periodicals *The Latter-day Saints' Millennial Star* and *Skandinaviens Stjerne*, with their pronouncements on program and doctrine, news of emigrant companies, correspondence, and annual statistical reviews. The library of the Historian's Office, furthermore, has copies of all Mormon publications in Scandinavia – tracts, pamphlets, periodicals, and books – and the only complete file of Utah's immigrant press, indispensable for the settlement story.

Other useful repositories are the Utah State Historical Society in Salt Lake City, particularly rich in county histories and biographical materials, with its relatively untouched WPA Writers' Project collection; the Daughters of Utah Pioneers, somewhat given to grandfather worship but avid collectors of biography and local lore; the remarkable Genealogical Society of Utah with a completely indexed collection of individual and family histories; the Salt Lake Public Library with a specially cataloged periodical and pamphlet collection bearing on Utah;

and the Utah Humanities Research Foundation Archives at the University of Utah, small but significant.

The personal literature of the immigrants – their letters, journals, and memoirs – continues to turn up as descendants make annual housecleanings. Richest of all the sources in human terms, it has been the most difficult to secure, the best finds often accidental. Huntington and Bancroft libraries preserve a number of fine immigrant diaries besides those found in Utah.

For the propaganda countering Mormon activity in Scandinavia, the Royal Library in Copenhagen and the New York Public Library have the most complete holdings. The "America Letters" collections in the emigrant archives at Copenhagen, Stockholm, and Oslo as yet contain very few Mormon items.

The denominational struggle in Utah for the soul of the immigrant after 1869 and the efforts of the federal government to outlaw polygamy and control Mormon immigration are best reflected in the published reports of various Christian conventions in Utah for the one, and, for the other, in the United States consular reports and the reports of the governors of Utah and the Utah Commission.

Notes

PROLOGUE: PROMISE

[1] Carrie Peterson Tanner, "A Story of the Life of Canute Peterson As Given by Himself and Some Members of His Family," MS., p. 1. Typescript copy in Historian's Office, Church of Jesus Christ of Latter-day Saints, Salt Lake City, Utah. The facts and inferences in the Prologue are based on the autobiographical passages in this account.

CHAPTER 1. FORERUNNERS

[1] Goudy Hogan on a visit to the old homestead Surgaarden, in Telemarken, Norway, in 1878. In "History of Goudy E. Hogan, by Himself and Daughter," MS., p. 56. Typescript in library, Brigham Young University, Provo, Utah.

[2] George P. Dykes to Joseph Smith, May 18, 1843, Latter-day Saint Journal History, MS.; hereafter cited as Journal History; in Historian's Office, Church of Jesus Christ of Latter-day Saints, Salt Lake City, Utah; hereafter cited as Church Historian's Office. Rasmus B. Anderson, *The First Chapter of Norwegian Immigration* (Madison, Wisc., 1895), pp. 399–408; Theodore Blegen, *Norwegian Migration to America* (Northfield, Minn., 1931, 1940), 2 vols., I, 248–49, II, 112–14; Carl M. Hagberg, *Den Norske Misjonshistorie* (Oslo, 1928), pp. 55–56; Andrew Jenson, "De förste norske Hellige," *Skandinaviens Stjerne* (Copenhagen), 51:235–38 (August 1, 1902).

[3] Carrie Peterson Tanner, "A Story of the Life of Canute Peterson As Given by Himself and Some Members of His Family," MS., p. 3. Typescript in Church Historian's Office.

[4] "Ellen Sanders Kimball," in Orson F. Whitney, *History of Utah* (Salt Lake City, 1902), 4 vols., IV, 67–69.

[5] Dykes, *op. cit.* Micah 4:2 was a favorite Mormon quotation: "And many nations shall come, and say, Come, and let us go up to the mountain of the Lord, and to the house of the God of Jacob; and he will teach us of his ways, and we will walk in his paths: for the law shall go forth of Zion and the word of the Lord from Jerusalem."

[6] Hagberg, p. 56.

[7] Goudy Hogan, Diary, MS., pp. 5, 6. Typescript in library, Brigham Young University, Provo, Utah.

[8] "Historical Sketch of J. E. Forsgren," *Box Elder News*, August 1, 1916; "Hans Christian Hansen," in Andrew Jenson, *Latter-day Saint Biographical Encyclopedia*

(Salt Lake City, 1901–26), 4 vols., II, 766, IV, 706; Peter O. Hansen, "Autobiografi," *Morgenstjernen*, 3:330–36 (1884).

[9] J. W. C. Dietrichson, *Reise blandt de norske Emigranter i "De forenede nordamerikanske Fristater"* (Stavanger, 1846; Madison, Wisc., 1896), pp. 102–8; Anderson, p. 400; Blegen, I, 254, II, 113–14.

[10] Blegen, I, 181.

[11] *Ibid.*, I, 156–57.

[12] Gustaf Unonius, *A Pioneer in Northwest America, 1841–1858* (Minneapolis, 1950), I, 313.

[13] Journal History, May 13, 1844; December 31, 1844.

[14] Hogan, p. 4.

[15] Journal History, October 23, 1844. James J. Strang, contending with Brigham Young for the leadership of the Mormons, waxed sarcastic about this enterprise. Reviewing Reuben Miller's *James J. Strang weighed in the Balance of Truth, and found wanting etc.* (1846), he wrote in *Zion's Reveille* for January 14, 1847: "It is probably something new to most of the church that a Stake of Zion was ever organized in the vicinity of Ottawa, Ills. It is nevertheless true that at a time when writs and sheriffs were quite too thick for the convenience of B. Young, H. C. Kimball, and P. P. Pratt, that they went up to the Norwegian settlement, a few miles from Ottawa, to live on the fat of the land, and *paid* the brethren for all their attentions in the *promise* of a stake, from which, however, they ordered the bishop to Nauvoo before any gathering was ever commenced at their new stake." I am indebted to Dale L. Morgan for calling the Strangite material to my attention and making available his microfilm copies of the manuscript Chronicles of Voree and the periodicals *Voree Herald*, *Zion's Reveille*, and *Gospel Herald*.

[16] Tanner, p. 8.

[17] *Ibid.*, p. 15

[18] Hogan, p. 7. The account of the Hogan family's activities is drawn from the same source, *passim*.

[19] Chronicles of Voree, MS., January 31, 1846. In State Historical Society of Wisconsin.

[20] *Loc. cit.*

[21] "Conference at the Norwegian Settlement," *Voree Herald*, 1:3 (May 1846); Chronicles of Voree, April 17, 18, 1846.

[22] Louisa Sanger to James J. Strang, July 15, 1846, Strang MSS. In Coe Collection, Yale University.

[23] Bertha S. Anderson, *Joseph Smith III* (Independence, Mo., 1952), p. 180.

[24] Rasmus B. Anderson, *The First Chapter of Norwegian Immigration*, p. 399.

[25] *Loc. cit.*

[26] Interview with Joseph Peterson of Salt Lake City, whose father worked in the same shop with Shure Olson; U.S. Seventh Census, 1850, Utah Population Census Schedule, MS., p. 21.

[27] Tanner, p. 18.

[28] George W. Bratten to Brigham Young, February 26, 1848, Journal History, same date.

[29] Tanner, p. 21. Incidents in the journey are drawn from Canute's reminiscences in this account.

[30] *The Latter-day Saints' Millennial Star* (Liverpool), 11:364 (1850). Journal History under date of 1849, Supplement, records the following recognizably Scandinavian names – with ages – in Benson's camp: Hannah Doll [Dahl], 57; Andrew Doll, 16; Swen Jacobs, 25; John Jacobs, 23; Ellen Jacobs, 18; Shure Oleson, 30; Elizabeth Oleson, 24; Ola Oleson, inf.; Canute Petersen, 24; Sarah A. Petersen, 22; Rasmus Rasmussen, 28; Henry Saby [Sabe], 57; Magla Saby, 51; Ira Saby, 17;

J. Saby, 22; Walber Saby, 16; Peter Saby, 14; Betsy Saby, 8; Christian Hyer [Hoier or Heier], 32.

[31] Tanner, p. 27

CHAPTER 2. KEYS AND COVENANTS

[1] From Robert P. Tristram Coffin, "The Mormons," *Collected Poems* (New York, 1939), p. 51.

[2] This is clear from the order in which the *Book of Mormon* and the revelations contained in *Doctrine and Covenants* appeared; and George A. Smith, official church historian, made this explicit in an early sermon: "Among the first principles that were revealed to the children of men in the last days was the gathering; the first revelations that were given to the Church were to command them to gather, and send Elders to seek out a place for the gathering of the saints." Journal History, MS., March 18, 1855. In Historian's Office, Church of Jesus Christ of Latter-day Saints.

[3] Joseph Smith founded his Church of Christ, as it was first called, on April 6, 1830, in western New York, within a few weeks after the publication of the *Book of Mormon.* The name was soon afterward changed to Church of Jesus Christ of Latter-day Saints, though its members were at first commonly referred to as Mormonites and then, persistently ever since, as Mormons or the Saints. A conscious restorer of "the ancient order," Joseph Smith, like his contemporaries the Campbellites, sought to model his organization on the Primitive Church. But since in his thinking the gospel was as old as Adam, with his own restoration of it but the latest gospel dispensation, he followed not only the New Testament but also the suggestions in the Old. He created two orders of priesthood, the Aaronic or lesser, with offices of Deacon, Teacher, and Priest; and the Melchizedek or higher, with offices of Elder, Seventy, and High Priest. From the High Priests he chose twelve apostles, the Quorum of the Twelve, presided over by a First Presidency. These provided a highly centralized administration for the growing stakes and wards of Zion, which is to say the church. A Mormon ward is the equivalent of a parish or congregation, presided over by a bishop, whose work is more like that of a pastor in other churches; a Mormon stake is the equivalent of a diocese, presided over, not by an archbishop, but by a stake president, to whom the ward bishops are responsible. Mormonism is strongly anti-clerical, and all these priesthood offices are filled by laymen, and, except for the First Presidency and the Quorum of the Twelve, in frequent rotation.

[4] A neighbor in Salt Lake City, Mrs. J. H. Iverson, gave me her childhood recollection of the rocking chair game; Peter Nielsen, Diary, MS., December 31, 1857; A. Christensen, Letter from Aalborg, Denmark, February 2, 1863, *The Latter-day Saints' Millennial Star* (Liverpool), 25:143 (February 28, 1863). Hereafter *Millennial Star.*

[5] Early Mormon hymn books devoted a whole section to the "Gathering of Israel," and one to "The Second Coming of Christ." The all-pervading theme of the gathering got into folksong too. *The Californian Crusoe . . . A Tale of Mormonism* (London, 1854) reproduces the following verse "sung to a lively tune" at a prayer meeting aboard a sailing vessel on its way from Liverpool to New Orleans in 1841:

> A Church without a gathering is not the Church for me,
> The Saviour would not order it, whatever it might be;
> But I've a Church that's called out,
> From false tradition, fear, and doubt,
> A gathering dispensation – oh that's the Church for me;
> Oh that's the Church for me; oh that's the Church for me.

[6] Reproduced in "Biography of Maria Wilhelmina C. K. Madsen," MS., p. 2. In Utah State Historical Society, WPA Writers' Project Biographies.

[7] "Second General Epistle of the Presidency of the Church of Jesus Christ of Latter-day Saints, from the Great Salt Lake Valley, to the Saints Scattered throughout the Earth," *Millennial Star*, 12:122 (April 15, 1850).

[8] *Loc. cit.*

[9] Everywhere encountered in Mormon literature, the aphorism is attributed to Lorenzo Snow, who meant it to express Joseph Smith's doctrine of eternal progression. See Eliza R. Snow, *Biography and Family Record of Lorenzo Snow* (Salt Lake City, 1884), p. 46.

[10] Quoted in Andrew Jenson, *History of the Scandinavian Mission* (Salt Lake City, 1927), p. 170.

[11] This is the view of Daryl Chase, *Joseph the Prophet* (Salt Lake City, 1944), one of the few Mormon accounts willing to set the Prophet against the background of contemporary religious movements.

[12] Emerson called Mormonism "an after-clap of Puritanism" and the furthest reach of Father Abraham. James B. Thayer, *A Western Journey with Mr. Emerson* (Boston, 1884), pp. 39–40. The British traveler Hepworth Dixon concluded that for the Mormons "Abraham is their perfect man; who forsook his home, his kindred, and his country, for the sake of God. Sarah is their perfect woman; because she called her husband lord, and gave her handmaid Hagar into his bosom for a wife. Everything that Abraham did, they pronounce it right for them to do. . . ." *New America* (Philadelphia, 1867), p. 172. Mormon historian Edward Tullidge ventured the opinion that "The same religious stock which in the Seventeenth Century formed the Cromwellian Puritans, in the Eighteenth Century became Wesleyan Methodists, and, in the Nineteenth Century, Mormons." "Joseph Smith," *Tullidge's Quarterly Magazine* (Salt Lake City), 1:259 (January 1881). An enlightening discussion of Mormon ideology in this connection is David Brion Davis, "The New England Origins of Mormonism," *New England Quarterly*, 26:147–68 (June 1953).

[13] Unlike the pastor cited in Marcus Lee Hansen (*The Atlantic Migration*, p. 171) for whom the Israelites of his day were the poor laborers and artisans oppressed by the state of society as a collective Pharoah, Joseph Smith meant a literal Israel, the blood descendants of the dispersed tribes. Those who were not of this lineage but accepted the gospel were Israel by adoption.

[14] "The first men of talent who became converts . . . had nearly all been preachers, teachers, or exhorters, and they were not slow to discover that the Old Testament abounded with, to them, evidences of prediction about America, Joseph Smith, the *Book of Mormon*, and the reign of the Saints on earth." T. B. H. Stenhouse, *The Rocky Mountain Saints* (London, 1874), p. 3. Advent titles like *Times and Seasons*, *The Millennial Star*, *The Evening and the Morning Star* were Mormonism's equivalent of the *Harbinger* and *Watchman* of other sects.

[15] *The Doctrine and Covenants of the Church of Jesus Christ of Latter-day Saints* (Salt Lake City, 1921 ed.), Section 110, verses 11–16. Hereafter cited as *Doctrine and Covenants.*

[16] Goudy Hogan from the Norwegian settlement at Sugar Creek, Iowa, as a boy of fourteen remembered hearing the Prophet preach in "the grove" at Nauvoo. "In this meeting he said that North and South America would become Mount Zion and that the Constitution would hang on a single untwisted thread and that the Latter-day Saints would save it." Diary, MS., p. 6.

[17] John Bernard, "The Father of His Country," in Allan Nevins, *American Social History as Recorded by British Travelers* (New York, 1923), p. 32.

[18] *The Book of Mormon* made its appearance in 1830, at Palmyra, New York;

The Doctrine and Covenants was first published in 1833 at Zion, Jackson County, Missouri, as *Book of Commandments for the Government of the Church of Christ.*

[19] Spring Hill, Daviess County, Missouri, "named by the Lord Adam-ondi-Ahman, because, said he, it is the place where Adam shall come to visit his people, or the Ancient of Days shall sit, as spoken of by Daniel the prophet." *Doctrine and Covenants*, Section 116.

[20] Sermon, *Journal of Discourses*, I, 333. "Different portions of the earth have been pointed out by the Almighty, from time to time, to His children, as their everlasting inheritance. . . . In the resurrection, the meek of all ages and nations will be restored to that portion of the earth previously promised to them. . . . while those who cannot prove their heirship to be legal, or who cannot prove that they have received any portion of the earth by promise, will be cast out into some other kingdom or world, where, if they ever get an inheritance, they will have to earn it by keeping the law of meekness during another probation." *Loc. cit.*

[21] Bernard DeVoto, to whom Mormonism seemed "a system utilizing religious energy for financial ends," attacked this materialism as "the American monstrosity called 'practical mysticism.' A man is a better farmer or a better carpenter when he believes that by plowing an acre or shingling an outhouse he is making himself into an archangel, confounding the Gentiles and glorifying God. . . ." DeVoto pictured "Jens Christopherson, newly arrived from Norway and set to forking out his bishop's manure pile," sharing "glories that no Gentile can ever behold, and he will increase his share in them forever. Meanwhile, his church can take over another block of New York Central at the market." "The Centennial of Mormonism," *American Mercury*, 19:1–13 (January 1930). An astringent interpretation, but, its imputations right or wrong, it confirms an important point: the convert actively and devoutly identified himself with "a cooperation of energized believers working in the name of God for an earthly Kingdom that will persist into eternity. . . ."

[22] *Doctrine and Covenants*, Sections 28, 29.

[23] *Ibid.*, Section 41.

[24] *Ibid.*, Section 45.

[25] *Ibid.*, Section 52.

[26] *Ibid.*, Section 57. ". . . the line running directly between Jew and Gentile . . ." meant the Indian border. Jackson County has remained the seat of Zion in Mormon thinking to this day; the expectation is that it will eventually be "restored." The expulsion after the Missouri troubles beginning in 1833 and the final retreat to the Rocky Mountains were long regarded as temporary; the exiles looked to their momentary return. Folklore has it that in the big barn on his estate behind the Eagle Gate in Salt Lake City, Brigham Young kept one carriage in readiness for the event.

[27] "Newell Knight's Journal," *Scraps of Biography*, quoted in Andrew Jenson, "Church Emigration," *Contributor* (Salt Lake City), 12:376ff (August 1891). It is worth noting that Newell Knight's journal, which recounts the history of this early gathering, was reproduced in Danish in the Scandinavian Mission's periodical *Ungdommens Raadgiver*, 8:35ff (May 1, 1887) – part of the indoctrination which gave the convert his image of Zion. As early as 1853 Scandinavians could read Joseph Smith's full description of his blueprint for the ideal City of Zion when *Skandinaviens Stjerne* reproduced the Prophet's "plat of Zion" letter of June 25, 1833. *Stjerne*, 3:96ff (December 15, 1853).

[28] Jenson, pp. 401–2.

[29] This use of the word "stake" as a territorial and administrative division is peculiar to the Mormon Church and merits special quotation in M. M. Matthews, ed., *A Dictionary of Americanisms* (Chicago, 1951), II, 1633. "Stakes" and "Zion's

tent" reflect a characteristic Mormon absorption and mingling of agrarian and biblical influences.

[30] "The Elders Stationed in Zion to the Churches Abroad, in Love, Greeting," *The Evening and the Morning Star* (Independence, Mo.), 2:6–7 (July 1833).

[31] "British Emigration by Years," in Richard L. Evans, *A Century of Mormonism in Great Britain* (Salt Lake City, 1937), p. 245.

[32] "History of Joseph Smith," *Deseret News*, April 9, 1856, quoted in M. Hamlin Cannon, "The Gathering of British Mormons to Western America: A Study in Religious Migration" (unpublished doctoral dissertation, American University, 1950), p. 76. A few years later in Salt Lake City, despite the Mormons' severe setbacks, Jedediah M. Grant displayed a similar enthusiasm: "This piecemeal business of gathering Saints! we want it upon the wholesale principle. That's the doctrine. I tell you, a few more boys breaking the crust of nations, like brother Carn, after a while, by driving their little wedges, will bring them over by nations. . . ." Sermon, *Journal of Discourses*, II, 74.

[33] *Doctrine and Covenants*, Section 136. A militant "Song for Camp of Israel," sung to the tune of "Auld Lang Syne," expressed the same confidence:

We go where nations yet will come
In ships, from climes abroad;
To seek protection, and a home,
And worship Israel's God.

Millennial Star, 9:336 (November 1, 1847).

[34] This may be claiming too much for both the role of the gathering and for the influence of Brigham Young's "Camp of Israel" epistle, but in view of the factions into which Mormonism splintered at the death of Joseph Smith, and their failures, this emphasis seems justified. At any rate, the epistle is for this history a significant document, anticipating as it does the temper, the morality, and the practicality of the instructions that would govern the migrations from Europe.

[35] "Preface," *Cambridge History of American Literature* (New York, 1917), I, vi.

[36] Texts could backfire. A hostile editor quoted Jeremiah 17:5, 6: "Cursed be the man that trusteth in man, and maketh flesh his arm, and whose heart departeth from the Lord. For he shall be like the heath in the desert, and shall not see when good cometh; but shall inhabit the parched places in the wilderness, in a salt land and not inhabited." He found it fulfilled to the letter in "the followers of Joe Smith, that have gone to Utah Territory; there they are in a salt and barren land, and they do not know when good comes." Quoted by Orson Hyde in a sermon in Salt Lake City, October 8, 1854, *Journal of Discourses*, II, 68.

[37] *Millennial Star*, 11:342 (November 15, 1849).

[38] "Second General Epistle of the Presidency of the Church of Jesus Christ of Latter-day Saints," *Millennial Star*, 12:122 (April 15, 1850).

[39] From "The Handcart Song," in Utah Centennial Commission, *Arts Division Source Book* (Salt Lake City, 1947), p. C-15.

[40] "Second General Epistle . . ." p. 121.

[41] See Chapter 11, "Inroads: Conflict and Crusade."

[42] Stephen L. Richards, "Building Zion Today," *The Improvement Era*, 38:231, 267–70 (1935). In 1953 the church announced the purchase of temple sites in England and Switzerland and in 1955 dedicated a temple in Berne.

[43] "Seventh General Epistle of the Presidency of the Church of Jesus Christ of Latter-day Saints," *Millennial Star*, 14:325 (July 17, 1852).

[44] Editorial, *Millennial Star*, 53:264 (April 27, 1891).

[45] Richard F. Burton, *The City of the Saints and Across the Rocky Mountains to California* (London, 1861).

CHAPTER 3. SIEGE OF BABYLON

[1] Gustav Sundbärg, *Mormonvärfningen i Sverige* (*Emigrationsutredningen*, III, Stockholm, 1910), p. 20, quoting a Swedish official.

[2] "Deseret," *Book of Mormon* name for honeybee. The provisional State of Deseret became the Territory of Utah in 1850, a pawn in the Missouri Compromise, which saw California admitted to the Union.

[3] By 1850, Mormonism had won 35,816 followers in the British Isles, 5784 of whom had emigrated. The half century 1850–1900 saw 111,330 British conversions and a total emigration of 48,043, not counting children under eight who, unbaptized, were not "members of record." Richard L. Evans, *A Century of Mormonism in Great Britain* (Salt Lake City, 1937), Appendix. Total church membership in 1850 did not exceed 60,000, with only a decided minority of 11,380 in Utah, which was substantially the number – 11,250 – Col. Thomas L. Kane found in Winter Quarters in 1846 before the move west when he estimated 4750 were scattered in Iowa settlements and 35,000 in England. Thomas L. Kane, "Number, Characteristics, and Persecutions of the Mormons," in Oscar Osburn Winther, *Thomas Leiper Kane: A Friend of the Mormons* (San Francisco, 1937), pp. 30–31. See also Andrew Jenson, *Church Chronology* (Salt Lake City, 1899), *passim.*

[4] "Erastus Snow" in Andrew Jenson, ed., *Latter-day Saint Biographical Encyclopedia* (Salt Lake City, 1901–26), 4 vols., I, 103–15; Erastus Snow, *One Year in Scandinavia* (Liverpool, 1851), p. 4.

[5] Snow's diary, from which the accompanying account is drawn, describes the journey in great detail. It was published serially in *The Improvement Era* (Salt Lake City), 14 (1910), 15 (1911). "Uddrag af Erastus Snows Dagbog" translated generous excerpts from it for the Danish readers of *Morgenstjernen* (Salt Lake City), in 1882.

[6] Erastus Snow to Zerubbabel Snow, February 14, 1851, in *One Year in Scandinavia*, p. 11.

[7] P. O. Hansen, "Autobiografi," *Morgenstjernen*, 3:333 (1884).

[8] Snow's rare pamphlet *One Year in Scandinavia*, made up largely of his reports to Brigham Young, is a primary source for the description of early mission events from this point on.

[9] Snow to Brigham Young, August 17, 1850, in *One Year*, p. 5.

[10] Snow, "Denmark, General Observations on the Country and People," *One Year*, p. 20.

[11] *Loc. cit.*

[12] Snow to Brigham Young, August 17, 1850, in *One Year*, p. 7.

[13] "Historical Sketch of J. E. Forsgren," *Box Elder News*, August 1, 1916; "De Förste Hellige i Sverige," *Morgenstjernen*, 3:27–31 (1884); Snow, *One Year*, pp. 9, 10, 13.

[14] Snow to Brigham Young, August 17, 1850, in *One Year*, p. 6.

[15] Snow to Brigham Young, July 10, 1851, in *One Year*, p. 14.

[16] A profile of mission membership appears hereafter in Chapter 5, "Ugly Ducklings."

[17] Daniel Spencer to F. D. Richards, October 17, 1855, *Millennial Star*, 17:707 (November 10, 1855).

[18] John H. Bille, *History of the Danes in America*, Wisconsin Academy of Arts, Sciences, and Letters, Transactions (Madison, Wisc., 1898), II, 6.

[19] Snow to Brigham Young, August 17, 1850, in *One Year*, p. 6.

[20] Snow to Franklin D. Richards, December 15, 1851, *Millennial Star*, 14:3 (January 1, 1852).

[21] Snow, *One Year*, p. 20.

[22] Snow to Franklin D. Richards, *op. cit.*, p. 3.

[23] "Erindringer fra Missionen i Skandinavien," *Morgenstjernen*, 1:50 (1882).

[24] "Til vore höistaerede danske Rigsdagsmaend," *Skandinaviens Stjerne*, 1:102–3 (April 1, 1852); Erastus Snow to F. D. Richards, March 23, 1852, *Millennial Star*, 14:117 (April 15, 1852). Chief Justice L. G. Brandebury, Associate Justice P. D. Brocchus, and Territorial Secretary B. D. Harris, Utah's first federal appointees, packed their bags in September 1851, after a stay of barely two months soured by quarrels and misunderstanding which they exploited to Mormon disadvantage in their reports. Their highly colored accounts, which got into the European press, were only the beginning of falsifications that by 1857 would lead the President of the United States to send federal troops to Utah to quell a "rebellion." See Orson F. Whitney, *History of Utah* (Salt Lake City, 1892), I, *passim.*

[25] *Flyvepost* (Copenhagen), n.d., reported in *Skandinaviens Stjerne*, 2:349–50 (August 15, 1853). Hereafter cited as *Stjerne.*

[26] "Aeldste A. W. Winbergs Autobiografi," *Morgenstjernen*, 4:160 (1885); "Erindringer," *Morgenstjernen*, 2:33 (1883).

[27] Hector C. Haight, "Report of Scandinavian Mission," Scandinavian Mission General History, MS., July 10, 1856. Hereafter cited as Mission History.

[28] Andrew Jenson, *History of the Scandinavian Mission* (Salt Lake City, 1927), p. 219.

[29] "Diplomatic Correspondence, Circular No. 10, August 9, 1879, Sent to Diplomatic and Consular Offices of the United States," *Papers Relating to the Foreign Relations of the United States 1879* (Washington, D.C., 1880), pp. 11, 12; Baron Rosenörn-Lehn to Secretary Evarts, January 31, 1880, *Foreign Relations 1880*, p. 936. The episode is described in detail hereafter in Chapter 11, "Inroads: Conflict and Crusade."

[30] Jenson, *History*, pp. 283–88.

[31] Theodore C. Blegen, *Norwegian Migration to America, 1825–1860* (Northfield, Minnesota, 1931), pp. 30–31; Florence E. Janson, *The Background of Swedish Immigration, 1840–1930* (Chicago, 1931), pp. 167ff; Sundbärg, *Mormonvärfningen, passim*; George M. Stephenson, "The Background of the Beginnings of Swedish Immigration, 1850–1875," *American Historical Review*, 31:709–12 (July 1926).

[32] B. J. Hovde, *The Scandinavian Countries 1720–1865* (Boston, 1943), 2 vols., II, 595.

[33] Janson, p. 167; Stephenson, p. 709. Sweden recognized only 414 Mormons in 1880, for example, though mission records show 2168 members. "Statistisk Rapport," *Stjerne*, 30:96 (December 15, 1880).

[34] *Nordstjärnan* (Stockholm), 14:16 (1894).

[35] Jenson, *History*, p. 301.

[36] A Pastor Åslev, cited in Sundbärg, p. 21.

[37] Sundbärg, p. 25.

[38] *Moss Tilskuer*, October 12, 1852, in Carl M. Hagberg, *Den Norske Misjonshistorie* (Oslo, 1928), p. 17.

[39] John E. Christiansen, "H. F. Petersens Biografi," *Morgenstjernen*, 3:270 (1884).

[40] Hagberg, p. 36.

[41] "This information is gleaned from Norwegian papers," reported the *Deseret News*, May 3, 1883; clipping in Latter-day Saint Journal History, MS. Hereafter cited as Journal History.

[42] Carl Widerborg, "Report of Scandinavian Mission," Mission History, January 1, 1859.

[43] Janson, p. 201.

[44] Stephenson, p. 715.

[45] Hector C. Haight to Orson Pratt, July 16, 1857, Mission History.

[46] John E. Forsgren to Erastus Snow, July 1, 1851, in *One Year*, p. 17; George P.

Dykes to Franklin D. Richards, n.d., in "Erindringer," *Morgenstjernen*, 1:54 (1882); Christian J. Larsen, "Skrivelser," *Morgenstjernen*, 1:61 (1882).

[47] Snow to John E. Forsgren, July 11, 1851, in *One Year*, p. 18.

[48] Postscript, Erastus Snow to Brigham Young, August 17, 1850, in *One Year*, p. 9.

[49] Ola N. Liljenquist, "Autobiografi," *Morgenstjernen*, 2:30 (1883).

[50] J. J. M. Bohn, "Autobiografi," *Morgenstjernen*, 4:40 (1885); H. J. Jensen, "Biografiske Skizze," *Morgenstjernen*, 1:103 (1882); "Biografiske Skizzer: Svend Larsen," *Morgenstjernen*, 1:174 (1882).

[51] Ezra T. Benson to John Taylor, November 26, 1856, Mission History. On such special occasions, Mormon public meetings from 1500 to 2000 were not uncommon.

[52] Snow to Brigham Young, August 17, 1850, in *One Year*, p. 8. Native strength was also appreciated in the German Mission, which in 1854 planned to have its handful of sixty-nine members emigrate to Cincinnati, Ohio, to settle with other Germans, convert them, and from among them send missionaries back to Germany in the hope they might have better success than foreign-born elders. George Ellsworth, "The Extension of Missionary Activities into Western Europe, 1849–1860," MS., p. 24, citing the *Millennial Star*, 16:648, 680–83 (October 14, 28, 1854); 16:812–13 (December 23, 1854).

[53] Journal History, September 18, 1859.

[54] Snow to Brigham Young, July 10, 1851, in *One Year*, p. 15; Mission History, December 5, 1851; December 31, 1852.

[55] Snow, sermon, Journal History, September 18, 1859.

[56] George M. Stephenson so describes the missionaries, and their converts as "the ignorant, the dregs of society," (*The Religious Aspects of Swedish Immigration* [Minneapolis, 1932], p. 96), a contradictory interpretation when it is realized the converts themselves were the missionaries. "Enthusiasts" in the seventeenth-century meaning would be more accurate.

[57] Hans Christensen, Memoirs, MS., pp. 9–11. Microfilm in Utah Humanities Research Foundation Archives, University of Utah.

[58] Willard Snow, Journal, February 6, 1853, cited in Mission History.

[59] The account of Nielsen's activities is drawn from his *Dagbog*, or Diary. The original is in possession of Frederik J. Nielsen, Blue Water, New Mexico; Orson B. West of the Historian's Office, Church of Jesus Christ of Latter-day Saints kindly made his typescript translation available to me.

[60]

Et Par Mormoner gik omkring
og sagde mange smukke Ting
om Landet ved den store Söe
om Zions Bjerg og Fredens öe
Hvor der er Fryd og Herlighed
og Penge nok og Kjaerlighed.

Casper Rimsmed, *Tvende mormonske Profeters Mirakelgjerninger, komisk og letfattelig, skildret paa Versemaal* (Randers, 1859), copy in Folkemindesamling, or Folklore Collection, Royal Library, Copenhagen. The verse relates that a pair of Mormons went around saying many wonderful things about the land by the great sea and Zion's mountains where peace and joy and wealth abound.

[61] The painting, 79 by 110.5 centimeters, was presented in 1871 by the Selskabet for Nordisk Kunst to the Statens Museum for Kunst in Copenhagen, where I saw it in 1948. The catalogue entry, No. 143, translated, reads: "Two Mormons in their wandering have come to a carpenter's cottage in the country where by preaching and by citing some of the scriptures of their sect they seek to win new adherents. Christen Dalsgaard, 1856." See my "'Mormon-praedikanter' . . . the

Story of a Painting," *The Improvement Era* (Salt Lake City), 52:627ff (October 1949).

[62] *Stjerne*, 2:104–6 (January 1, 1853).

[63] "Erindringer," *Morgenstjernen*, 2:17ff (1883).

[64] "C. S. Winges Biografi," *Morgenstjernen*, 4:135–37 (1885).

[65] Hagberg, p. 30.

[66] "Biografiske Skizzer: Svend Larsen," *Morgenstjernen*, 1:174–75 (1882); Jenson, *History*, p. 349.

[67] Quoted in Hagberg, p. 19.

[68] These and the accompanying figures are based on an analysis of the Scandinavian Mission Missionary List, 1850–1904, MS., Church Historian's Office.

[69] Sundbärg, p. 20. Sundbärg notes the record of activity in Sweden for 1897: 48,707 tracting calls, 1638 invitations in, 13,775 gospel conversations, 39,727 tracts and 1235 books distributed, 2416 meetings held (p. 49, citing the mission's annual "Statistisk Rapport" in *Skandinaviens Stjerne*).

[70] "The Scandinavian Mission," *Millennial Star*, 47:680 (1885).

[71] In 1875, for example, priesthood strength in Scandinavia included 167 "Elders," 50 "Priests," 71 "Teachers," 25 "Deacons" in a total of 2020 lay members. "Statistisk Oversigt over den Skandinaviske Mission fra Aaret 1850 til 1883," *Morgenstjernen*, 3:350 (1885). Herman H. Sundström on a first mission to Sweden in 1882 traveled 10,000 miles on foot, baptized 55, sold 642 kronors' worth (about $160) of books. On a second mission in 1894 he traveled 4500 miles, baptized 27. Jenson, *History*, p. 339.

[72] Anthon L. Skanchy, *Autobiography*, John A. Widtsoe, trans. (Logan, Utah, 1915), p. 41.

[73] The Kvalbergs to August Carlson, April 1, 1878, *Nordstjärnan*, 2:110 (1878).

[74] "Autobiografi," *Morgenstjernen*, 2:42 (1883).

[75] Joseph W. Young, Letter, February 4, 1858, published as "The Mormons in Europe – Progress of Mormonism in Northern Europe," New York *Times*, March 10, 1858.

[76] "Tale af Aeldste Andrew Jenson," *Morgenstjernen*, 4:177 (1885).

[77] "Statistisk Rapport," *Stjerne*, 12:128 (January 15, 1863); "Emigration fra Skandinavien," *Morgenstjernen*, 3:371 (1884). Denmark's general dejection after the Schleswig-Holstein defeats of the early 1860s, with national pride at low ebb and all its political ambitions disappointed, and with the Establishment, moreover, hopelessly divided against itself, may also have stimulated emigration.

[78] "The Mormons in Europe. Causes of the Emigration from Wales and Scandinavia. Wiles and Tricks of the Mormons," New York *Times*, August 13, 1869, quoting the Montreal *Gazette* for August 11, 1869.

[79] The accompanying figures are based on an analysis of entries in the *Latter-day Saint Biographical Encyclopedia* (Salt Lake City, 1901–26), 4 vols., and the *Scandinavian Jubilee Album 1850–1900* (Salt Lake City, 1900).

[80] Scandinavian Mission Missionary List, *passim*; census reports show that Salt Lake County's Scandinavian population in 1880 was 2044, Sanpete County's (where Ephraim was located), 3115. Ephraim in 1870 showed a foreign population of 666 (almost exclusively Danish) against 501 native; little Hyrum showed 356 foreign (i.e., Scandinavian) against 352 native. Exact comparisons are difficult but make the point: the proportion of missionary service was high.

[81] Peter Hansen, "Levnetsbeskrivelse eller Dag Bog," MS., p. 4. Microfilm of original in Huntington Library.

[82] "Instruktioner til Missionairerne af Praesident Brigham Young," *Stjerne*, 9:353–57 (September 1, 1860).

[83] *Stjerne*, 3:62 (November 15, 1853).

[84] Niels Wilhelmsen, "Autobiografi," *Morgenstjernen*, 2:133 (1883).

[85] Ray S. Hansen, "A Brief History of the Life of Hans Christian Hansen," MS. Mr. Hansen kindly made a typescript copy available to me.

[86] Sermon, November 15, 1856, *Journal of Discourses* (Liverpool, 1854–86), IV, 92.

[87] "Nogle Bemaerkninger," *Stjerne*, 3:61–63 (November 15, 1853); "Sendebrev til praesiderende og omreisende Aeldste," *Stjerne*, 7:327 (August 1, 1858).

[88] "Til de Hellige," *Stjerne*, 8:219 (April 15, 1859).

[89] *Deseret News*, September 19, 1860, reporting a sermon by Brigham Young.

[90] "Sendebrev," *op cit.*, p. 328.

[91] Sermon, History of Brigham Young, MS., September 13, 1860, quoted in B. H. Roberts, *A Comprehensive History of the Church* (Salt Lake City, 1930), 6 vols., V, 85.

[92] C. F. Olsen to N. C. Flygare, July 20, 1886, *Stjerne*, 35:348 (August 15, 1886).

[93] P. F. Madsen to C. G. Larsen, September 1, 1873, *Stjerne*, 23:41 (November 1, 1873).

[94] Quoted in Andreas Mortensen, *Fra mit Besog blandt Mormonerne* (Christiania, 1887), p. 265.

[95] Andrew M. Israelsen, *Autobiography* (Salt Lake City, 1938), p. 96, quoting a letter to the Drammen *Tidende*, n.d.

CHAPTER 4. "ZION, WHEN I THINK OF THEE"

[1] John Taylor, sermon, *Journal of Discourses* (Liverpool, 1854–86), I, 19.

[2] According to Gunnar Hansen, "Dansk Udvandring til U.S.A. tog Fart for 100 Aar siden," *Danmarksposten*, June 1948.

[3] "Peter O. Hansens Autobiografi," *Morgenstjernen*, 3:331.

[4] Taylor, p. 19. A generation later, missionary A. L. Skanchy succeeded in having a Bergen, Norway, newspaper run Governor Caleb West's report on Utah to correct a fanciful history of Brigham Young which the paper had published. Skanchy to N. C. Flygare, March 16, 1887, *Skandinaviens Stjerne*, 36:203 (April 1, 1887).

[5] Taylor, p. 19.

[6] Sermon, Latter-day Saint Journal History, MS., January 24, 1858. Hereafter cited as Journal History.

[7] Quoted in Orson F. Whitney, *History of Utah* (Salt Lake City, 1892), 4 vols., I, 288.

[8] Whitney, I, 195; Joseph Smith, "An Ordinance for the Protection of the Citizens of the United States Emigrating to the Territories, and for the Extension of the Principles of Universal Liberty," March 26, 1844, in *History of the Church* (Salt Lake City, 1950, 2nd ed.), 7 vols., VI, 274–77.

[9] November 25, 1850, cited in Theodore C. Blegen, *The America Letters* (Oslo, 1928), p. 23.

[10] See Carl G. W. Vollmer, *Kalifornien och guldfebern. Guldgräfvarnes, Mormonernas och Indianernas seder och bruk . . .* (Stockholm, 1862); and Paul Toutain, *Un Français en Amerique* (Paris, 1876). Dale L. Morgan's Mormon bibliography, on cards at the Utah State Historical Society, conveniently brings together a number of foreign titles on the Mormons and the Far West.

[11] See, for example, O. J. Hollister, *Resources and Attractions of Utah* (Salt Lake City, 1882), and *Utah Revealed* (Salt Lake City, 1896), which declared: "There is now no reason why the State should be ignored on account of any fear of the Mormon Church. Her citizens . . . assimilate socially and in business, and the visitor to Utah will be unable to distinguish the Mormon from the Gentile . . ." (p. 45).

[12] Whitney, I, 450.

[13] *Millennial Star*, 3:76 (August 1, 1842).

[14] Brigham Young and others, "Thirteenth General Epistle," *Millennial Star*, 18:49 (January 26, 1856).

[15] See William A. Linn, *The Story of the Mormons* (New York, 1902), p. 411.

[16] Parley P. Pratt to Orson Pratt, *Millennial Star*, 11:24 (January 15, 1849).

[17] "Governor's Message," December 13, 1852, in "Governors' Messages," MS., pp. 34–35. Typescript in Utah State Historical Society.

[18] August 12, 1879, quoted in *Millennial Star*, 41:513 (August 18, 1879).

[19] "Governor's Message," December 11, 1854; December 15, 1857, in Governors' Messages," pp. 53, 59.

[20] Described later in the chapter. It should be noted in passing that Utah's mines sought European investors, almost wholly a non-Mormon interest and, it goes without saying, non-immigrant. Not until 1911 did Utah establish a state bureau concerned, according to Commissioner H. T. Haines, with "securing for Utah a fair share of the admitted aliens to the United States." During its first year, the bureau answered "hundreds of inquiries" and mailed "several thousand pieces of literature" from commercial clubs and railroads; but it complained its budget of $2000 a year was too small to do much advertising. State of Utah, *First Report of State Bureau of Immigration, Labor and Statistics, 1911* Salt Lake City, 1911), p. 16.

[21] *Millennial Star*, 23:232–34 (April 13, 1861).

[22] *Salmer til Brug for Jesu Kristi Kirke af Sidste-Dages Hellige* (Copenhagen, 1885, 12th ed.), pp. 80–82. "Zion, When I Think of Thee," the title of the present chapter, is taken from the hymn by Hans F. Petersen, "Zion, naar paa Dig jeg taenker," which first appeared in *Skandinaviens Stjerne*, 1:48 (December 1, 1851) and was included in every edition of the Danish Mormon hymnal thereafter.

[23] "There Is a Place in Utah," *Sacred Hymns and Spiritual Songs for the Church of Jesus Christ of Latter-day Saints* (Salt Lake City, 1891, 20th ed.), p. 382.

[24] *Salmer til Brug*, p. 286.

[25] Gustav Sundbärg, *Mormonvärfningen i Sverige* (*Emigrationsutredningen*, III, Stockholm, 1910), p. 15.

[26] Scandinavian Mission General History, MS., March 31, 1851. Hereafter cited as Mission History.

[27] Publication figures to 1882 for this and other titles to be cited are drawn from the printer's account books and tabulated in Andrew Jenson's "Bogtrykker F. E. Bording," *Morgenstjernen*, 3:104 (1884).

[28] Jenson, p. 104. By 1890 they spent another 26,000 kroner on printing. "The Scandinavian Mission," *Millennial Star*, 53:62 (January 26, 1891).

[29] Erastus Snow, *One Year in Scandinavia* (Liverpool, 1851), pp. 7, 8, 12.

[30] "Peter O. Hansens Autobiografi," p. 334.

[31] Mission History, May 22, 1851.

[32] Snow, p. 12.

[33] *Ibid.*, p. 8.

[34] A copy of the *Tabel* survives in the Royal Library, Copenhagen, where I discovered it in 1948. Originals of all the other official titles may be found in the Historian's Office, Church of Jesus Christ of Latter-day Saints, in Salt Lake City – and many, incidentally, still in the homes of Scandinavian converts and their descendants.

[35] See, for example, "The Mormon Embargo," London *Examiner*, August 16, 1879, from which these phrases are quoted; the article was reprinted in the *Millennial Star*, 35:545–47 (September 1, 1879), and *Skandinaviens Stjerne*, 29:9–12 (October 1, 1879).

[36] So advertised in *Indbydelse til Guds Rige*, 10th ed.

[37] *Skandinaviens Stjerne*, 1:58 (January 1, 1852). Hereafter cited as *Stjerne*.

[38] *Stjerne*, 1:172 (August 1, 1852).

[39] Peder Nielsen, Diary, MS., July 7–10, 1857.

[40] "Erindringer fra Missionen i Skandinavien," *Morgenstjernen*, 4:174 (1885).

[41] *Stjerne*, 20:41 (November 1, 1870); J. C. Nielsen to J. Van Cott, September 18, 1855, *Stjerne*, 5:29 (October 15, 1855).

[42] To Edward H. Anderson, January 24, 1892, *Nordstjärnan*, 16:78 (March 1, 1892).

[43] Anthon L. Skanchy, *Autobiography*, John A. Widtsoe, trans. (Logan, Utah, 1915), p. 37.

[44] Christian Michelsen, *Fra Danmark til Saltsøen* (Copenhagen, 1885), p. 8.

[45] Andrew Jenson, *History of the Scandinavian Mission* (Salt Lake City, 1927), p. 282.

[46] Snow to Samuel W. Richards, July 16, 1852, *Deseret News*, December 11, 1852.

[47] "Eiendomme tilkjøbs i Utah Territorium," *Stjerne*, 6:42–43 (November 1, 1856).

[48] *Stjerne*, 2:111 (January 1, 1853). "Bros N C Neilsen, H P Peel & Bro Godfreysen also seemed pretty well in spirits corroborated the testimony of Bro Staker Spoke of the war in Denmark and the conduct of his countrymen believed that the hand of the Lord was in it to give effect to the testimony of his Servants in that land." High Priests Quorum Minute Book, MS., Mt. Pleasant, Utah, entry for March 28, 1864. O. N. Liljenquist wrote from Hyrum, Utah, in 1869: "In Scandinavia I was frequently asked how long it would be before God's judgments would 'overtake the nations.' Maybe they asked so they could delay their repentance till the last moments. But could they realize how much they have lost by their delay. . . . they could have been united with God's folk here and received the blessings and teachings which will prepare us for the great day." Liljenquist to J. N. Smith, April 15, 1869, *Stjerne*, 18:286 (June 15, 1869).

[49] *Stjerne*, 18:313 (July 15, 1869). Missionary Joseph W. Young reflected Zion's confidence when he wrote satirically from Copenhagen on February 4, 1858: "James Buchanan's sending troops to Utah seems to me the greatest piece of humbug that has been got up since Barnum's 'Baby Show.' However, if Uncle Sam has a few millions of dollars to spend, and a few thousand soldiers to freeze and starve to death in the mountains, all right, – the game has been his own seeking after. The old gentleman will learn, perhaps when it is too late to repent, that he is fighting against God. Yes, the Almighty built the batteries, bastions, towers, and parapets, and dug the trenches which form the bulwarks around his people, and I entertain the idea that Uncle will find He is a better engineer than the old man had taken him to be." "The Mormons in Europe – Progress of Mormonism in Northern Europe," New York *Times*, March 10, 1858.

[50] Journal History, May 31, 1855.

[51] See Chapter 3, "Siege of Babylon." "The Scandinavian Elders from the Valley," Carl Widerborg wrote in 1865, "are exciting considerable interest among their friends and acquaintances, and are pretty busy in traveling, holding meetings and conversing with those who are seeking information about the things and matters in famous Utah. Some strangers only wish to satisfy their curiosity, I admit, but still many of the honest will be led to investigate the truth of the gospel and obey it." Widerborg to Brigham Young, Jr., September 27, 1865, Mission History, same date.

[52] Larsen to John Van Cott, May 29, 1854, *Stjerne*, 3:318 (July 15, 1854); Sandberg to August Carlson, October 10, 1877, *Nordstjärnan*, 1:331 (November 1, 1877); Kempe to Carl Widerborg, November 14, 1865, *Stjerne*, 15:122 (January 15, 1866).

[53] *Stjerne*, 11:9 (October 1, 1861).

[54] See my article, "Through Immigrant Eyes," *Utah Historical Quarterly*, 22:41–55 (January, 1954), which summarizes a letter from Christian Nielsen written April 27, 1856, from Manti, Utah, and preserved in the Royal Library at Copenhagen as one of several Danish Mormon immigrant letters. *Stjerne* and *Nordstjärnan*, of course, published but a fraction of all the letters that must have been written.

[55] Lautrup to the Editor, *Stjerne*, 7:123–27 (January 15, 1858).

[56] Nielsen to John Van Cott, September 18, 1855, *Stjerne*, 5:27-29 (October 15, 1855).

[57] Madsen to Carl Widerborg, July 25, 1858, *Stjerne*, 8:26 (October 15, 1858).

[58] Kragskov to J. C. A. Weibye, April 15, 1860, *Stjerne*, 9:345 (August 15, 1860).

[59] Pedersen to Jesse N. Smith, February 25, 1869, *Stjerne*, 18:221 (April 15, 1869).

[60] Weibye to Jesse N. Smith, February 10, 1870, *Stjerne*, 19:188 (March 15, 1870).

[61] Pedersen to Jesse N. Smith, February 25, 1869, *Stjerne*, 18:221 (April 15, 1869).

[62] Christensen to Jesse N. Smith, September 18, 1863, *Stjerne*, 13:60 (November 15, 1863). Franklin D. Richards, attending the Royal Theatre in Stockholm in 1867, found it "about the same size as the one in Salt Lake City." Letter, February 6, 1867, Mission History.

[63] N. C. Edlefsen to Sidste-Dages Hellige, November 3, 1868, *Stjerne*, 18:123 (January 15, 1869).

[64] C. J. Kempe to J. N. Smith, August 17, 1869, *Stjerne*, 19:30 (October 15, 1869).

[65] "What to Do with the Immigrants?" *Deseret News Weekly*, June 19, 1878; reprinted in *Stjerne*, 27:347–48 (August 1, 1878).

[66] *Millennial Star*, 11:342 (November 15, 1849).

[67] "Brigham Youngs Svar til New York Herald," *Stjerne*, 22:269–70 (June 1, 1873).

[68] Thomassen to C. A. Larsen, February 26, 1875, *Stjerne*, 24:217–20 (April 15, 1875).

[69] *Nordstjärnan*, 9:48 (February 1, 1885); 16:47 (February 1, 1892).

[70] Carlquist to P. Sundwall, August 12, 1894, *Stjerne*, 43:362 (September 1, 1894).

[71] *Millennial Star*, 53:264–67 (April 27, 1891).

[72] "Insamlingens ändamål," *Nordstjärnan*, 28:41 (February 1, 1904).

[73] Sermon, September 24, 1854, *Journal of Discourses*, III, 65–66.

[74] Sermon, September 2, 1860, Journal History, same date.

[75] "Taenk ej, naar til Zion I drage," *Salmer til Brug*, p. 36; *Sacred Hymns*, p. 393.

[76] American Social Science Association, *Handbook for Immigrants to the United States* (New York, 1871), p. 106.

[77] Snow to F. D. Richards, December 15, 1851, *Millennial Star*, 14:3 (January 1, 1852). Snow refers to the following anti-Mormon works: John C. Bennett, *The History of the Saints; or an Exposé of Joe Smith and Mormonism* (Boston, 1842); Henry Caswall, *The City of the Mormons, or Three Days at Nauvoo* (London, 1842); J. B. Turner, *Mormonism in All Ages* (New York, 1842); and John Bowes, *Mormonism Exposed in Its Swindling and Licentious Abominations* (London, 1851).

[78] Originals of these and of most of the titles that follow may be found in the New York Public Library – a collection of some twenty-five titles in all. I have deposited a microfilm of these with the Church Historian's Office.

[79] Mission History, October 30, 1850.

[80] A number of street ballads are preserved in the Dansk folkemindesamling, the Danish Folklore Collection, at the Royal Library in Copenhagen.

[81] Some members of the church in Scandinavia had learned of it privately beforehand. Willard Snow, who was in Liverpool when the news of the announcement in Salt Lake City reached him, brought a copy back to Copenhagen in

February 1853 to read to the lay priesthood. Mission History, February 6, 1853. Canute Peterson, missionary fresh from Zion with a copy of the *Deseret News* "extra" in his pocket, "read and interpreted" it for some brethren "on one of the high hills near Risør," who asked if they were to preach the doctrine. "I told them 'No, not even to talk of it privately before they were better informed concerning it.' This gave them new light and also satisfied them." Carrie Peterson Tanner, "Life Story of Canute Peterson," MS., p. 32. The first company of emigrating Saints heard the revelation read at sea aboard the *Forest Monarch*. J. J. Christensen, Journal, MS., January 23, 1853, quoted in Mission History, same date.

[82] Christian Fonnesbeck, *Svar paa Sognepraesten A. Bulows Angreb paa Mormonerne* (Copenhagen, 1903).

[83] More fully discussed in Chapter 11, "Inroads: Conflict and Crusade."

[84] *Fra mit Besog blandt Mormonerne* (Christiania, 1887), p. 181.

[85] Andrew Jenson, "Missionary Reminiscences," *The Historical Record*, 9:31 (1890).

[86] George M. Stephenson, *A History of American Immigration* (Boston, 1926), p. 39. Consular officer M. J. Cramer wrote Secretary of State William Evarts from Denmark in 1881 complaining of erroneous ideas in Scandinavia concerning America. He found the secular press to some extent "unfriendly, not to say hostile, towards our country." The reason was threefold: (1) resentment at the loss of thousands of the "thriftiest, most energetic, and intelligent" and the spread of "republicanism" among those unable to emigrate, engendering dissatisfaction with "large standing armies and consequent heavy taxes"; (2) dislike of the protective tariff; (3) the bad influence of "second and third rate writers unable to make good at home" who had emigrated to the United States, failed there also, and now wrote diatribes home to the "gossip chronicles" blaming the country. Cramer to Evarts, March 2, 1881, *Foreign Relations, 1881*, pp. 388–90. Mormon activity certainly contributed to reasons one and three.

[87] Missionary reports in *Stjerne* frequently mentioned encounters with Mortensen and Ingerøe [or Ingerød], whose latest charges were forthwith met in the editorials. C. Christensen, for example, related that "Frue Ingerød" had declared in public that Utah had no government and was the scene of murders and abominations – accusations which gave *Stjerne* a chance to explain Utah's territorial government and to note that there were "a good many American citizens in Scandinavia from Utah who can testify of true conditions." "Om Apostater og deres Virken," *Stjerne*, 17:73 (December 1, 1867). A speech by Pastor Mortensen in Randers, reported in Fyens *Stiftstidning* met a strong reply in *Nordstjärnan*, 9:53–54 (February 15, 1885).

[88] *Brev fra en Mormonerinde. Brev fra en Guldgraver i Melbourne. Til Advarsel for hans Landsmaend i Danmark* (Copenhagen, 1855). Copies of this and the letters named may be found in the Royal Library and the University Library in Copenhagen. A few of them are quoted in Harald Jensen Kent's unfavorable *Danske Mormoner* (Copenhagen, 1913). A Professor Thomas A. Becker at one time collected twelve letters written from America by Scandinavian Mormon emigrants, intending to use them in an anti-Mormon work, but he found them too favorable and left them with the Royal Library. Andrew Jenson, foreword to one of the letters published in *Bikūben* (Salt Lake City), December 14, 1912.

[89] *Maerkvaerdigt Brev om Mormonernes Skjaendigheder* (Copenhagen, 1854).

[90] *Fra Danmark til Saltsøen* (Copenhagen, 1885).

[91] *Brev fra Jens Laursen Lund* (Aalborg, 1863).

[92] *Oplysninger om Mormonsamfundet i Utah*, Nos. 1, 2, (Copenhagen, 1863–64).

[93] Letter from Omaha, March 17, 1863, cited in Kent, *Danske Mormoner*, p. 39.

[94] Cited in Jenson, *History*, p. 357. The editor of the *Millennial Star*, following

a visit to Scandinavia in 1885, believed that letters from disaffected Saints enjoyed a much larger circulation than those sent by "faithful and contented Saints." *Millennial Star*, 47:680 (October 26, 1885).

[95] *Tre År i Mormonlandet* (Malmö, 1867), pp. 129–33.

[96] Ahmanson, Ingerøe, and Michelsen, among others, are more fully dealt with in Chapter 7, "Journey to Zion."

[97] *Et Tilbud til danske Landbrugere og Mejerister fra Lucerne Land and Water Company i Utah* (Copenhagen, c. 1895). A copy, the only one I know of, is available in the Royal Library, Copenhagen.

[98] *Journal of Discourses*, I, 137–43, for this and the succeeding quotations.

[99] Arthur L. Thomas, *Report of the Governor of Utah to the Secretary of the Interior, September 9, 1890* (Washington, D.C., 1890).

CHAPTER 5. UGLY DUCKLINGS

[1] C. C. A. Christensen to Edward H. Anderson, December 29, 1891, *Nordstjärnan*, 16:47 (February 1, 1892).

[2] See Table I, "Mormon Conversion, Disaffection, and Emigration in Scandinavia by Decades, 1850–1904," in my manuscript dissertation, "Mormons from Scandinavia, 1850–1905," copies in the Harvard University Library and Utah State Historical Society.

[3] P. S. Vig notes that economic conditions improved in Denmark after 1850, especially for farmers, only indirectly for laborers and artisans. Three factors making for emigration from Denmark, he says, were Mormonism, gold fever, and America letters. *Danske i Amerika* (Minneapolis, 1907), 2 vols., I, 284ff.

[4] "Tale af Aeldste Andrew Jenson," *Morgenstjernen*, 4:179 (1885).

[5] C. A. Madsen to John Van Cott, July 24, 1861, in Scandinavian Mission General History, MS. Hereafter Mission History.

[6] Anders Christensen to John Van Cott, January 4, 1861, in Mission History.

[7] A. M. Lyman to G. Q. Cannon, September 29, 1861, in Mission History.

[8] *Loc. cit.*

[9] Letter, February 4, 1858, in New York *Times*, March 10, 1858, under the heading "The Mormons in Europe – Progress of Mormonism in Northern Europe."

[10] See Table II, "Mormon Conversion, Disaffection, and Emigration in Scandinavia by Districts, 1850–1904," in "Mormons from Scandinavia, 1850–1905," cited in note 2 above.

[11] "Spread of the Gospel," *Millennial Star*, 40:603 (September 23, 1878).

[12] United States Immigration Commission, *Statistical Review of Immigration 1820–1910*; *Distribution of Immigrants 1850–1900* (U.S. Im. Comn. Reports, III, Washington, D.C., 1911), p. 15; Scandinavian Mission Emigration Records, MS., Book A (1854–63), Book B (1864-65), Book C (1866), Book D (1867-69), Historian's Office, Church of Jesus Christ of Latter-day Saints; annual "Statistisk Rapport," *Skandinaviens Stjerne*, *passim*.

[13] U.S. Seventh (1850), Eighth (1860), Ninth (1870), and Eleventh (1890) Censuses, tables on foreign-born, states and territories; John H. Bille, *History of the Danes in America* (Madison, Wisc., 1898) pp. 12, 13.

[14] U.S. Eighth Census, *Population*, Introduction, p. xxxii.

[15] See Chapter 3, "Siege of Babylon."

[16] F. D. Richards to First Presidency, February 6, 1867, in Mission History.

[17] Carl Widerborg to G. Q. Cannon, June 25, 1858, in Mission History.

[18] Helge Nelson, *The Swedes and the Swedish Settlements in North America*. (New York, 1943), 2 vols., I, 310–11.

[19] A. L. Skanchy to N. C. Flygare, March 16, 1887, *Stjerne*, 36:202 (April 1, 1887).

[20] "A Visit to Scandinavia," *Millennial Star*, 17:705 (November 10, 1855).

[21] See Table I, "Mormon Conversion, Disaffection, and Emigration in Scandinavia by Decades, 1850–1904," and Table III, "Mormon Membership in Scandinavia, 1850–1904," in "Mormons from Scandinavia 1850–1905," cited in note 2 above.

[22] The next chapter describes the assistance.

[23] Some Mormon proselytes were made in Iceland as early as 1851 when two natives, Thorarinn Halflidason, a cabinetmaker, and Gudmundur Gudmundson, a jeweler, learning their trades in Copenhagen, were baptized there and on returning to Iceland won several followers. Numbering fewer than 400 during the half century, Icelandic Mormons emigrated a handful at a time, usually via Liverpool. A group of sixteen settled in Spanish Fork, Utah, in 1855–56, forming the nucleus of what is claimed to be the first Icelandic colony in America in modern times. Possessed of literary and musical gifts, and skilled in a variety of crafts, the small but influential settlement deserves separate study. Kate Bjarnason Carter, perennial president of the Daughters of Utah Pioneers, is a descendant of the first settlers and holds valuable manuscript collections about them. See Kate B. Carter, "The Gospel in Iceland," *The Improvement Era*, 40:88–90 (February 1951).

[24] N. C. Flygare, "Autobiografi," *Morgenstjernen*, 3:232 (1884).

[25] "Dagbog," *Morgenstjernen*, 3:151–52 (1884).

[26] This count includes every company to leave during the 1860s, when Mormonism was at floodtide in Scandinavia and most characteristic; beyond this, the count–which takes in over a third of the total emigration, a generous representation – samples companies leaving in the 1850s, 1870s, and 1880s as recorded in the Scandinavian Mission Emigration Records, MS., Books A to G (1854–86), supplemented by passenger manifests from the National Archives of certain vessels whose records were missing from the Mormon files.

[27] P. A. M. Taylor, "Mormon Emigration from Great Britain to the United States 1840–1870" (unpublished doctoral dissertation, University of Cambridge, 1950), p. 223.

[28] Imre Ferenczi, *International Migrations* (New York, 1929), 2 vols., I, 667–68, 748–50, 757–58.

[29] Taylor, p. 224; Ferenczi, I, 410.

[30] U.S. Eleventh Census, I, 556.

[31] Gustav Sundbärg, *Mormonvärfningen i Sverige* (*Emigrationsutredningen*, III, Stockholm, 1910), p. 50. Swedish statistics for this period are especially welcome since Mormon passenger lists were discontinued as organized emigration dwindled, and it is an impossible task to separate Mormon from general passengers in the manifests recorded at U.S. ports of entry.

[32] "Of Plantations," *Bacon's Essays* (Cornell Series, n.d.), p. 178.

[33] Records of the Bureau of Customs, Office of the Collector of Customs, Port of New Orleans, Passenger List of the *Forest Monarch*, March 17, 1853. Microfilm from the National Archives and Records Service, Washington, D.C. Danish immigrants were such a novelty the customs officials must have mistaken their tongue for Gaelic.

[34] "The Forsgren Company," MS. compilation, Church Historian's Office.

[35] T. H. Hauch-Fausboll, "How is Genealogy to be Studied?" *Utah Genealogical Magazine*, 22:6 (January 1931). Hauch-Fausboll was director of the Danish Genealogical Institute and wrote several articles for the benefit of Danish Mormons on resources and procedures in Denmark for tracing family pedigrees.

[36] *Scandinavian Jubilee Album* (Salt Lake City, 1900), p. 228; "Across the Plains in 1863," *Heart Throbs of the West* (Salt Lake City, 1944), IV, 351; C. N. Lund, "Autobiography," MS.; Hans Christensen, "Memoirs," MS.; Jens Nielsen, letter to son Uriah, in Albert R. Lyman, "Sketch of Bishop Jens Nielsen," MS., Utah

State Historical Society, WPA Writers' Project Biographies; Hans Jensen Hals, "Autobiography," MS.

[37] Scandinavian Mission Emigration Records, *passim.*

[38] Journal History, April 26, 1858, quoting the New York *Times*, same date. The great difference in the amounts between 1856 and 1857 may be attributed to hard times in 1857: Carl Widerborg in 1858 reported "the past and present season have been rather unfavorable for many of the Saints, who are out of employment and are scarcely able to procure the most necessary articles for their support." He found some conferences "almost too weak and poor to defray the necessary expenses and pay some debts accumulated in times past, not through mismanagement, but rather on account of the great willingness to borrow money and donate to emigrating Elders, Saints and traveling Elders." Letter to Asa Calkin, June 25, 1858, in Mission History.

[39] J. M. Tanner, *Biographical Sketch of James Jensen* (Salt Lake City, 1911), p. 6.

[40] Hans Peter Jensen, "Biographi and Jurnal [*sic*]," MS.; Jens Weibye, "Dagbog," *Morgenstjernen*, 3:152 (1884); J. C. Kempe, "Autobiography," MS.; Hans Zobell, "Autobiography," MS.; O. N. Liljenquist, "Autobiography," *Tullidge's Quarterly Magazine*, 1:564 (July 1881).

[41] Carl M. Hagberg, *Den Norske Misjonshistorie* (Oslo, 1928), pp. 23–26.

[42] Arthur Schmidt Larsen, "Life Sketch of Hans Larsen," MS., Utah State Historical Society, WPA Writers' Project Biographies.

[43] C. C. A. Christensen, "Levnedsløb," *Digte og Afhandlinger* (Salt Lake City, 1921), pp. 329–81.

[44] C. C. A. Christensen to K. Peterson, November 10, 1872, *Stjerne*, 22:123–24 (January 15, 1873).

[45] C. C. A. Christensen to Edward H. Anderson, December 29, 1891, *Nordstjärnan*, 16:47 (February 1, 1892).

[46] William M. Evarts, "Diplomatic Correspondence, Circular No. 10, August 9, 1879, Sent to Diplomatic and Consular Officers of the United States," *Papers Relating to the Foreign Relations of the United States 1879* (Washington, D.C., 1880), p. 11.

[47] Samuel Bowles, *Across the Continent* (Springfield, Mass., 1865), p. 398.

[48] "The Scandinavian Element," *Deseret News*, June 25, 1886. Chapter 11 of the present study discusses the popular and official measures aimed at drying up the stream of Utah's immigrant proselytes.

[49] John M. Coyner, ed., *Handbook on Mormonism* (Salt Lake City, 1882), p. 40; C. C. Goodwin, "The Mormon Situation," *Harper's*, 63:756 (October 1881).

[50] John W. Hill, *Mormonism vs. Americanism* (Salt Lake City, 1889), p. 22.

[51] *Hearings before the Committee on Territories in Regard to the Admission of Utah as a State, 1889*, (Washington, D.C., 1889), p. 128.

[52] John C. Kimball, *Mormonism Exposed, the Other Side* (Hartford, Conn., 1884), p. 3.

[53] Interview, March 27, 1881, New York *Times*, April 11, 1881.

[54] A. H. M., "Ancient and Modern Mormonism," *The Western Examiner* (St. Louis), December 10, 1835. In Utah State Historical Society typescript collection, Articles on Mormonism Appearing in Missouri and Illinois Papers 1830–47.

[55] August 16, 1879.

[56] Coyner, p. 94.

[57] Thomas S. Forsath, Letter, June 27, 1882, New York *Times*, July 4, 1882. Forsath, on his way from New Zealand to Europe, stopped over in Salt Lake City and heard Apostle George Q. Cannon speak in the Tabernacle.

[58] Ernest Ingersoll, "Salt Lake City," *Harper's*, 69:397 (August 1884).

[59] New York *Times*, July 16, 1873; July 7, 1877.

[60] New York *Daily Graphic*, October 19, 1887, quoted in *Millennial Star*, 49:757–58 (November 28, 1887).

[61] Edward Stephenson to the secretary of the treasury, July 15, 1886, in "Paupers and Mormons," New York *Times*, August 2, 1886, describing the arrival of 497 Mormon immigrants on the *S.S. Nevada*, July 7, 1886, "bound for Utah with passage prepaid." Stephenson urged that future shiploads not be allowed to land.

[62] "Our Western Patriarchs," New York *Times*, July 9, 1877.

[63] London *Times*, August 12, 1879.

[64] J. B. Sweet, *A Lecture on the Book of Mormon and the Latter-day Saints, with Notes* (London, 1855), p. 15.

[65] *New America* (Philadelphia, 1867), p. 169.

[66] Gunnar Hansen, "Dansk Udvandring til U.S.A. tog Fart for 100 Aar siden," *Danmarksposten* (Aalborg, Denmark), June 1948.

[67] A. O. Assar, *Mormonernas Zion* (Stockholm, 1911), p. 57.

[68] John L. Stevens to William M. Evarts, September 23, 1879, in *Papers Relating to the Foreign Relations of the United States 1879*, p. 964.

[69] Sundbärg, pp. 10–28. The report considered polygamy a threat to family morals, accused the priesthood of having temporal as well as spiritual authority, feared a state within a state, and thought it not unlikely that, unless the proselytes continued to emigrate, Sweden might some day be treated to terrorists as in the days of Brigham Young. Even Mormon apostates were considered "a dangerous influence in society" because they became "free thinkers."

[70] Jens Nielsen, *op. cit.*; Hannah Sorensen, "Life Sketch," *The Young Woman's Journal* (Salt Lake City), 1:392 (August 1890); Hans Christensen, *op. cit.*; John A. Widtsoe, *In the Gospel Net* (Salt Lake City, 1941), p. 64; Olof Hanson, "Autobiography," MS.

[71] Hannah Sorensen, *op. cit.*, p. 393; "Zion's Daughters Sing," *Heart Throbs of the West* (Salt Lake City, 1948), IX, 13–18; Annie Catrine Christensen Olsen, "Autobiography," MS., and Christina Oleson Warnick, "Autobiography," MS., Utah State Historical Society, WPA Writers' Project Biographies.

[72] F. D. Richards to First Presidency, February 6, 1867, in Mission History. Farmer Hans Jensen Hals noted the inability of the poor to afford a dowry or the "church marriage tax." Diary, MS., August 12, 1867.

[73] J. Christopher Kempe, Diary, MS., January 30, 1899. The Mormons could have echoed a Minnesota immigrant: "As long as I cursed, danced, drank a little, and responded well at catechetical meetings – which I always did – I was praised by the worthy fathers. But when I abandoned the life of sin and took Christianity seriously, with the Bible for my guide, I was threatened with imprisonment." *Emigrationsutredningen*, Bilaga VII, *Utvandrarnes egna Uppgifter* (Stockholm, 1908), pp. 168–69, quoted in George M. Stephenson, "The Background of the Beginnings of Swedish Immigration, 1850–1875," *American Historical Review*, 31:712 (July 1925).

[74] The archives of the Dansk folkemindesamling, the Danish Folklore Collection, at the Royal Library in Copenhagen contain a number of reminiscences about the Mormons. I am grateful to Mr. Henning Henningsen for calling them to my attention during my visit to the library in 1948.

[75] P. E. Åslev in Sundbärg, p. 21.

[76] Olina Törasen Kempe, "Autobiography," MS. Another Norwegian girl ordered out of the house by parents who could not be reconciled to her joining the Mormons was Kristine Mauritzdatter, who as the plural wife of Abraham O. Smoot became the mother of Reed Smoot, U.S. senator from Utah for five unbroken terms at the same time he was an apostle, member of the leading council of the Mormon Church. For Kristine's moving letter from Drammen to her par-

ents in Fredrikstad in 1854 at the time of her dismissal, see Carl Hagberg, *Den Norske Misjonshistorie*, p. 12.

[77] The Danish minister to the secretary of state, May 14, 1858, set off a series of communications involving – besides the State Department and the Danish legation – the secretary of war, army commands at Ft. Leavenworth and Camp Floyd, Utah, the governor of Utah Territory, and the U.S. attorney for Utah, who finally succeeded in obtaining an interview with Mary and Thea Hastrup, the young women in question. See *Notes from the Danish Legation, Notes to the Danish Legation*, and *Domestic Letters Series of the Department of State* beginning May 14, 1858, and extending to May 30, 1859. I am grateful to John P. Harrison of the National Archives and Records Service for calling this correspondence to my attention.

[78] Hannah Sorensen, *op. cit.*, pp. 391–404.

[79] "Biography of Maria Wilhelmina C. Krause Madsen," MS., Utah State Historical Society, WPA Writers' Project Biographies.

[80] George Q. Cannon, visiting Scandinavia in September, 1862. Quoted in Andrew Jenson, *History of the Scandinavian Mission* (Salt Lake City, 1927), p. 170.

[81] "Foreign Missions," *Deseret News*, November 16, 1860.

[82] *Stjerne*, 12:40–43 (November 1, 1862).

[83] Ansine M. Peterson, "Autobiography," MS., Utah State Historical Society, WPA Writers' Project Biographies.

[84] Christina Oleson Warnick, *op. cit.*

[85] Jens Nielsen, *op. cit.*

[86] George Q. Cannon, in Jenson, p. 170.

[87] F. D. Richards to First Presidency, February 6, 1867, in Mission History.

[88] O. N. Liljenquist, "Autobiography," p. 568.

[89] Sarah Josephine Jensen, "Autobiography," MS., describing events in 1852. She felt she would "in due time obey this command." Looking back in her eighty-eighth year, she could write: "I lived in this Order for 33 years until my husband's death."

[90] Hans Christensen, *op. cit.*; J. Christopher Kempe, *op. cit.*; Hannah Sorensen, *op. cit.*, p. 392; Peder Nielsen, Diary, MS., reviewing the period 1841–46; Sarah Josephine Jensen, *op. cit.*

[91] Carl Madsen, "My Conversion to Mormonism," MS.

[92] Jens Nielsen, *op. cit.*; Carl Madsen, *op. cit.*; Hannah Sorensen, *op. cit.*, p. 392; Hans Jensen Hals, *op. cit.*, entry describing events in 1852.

[93] Jens Nielsen, *op. cit.*; Hans Jensen Hals, *op. cit.*

[94] *Loc. cit.*

[95] Hans Christensen, *op. cit.*; J. Christopher Kempe, *op. cit.*; Jens Nielsen, *op. cit.*; Hans Christensen, *op. cit.*; Carl Madsen, *op. cit.*; Hannah Sorensen, *op. cit.*, p. 393.

[96] C. C. A. Christensen, "Beretning," *Morgenstjernen*, 3:203 (1884).

[97] "The Outgathering of the Saints," *Millennial Star*, 24:200–2 (March 29, 1862).

[98] "Why Are So Many of the Saints Not Gathered?" *Millennial Star*, 24:649–52 (October 11, 1862), and *Skandinaviens Stjerne*, 12:40–43 (November 1, 1862); "Vink til de Hellige, som skulle emigrere," *Stjerne*, 12:216 (April 15, 1863); *Stjerne*, 12:296–98 (July 1, 1863); "Emigration and the Motives Which Prompt It," *Millennial Star*, 26:57–60 (January 23, 1864); "Mormon Proselytism and Immigration," *Deseret News*, June 25, 1886.

[99] "The Outgathering of the Saints," p. 201. Adding "to the treasury of the Church" meant money as well as experience; Europe sustained Zion through tithing and temple contributions from the proselytes, for whom these funds were their Bell for Adano, a spiritual asset placed even ahead of their own emigration savings. Their contributions were less an indication of wealth – for they were

widows' mites – than an expression of a devotion the cathedral builders of the Middle Ages would have understood.

[100] "Erindringer fra Missionen i Skandinavien," *Morgenstjernen*, 1:130–31 (1882).

[101] Diary, MS., April 23, 1859. Martin Petersen Kuhre notes the same activity: "Fast Day. English school in the forenoon in Honsinge and meeting in the afternoon. We participated in the Holy Sacrament." Diary, MS., July 7, 1861. The mission periodicals frequently admonished converts to study English: "Det Engelske Sprog," *Stjerne*, 5:244–47 (January 15, 1856); 9:25 (October 15, 1859); *Nordstjärnan*, 6:24 (January 15, 1883).

[102] Olof Hanson, *op. cit.*; John Nielsen, "Autobiography," MS.

[103] Peter Thomassen, "Hilsen til vore Laesere," *Utah Posten* (Salt Lake City), December 24, 1873.

[104] "Et Vink til Emigranterne," *Stjerne*, 11:200–1 (April 1, 1862).

[105] William R. Palmer, "Questions to Be Asked the Latter-Day Saints," *The Improvement Era*, 42:210-11 (April 1939).

[106] Hans Christensen, *op. cit.*; Carl Fjeld, "Beretning," *Morgenstjernen*, 3:91 (1884); N. C. Flygare, "Autobiografi," *Morgenstjernen*, 3:233 (1884).

[107] Tanner, p. 8.

[108] O. N. Liljenquist, "Autobiografi," *Morgenstjernen*, 2:25–32 (1883).

[109] High Priests Quorum Minute Book, Mt. Pleasant, Utah, MS., entry for December 23, 1894. Episcopal Bishop Daniel S. Tuttle noted that the Mormon young men and women "have been taught that all Gentiles are a cheating, blasphemous, licentious set of men." Quoted in Brigham H. Roberts, *Comprehensive History of the Church* (Salt Lake City, 1930), 6 vols., V, 491.

[110] E. L. T. Harrison, "The Question of the Hour: or, Radical or Conservative Measures for Utah?" *Tullidge's Quarterly Magazine*, 1:131 (1881).

[111] *Loc. cit.*

[112] *Sacred Hymns and Spiritual Songs for the Church of Jesus Christ of Latter-day Saints*, 20th ed. (Salt Lake City, 1891), p. 154.

[113] John White, *Planter's Plea*, quoted in Ola Elizabeth Winslow, *Meetinghouse Hill: 1630–1783* (New York, 1952), pp. 16–17.

[114] Letter, April 27, 1856, in *Bikûben* (Salt Lake City), December 19, 1912. Original in Royal Library, Copenhagen.

[115] *Stjerne*, 1:141 (June 1, 1852).

CHAPTER 6. BOOTSTRAP REDEMPTION

[1] Christian A. Madsen to John Van Cott, July 24, 1861, in Scandinavian Mission General History, MS. Hereafter cited as Mission History.

[2] Thomas Margetts to F. D. Richards, July 4, 1852, *Skandinaviens Stjerne*, 2:15, 16 (October 1, 1852); Erastus Snow to Willard Snow, July 15, 1852, *Stjerne*, 2:21 (October 15, 1852).

[3] Mission History, February 21, 22, 1852; Erastus Snow, Letter, March 23, 1852, in Latter-day Saint Journal History, MS.; *Stjerne*, 1:95 (March 1, 1852). A Danish rigsdaler was then worth about half an American dollar. The Perpetual Emigrating Fund, both in the church at large and in the Scandinavian Mission, is more fully described hereafter.

[4] Mission History, August 12–14, 1852; *Stjerne*, 2:2 (October 1, 1852).

[5] Letter, September 2, 1852, in Mission History.

[6] Non-Mormon emigrants sometimes joined church companies for the benefits of organization. "We are continually called upon to know if we will not forward people to Zion. Strangers call and confess their willingness to fight for us if we will send them; we are not engaged in this business. The Saints . . . gather because it is a commandment of God." *Millennial Star*, 49:140 (February 28, 1887).

Sven J. Jonasson and Christian Hansen wrote that five Danes aboard the *Humboldt*, carrying a party of 328 Scandinavian Mormons, said they were headed for the Far West and asked to be included in the group and follow its itinerary. Letter, July 19, 1866, *Stjerne*, 15:364 (September 1, 1866).

[7] Willard Snow, Journal, MS., September 24, 1852, excerpted in Mission History.

[8] Samuel W. Richards, Letter, which Willard Snow records in his journal as having been received on September 23, 1852.

[9] Erastus Snow to Willard Snow, July 15, 1852, *Stjerne*, 2:21 (October 15, 1852).

[10] Willard Snow, Journal, October 16, 23, November 16, 1852, in Mission History.

[11] Willard Snow, Journal, November 19, 1852, in Mission History.

[12] The Scandinavian converts appear on two sets of church emigration records: those kept in Copenhagen as each season's emigration was organized and those kept in Liverpool, where the Scandinavians were added to the passenger lists of the church-chartered vessels. The extant Emigration Records of the Scandinavian Mission, Books A to G (1854–86), MS., with names entered by families and by districts and with deposits itemized in detail, are preserved in the Historian's Office, Church of Jesus Christ of Latter-day Saints, Salt Lake City, as are the Emigration Records of the British Mission, particularly useful for their statistical and financial summaries of the whole companies of which the Scandinavians formed a part. The Scandinavian records will be cited as Emigration Records (Copenhagen), the British as Emigration Records (Liverpool).

[13] Mission History, December 7, 20, 1852.

[14] "Mr. Morris rendered us every attention that we could ask or expect and treated us with the utmost respect. Bro. Daniel Garn also came in and we all took supper with Mr. Morris . . . and I never saw a better table spread. . . ." Willard Snow, Journal, December 20, 1852, in Mission History.

[15] O. N. Liljenquist, "Autobiografi," *Morgenstjernen*, 2:38 (1883).

[16] The figure comes from multiplying 22,000 adult emigrants by the average travel costs of $75, and 8000 children by half costs. Some notion of the extent to which Mormon emigration as a whole was a multimillion dollar operation may be gained from the statement of official church historian A. Milton Musser that from 1847 to 1887 some $8,000,000 had been expended in assisting poor immigrants alone (from the States as well as from Europe) and that during the same period it was estimated immigrants had brought some $20,000,000 in personal property into Utah. William E. Smythe, "Utah as an Industrial Object Lesson," *Atlantic Monthly*, 78:610–18 (November 1896).

[17] American Social Science Association, *Handbook for Immigrants to the United States* (New York, 1871), pp. 15, 16.

[18] The Fund, its nature and operation, is most completely discussed by Gustive O. Larson in "The Story of the Perpetual Emigration Fund," *Mississippi Valley Historical Review*, 18:184–94 (1931), and in *Prelude to the Kingdom* (Francestown, N. H., 1947), *passim.*

[19] "I wish the brethren to whisper this around among their neighbors, when they go out of this tabernacle, and say, 'What can we give to the Perpetual Emigrating Fund?' . . . We will take from a pin to a bed quilt; but be sure, when you bring a pin, that you have not many other things in your trunk that would be useful, more than you at present need; for if you bring a pin under such circumstances you cannot receive a blessing. . . ." Brigham Young, sermon, October 6, 1853, *Journal of Discourses* (Liverpool, 1854–86), I, 327.

[20] Brigham Young to Orson Hyde, October 16, 1849, *Millennial Star*, 12:124–25 (April 15, 1850). Presiding Bishop Edward Hunter was the agent who carried with him the first contributions to help remove the Saints from the Pottawattamie lands.

[21] James Brown to his family, February 22, 1854, MS. Typescript copy in Utah Humanities Research Foundation Archives, University of Utah.

[22] Doubtless some poor converts were shocked to find the assistance so business-like, with I.O.U.'s securing every kind of loan, while converts better off were shocked when they may have put their surplus into the hands of emigrant leaders as a loan only to discover it had been regarded as a donation. Misunderstandings were often bitter enough to lead to apostasy on the spot. N. Bourkersson, *Tre År i Mormonlandet* (Malmö, 1867) and Andreas Mortensen, *Fra mit Besog blandt Mormonerne* (Christiania, 1887), both disillusioned accounts, relate several unsavory episodes; even the memoirs of the faithful frequently describe touchy money incidents.

[23] Emigration Records (Liverpool), Book No. 1042 (1875–85).

[24] Photostat copies of these notes and the voucher are preserved in the Utah Humanities Research Foundation Archives, University of Utah.

[25] Latter-day Saints Church Tithing Office, Invoice Book, April 23, 1857 to December 11, 1863, MS., containing nearly 1000 receipts.

[26] Emigration Records (Liverpool) and Emigration Records (Copenhagen), *passim.*

[27] Daughters of Utah Pioneers, *Heart Throbs of the West* (Salt Lake City, 1944), IV, 151, reproduces a typical contract.

[28] William A. Linn, *The Story of the Mormons* (New York, 1902), p. 415.

[29] Christensen to his family, September 30, 1853, *Stjerne,* 4:59 (November 15, 1854).

[30] Sermon, October 7, 1854, *Journal of Discourses,* II, 72.

[31] First Presidency to Orson Hyde, October 16, 1849, quoted in Andrew Jenson, "Church Emigration," *The Contributor* (Salt Lake City), 13:81 (1891).

[32] Under the confiscation proceedings of the Edmunds-Tucker Act, more fully discussed in Chapter 11.

[33] Brigham Young, sermon, September 16, 1855, *Journal of Discourses,* III, 3.

[34] *Names of Persons and Sureties Indebted to the Perpetual Emigrating Fund Company from 1850 to 1877 Inclusive* (Salt Lake City, 1877). Alphabetically arranged, the list provides only names and the year the debt was incurred, not the amount. Most help, in terms of number, was extended the Scandinavians in 1866, when 718 names appear, without doubt for assistance from the frontier to the Salt Lake Valley in church wagon trains. It is ironic to find among the Scandinavian debtors notorious apostates like Johan A. Ahmanson and N. Bourkersson. The church might well complain they bit the hand that fed them.

[35] Letter in *Names and Sureties.* The copy preserved in the Church Historian's Office contains the letter addressed to the bishop of the Fourth Ward, Ogden City, September 19, 1878.

[36] Larson, *Prelude,* pp. 233–34.

[37] Christian A. Madsen, Letter, July 24, 1861, in Mission History, MS.

[38] See Emigration Records (Copenhagen), *passim.*

[39] John A. Widtsoe, *In the Gospel Net: The Story of Anna Karine Widtsoe, 1849–1919* (Salt Lake City, 1941), p. 74; H. J. Zobell, "Autobiography," MS., typescript in possession of Albert Zobell, Jr., Salt Lake City; Andrew M. Israelsen, *Utah Pioneering, An Autobiography* (Salt Lake City, 1938), p. 12; Martin Petersen Kuhre, "Dagbog," MS., January 3, 9, March 17, 28, 30, April 9, June 21, 1862, original in possession of William D. Kuhre, Sandy, Utah.

[40] Quoted in Andrew Jenson, *History of the Scandinavian Mission* (Salt Lake City, 1927), p. 90.

[41] Emigration Records (Copenhagen), *passim.*

[42] *A Pioneer Journal, Forsgren Company,* Daughters of Utah Pioneers, Historical Pamphlet (Salt Lake City, 1944), p. 11.

[43] Emigration Records (Copenhagen), *passim.*

[44] Niels Wilhelmsen, "Autobiografi," *Morgenstjernen,* 2:135 (1883); Jenson, *History,* p. 164; "Hans Rasmussen," *Scandinavian Jubilee Album* (Salt Lake City, 1900), p. 204; Jennie E. Hansen, "Across the Plains in 1863," *Heart Throbs of the West,* IV, 359; J. J. M. Bohn, "Autobiografi," *Morgenstjernen,* 4:42 (1885); Zobell, "Autobiography."

[45] "The Life History of Our Father John Nielsen," MS., pp. 17–19, microfilm in Utah State Historical Society.

[46] Knud Svendsen, "Mit Levningsløb," MS., May 5, 1858, microfilm in Huntington Library; Hans Jensen Hals, Diary, MS., summary entry for 1869, typescript translation in possession of Nicholas G. Morgan, Salt Lake City.

[47] "Betal Eders Emigrationsgjaeld," *Morgenstjernen,* 1:168 (1882).

[48] Svendsen, "Mit Levningsløb," July 9, August 11, 1858.

[49] "This Season's Emigration," *Millennial Star,* 30:488–91 (August 1, 1868); S. J. Jonasson to Carl Widerborg, October 10, 1867, *Stjerne,* 17:75 (December 1, 1867); O. F. Whitney, *History of Utah* (Salt Lake City, 1892), 4 vols., II, 183; "Emigrationen," *Stjerne,* 18:313 (July 15, 1869).

[50] Zobell, "Autobiography"; Emigration Records (Copenhagen), after 1870; *Deseret News,* April 29, 1873; C. C. A. Christensen to A. Lund, July 25, 1871, *Stjerne,* 20:362 (September 1, 1871); H. F. Petersen to K. Peterson, September 14, 1871, *Stjerne,* 21:47 (November 1, 1871); A. H. Lund, "Sarah Ann Nelson Peterson," in *Daughters of Utah Pioneers and Their Mothers* (Salt Lake City, 1897), p. 207.

[51] Hans Jensen Hals, Diary, various entries for 1872; Mt. Pleasant, Utah, High Priests Quorum Minute Book, MS., December 30, 1871; W. W. Cluff to K. Peterson, January 16, 1872, *Stjerne,* 21:173–74 (March 1, 1872); *Nordstjärnan* (Stockholm), 7:24 (January 15, 1883).

[52] J. C. Nielsen to N. C. Flygare, March 4, 1888, *Stjerne,* 37:203–5 (April 1, 1888).

[53] Emigration Records (Copenhagen), Books F, G.

[54] *Svenska Härolden* (Salt Lake City), June 18, 1885.

[55] *Stjerne,* 21:186 (March 15, 1872).

[56] *Stjerne,* 22:333 (August 1, 1873).

[57] Mission History, February 21, 22, April 9, May 3, 1852; Willard Snow, Letter, July 4, 1853, in "Erindringer fra Missionen i Skandinavien," *Morgenstjernen,* 2:23 (1883); *Stjerne,* 1:95 (March 1, 1852). An article on "The Poor" in *Stjerne* for August 1, 1852, differentiates between the Lord's poor and the Devil's poor: the former were unfortunate but blameless in their walk; the latter were those who could work but would rather be assisted. "You shall not give the food of the children to dogs."

[58] Peder Nielsen, "Dagbog," MS., August 1854, typescript translation in possession of Orson B. West, Salt Lake City.

[59] *Stjerne,* 1:112 (April 1, 1852).

[60] Mission History, June 30, 1859; Jenson, *History,* p. 237; most of the surviving account books of the Scandinavian Mission are now in the Church Historian's Office at Salt Lake City.

[61] The individual savings fund idea received considerable impetus after President Asa Calkin of the British Mission visited Scandinavia and told the Saints it would be easier to get help if they had saved a third, a half, or three fourths of their passage. *Stjerne,* 8:57 (November 15, 1858); 8:183 (March 15, 1859).

[62] "Hvorledes skal jeg komme til Zion?" *Ungdommens Raadgiver* (Copenhagen), 1:20–21 (1880).

CHAPTER 7. JOURNEY TO ZION

[1] Christoffer J. Kempe to Carl Widerborg, November 14, 1865, *Stjerne*, 15:122 (January 15, 1866).

[2] Emigration Shipping Book B (Liverpool), Promiscuous Emigration, February 28, 1851 to February 2, 1855, MS., in Historian's Office, Church of Jesus Christ of Latter-day Saints; *Stjerne*, 1:112 (April 1, 1852); 1:190 (September 1, 1852); 2:15, 16 (October 1, 1852); 2:21 (October 15, 1852); 2:110 (January 1, 1853).

[3] "Efterretninger fra Emigranterne," *Stjerne*, 2:288 (June 15, 1853); "Fra Vesten," *Stjerne*, 3:187 (March 15, 1854); "Niels Jensen," *Stjerne*, 19:314 (July 15, 1860); Andrew Jenson, *Latter-day Saint Biographical Encyclopedia* (Salt Lake City, 1901–1926), 4 vols., II, 67, III, 126; "O. U. C. Mönster," *Morgenstjernen*, 3:192 (1884); *Scandinavian Jubilee Album 1850–1900* (Salt Lake City, 1900), p. 220; Salt Lake City Second Ward, Historical Record, MS., in Church Historian's Office.

[4] The ensuing account of the Forsgren company is drawn from several sources: *A Pioneer Journal, Forsgren Company*, Daughters of Utah Pioneers, Historical Pamphlet (Salt Lake City, 1944), pp. 1–40; Willard Snow, Journal, MS., excerpted in Scandinavian Mission General History, MS., in Church Historian's Office, which also quotes a number of journals by members of the company – especially by Herman Julius Christensen and Christian I. Munk – and provides a partial list of the emigrants; Christian Nielsen, Letter, April 27, 1856, MS., original in Royal Library, Copenhagen; "History of Anders Thomsen, Sr., by Himself," MS., typescript in possession of Woodruff Thomsen; letters from the emigrants published in *Stjerne*, *passim* for 1852–54; "Aeldste Lars Poulsens Död," *Morgenstjernen*, 3:95–96 (1884). The story of the Forsgren company also survives in fleeting references in many memoirs and in the oral tradition of Mormon families who take pride in their descent from the emigrants; Scandinavian reunions frequently hear bits of it. In 1953 a float creation of the *Forest Monarch* formed part of the Pioneer Day parade (July 24) in Salt Lake City.

[5] In almost every company someone would suffer a last-minute disappointment or disaster, like Soren Sorenson, forty-four, a farmer, who, with his wife and three children, was held up in Liverpool: "This family did not go per *John J. Boyd* in consequence of the Surgeon refusing to pass them, children being sick with measles." Laborer Niels Christian Nielsen's family was similarly afflicted; his little Anne Marie "Died at Chapman's Temperance Hotel 17 Dec 1855. Interred at St. Johns Church 20 Dec 1855." Emigration Records (Liverpool), Book D.

[6] Records of the Bureau of Customs, Office of the Collector of Customs, Port of New Orleans, Passenger List of *Forest Monarch*, arriving March 17, 1853. Besides the Forsgren company the manifest shows fifty-three other passengers, most of them with Irish names; but the manifest enters "Ireland" for the whole company, and labels them all "Labourers" and "Shoemakers." See Chapter 5, "Ugly Ducklings," for the emigrants' varied occupations.

[7] Hans Jensen Hals, Diary, MS., entries for 1865–68.

[8] "Til Emigranterne," *Stjerne*, 2:30, 46–47, 62–63, 72–73 (1852).

[9] "Instruktioner til Emigranterne," *Stjerne*, 34:201ff (April 1, 1885). N. C. Flygare noted in 1877 that during the previous summer many emigrants had to leave their baggage in the hands of the railroad because they could not pay excess freight charges. Letter, February 25, 1877, *Nordstjärnan* (Stockholm), 1:17 (January 1, 1877). Lars J. Halling, arriving with his family in Salt Lake in 1856 as a lad of fifteen, was sent back on foot 113 miles to Fort Bridger to recover a stray ox. MS. letter, n.d., Utah Humanities Research Foundation Archives.

[10] "Angaaende Emigrationen," *Stjerne*, 21:186 (March 15, 1872); "Vor Emigration," *Stjerne*, 34:200 (April 1, 1885).

[11] *Stjerne*, 1:9 (October 1, 1852); 3:62, 73 (November 15, 1853); 34:201 (De-

cember 1, 1885). Bound apprentices and servant girls sometimes had difficulty securing release from their contract before they could emigrate. Fourteen-year-old Frederick Christenson petitioned the mayor of his town, describing his master's ill treatment and his persecution by the other apprentices. The mayor, impressed that Frederick had written his own request, investigated his claims, found them true, and granted him his freedom. Frederick Christenson to Joseph Christiansen, November 29, 1892, *Stjerne*, 42:107–8 (January 1, 1893).

[12] Andrew M. Israelsen, *Autobiography* (Salt Lake City, 1938), p. 19.

[13] Andrew Jenson, "Erindringer fra Missionen i Skandinavien," *Morgenstjernen*, 2:54 (1883).

[14] *Millennial Star*, 18:206 (March 22, 1856); 28:345 (June 2, 1866); Jenson, "Erindringer," *Morgenstjernen*, 3:286 (1884).

[15] Hans Zobell, "Autobiography," p. 60; Julie Ingerøe, *Et Aar i Utah* (Copenhagen, 1868), p. 15; private journals cited in Scandinavian Mission General History, MS. For a hypersensitive person like Miss Ingerøe, who later apostatized, the whole journey was an unrelieved nightmare. Throughout her disillusioned account she complains of hardships which were the lot of all pioneering and not the special curse of Mormonism.

[16] Andrew Jenson, "En Zionsrejse," *Morgenstjernen*, 3:364–66, 374-76 (1884).

[17] Zobell, "Autobiography," p. 52.

[18] O. N. Liljenquist, "Autobiografi," *Morgenstjernen*, 2:37 (1883); Hans Jensen Hals, Diary, June 12, 1868.

[19] "Emigranternes Afreise," *Stjerne*, 21:296 (July 1, 1872).

[20] *Edinburgh Review*, 115:198 (1862).

[21] "Lars Peter Christensen," *Sevier Stake Memories* (Springville, Utah, 1949), p. 446.

[22] Hans Jensen Hals, Diary, July 13, 1868.

[23] Andrew Jenson, "Church Emigration," *The Contributor* (Salt Lake City), 13:182 (1892).

[24] New York *Times*, July 8, 1877; July 16, 1873; July 3, 1882.

[25] "Diplomatic Correspondence, Circular No. 10, August 9, 1879, Sent to Diplomatic and Consular Officers of the United States," *Papers Relating to the Foreign Relations of the United States 1879* (Washington, D.C., 1880), pp. 11, 12.

[26] New York *Times*, September 17, 1879.

[27] *Ibid.*, September 17, 1880.

[28] Jenson, "Church Emigration," *The Contributor*, 13:183 (1892).

[29] C. C. A. Christensen, "Beretning," *Morgenstjernen*, 3:205 (1884).

[30] The ensuing handcart account is drawn from Jensen's recollections in J. M. Tanner, *Biographical Sketch of James Jensen* (Salt Lake City, 1911), pp. 19–40.

[31] It is estimated that 4000 Mormon converts (all nationalities) crossed the plains by handcart from 1856 to 1860; and between 1861 and 1868, some 2016 "teams," each consisting of a wagon and four yoke of oxen and accommodating from eight to ten persons, were sent out from Utah as "church trains" to aid the emigrants. Latter-day Saint Journal History, MS., entry for September 25, 1868, in Church Historian's Office. Outfitting points – where Mormon agents temporarily established themselves to make advance preparations – until the completion of the railroad in 1869 were as follows: 1853, Keokuk, Iowa; 1854, Westport (near Kansas City), Missouri; 1855, Mormon Grove, Kansas (five miles west of Atchison); 1856–58, Iowa City, Iowa; 1859–63, Florence, Nebraska; 1864–66, Wyoming, Nebraska (on the Missouri River); 1867, North Platte, Nebraska; 1868, Benton, Wyoming (on the Platte River).

[32] A. W. Winberg to Carl Widerborg, August 22, 1865, *Stjerne*, 15:10, 11 (October 1, 1865).

[33] "Life History of Our Father John Nielsen," MS., pp. 30, 34, microfilm in Utah State Historical Society.

[34] Folkmann to Carl Widerborg, May 23, 1858, *Stjerne*, 7:299 (July 1, 1858).

[35] M. Pedersen to J. N. Smith, February 25, 1869, *Stjerne*, 18:220 (April 15, 1869).

[36] Jenson, "Erindringer," *Morgenstjernen*, 3:214, 242 (1884); Andrew Jenson, *History of the Scandinavian Mission* (Salt Lake City, 1927), p. 150.

[37] Peter O. Thomassen, Letter, n.d., quoted in Jenson, *History*, p. 175.

[38] Olsen to N. C. Flygare, July 20, 1886, *Stjerne*, 35:348 (August 15, 1886).

[39] Zobell, "Autobiography," p. 71; Nils Pehrsson, Letter, March 12, 1872, MS., original in Nordiska Museet, Stockholm.

[40] Jonas Stadling, *Hvad Jag Hörde och Såg i Mormonernas Zion* (Stockholm, 1884), p. 28. The general insinuation – which the evidence here proves untenable – about the whole movement from Scandinavia seems to be that the Mormons were "segregated on the boat and on arrival at New York were herded in separate railway cars and locked in. When they arrived in Salt Lake City they were conducted to an emigrant house, from which they were distributed to different parts of the territory." George M. Stephenson, *The Religious Aspects of Swedish Immigration* (Minneapolis, 1932), p. 99. Even reputable historians persist in this misinterpretation which makes Mormon immigration sound like a deal in cattle.

[41] Andreas Mortensen, *Fra mit Besog blandt Mormonerne* (Christiania, 1887), p. 279.

[42] "Life History of Our Father John Nielsen," p. 35.

[43] Christoffer J. Kempe to Carl Widerborg, November 14, 1865, *Stjerne*, 15:122 (January 15, 1866).

[44] John A. Widtsoe, *In the Gospel Net* (Salt Lake City, 1941), p. 79.

[45] Ingerøe, *Et Aar*, p. 19; Zobell, "Autobiography," pp. 71–74.

[46] Peder Nielsen, Diary, September 21, 1861, typescript translation in possession of Orson B. West.

[47] None of these names survives today; even Emigration Road has been robbed of its romance: it is today colorless Fifth South Street.

[48] Manuscript History of Brigham Young, November 30, 1856, quoted in Milton R. Hunter, *Brigham Young the Colonizer* (Salt Lake City, 1940), p. 108.

[49] P. O. Thomassen to K. Peterson, September 28, 1872, *Stjerne*, 22:44 (November 1, 1872).

[50] Andrew M. Israelsen, *Utah Pioneering* (Salt Lake City, 1938), p. 21; Ingerøe, *Et Aar i Utah*, p. 20; Stadling, *Hvad Jag Hörde*, p. 27.

[51] William Hepworth Dixon, *New America* (Philadelphia, 1867), pp. 149, 150.

[52] Sermon, October 6, 1853, *Journal of Discourses*, I, 316. Richards understood human nature: Mons Pedersen noted in 1870 that some who were good Saints in the Old Country turned their backs on the gospel because Zion did not come up to their expectations. Some of their reasons made him smile. "The emigrants go about looking for faults to get a true picture of conditions in Utah." They complained most over not having "a house, land, animals, and so forth, like the old settlers, and these are unwilling to turn their possessions, which they have earned through thrift and industry, over to the immigrants. Those who come in the right spirit will in due time acquire what the earlier immigrants have." Pedersen to Jesse N. Smith, March 16, 1870, *Stjerne*, 19:235–36 (May 1, 1870).

[53] Sermon, September 24, 1854, *Journal of Discourses*, III, 67.

[54] John M. Coyner, ed., *Handbook on Mormonism* (Salt Lake City, 1882), p. 19.

[55] Emigration Records (Liverpool), Book E, 1856–60.

[56] Frederick Loba in the New York *Times*, April 27, May 1, May 8, 1858; "Breaking up of Mormondom," New York *Times*, July 18, 1857, quoting Plattsmouth (Nebraska) *Jeffersonian*.

[57] *Bikūben*, August 9, 1877.

[58] N. Bourkersson, *Tre År i Mormonlandet* (Malmö, 1867), pp. 27, 170.

[59] Ingerøe, *Et Aar i Utah, passim.*

[60] Christian Michelsen, *Livet ved Saltsøen* (Odense, 1872), *passim.*

[61] New York *Times*, August 2, 1863; *A Voice from the West to the Scattered People of Weber* (np., nd.), *passim.* Of 430 baptized followers of Morris, at least 174 were Scandinavians, a proportionate number of whom must have figured in the exodus to Soda Springs and Carson. See *Roll of Membership. Names of Persons Baptized into the Fulness of the Gospel* (San Francisco, 1886), *passim.* I am indebted to Dale L. Morgan for a copy of the list.

[62] P. S. Vig, "Danske i Amerika, 1851–60," in *Danske i Amerika* (Minneapolis, 1907), 2 vols., I, 286; George T. Flom, "The Danish Contingent in Early Iowa," *Iowa Journal of History and Politics*, 4:238–40 (April 1906).

[63] Lamont Poulter Knapp, "The History of Solon Hannibal Borglum" (unpublished M.A. thesis, University of Utah, 1950), pp. 29–31.

[64] Johan Ahmanson, *Vor Tids Muhammed* (Omaha, 1876), *passim.*

[65] Diary, MS., May 26, 1858.

[66] *Stjerne*, 22:45 (November 1, 1872); 20:377 (September 15, 1871).

[67] *Millennial Star*, 26:72 (January 30, 1864).

[68] Geertsen to W. W. Cluff, July 25, 1870, *Stjerne*, 19:365 (September 1, 1870). Andrew Jenson, a Dane who became assistant historian of the Mormon Church, told a Scandinavian gathering in Salt Lake City that "Although many of our countrymen who have taken up Christ's cross to follow him have fallen – some in the Old Country and others after they arrived in these valleys – the per cent of the apostates is still much less than in any other country where the gospel has been preached. Of the tens and hundreds of thousands baptized in America and Great Britain since the organization of the Church, only a lesser part has remained faithful." "Tale," *Morgenstjernen*, 4:180 (1885).

CHAPTER 8. MORMON VILLAGERS

[1] Mt. Pleasant High Priests Quorum, Minute Book, MS., January 26, 1860. In Historian's Office, Church of Jesus Christ of Latter-day Saints.

[2] "History of Anders Thomsen, Sr., by Himself," MS. Typescript in possession of Woodruff Thomsen, a grandson. The ensuing details about Thomsen are drawn from this manuscript.

[3] John Codman, "Through Utah," *Galaxy*, 20:620 (November 1875).

[4] *Laws and Ordinances of the State of Deseret, Compilation of 1851* (Reprint, Salt Lake City, 1919), pp. 78–89; Milton R. Hunter, *Brigham Young the Colonizer* (Salt Lake City, 1940), p. 15. *Skandinaviens Stjerne* in its early issues speculated on the possibility of a round-the-Horn passage.

[5] Hunter, pp. 361–66.

[6] *Report of the Utah Commission to the Secretary of the Interior, September 24, 1888* (Washington, D.C., 1888), p. 16. Mormon land policy at first envisioned no buying or selling of land. No man had right to more than he could use. Holdings were necessarily small: farms in Utah during the 1860s and 1870s, when Scandinavian rural settlement was at its height, averaged 25 to 30 acres, which were in more intensive use than larger acreages later. "Give me the wives, I'll get the land somehow," was a common toast. Land taken up under the Desert Land Act increased the average acres per farm from 25 in 1860 to 126 in 1890, but the percentage unimproved in farm land went from 14.12 per cent to 58.58 per cent. (U.S. Eleventh Census, III, 108.) When the government survey was made, the Mormons had to resort to unusual stratagems to obtain title to their tracts: it was agreed among the claimants of a quarter section that one of them would file for a home-

stead patent on the whole 160 acres, put up a shanty on the land and occupy it the minimum time to fulfill the law (the Mormons as villagers did not live on the farms), and give quit claim deeds to the other claimants, who paid him a small sum for having used up his homestead right. Lowry Nelson, *The Mormon Village* (Salt Lake City, 1952), pp. 140–41.

[7] See Joseph Smith, *History of the Church* (Salt Lake City, 1921), I, 357–62, for the plat of the City of Zion and its specifications. Lowry Nelson's *The Mormon Village* is the most comprehensive study.

[8] Mt. Pleasant High Priests Quorum, April 16, 1871.

[9] *Ibid.*, March 25, 1877.

[10] Mendon Ward Historical Record, MS., July 7, 1872. Typescript in Utah State Historical Society.

[11] Edward L. Sloan, ed., *Gazetteer of Utah and Salt Lake City Directory, 1874*, p. 83; *ibid.*, *1884*, p. 142.

[12] Nielsen to Fisherman Carl, April 27, 1856, in *Bikûben* (Salt Lake City), December 19, 1912. Original in Royal Library, Copenhagen.

[13] Albert R. Lyman, "Jens Nielsen," MS., WPA Writers' Project Biographies, Utah State Historical Society. The Hole-in-the-Rock story is often retold in Mormon circles. Hoffman Birney's *Zealots of Zion* (Philadelphia, 1931) and Wallace Stegner's *Mormon Country* (New York, 1942) contain dramatic accounts.

[14] Hans Jensen Hals to N. C. Flygare, August 22, 1878, *Stjerne*, 28:25–26 (October 15, 1878).

[15] Daughters of Utah Pioneers, *Heart Throbs of the West* (Salt Lake City, 1946), VII, 505–21.

[16] Utah Writers' Project, *Utah Place Names* (n.p., n.d.), *passim*; also various county histories.

[17] *Svenska Härolden* (Salt Lake City), scattered advertisements for 1885; in May 5, 1892, it advertised a Folsom Addition as "the Scandinavian Suburb."

[18] U.S. Eighth Census, Schedule 1., "Free Inhabitants in 2nd Ward Great Salt Lake City in the County of Salt Lake, Territory of Utah," MS., pp. 125–30. On one block lived two Danish families, a Canadian, an English, and one from Maine; on another, the order of houses was Scotch, Danish, English, two Danish, Irish, English, two Danish; on a third, Danish, Pennsylvania, Vermont, three Danish, New York, English, English. The most Scandinavian block contained one family from New York, two from Sweden, nine in a row from Denmark, one from Scotland. Scandinavian occupations, incidentally, included farmers (the parish, or ward, only nine blocks from the center of the city, was still decidedly rural, devoted to dairying), potter, shoemaker, cabinetmaker, blacksmith, wheelwright, laborer, carpenter.

[19] Charles L. Walker, Journal, MS., entries for October 20, 23, 1859; October 21, 1860. Typescript in Utah State Historical Society.

[20] Hans Jensen Hals, Diary, MS., summary entry for 1859. Typescript translation in possession of Nicholas G. Morgan, Sr.

[21] *Compendium of Eleventh Census, Part I*, Table 16; U.S. Immigration Commission, *Statistical Review of Immigration 1820–1910* (U.S. Im. Com., *Reports*, III), p. 521.

[22] United States Sixteenth Census, *Population*, II, 31.

[23] *Utah Korrespondenten*, August 1, 1902. The U.S. Twelfth Census (1900) shows 24,751 inhabitants of Danish stock, 14,578 of Swedish, and 4554 of Norwegian in Utah for a total of 43,883 of Scandinavian stock, or very close to Lund's 45,000.

[24] Daughters of Utah Pioneers, *Scandinavia's Contribution to Utah* (Salt Lake City, 1939), pp. 25–26.

[25] Julie Ingerøe, *Et Aar i Utah* (Copenhagen, 1868), p. 24.

[26] John A. Widtsoe, *In the Gospel Net. The Story of Anna Karine Widtsoe, 1849–1919* (Salt Lake City, 1941), p. 84.

[27] Niels Wilhelmsen, "Autobiografi," *Morgenstjernen*, 2:136 (1883); Wilhelmsen to John Van Cott, December 29, 1861, *Stjerne*, 11:172 (March 1, 1862).

[28] Sermon, October 7, 1853, Journal History, MS., same date.

[29] "History of Gustave Anderson," MS., typescript in possession of Emma A. Liljenquist.

[30] Carrie P. Tanner, "A Story of the Life of Canute Peterson as Given by Himself," MS., typescript in Church Historian's Office.

[31] Hals, Diary; Irvin L. Warnock, *Memories of Sevier Stake, 1874–1949* (Springville, 1949), p. 450; "History of Spanish Fork," *Tullidge's Quarterly*, 3:151 (April 1884).

[32] Andrew Jenson, *Latter-day Saint Biographical Encyclopedia* (Salt Lake City, 1901–26), 4 vols., III, 423; C. E. Forsberg to Andreas Peterson, n.d., *Nordstjärnan*, 25:58 (February 15, 1901).

[33] See, for example, W. W. Cluff to K. Peterson, January 16, 1872, *Stjerne*, 21:173 (March 1, 1872). Ohio-born Cluff, who had presided over the Scandinavian Mission in 1870–71, said the Scandinavians seemed to be getting along better "temporally" than any other nationality.

[34] *Latter-day Saint Biographical Encyclopedia*, I, 186, 202–3.

[35] N. C. Edlefson to Jesse N. Smith, September 3, 1869, *Stjerne*, 19:42 (November 1, 1869).

[36] Hals, Diary, entries for 1854–60.

[37] J. M. Tanner, *Biographical Sketch of James Jensen* (Salt Lake City, 1911), pp. 40–61.

[38] "Leaves from the Journal of C. L. Christensen," MS., typescript in Utah Humanities Research Foundation Archives.

[39] "The Life History of Our Father, John Nielsen," MS., microfilm in Utah State Historical Society.

[40] Peder Nielsen, Diary, MS., entries for 1861–66. Typescript translation in possession of Orson B. West.

[41] Martin P. Kuhre, Diary, MS., entries for 1863. Original and typescript translation in possession of William D. Kuhre.

[42] The ensuing account is based on Hans Christensen's "Memoirs" written in 1890. Typescript in Utah Humanities Research Foundation Archives. The spelling has been corrected in the direct quotes.

[43] The United Order and Scandinavian participation in it are more fully described in the next chapter.

[44] "Life History of Our Father John Nielsen"; "Christian Hansen," *Scandinavian Jubilee Album* (Salt Lake City, 1900), p. 112; "Olof Nilson," *ibid.*, p. 177; Hannah Sorensen, "Letters to the Young Women of Zion," *Young Woman's Journal*, 1:468–72 (September 1890); the soil chemist was John A. Widtsoe, who became president of the Utah State Agricultural College and later of the University of Utah; at least three Scandinavians have headed the Agricultural College: John A. Widtsoe, Elmer G. Peterson, and Louis L. Madsen.

[45] Nielsen to Fisherman Carl, April 27, 1856, *Bikūben*, December 19, 1912.

[46] Sloan, *Gazetteer 1874*, pp. 63–64; Sloan, *The Salt Lake City Directory and Business Guide for 1869* (Salt Lake City, 1869), pp. 87–171.

[47] Leonard J. Arrington, "Mormon Economic Policies and Their Implementation on the Western Frontier, 1847–1900," MS. (unpublished Ph.D. dissertation, University of North Carolina, 1952), pp. 270–329.

[48] Kempe to Carl Widerborg, November 14, 1865, *Stjerne*, 15:122 (January 15, 1866). Flour was then worth $6 cwt.

[49] Journal History, February 26, 1854.

[50] Arrington, *op. cit.*

[51] C. C. A. Christensen, *Digte og Afhandlinger* (Salt Lake City, 1926), p. 356; Alice M. Horne, *Devotees and Their Shrines; A Handbook of Utah Art* (Salt Lake City, 1914).

[52] "Br S Larsen exhorted the brethren to do all in their power to help to bild the Temple & sustain the 2 brethren with provision that we sent with unanemus woth [vote] to help to bild the Temple in Salt Lake City. Spoke of President Youngs request last Sommer in Fort Ephraim in regard to the bilding of the Sanpete Temple. . . . $36 was obtaind in provision & mony etc & sent to the brethren Johnsen & Nilsen." Mount Pleasant High Priests Quorum, Minute Book, June 25, 1876.

[53] "Til de unge Søstre," *Utah Posten*, January 24, 1874.

[54] O. C. Larsen to the Editor, January 24, 1874, *Utah Posten*, January 31, 1874.

[55] *Loc. cit.*

[56] "What to Do with the Immigrants?" *Deseret News Weekly*, June 1, 1878, reprinted in *Skandinaviens Stjerne*, 27:347–48 (August 1, 1878).

[57] "Arbejdsløsheden," *Morgenstjernen*, 3:56 (1884).

[58] Christensen to the Editor, February 24, 1884, *Morgenstjernen*, 3:90 (1884).

[59] Hermina Thuesen, "Notes," MS., typescript in possession of Anna K. Lewis; Carl Madsen, "My Conversion to Mormonism," MS., typescript in possession of Dr. Brigham Madsen.

[60] The ensuing account of Hyrum is based on my biographical essay "Ola Nilsson Liljenquist and His Cooperative City" in Adolph B. Benson, ed., *The Will to Succeed: Stories of Swedish Pioneers* (Stockholm, 1948), pp. 88–99. Original sources include a manuscript diary of Liljenquist; a manuscript history of Hyrum in "Cache Stake History," found in the Church Historian's Office; and contemporary reports in the *Deseret News*.

[61] Nelson, *The Mormon Village*, pp. 138–39.

[62] Mt. Pleasant Ward Historical Record, MS., May 30, 1859. In Church Historian's Office.

[63] Lucinda P. Jensen, *History of Bear River City* (Brigham City, Utah, 1947), p. 58; John A. Widtsoe, *Dry Farming* (New York, 1911), p. 355.

[64] Lucinda P. Jensen, pp. 59–64.

[65] Mt. Pleasant High Priests, February 11, 1861.

[66] North Sanpete Stake History, MS., April 15, October 20, 1866. In Church Historian's Office.

[67] Mt. Pleasant High Priests, August 6, 1865.

[68] Mendon Ward Historical Record, September 20–22, 1869.

[69] Kate C. Snow, "Early Day Freighting in Sanpete County," in *Heart Throbs of the West* (Salt Lake City, 1949), X, 78.

[70] B. N. S. Nielsen, quoted in Elice M. Moffitt, "Freighting Goods from Manti," *Heart Throbs of the West*, X, 82.

[71] Moffitt, p. 81.

[72] Ogden *Herald*, December 13, 1886; *Deseret News*, September 7, 1882; June 13, 1883; in Leonard J. Arrington, "The Economic Role of Pioneer Mormon Women," *Western Humanities Review*, 9:145–64 (Spring 1955).

[73] Mendon Ward Historical Record, summary entry for 1891.

[74] "Minutes," in Warnock, *Memories of Sevier Stake*, p. 18.

[75] Ephraim *Enterprise*, October 14, 1891.

[76] Mendon Ward Historical Record, summary entry for 1893.

CHAPTER 9. SEED OF ABRAHAM

[1] W. L. Muir, inscription, March 17, 1888, in Mads Christensen, Autograph Album, MS., in possession of P. A. Christensen.

[2] Sanpete Stake Quarterly Conference, Manti, August 17, 1878, reported in *Deseret News*, August 28, 1878.

[3] Orson Hyde, sermon, July 1, 1860, reported in Mt. Pleasant Branch, Church Record, MS., pp. 10–18. In Historian's Office, Church of Jesus Christ of Latter-day Saints.

[4] Mt. Pleasant High Priests Quorum, Minute Book, 1859–1915, MS. In Church Historian's Office.

[5] *Ibid.*, November 27, 1870.

[6] *Ibid.*, December 15, 1859.

[7] *Ibid.*, December 31, 1876, January 6, 1877.

[8] See Chapter 11, "Inroads: Conflict and Crusade."

[9] High Priests Quorum, Minute Book, May 11, 1862.

[10] *Ibid.*, July 7, 1861; January 5, 1864; June 1, October 5, 1873; February 28, 1874.

[11] *Ibid.*, February 26, August 25, October 22, 1860.

[12] Mt. Pleasant Branch, Church Record, n.d., p. 68.

[13] *Ibid.*, December 22, 1861; October 31, 1862.

[14] *Ibid.*, October 31, 1863.

[15] High Priests Quorum, Minute Book, January 8, September 10, 1871; January 12, November 2, 1873; February 13, 27, 1875; January 5, February 19, 26, March 4, 11, 1876.

[16] *Ibid.*, March 25, 1877; May 14, 1882; April 1, 15, 1883.

[17] *Ibid.*, November 26, 1860.

[18] Mt. Pleasant Ward History, MS., July, 1861; October 20, 28, 1861. In Church Historian's Office.

[19] High Priests Quorum, Minute Book, May 24, 1863; October 2, 1864.

[20] Mt. Pleasant Ward History, January 4, February 17, November 1, 1865; High Priests Quorum, Minute Book, August 25, 1877.

[21] Mt. Pleasant Branch, Church Record, June 1, 1861, p. 67; *Deseret News*, June 8, 1861.

[22] High Priests Quorum, Minute Book, March 10, 1883.

[23] *Tullidge's Quarterly*, 1:366 (April 1881).

[24] I have this anecdote from Lucinda P. Jensen of Bear River City.

[25] Lorenzo Snow to F. D. Richards, November 1, 1879, in "The United Order of Brigham City," *Tullidge's Quarterly*, 2:405 (January 1883).

[26] "Our Brigham City Letter: Cooperation What It Has Done and Is Doing for the People of That Burg," October 30, 1874, in Salt Lake *Daily Herald*, October 31, 1874.

[27] History of Mendon Ward, MS., entries for 1869–72. Typescript in Utah State Historical Society.

[28] Lucille Butler, "Ephraim Humor" (unpublished master's thesis, University of Utah, 1950), p. 83.

[29] See Leonard J. Arrington, "Early Mormon Communitarianism: The Law of Consecration and Stewardship," *Western Humanities Review*, 7:341–69 (Autumn 1953). See also Edward J. Allen, *The Second United Order among the Mormons* (New York, 1936).

[30] See F. Y. Fox, "The Consecration Movement of the Middle Fifties," *The Improvement Era* (Salt Lake City), 47:80ff, 146ff (February, March 1944).

[31] See Chapter 7, "Journey to Zion," for further mention of the Morrisites.

[32] See Leonard J. Arrington, *Orderville, Utah: A Pioneer Mormon Experiment in Economic Organization*, Utah State Agricultural College Monograph Series, II, No. 2 (Logan, Utah, 1954); Goudy Hogan, "History of Goudy Hogan," MS., typescript in Brigham Young University Library.

[33] *The Daily Press* (Salt Lake City), May 16, 1874, a satirical account.

[34] Mt. Pleasant High Priests Quorum, Minute Book, May 31, 1874.

[35] Jacobsen to C. G. Larsen, November 23, 1874, *Skandinaviens Stjerne*, 24:106–8 (January 1, 1875).

[36] Mendon Ward Historical Record, p. 15.

[37] *Ibid.*, p. 16.

[38] *Loc. cit.*

[39] Hans Christensen, "Memoirs," MS., microfilm in Utah Humanities Research Foundation Archives; see Chapter 8, "Mormon Villagers," for a description of his reception of the Order when it was first announced.

[40] "Articles of Agreement and Minutes of the United Order in Oak City [Creek], Utah, 1874," MS., typescript in Utah Humanities Research Foundation Archives.

[41] *Ibid.*, May 3, June 14, 1874.

[42] High Priests Quorum Minute Book, November 3, 1872; December 21, 1873.

[43] Jonas Stadling, *Hvad Jag Hörde och Såg i Mormonernas Zion* (Stockholm, 1884), p. 25.

[44] Hans Zobell, "Autobiography," MS., p. 95, typescript in possession of Albert L. Zobell, Jr.; Knud Svendsen, Diary, MS., August 1858, microfilm in Huntington Library.

[45] "Patriarch H.," *Bikûben*, March 1, 1877.

[46] Andrew Jenson, *Latter-day Saint Biographical Encyclopedia* (Salt Lake City, 1901–26), 4 vols., II, 361; "Jens Hansen," in "Biografiske Skizzer," *Morgenstjernen*, 1:124 (1882). The original schedule for Spanish Fork in the U.S. Ninth Census (1870) provides an interesting statistical profile of Hansen's family some seven years before the Danish editor's visit: He is listed as James Hanson, 46, farmer and citizen, worth $1200 in real estate and $1000 in personal property. His first wife Caroline, 46, is described as "Keeping house" and is followed by the names of twenty children ranging from 16 years of age down to 26 days, all the school-age children literate. The seven plural wives, all Danish and described as "Keeping house," follow these, their ages 51, 45, 36, 33, 32, 27, 27. Also in the household were Yorgen Peter, 44, a laborer, remarked as insane, and Emma Tristram, 15, a Danish schoolteacher.

[47] Frank Esshom, *Pioneers and Prominent Men of Utah* (Salt Lake City, 1913), p. 965; *Latter-day Saint Biographical Encyclopedia*, III, 433; U.S. Tenth Census, original schedule for Ephraim, Sanpete County.

[48] John Codman, *A Solution of the Mormon Problem* (New York, 1885), p. 7.

[49] Statistics are hard to come by, since polygamous marriages were not licensed and church records are not made public. The common assumption has grown up that not more than 2 or 3 per cent of the church membership practiced polygamy, a figure seemingly based on the report of the Utah Commission for 1882 as cited by a church official in the Reed Smoot investigation. The application of the anti-polygamy law had disfranchised 12,000 Mormons. Two thirds of these must have been women, leaving only 4000 male polygamists, which constituted about 2 per cent of the entire church membership. The miscalculation is obvious. It is closer to the truth that 23 per cent of the Mormons over eighteen years of age were involved in polygamy. In 1890 there were 2451 polygamous families in the United States, some 3000 with those in Mexico and Canada – altogether some 30,000 individuals. Thus, 10 per cent or more of the Mormon membership in the early 1880s were involved in polygamy. See Stanley S. Ivins, "Notes on Mormon Polygamy," *Western Humanities Review*, 10:229–39 (Summer 1956).

[50] U.S. Ninth Census, original schedule for Spanish Fork, Utah County.

[51] U.S. Tenth Census, original schedule for Ephraim, Sanpete County.

[52] Stanley S. Ivins, "Notes on Mormon Polygamy," provides a general tabulation; I have tabulated the figures for the Scandinavians independently, going be-

yond Ivins in counting the number of Scandinavian women listed in Esshom who were involved in polygamy. Ivins says that of 1784 polygamists 66.3 per cent married one plural wife; 21.2 per cent were three-wife men; 6.7 per cent took four; less than 6 per cent married five or more women. "The typical polygamist . . . was content to call a halt after marrying the one extra wife required to assure him his chance at salvation." Of 1642 polygamists. Ivins found that 10 per cent married one or more pairs of sisters. Of 1229 polygamists, more than 10 per cent married their last wives while still in their twenties, and more than one half before arriving at the age of 40. Not one in five took a wife after passing his fiftieth year. Of 1348 plural wives, 38 per cent were in their teens, 67 per cent under 25, and only 13 per cent over 30. A few had passed 40, and about one in a hundred were married after 50 "for their soul's sake."

[53] In 1870 males in Utah numbered 44,122, females 42,665; foreign-born males 15,127, females 15,575. In 1890 the ratio was 92 males to every 100 females among the Swedes, 87.2 among the Norwegians (no figure for the Danish). U.S. Eleventh Census, 1, 556. Sanpete's female preponderance was slight: but thirteen. Edward L. Sloan, ed., *Gazetteer of Utah and Directory of Salt Lake City 1884* (Salt Lake City, 1884), p. 142. Logan's males numbered 799, females 925; in contrast, Park City, a gentile mining community, numbered 592 males, 300 females. U.S. Eleventh Census, I, 556.

[54] "Convictions for Polygamy in the Territory of Utah," in Orson F. Whitney, *History of Utah* (Salt Lake City, 1892–98), 4 vols., III, 643–48.

[55] "Nyheter," *Nordstjärnan*, 9:183 (June 15, 1885).

[56] "Utah Penitentiary Report," cited in *Hearings before the Committee on Territories 1889* (Washington, D.C., 1889), pp. 27–31.

[57] *Millennial Star*, 50:159 (March 15, 1888).

[58] Mendon Ward Historical Record, p. 20.

[59] Andrew Jenson, compiler, "Prisoners for Conscience' Sake," MS., in Church Historian's Office.

[60] The album, in the possession of a son, Professor P. A. Christensen of Brigham Young University, contains 88 inscriptions – 18 of them by Scandinavians – entered from February 12 to August 25, 1888.

[61] "Back to the Fold – A Glimpse of Prison Life in the Utah Pen," *Young Woman's Journal* (Salt Lake City), 7:165, 220, 265 (January 1896).

[62] Mendon Ward Historical Record, summary entry for 1885, p. 19.

[63] Whitney, III, 672–74.

[64] "The Mormons and the Law," New York *Times*, October 14, 1889. See Chapter 11, "Inroads: Conflict and Crusade," for a fuller discussion of the antipolygamy agitation.

[65] "Life History of Gustave Anderson," MS., typescript in possession of Emma Anderson Liljenquist; Hans Jensen Hals, Diary, MS., summary entry for 1858. Hals' close friend and neighbor was E. E. Kjaerulf, killed by Indians on June 4, 1858. "This gave me much sorrow, to my wife as well as his wife. The Lord gave us strength to bear this together. After awhile I drove to the City with others who were going to be married, and I married his wife for time. This took place in Brigham Young's home by Erastus Snow, who sealed her to her husband for time and eternity and to me for time. This was my and my wifes decision as well as Marie's wishes."

[66] John A. Widtsoe, *In the Gospel Net* (Salt Lake City, 1941), *passim*; "Life Sketch of Sister Hannah Sorensen," *Young Woman's Journal*, 1:391–405 (August 1890).

[67] Peder Nielsen, Diary, MS., May 1866; Emma Anderson Liljenquist, "The Story of My Life," MS., typescript in family's possession.

[68] Goudy Hogan, "History of Goudy Hogan," entry for December 1853.

[69] Ray S. Hansen, "A Brief History of the Life of Hans Christian Hansen," MS., typescript in possession of Ray S. Hansen.

[70] Esshom, pp. 846, 866, and *passim*.

[71] According to Stanley S. Ivins, a grandson.

[72] U.S. Eighth Census, original schedule for Salt Lake County; "Ellen Sanders Kimball," in Whitney, IV, 67–69; "Anna Kirstine Mauritzdatter," in Carl M. Hagberg, *Norske Misjonshistorie* (Oslo, 1928), p. 12; "Minnie Jensen Snow," *Utah Posten*, August 15, 1901; Sarah Josephine Jensen, "Autobiography," MS., typescript in possession of LeRoi C. Snow, a grandson.

[73] Reminiscence of James B. Morrison in Olena Kempe Lewis, "Notebook," MS., in family's possession.

[74] U.S. Eighth Census, original schedule for Salt Lake County.

[75] Mt. Pleasant Ward Record, MS., August 11, 1864.

[76] Reminiscence of Professor Lowry Nelson, a grandson.

[77] Carrie P. Tanner, "A Story of the Life of Canute Peterson as Told by Himself," MS., typescript in Church Historian's Office; U.S. Ninth Census, original schedule for Ephraim, Sanpete County.

[78] "Maria Wilhelmina Krause Madsen," MS., WPA, Utah Writers' Project Biographies, in Utah State Historical Society.

[79] Peter Hansen, "Levnetsbeskrivelse," MS., microfilm in Huntington Library.

[80] Mendon Ward Historical Record, July 7, 1872.

CHAPTER 10. MOTHER TONGUE

[1] C. C. A. Christensen, "Rimbrev," *Digte og Afhandlinger* (Salt Lake City, 1921), p. 314.

[2] Said the first number of *Utah Posten*, Danish-Norwegian weekly: "It is by no means our intention to push English into the background or to cast reflections on it, because it is desirable that everyone should understand the language in which it pleased the Almighty to manifest His will in this last dispensation." December 24, 1873.

[3] H. F. Liljenquist, noting the time consumed in the mission to learn the language, thought it a shame the young were not taught the mother tongue, that they considered it "simple" to be a Dane. *Skandinaviens Stjerne*, 42:41 (November 1, 1892). I am indebted to Lowry Nelson, well-known sociologist and author of *The Mormon Village*, for pointing out that mother-tongue surveys – that is, census accounts of what people report their mother tongue to be – show that the old language died out more quickly in Utah than in any other state; in Minnesota, he told me, it is not uncommon to find third- and fourth-generation Scandinavians still giving the old speech as their mother tongue.

[4] "To the Saints," *Deseret News*, February 5, 1853.

[5] Hans Jensen Hals, Diary, MS., summary entry for 1885. Typescript translation in possession of Nicholas G. Morgan, Sr.

[6] Knud Svendsen, "Dagbog," MS., April 11, 1868. Microfilm of original in Huntington Library.

[7] Hals, September 26, 1884.

[8] Edward H. Anderson, "Scandinavia," *The Contributor* (Salt Lake City), 12:109 (December 1890).

[9] "We have to learn the English language now, which is a bit difficult for the elders; the children learn it quickly. Most of the Danish children and young folk talk fairly good English and Indian. Fritz conducts an English school for a few Danes. We can just as readily learn Indian, because we come into conversation with them more often than we have opportunity to talk with Americans. We can begin to talk a little in both tongues; our children constantly talk English or In-

dian." Nielsen to Fisherman Carl Nielsen, April 27, 1856, in *Bikúben*, December 19, 1912. Original in Royal Library, Copenhagen.

[10] "Governor's Message, December 12, 1853," in "Governors' Messages," typescript in Utah State Historical Society, pp. 42–43.

[11] *Deseret News*, January 19, 1854.

[12] "Eleventh General Epistle of the Presidency of the Church of Jesus Christ of Latter-day Saints," in *Deseret News*, April 13, 1854.

[13] See Stanley S. Ivins, "The Deseret Alphabet," *Utah Humanities Review*, 1:223–39 (July 1947), and Leah R. Frisby and Hector Lee, "The Deseret Readers," *ibid.*, pp. 240–44.

[14] See Chapter 11, "Inroads: Conflict and Crusade."

[15] Thomassen to N. C. Flygare, January 21, 1887, *Stjerne*, 36:155 (February 15, 1887).

[16] Anderson, p. 108.

[17] "Skandinavisme," *Utah Korrespondenten*, July 25, 1902.

[18] *Utah Korrespondenten*, *passim*, particularly for 1901–3. A complete file has been preserved at the Historian's Office, Church of Jesus Christ of Latter-day Saints.

[19] See *Utah Posten* and *Utah Korrespondenten* for August 1902, for the charges and countercharges.

[20] The event was striking enough for the Swedish observer A. O. Assar to make note of it in his *Mormonernas Zion* (Stockholm, 1911), pp. 45–49. See *Utah Korrespondenten*, January 9, 1903, for Rydman's account of the petitioners.

[21] *Deseret Evening News*, April 4, 1903.

[22] See Rydman's valedictory in *Utah Korrespondenten*, April 14, 1915: "We finish our work without bad feelings toward anyone. . . ."

[23] Andrew Jenson, *History of the Scandinavian Mission* (Salt Lake City, 1927), pp. 411ff, 444ff, 501ff.

[24] A. W. Winberg called it a "Laeseforening," a Reading Society. Winberg to J. N. Smith, February 18, 1870, *Stjerne*, 19:205 (April 1, 1870).

[25] "Salt Lake's Norske Klub," *Utah Posten*, March 28, 1874.

[26] N. Bourkersson, *Tre Ar i Mormonlandet* (Malmö, 1867), p. 119.

[27] Letter to the Editor, n.d., *Bikúben* (Salt Lake City), October 1, 1876.

[28] *Loc. cit.*

[29] Ephraim *Enterprise*, October 28, 1891; February 10, March 2, 1892.

[30] Christensen to Knud Peterson, September 14, 1871, *Stjerne*, 21:36 (November 1, 1871).

[31] C. C. A. Christensen to K. Peterson, July 25, 1871, *Stjerne*, 20:362 (September 1, 1871); M. Pederson to J. N. Smith, February 25, 1869, *Stjerne*, 18:221 (April 15, 1869).

[32] *Bikúben*, January 10, 1878.

[33] *Korrespondenten*, January 28, 1891.

[34] Raymond E. Lindgren, "The Swedes Come to Utah," American Swedish Historical Foundation, *Yearbook 1949* (Philadelphia, 1949), p. 25; *Danske i Salt Lake City* (Salt Lake City, 1910), p. 30.

[35] *Stjerne*, 11:59–60 (February 15, 1902).

[36] Emma Anderson Liljenquist, "The Story of My Life," MS.

[37] Wanda Clayton Thomas of Salt Lake City tells me this about her grandfather.

[38] The Archive of American Folk Song in the Library of Congress contains a number of Danish folk songs in the Fife Mormon Collection. For a collection of local Scandinavian anecdotes see Lucille Butler, "Ephraim Humor" (unpublished master's thesis, University of Utah, 1950).

[39] *Utah Posten*, December 20, 1873. A complete file of this and the other Scandi-

navian periodicals published in Utah which are named hereafter may be found in the Church Historian's Office.

[40] *Utah Posten*, January 24, 1874.

[41] *Ibid.*, February 28, 1874.

[42] *Ibid.*, August 1, 1874.

[43] Salt Lake *Herald*, October 23, 1874. No copies of *Utah Skandinav* are extant; what is known about it has to be gleaned from contemporary descriptions in other papers.

[44] *Biküben*, August 2, September 6, 1877.

[45] *Ibid.*, June 1, 1877.

[46] Andrew Jenson, *Autobiography* (Salt Lake City, 1938), pp. 103–6.

[47] *Biküben*, May 2, 1878.

[48] *Utah Posten*, January 1, 1885.

[49] *Biküben*, October 16, 1884; January 22, 1885.

[50] Advertisement in *Korrespondenten*, March 15, 1893.

[51] Jenson, *Autobiography*, p. 391.

[52] *Biküben*, December 18, 1913.

[53] *Joseph Smiths Levnetsløb* (Salt Lake City, 1879).

[54] His collection in the Andrew Jenson Memorial Room in the Church Historian's Office is still uncatalogued.

[55] *Biküben*, April 13, 1885.

[56] *Svenska Härolden*, September 18, 1890.

[57] *Utah Korrespondenten*, September 20, 1900. (Rydman changed the name of his paper from *Korrespondenten* to *Utah Korrespondenten* in July, 1894.)

[58] *Utah Posten*, March 28, 1874.

[59] *Svenska Härolden*, February 16, 1888. The *Box Elder News* for July 31, 1902, noted that "The Scandinavian people of this city [Brigham City] don't seem to take much stock in a Scandinavian play. The patronage has always been light and that received by the Scandinavian Dramatic Club of Salt Lake City last Saturday night at the opera house was no exception to the rule."

[60] *Biküben*, April 16, 1885; J. J. M. Bohn, "Autobiografi," *Morgenstjernen*, 4:25 (February 1885).

[61] C. C. A. Christensen, "Man kalder mig Digter," *Digte og Afhandlinger* (Salt Lake City, 1921), p. 269.

[62] *Digte*, p. 266.

[63] *Utah Posten*, March 28, 1874. My translation.

[64] *Maer* in Danish is a mare, a jade. With the definite article *en*, *Maeren* becomes an obvious play on "mayor."

[65] Burgomaster: Mayor Ravn.

[66] "Rimbrev," *Digte*, p. 314. "Kurikurium" is a reference to "Dr. Peter's Kuriko," an eastern patent medicine widely advertised and rather piously believed in.

[67] "Aandeverdenen," *Digte*, p. 89.

[68] "Humoreske," *Digte*, p. 304.

[69] "Politisk Økonomisang," *Digte*, p. 312.

[70] *Digte*, p. 321.

[71] "Levnedsløb," *Digte*, p. 329ff.

CHAPTER 11. INROADS: CONFLICT AND CRUSADE

[1] C. C. A. Christensen, *Digte og Afhandlinger*, John S. Hansen, ed. (Salt Lake City, 1921), p. 294. The words form the refrain of a humorous Danish verse reciting various notions "the world" entertained of Utah.

[2] A. S. Bailey, "Anti-American Influences in Utah," in *The Situation in Utah: Proceedings of the Christian Convention 1888* (Salt Lake City, 1889), p. 18.

3 *Ibid.*, p. 23.

4 Edward Dicey, "Religion in America," *Macmillan's Magazine*, 15:443 (1867). Dicey was reviewing Hepworth Dixon's book, *New America*.

5 John M. Coyner, "Letters on Mormonism," in J. M. Coyner, ed., *Handbook on Mormonism* (Salt Lake City, 1882), p. 7.

6 C. C. Goodwin, "The Mormon Situation," *Harper's Magazine*, 63:763 (October 1881).

7 *Remarks of the Honorable Stephen A. Douglas on Kansas, Utah, and the Dred Scott Decision, Delivered at Springfield, Illinois, June 12, 1857* (Chicago, 1857). Brigham Young severely criticized the territorial policies of the federal government, calling the Ordinance of 1787 "unconstitutional" and "a relic of colonial barbarism" because it forced unwanted officers upon a "free people" and denied them the privilege of self-government. "Governor's Message, December 15, 1857," in "Governors' Messages," typescript in Utah State Historical Society.

8 Orson F. Whitney, *History of Utah* (Salt Lake City, 1892), 4 vols., I, 725.

9 Samuel Bowles, *Across the Continent* (Springfield, Mass., 1865), p. 398.

10 William Hepworth Dixon, *New America* (Philadelphia, 1867), p. 241.

11 "The Republicans long ago put into their platform that there were two twin relics that had to be moved out of the way – the one was slavery, and the other polygamy. They have removed slavery out of the way, but polygamy seems to be rather a hard nut for them to crack. It seems to bother them. They are in a good deal of trouble about it. . . ." John Taylor, sermon, February 10, 1884, *Journal of Discourses*, XXV, 92.

12 Christensen, p. 294.

13 Speech in the House of Representatives, March 23, 1870, 41st Cong., 2nd sess., *Congressional Globe*, Part 7, Appendix, p. 173. A Connecticut clergyman who had something favorable to say of the Mormons reported that an editor threw up his hands: "I have no doubt that what you say is all true, but it would ruin us to publish it." Rev. John C. Kimball, *Mormonism Exposed, the Other Side* (Hartford, 1884), p. 5.

14 The Liberals sang "Marching through Zion" to the tune of "Marching through Georgia":

> Orlond's boys with carpet bags can never take Salt Lake!
> So the royal families said, but that was their mistake,
> We'll show them at the ballot boxes who will "take the cake,"
> While we go marching through Zion.

Daughters of Utah Pioneers, "Political Parties," in *Heart Throbs of the West* (Salt Lake City, 1949), X, 18, reproduces a version with five verses and a chorus.

15 "The Massachusetts gentlemen who propose to overthrow the Mormon power in Utah by filling the waste places of the Territory with immigrants from the East . . ." were personages no less than Edward Everett Hale, Amos A. Lawrence, and Eli Thayer. The New York *Times* was admiring but skeptical: "Only a phenomenally successful emigration society can keep pace with the immigration of converts, especially in view of the fact that the most attractive parts of the Territory have long been in the hands of the Mormons." Editorial, April 20, 1885. At the death of Brigham Young in 1877, the Reverend DeWitt Talmage told a Brooklyn Tabernacle audience: "Now is the time for the United States Government to strike. Let as much of their rich lands be confiscated as will pay for their subjugation. . . . Set Phil Sheridan after them. Give him enough troops, and he will teach all Utah that forty wives is thirty-nine too many." New York *Times*, October 28, 1877. He would have "cannon of the biggest bore thunder into them the seventh commandment." A decade earlier the *Times* had taken issue with fire-eaters who would force Mormon loyalty and monogamy at the point of the

sword: "If an imperial Zouave on the other side of the Rio Grande 'makes faces' at a blue uniform on this side, our hot-heads would at once raise a 'million' men to fight the French Emperor. . . . If the redskins of the plains have a war-dance . . . these belligerent citizens would never attempt the policy of William Penn." Editorial, November 28, 1865.

[16] Dixon, p. 247.

[17] Lewis Hartsough, quoted in *Church Review* (Salt Lake City), 4:12 (December 29, 1895).

[18] M. T. Lamb, "Lessons from Mormonism," in *The Situation in Utah*, p. 88.

[19] Christoffer J. Kempe to Carl Widerborg, November 14, 1865, *Skandinaviens Stjerne*, 15:122 (January 15, 1866).

[20] Robert J. Dwyer, *The Gentile Comes to Utah* (Washington, D.C., 1941), pp. 30–33.

[21] Quoted in "Scandinavian Work in Utah," *Church Review*, 4:54 (December 29, 1895).

[22] R. G. McNiece, "The Christian Conflict with Mormonism," in J. M. Coyner, ed., *Handbook on Mormonism*, p. 60; *Report of the Governor of Utah to the Secretary of the Interior, 1890* (Washington, D.C., 1891), p. 17.

[23] Andreas Mortensen, *Fra mit Besog blandt Mormonerne* (Christiania, 1887), p. 283.

[24] D. J. McMillan, "Historical Sketch," MS., Minutes of Session, First Presbyterian Church, Mt. Pleasant, Utah, cited throughout in G. Grey Dashen, "A History of the First Presbyterian Church, Mt. Pleasant," in Hilda Madsen Longsdorf, compiler, *Mount Pleasant 1859–1939* (Salt Lake City, 1939), pp. 248–52; "Scandinavian Work in Utah," *Church Review*, 4:39ff (December 29, 1895).

[25] The account in Jennie A. Froiseth, *Women of Mormonism* (Detroit, 1882), pp. 414–16, claims to be "vouched for by Rev. McMillan." Mrs. Froiseth's antipolygamy book, incidentally, appeared in a Swedish edition as *Mormonismens Kvinnor* (Stockholm, 1883). C. C. Goodwin's "The Situation in Utah" retold the affair for *Harper's*, 63:758 (October 1881). The official Latter-day Saint Journal History is silent on this episode.

[26] Hans P. Freece, "Are You That Damned Presbyterian Devil?" reprint from *Presbyterian Magazine*, October 1931.

[27] McMillan, p. 249.

[28] Mt. Pleasant High Priests Quorum, Minute Book, MS., entries from January 5 to March 11, 1876.

[29] "Scandinavian Work in Utah," p. 41.

[30] "The History of Presbyterian Work in Utah," in *World's Fair Ecclesiastical History of Utah* (Salt Lake City, 1893), p. 230.

[31] *Ibid.*, pp. 223–38. McMillan labored in Mt. Pleasant for eight years, serving at one time as superintendent of home missions in Utah, until he was called to preside over the new Presbyterian College at Deer Lodge, Montana. He eventually became one of the secretaries of the Home Mission Board in New York. One of his successors in Mt. Pleasant was J. H. Kyle, who in 1898 served as United States senator from South Dakota.

[32] "Scandinavian Work in Utah," p. 47.

[33] A grandson, Lowry Nelson, the distinguished sociologist now at the University of Minnesota, told me in 1953 that his grandfather and a number of Danish cronies were excommunicated by their bishop for playing casino – not for drinking Danish beer and smoking, forms of socializing common among the Danes despite church taboos. Andrew had two wives when he went on his mission, but came back with two girls whom he married in the Endowment House in Salt Lake City on the way home. On his arrival his second wife, Christena Jensen, Professor Nelson's grandmother, took her two children and went out the back

door, not to return. She went to her mother's in nearby Ephraim and later to Salt Lake, where she married a Swede, Sven Lovendahl of Cottonwood. She did send her two sons to their father for a time, where they were educated at the Presbyterian mission school along with the other children – their only schooling. For a biographical sketch see W. H. Lever, *History of Sanpete and Emery Counties* (Ogden, 1898), p. 163.

[34] Lever, pp. 83–84; "The History of Presbyterian Work in Utah," p. 230.

[35] "Scandinavian Work in Utah," pp. 55–57; "The History of Presbyterian Work in Utah," pp. 223–38.

[36] "Scandinavian Work in Utah," p. 55.

[37] Mendon Ward Historical Record, MS., p. 33. Typescript in Utah State Historical Society.

[38] "Scandinavian Work in Utah," p. 55.

[39] V. S. Peet, "The Biggest Presbyterian Pumpkins," in *Truth*, April 2, 1907, clipping in Journal History, same date.

[40] *Loc. cit.*; "Mormon to Presbyterian," reprint from *Presbyterian Magazine*, October 1931; "Light from the Home Paper of Hans Peter Freece," *The Richfield Reaper*, May 28, 1908; Dr. Margaret A. Freece, Letter, May 25, 1908, in *The Richfield Reaper*, June 4, 1908.

[41] McMillan, p. 251.

[42] "De sekteriska skolornas verksamhet i Utah," *Nordstjärnan* (Stockholm), 9:40–41 (February 1, 1885). A didactic short story, "Back to the Fold," dealing with sectarian school influences, includes a humorous episode: a boy in a Presbyterian school taught by "Miss Memquist" in a small town in Sevier Valley was referred to Webster's dictionary, which stood on its stand on the platform. After fumbling with the leaves for some time he said to the teacher, "I like your school first rate, but durned if I can understand that Presbyterian Bible of yourn." *Young Woman's Journal* (Salt Lake City), 7:267 (January 1896).

[43] Kate C. Snow on Manti, Sanpete County, in "Non-Mormon Religious Denominations in Utah," Daughters of Utah Pioneers, *Heart Throbs of the West* (Salt Lake City, 1946), VII, 262–64.

[44] Mrs. M. M. Green, quoted in "The History of Presbyterian Work in Utah," pp. 235–37.

[45] "Scandinavian Work in Utah," p. 58.

[46] "Scandinavian Methodists in Utah," MS., Utah Writers' Project, Historical Records Survey, Church Inventory Files, typescript in Utah State Historical Society; "Scandinavian Work in Utah," p. 39.

[47] "Scandinavian Work in Utah," pp. 13, 15, 19, 39ff.

[48] "Scandinavian Methodist Episcopal Missions in Utah," in *World's Fair Ecclesiastical History of Utah*, pp. 273–75.

[49] Mary G. Burdette, *Twenty-Two Years' Work among the Mormons* (Chicago, n.d.), pp. 17–35.

[50] "The Baptist Church," in *World's Fair Ecclesiastical History of Utah*, p. 284.

[51] George M. Stephenson, *The Religious Aspects of Swedish Immigration* (Minneapolis, 1932), pp. 101–2.

[52] Gustav Sundbärg, *Mormonvärfningen i Sverige* (*Emigrationsutredningen*, III, Stockholm, 1910), p. 15.

[53] "Elim Lutheran Church," MS., Utah Writers' Project, Historical Records Survey, Church Inventory Files, citing Carl A. Glad, "Our Missionary Work in Utah," *Missionary Calendar*, n.d. Typescript in Utah State Historical Society.

[54] Andrew M. Israelsen, *Utah Pioneering, An Autobiography* (Salt Lake City, 1938), p. 99.

[55] John H. Bille, *History of the Danes in America* (Madison, Wisc., 1898), pp. 13–17.

[56] *Danske i Salt Lake City* (Salt Lake City, 1910), p. 18.

[57] Hans P. and Blanch K. Freece, *How Mormons Recruit Abroad* (New York, 1911), p. 21.

[58] An antipolygamy work, it was published in Detroit in 1882.

[59] *The Anti-Polygamy Standard*, a monthly magazine, flourished for three years, from April 1880 to April 1883. The Salt Lake Public Library has a file of this most curious publication.

[60] Dwyer, p. 190.

[61] *Constitutional and Governmental Rights of the Mormons as Defined by Congress and the Supreme Court of the United States* (Salt Lake City, 1890) conveniently reproduces the texts of the antibigamy law of 1862, the Poland bill of 1874, and the Edmunds and the Edmunds-Tucker enactments of the 1880s, together with reviews of Supreme Court cases. The *United States Statutes at Large*, of course, and the *Congressional Record* are primary sources for this legislation in all its stages. The *Reports* of the Utah Commission after 1882 provide complete descriptions of political and social affairs in Utah for the period.

[62] James D. Richardson, ed., *Messages and Papers of the Presidents* (New York, 1897), X, 4105.

[63] *Stjerne*, 22:140–42 (February 1, 1873); 21:107–9 (January 1, 1872).

[64] Richardson, XI, 4458.

[65] *Ibid*., XI, 4601.

[66] Salt Lake *Daily Tribune*, December 11, 1883, quoted in Dwyer, p. 222.

[67] Richardson, XI, 4947.

[68] John Bassett Moore, ed., *The Works of James Buchanan* (Philadelphia, 1908–11), X, 318, quoted in M. H. Cannon, "The Gathering of British Mormons to Western America" (unpublished doctoral dissertation, American University, 1950), p. 158.

[69] "Diplomatic Correspondence, Circular No. 10, August 9, 1879, Sent to Diplomatic and Consular Officers of the United States," *Papers Relating to the Foreign Relations of the United States 1879*, pp. 11, 12.

[70] In the celebrated George Reynolds case the United States Supreme Court ruled that "Religious belief cannot be accepted as a justification of an overt act made criminal by the law of the land. The Constitutional guaranty of religious freedom was not intended to prohibit legislation in respect to polygamy. . . . A criminal intent is generally an element of crime; but every man is presumed to intend the necessary and legitimate consequences of what he knowingly does. Ignorance of a fact may sometimes be taken as evidence of a want of criminal intent, but not ignorance of the law." Reynolds v. United States, 98 U.S., 145–68, in *Constitutional and Governmental Rights of the Mormons*, p. 100. Violation of the Anti-Polygamy Act of 1862 called for a fine of $500 and a prison sentence of five years.

[71] Noted in B. H. Roberts, *Comprehensive History of the Church* (Salt Lake City, 1930), 6 vols., VI, 142; London *Examiner*, August 16, 1879, quoted in New York *Times*, August 30, 1879.

[72] New York *Times*, September 17, 1879.

[73] Baron Rosenörn-Lehn to Secretary Evarts, January 31, 1880, *Foreign Relations 1880*, p. 936.

[74] John L. Stevens to Secretary Evarts, September 23, 1879, *Foreign Relations 1879*, p. 964.

[75] M. J. Cramer to Secretary Evarts, October 17, 1879, *Foreign Relations 1879*, p. 345.

[76] *Millennial Star*, 47:683 (October 26, 1885).

[77] See Table I, "Mormon Conversion, Disaffection, and Emigration by Decades,

1850–1904," in my manuscript dissertation, "Mormons from Scandinavia, 1850–1905," copies in Harvard University Library and Utah State Historical Society.

[78] Quoted without date in "De skandinaviske Emigranter," *Skandinaviens Stjerne*, 35:93 (December 15, 1885).

[79] Reported in the New York *Times* during January 1882.

[80] *Ibid*., January 30, 1882.

[81] *Ibid*., February 14, 1882.

[82] "Defying the Laws in Utah. Governor Murray asks for military aid in enforcing the acts of Congress," New York *Times*, October 16, 1883.

[83] Cannon, p. 184, citing *Congressional Record*, House, January 12, 1887.

[84] New York *Times*, June 24, 1884. On May 27, 1886, the *Times* dramatized the relationship of polygamy and immigration in a news story "Convicts and Converts": "Somewhere in the course of their westward journey to the land of the polygamists the 17 Mormon converts from Iceland whom the *Arizona* brought to this port on Monday may meet the special car in which the 13 Mormons are journeying eastward to Detroit. If these two groups of Mormons could be brought face to face, the deluded immigrants from Iceland might enlarge their small stock of knowledge about the nature and perils of Mormonism, for the thirteen occupants of the special car are convicts [polygamists indicted under the Edmunds law] on their way to the penitentiary in Detroit."

[85] John Codman, "Mormonism," *International Review* (September 1881), p. 232.

[86] First Presidency, *To the Church of Jesus Christ of Latter-day Saints in General Conference Assembled, April 6, 1886* (Salt Lake City, 1886), p. 3.

[87] "Annual Report of the Governor of Utah," Secretary of the Interior, *Annual Report, 1883* (48th Cong., 1st sess., *House Executive Documents*, No. 1, Part 5, XI, 627–37).

[88] *United States Statutes at Large*, XXIV, 634–41.

[89] Gustive O. Larson, *Prelude to the Kingdom* (Francestown, N.H., 1947), p. 278.

[90] "How Aliens Were Naturalized in Utah – Letter from Judge Drummond," New York *Times*, August 24, 1857.

[91] "Saints of Mormondom. Visit to John Taylor and George Q. Cannon," New York *Times*, April 11, 1881.

[92] "Polygamy and Citizenship. The Courts of Utah Have No Power to Issue Naturalization Papers," New York *Times*, June 7, 1866.

[93] Whitney, II, 558.

[94] Ballard G. Dunn, *How to Solve the Mormon Problem. Three Letters* (Chicago, 1877), pp. 15–16.

[95] Quoted in John Codman, "Through Utah," *Galaxy*, 20:624 (November 1875). Said Codman, "We have listened to worse sermons than this."

[96] *Circular* (Salt Lake City), February 16, 1874.

[97] Goodwin, p. 757.

[98] *Circular*, February 9, 1874.

[99] *Ibid*., April 13, 1874.

[100] Andrew Jenson, *Church Chronology* (Salt Lake City, 1899), entries for November 11, 29, 1889; *The Herald and Presbyter*, May 28, 1913.

[101] Quoted in George Q. Cannon, *History of the Mormons* (Salt Lake City, 1891), p. 19; see also First Presidency and Council of the Twelve, "Petition for Amnesty Sent to the President of the United States, December 19, 1891," *The Contributor* (Salt Lake City), 12:196–97 (February 1892).

[102] Jenson, *Church Chronology*, entries for October 7, 1890, and December 3, 1890.

[103] Kate C. Snow, "Political Parties, Sanpete County," in Daughters of Utah Pioneers, *Heart Throbs of the West* (Salt Lake City, 1949), X, 43.

[104] "Mormons with Little Money," New York *Times*, July 19, 1886.

[105] Jenson, *Church Chronology*, entry for August 21, 1886.

[106] *Ibid.*, entry for September 1, 1886; "Emigranter standsede i New York," *Skandinaviens Stjerne*, 36:10 (October 1, 1886).

[107] "Paupers and Mormons," New York *Times*, August 2, 1886.

[108] *Loc. cit.*

[109] "The Delayed Emigrants," *Millennial Star*, 50:702 (October 29, 1888), quoting a variety of contemporary newspaper accounts.

[110] *Loc. cit.*

[111] "Dupes of Mormon Missionaries," New York *Times*, May 15, 1890.

[112] Liverpool *Courier*, July 23, 1891, quoted in "American Immigration Commissioners," *Millennial Star*, 53:491 (August 3, 1891).

[113] Hans P. and Blanch K. Freece, p. 18. As late as 1913 the Danish yearbook, *De Forenede Staters danske Almanak, Haand- og Aarbog* (Seattle, 1913), was telling Danes applying for citizenship that, among other things, they had to declare they were "neither anarchist nor Mormon."

[114] Sundbärg, p. 3.

[115] Bruce Kinney, *Frontier Missionary Problems* (New York, 1918), pp. 83–96, held that since 1890 the whole country catered to the Mormons.

[116] This is the figure Milton Musser, assistant church historian, gave William E. Smythe, "Utah as an Industrial Object Lesson," *Atlantic Monthly*, 78:610–18 (November 1896).

[117] State of Utah, *First Report of the State Bureau of Immigration, Labor, and Statistics* (Salt Lake City, 1911), p. 16.

[118] George M. Stephenson, "The Background of the Beginnings of Swedish Immigration, 1850–1875," *American Historical Review*, 31:723 (July 1926).

Index

William Mulder, a native of Holland, is emeritus professor of English at the University of Utah, where he taught for forty-one years. He was the founding director of the university's Institute for American Studies and of the Center for Intercultural Studies, and he was for many years the editor of *Western Humanities Review.* He is the coeditor (with A. Russell Mortensen) of *Among the Mormons: Historic Accounts by Contemporary Observers,* and he has also written on such American literary figures as Robert Frost, Emily Dickinson, John Steinbeck, and Wallace Stegner; on India; and on a wide range of topics in Western and Mormon history. He received the Governor's Award in the Humanities from the Utah Humanities Council in 1999.